SKILLS · FOR · FLIGHT

Aeroplanes

Airframes & Systems – Instruments – Mass & Balance

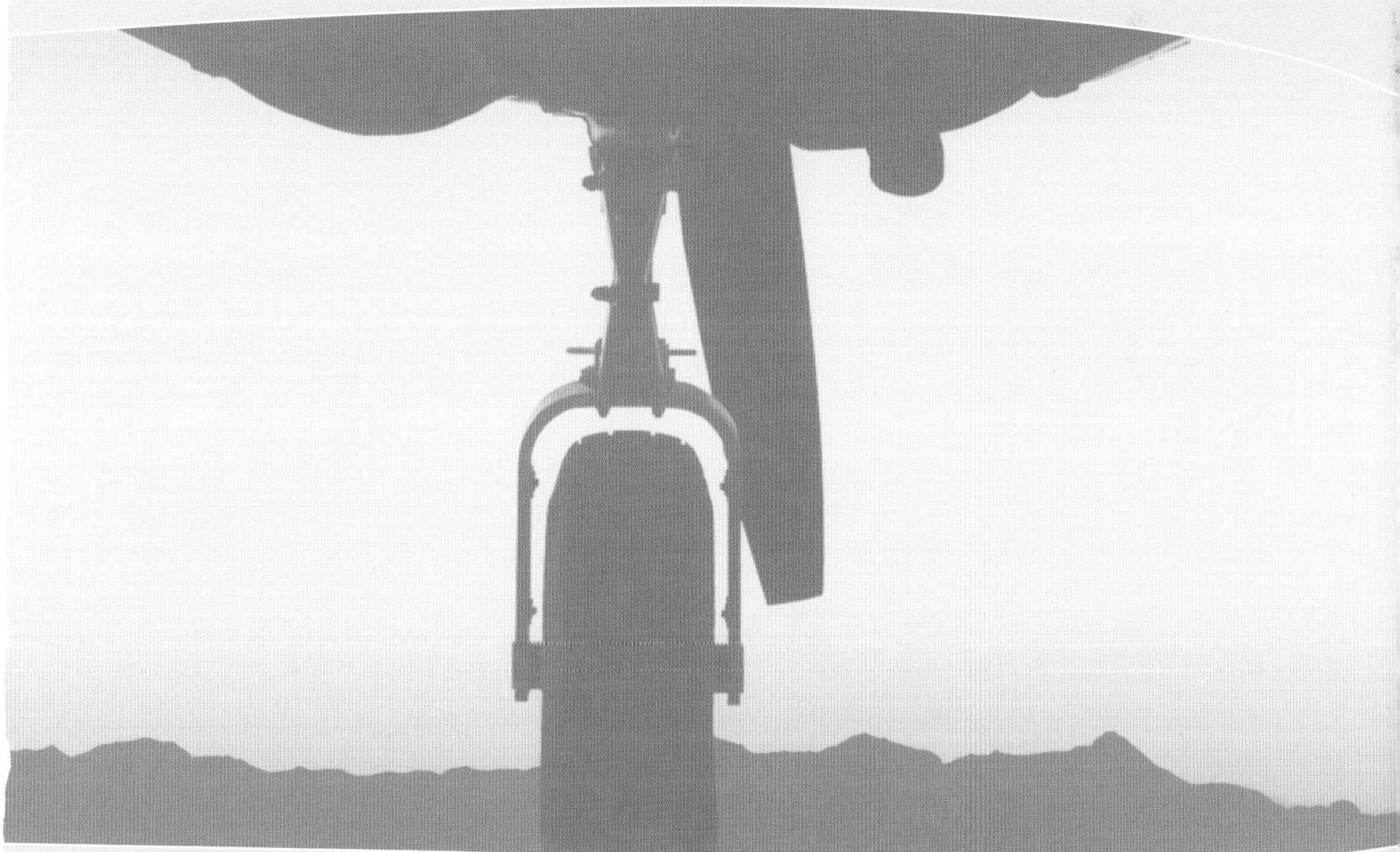

6

OXFORD AVIATION TRAINING

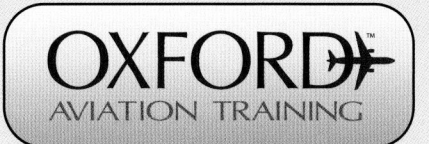

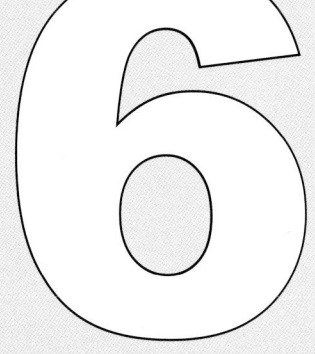

Copyright © Oxford Aviation Training Ltd 2007. All Rights Reserved.

This text book is to be used only for the purposes of private study by individuals and may not be reproduced in any form or medium, copied, stored in a retrieval system, lent, hired, rented, transmitted, or adapted in whole or part without the prior written consent of Oxford Aviation Training Limited.

Copyright in all documents and materials bound within these covers or attached hereto, excluding that material which is reproduced by the kind permission of third parties and acknowledged as such, belongs exclusively to Oxford Aviation Training Limited.

Certain copyright material is reproduced with the permission of the International Civil Aviation Organisation, the United Kingdom Civil Aviation Authority and the Joint Aviation Authorites (JAA).

This text book has been written and published as a reference work for student pilots with the aims of helping them prepare for the PPL theoretical knowledge examinations, and to provide them with the aviation knowledge they require to become safe and competent pilots of light aeroplanes. The book is not a flying training manual and nothing in this book should be regarded as constituting practical flying instruction. In practical flying matters, students must always be guided by their instructor.

Oxford Aviation Training Limited excludes all liability for any loss or damage incurred as a result of any reliance on all or part of this book except for any liability for death or personal injury resulting from negligence on the part of Oxford Aviation Training Limited or any other liability which may not legally be excluded.

This book has been produced by Oxford Aviation Training.

Production Team

Subject Specialist - Aeroplanes:
Dave Clayton

Subject Specialists - Mass & Balance:
Dave Clayton, Les Fellows, Glyn Rees

Contributors:
Rhodri Davies, Dick Hughes, Steve Partridge, Lesley Smith

Created and Compiled by:
James Kenny

Assisted by:
Andrea Goddard, Hailey Masterson, Monica Messaggi de Souza, Samuel Tierney

Design Team:
Mohammed Afzal-Khan, Andrea Goddard, Chris Hill,
Jon Kalicki, James Kenny, Hailey Masterson, Monica Messaggi de Souza, Samuel Tierney

Editor:
Les Fellows

Cover Design by: Chris Hill

First Published by: Oxford Aviation Training, Oxford, England, 2007
Printed in Singapore by: KHL Printing Co. Pte Ltd

Contact Details:
OATmedia
Oxford Aviation Training
Oxford Airport
Kidlington
Oxford
OX5 1QX
England
Tel: +44 (0)1865 844290
Email: info@oatmedia.com

Innovative learning solutions for

www.oatmedia.com   ISBN 978-0-9555177-5-4   www.oxfordaviation.net

TABLE OF CONTENTS

GENERAL

FOREWORD	v
TO THE PILOT	xiii

AEROPLANES

THE AEROPLANE (GENERAL LAYOUT)	xv
CHAPTER 1: AIRFRAMES	1
CHAPTER 2: LANDING GEAR, TYRES AND BRAKES	23
CHAPTER 3: ENGINES GENERAL	37
CHAPTER 3A: AERO DIESEL ENGINES	51
CHAPTER 4: ENGINE COOLING	63
CHAPTER 5: ENGINE LUBRICATION	71
CHAPTER 6: IGNITION SYSTEMS	83
CHAPTER 7: CARBURATION	93
CHAPTER 8: AERO ENGINE FUELS AND FUEL SYSTEMS	115
CHAPTER 9: PROPELLERS	127
CHAPTER 10: ENGINE HANDLING	145
CHAPTER 11: ELECTRICAL SYSTEMS	157
CHAPTER 12: VACUUM SYSTEMS	179
CHAPTER 13: ENGINE INSTRUMENTS	187
CHAPTER 14: PRESSURE INSTRUMENTS	199
CHAPTER 15: GYROSCOPIC INSTRUMENTS AND THE MAGNETIC COMPASS	223
CHAPTER 16: AIRWORTHINESS	251
AIRCRAFT (GENERAL) EXAMINATION SYLLABUS	267
ANSWERS TO AEROPLANES QUESTIONS	269
AEROPLANES GENERAL INDEX	273

FOREWORD TO THE FIRST EDITION.

INTRODUCTION.

Whether you are planning to fly microlights, space shuttles, gliders, combat aircraft, airliners or light aircraft, it is essential that you have a firm grasp of the theoretical knowledge which underpins practical piloting skills. This Oxford Aviation Training "Skills for Flight" series of text books covers the fundamental theory with which all pilots must come to grips from the very beginning of their pilot training, and which must remain with them throughout their flying career, if they are to be masters of the art and science of flight.

JOINT AVIATION AUTHORITIES PILOTS' LICENCES.

Joint Aviation Authorities (JAA) pilot licences were first introduced in Europe in 1999. By 2006, almost every JAA member state, including all the major countries of Europe, had adopted this new, pan-European licensing system at Air Transport Pilot's Licence, Commercial Pilot's Licence and Private Pilot's Licence levels, and many other countries, world-wide, had expressed interest in aligning their training with the JAA pilot training syllabi.

These syllabi, and the regulations governing the award and the renewal of licences, are defined by the JAA's licensing agency, 'Joint Aviation Requirements - Flight Crew Licensing', (JAR-FCL). JAR-FCL training syllabi are published in a document known as 'JAR-FCL 1.'

The United Kingdom Civil Aviation Authority (UK CAA) is one of the founder authorities within the JAA. The UK CAA has been administering examinations and skills tests for the issue of JAA licences since the year 2000, on behalf of JAR-FCL.

The Private Pilot's Licence (PPL), then, issued by the UK CAA, is a JAA licence which is accepted as proof of a pilot's qualifications throughout all JAA member states.

Currently, the JAA member states are: *United Kingdom, Denmark, Iceland, Switzerland, France, Sweden, Netherlands, Belgium, Romania, Spain, Finland, Ireland, Malta, Norway, Czech Republic, Slovenia, Germany, Portugal, Greece, Italy, Turkey, Croatia, Poland, Austria, Estonia, Lithuania, Cyprus, Hungary, Luxembourg, Monaco, Slovakia.*

As a licence which is also fully compliant with the licensing recommendations of the International Civil Aviation Organisation (ICAO), the JAA PPL is also valid in most other parts of the world.

The JAA PPL in the UK has replaced the full UK PPL, formerly issued solely under the authority of the UK CAA.

Issue of the JAA PPL is dependent on the student pilot having completed the requisite training and passed the appropriate theoretical knowledge and practical flying skills tests detailed in 'JAR-FCL 1'. In the UK, the CAA is responsible for ensuring that these requirements are met before any licence is issued.

FOREWORD

EUROPEAN AVIATION SAFETY AGENCY.

With the establishment of the European Aviation Safety Agency (EASA), it is envisaged that JAA flight crew licensing and examining competency will be absorbed into the EASA organisation. It is possible that, when this change has taken place, the PPL may even change its title again, with the words "EASA" replacing "JAA". However, we do not yet know this for certain. In the UK, such a step would require the British Government to review and, where necessary, revise the Civil Aviation Act. But, whatever the future of the title of the PPL, the JAA pilot's licence syllabi are unlikely to change fundamentally, in the short term. So, for the moment, the JAA Licence remains, and any change in nomenclature is likely to be just that: a change in name only.

OXFORD AVIATION TRAINING AND OATMEDIA.

Oxford Aviation Training (OAT) is one of the world's leading professional pilot schools. It has been in operation for over forty years and has trained more than 15 000 professional pilots for over 80 airlines, world-wide.

OAT was the first pilot school in the United Kingdom to be granted approval to train for the JAA ATPL. OAT led and coordinated the joint-European effort to produce the JAR-FCL ATPL Learning Objectives which are now published by the JAA, itself, as a guide to the theoretical knowledge requirements of ATPL training.

OAT's experience in European licensing, at all levels, and in the use of advanced training technologies, led OAT's training material production unit, OATmedia, to conceive, create and produce multimedia, computer-based training for ATPL students preparing for JAA theoretical knowledge examinations by distance learning. Subsequently, OATmedia extended its range of computer-based training CD-ROMs to cover PPL and post-PPL studies.

This present series of text books is designed to complement OATmedia's successful PPL CD-ROMs in helping student pilots prepare for the theoretical knowledge examinations of the JAA PPL and beyond, as well as to provide students with the aviation knowledge they require to become safe and competent pilots.

The OAT expertise embodied in this series of books means that students working towards the JAA PPL have access to top-quality, up-to-date, study material at an affordable cost. Those students who aspire to becoming professional pilots will find that this series of PPL books takes them some way beyond PPL towards the knowledge required for professional pilot licences.

THE JAA PRIVATE PILOT'S LICENCE (AEROPLANES).

The following information on the Joint Aviation Authorities Private Pilot's Licence (Aeroplanes); (JAA PPL(A)) is for your guidance only. Full details of flying training, theoretical knowledge training and the corresponding tests and examinations are contained in the JAA document: **JAR–FCL 1, SUBPART C – PRIVATE PILOT LICENCE (Aeroplanes) – PPL(A).**

The privileges of the JAA PPL (A) allow you to fly as pilot-in-command, or co-pilot, of any aircraft for which an appropriate rating is held, but not for remuneration, or on revenue-earning flights.

FOREWORD

For United Kingdom based students, full details of JAA PPL (A) training and examinations can be found in the CAA publication, **Licensing Administration Standards Operating Requirements Safety (LASORS),** copies of which can be accessed through the CAA's Flight Crew Licensing website.

Flying Training.

The JAA PPL (A) can be gained by completing a course of a minimum of 45 hours flying training with a training organisation registered with the appropriate National Aviation Authority (the Civil Aviation Authority, in the case of the United Kingdom).

Flying instruction must normally include:

- **25 hours** dual Instruction on aeroplanes.

- **10 hours** supervised solo flight time on aeroplanes, which must include **5 hours** solo cross-country flight time, including one cross-country flight of at least 150 nautical miles (270km), during which full-stop landings at two different aerodromes, different from the aerodrome of departure, are to be made.

The required flying-instructional time may be reduced by a maximum of 10 hours for those students with appropriate flying experience on other types of aircraft.

The flying test (Skills Test), comprising navigation and general skills tests, is to be taken within 6 months of completing flying instruction. All sections of the Skills Test must be taken within a period of 6 months. A successfully completed Skills Test has a period of validity of 12 months for the purposes of licence issue.

Theoretical Knowledge Examinations.

The procedures for the conduct of the JAA PPL (A) theoretical knowledge examinations will be determined by the National Aviation Authority of the state concerned, (the Civil Aviation Authority, in the case of the United Kingdom).

The JAA theoretical knowledge examination must comprise the following 9 subjects: *Air Law, Aircraft General Knowledge, Flight Performance and Planning, Human Performance and Limitations, Meteorology, Navigation, Operational Procedures, Principles of Flight, Communication.*

A single examination paper may cover several subjects.

The combination of subjects and the examination paper titles, as administered by the UK CAA, are, at present:

1. Air Law and Operational Procedures.
2. Human Performance and Limitations.
3. Navigation & Radio Aids.
4. Meteorology.
5. Aircraft (General) & Principles of Flight.
6. Flight Performance and Planning.
7. JAR-FCL Communications (PPL) (i.e. Radiotelephony Communications).

The majority of the questions are multiple choice. In the United Kingdom, examinations

FOREWORD

are normally conducted by the Flying Training Organisation or Registered Facility at which a student pilot carries out his training.

The pass mark in all subjects is 75%.

For the purpose of the issue of a JAA PPL(A), a pass in the theoretical knowledge examinations will be accepted during the 24 month period immediately following the date of successfully completing all of the theoretical knowledge examinations.

Medical Requirements.
An applicant for a JAR-FCL PPL(A) must hold a valid JAR-FCL Class 1 or Class 2 Medical Certificate.

THE UNITED KINGDOM NATIONAL PRIVATE PILOT'S LICENCE (AEROPLANES).

One of the aims of the United Kingdom National Private Pilot's Licence (UK NPPL) is to make it easier for the recreational flyer to obtain a PPL than it would be if the requirements of the standard JAA-PPL had to be met. The regulations governing medical fitness are also different between the UK NPPL and the JAA PPL.

Full details of the regulations governing the training for, issue of, and privileges of the UK NPPL may be found by consulting LASORS and the Air Navigation Order. Most UK flying club websites also give details of this licence.

Basically, the holder of a UK NPPL is restricted to flight in a simple, UK-registered, single piston-engine aeroplane (including motor gliders and microlights) whose Maximum Authorized Take-off Weight does not exceed 2000 kg. Flight is normally permitted in UK airspace only, by day, and in accordance with the Visual Flight Rules.

Flying Training.
Currently, 32 hours of flying training is required for the issue of a UK NPPL (A), of which 22 hours are to be dual instruction, and 10 hours to be supervised solo flying time.

There are separate general and navigation skills tests.

Theoretical Knowledge Examinations.
The UK NPPL theoretical knowledge syllabus and ground examinations are the same as for the JAA PPL (A). This series of books, therefore, is also suitable for student pilots preparing for the UK NPPL.

THE UNITED KINGDOM FLIGHT RADIOTELEPHONY OPERATOR'S LICENCE.

Although there is a written paper on Radiotelephony Communications in the JAA PPL theoretical knowledge examinations, pilots in the United Kingdom, and in most other countries, who wish to operate airborne radio equipment will need to take a separate practical test for the award of a Flight Radiotelephony Operators Licence (FRTOL). For United Kingdom based students, full details of the FRTOL are contained in LASORS.

FOREWORD

NOTES ON CONTENT AND TEXT.

Technical Content.
The technical content of this OAT series of pilot training text books aims to reach the standard required by the theoretical knowledge syllabus of the JAA Private Pilot's Licence (Aeroplanes), (JAA PPL(A)). This is the minimum standard that has been aimed at. The subject content of several of the volumes in the series exceeds PPL standard. However, all questions and their answers, as well as the margin notes, are aimed specifically at the JAA PPL (A) ground examinations.

An indication of the technical level covered by each text book is given on the rear cover and in individual subject prefaces. The books deal predominantly with single piston-engine aeroplane operations.

Questions and Answers.
Questions appear at the end of each chapter in order that readers may test themselves on the individual subtopics of the main subject(s) covered by each book. The questions are of the same format as the questions asked in the JAA PPL (A) theoretical knowledge examinations, as administered by the UK CAA. All questions are multiple-choice, containing four answer options, one of which is the correct answer, with the remaining three options being incorrect "distracters".

Students Working for a Non-JAA PPL.
JAA licence training syllabi follow the basic structure of ICAO-recommended training, so even if the national PPL you are working towards is not issued by a JAA member state, this series of text books should provide virtually all the training material you need. Theoretical knowledge examinations for the JAA PPL are, however, administered nationally, so there will always be country-specific aspects to JAA PPL examinations. 'Air Law' is the most obvious subject where country-specific content is likely to remain; the other subject is 'Navigation', where charts will most probably depict the terrain of the country concerned.

As mentioned elsewhere in this Foreword, this series of books is also suitable for student pilots preparing for the United Kingdom National Private Pilot's Licence (UK NPPL). The theoretical examination syllabus and examinations for the UK NPPL are currently identical to those for the JAA PPL.

Student Helicopter Pilots.
Of the seven book in this series, the following are suitable for student helicopters pilots working towards the JAA PPL (H), the UK NPPL (H) or the equivalent national licence:

Volume 1: 'Air Law & Operational Procedures'; Volume 2: 'Human Performance'; Volume 3: 'Navigation & Radio Aids'; Volume 4: 'Meteorology', and Volume 7: 'Radiotelephony'.

The OATmedia Website.
If any errors of content are identified in these books, or if there are any JAA PPL (A) theoretical knowledge syllabus changes, Oxford Aviation Training's aim is to record those changes on the product support pages of the OATmedia website, at: www.oatmedia.com

FOREWORD

Grammatical Note.
It is standard grammatical convention in the English language, as well as in most other languages of Indo-European origin, that a single person of unspecified gender should be referred to by the appropriate form of the masculine singular pronoun, *he*, *him*, or *his*. This convention has been used throughout this series of books in order to avoid the pitfalls of usage that have crept into some modern works which contain frequent and distracting repetitions of *he or she*, *him or her*, *etc*, or where the ungrammatical use of *they*, and related pronouns, is resorted to. In accordance with the teachings of English grammar, the use, in this series of books, of a masculine pronoun to refer to a single person of unspecified gender does not imply that the person is of the male sex.

Margin Notes.
You will notice that margin notes appear on some pages in these books, identified by one of two icons:

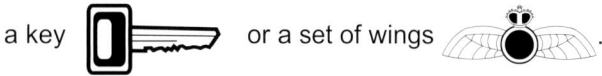

a key   or a set of wings   .

The key icon identifies a note which the authors judge to be a key point in the understanding of a subject; the wings identify what the authors judge to be a point of airmanship.

The UK Theoretical Knowledge Examination Papers.
The UK CAA sets examination papers to test JAA PPL (A) theoretical knowledge either as single-subject papers or as papers in which two subjects are combined.

Two examination papers currently cover two subjects each:

- **Aircraft (General) & Principles of Flight**: The 'Aircraft (General) & Principles of Flight' examination paper, as its title suggests, covers 'Principles of Flight' and those subjects which deal with the aeroplane as a machine, 'Airframes', 'Engines', 'Propellers' and 'Instrumentation', which JAR-FCL groups under the title 'Aircraft General Knowledge'.

- **Flight Performance & Planning:** The examination paper entitled 'Flight Performance & Planning' covers both 'Aeroplane Performance, and 'Mass & Balance'.

When preparing for the two examinations named above, using this Oxford series of text books, you will need **Volume 5, 'Principles of Flight'**, which includes 'Aeroplane Performance', and **Volume 6, 'Aeroplanes'**, which includes 'Mass & Balance' as well as 'Airframes', 'Engines', 'Propellers', and 'Instrumentation'. So to prepare for the 'Aircraft (General) & Principles of Flight' examination, you need to take the **'Aeroplanes'** infomation from **Volume 6** and the **'Principles of Flight'** information from **Volume 5**. When you are preparing for the 'Flight Performance & Planning' examination you need to take the **'Aeroplane Performance'** information from **Volume 5** and the **'Mass & Balance'** information from **Volume 6**.

It has been necessary to arrange the books in this way for reasons of space and subject logic. The titles of the rest of the volumes in the series correspond with the titles of the examinations. The situation is summed up for you in the table on the following page:

FOREWORD

JAA Theoretical Examination Papers	Corresponding Oxford Book Title
Air Law and Operational Procedures	Volume 1: Air Law
Human Performance and Limitations	Volume 2: Human Performance
Navigation and Radio Aids	Volume 3: Navigation
Meteorology	Volume 4: Meteorology
Aircraft (General) and Principles of Flight	Volume 5: Principles of Flight Volume 6: Aeroplanes
Flight Performance and Planning	Volume 5: Aeroplane Performance Volume 6: Mass and Balance
JAR-FCL Communications (PPL)	Volume 7: Radiotelephony

Regulatory Changes.
Finally, so that you may stay abreast of any changes in the flying and ground training requirements pertaining to pilot licences which may be introduced by your national aviation authority, be sure to consult, from time to time, the relevant publications issued by the authority. In the United Kingdom, the Civil Aviation Publication, LASORS, is worth looking at regularly. It is currently accessible, on-line, on the CAA website at **www.caa.co.uk**.

Oxford,
England

April 2007

TO THE PILOT.

The book is intended specifically to meet the needs of the **light aeroplane pilot**. Its content and self assessment tests satisfy the demands of the **theoretical knowledge syllabus** of both the **JAR-FCL/EASA Private Pilot's Licence** and the **United Kingdom National PPL** in the subjects **of 'Aircraft (General)'** and '**Mass and Balance'**.

The **'Aeroplanes'** section of this book satisfies the **PPL** syllabus for the examination **'Aircraft (General)'**, and covers all of the systems which go to make up a modern light aeroplane: **the electrical, electronic, mechanical and hydraulic systems, its flight instruments and its engine, propeller and engine instrumentation**. Using this book, you should acquire the theoretical and practical knowledge of your aeroplane's systems that you will need in order to fly your aeroplane efficiently and safely.

The second section of the book, on **'Mass & Balance'**, covers all the necessary knowledge and principles that the pilot needs to master in order to check that his aircraft is correctly **loaded** and **balanced** for safe and efficient operations.

The **loading** of an aircraft not only affects the position of an aircraft's **centre of gravity**, but also determines whether the aircraft will achieve the required take-off performance, whether it can be landed safely, and at what speeds it can be safely manoeuvred.

Pilots need to understand thoroughly the role played by the position of the aeroplane's **centre of gravity**. In whatever phase of flight the aircraft happens to be, it is vitally important that the location of the aircraft's **centre of gravity** always remains within the limits specified by the designer of the aircraft. If the **centre of gravity** falls outside these limits, the aircraft's flying characteristics will be adversely affected and the aircraft may ultimately become uncontrollable.

While we have attempted, in this book, to relate the subjects of **'Aeroplanes'** and **'Mass & Balance'** to the practical aspects of piloting, it is a primary aim of the book to prepare the student pilot for the **PPL theoretical knowledge examinations**. Appropriate emphasis, therefore, has been given to the pure theory of the two subjects which is demanded by the **PPL ground examinations**.

Readers should note that, **at PPL level**, the United Kingdom Civil Aviation Authority (UK CAA) examines the subject of **'Aircraft (General)'** along with the subject of **'Principles of Flight'** in one paper, currently entitled **'Aircraft (General)' and 'Principles of Flight'**. Similarly, **'Mass & Balance'** is examined by the UK CAA in a separate paper called **'Flight Performance & Planning'**, along with the subject **'Aeroplane Performance'**.

Volumes 5 and **6** of this series of books, entitled respectively **'Principles of Flight'** and **'Aeroplanes'**, will prepare you for both examinations.

THE AEROPLANE (GENERAL LAYOUT)

THE AEROPLANE (GENERAL LAYOUT)

THE AEROPLANE (GENERAL LAYOUT)

THE PIPER PA28 WARRIOR.

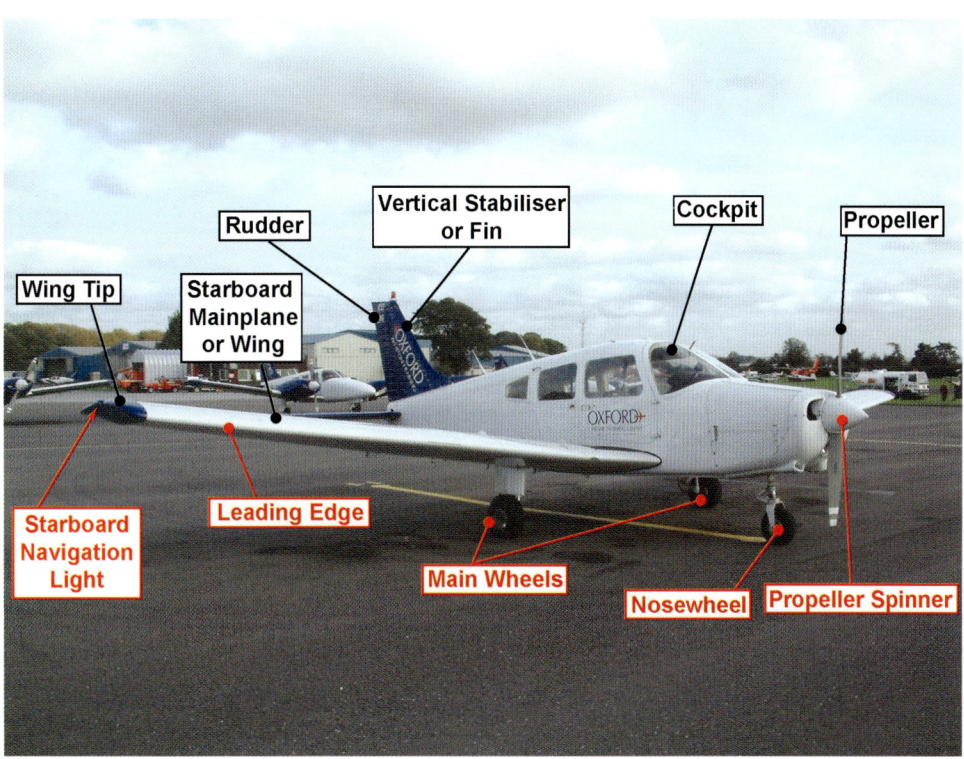

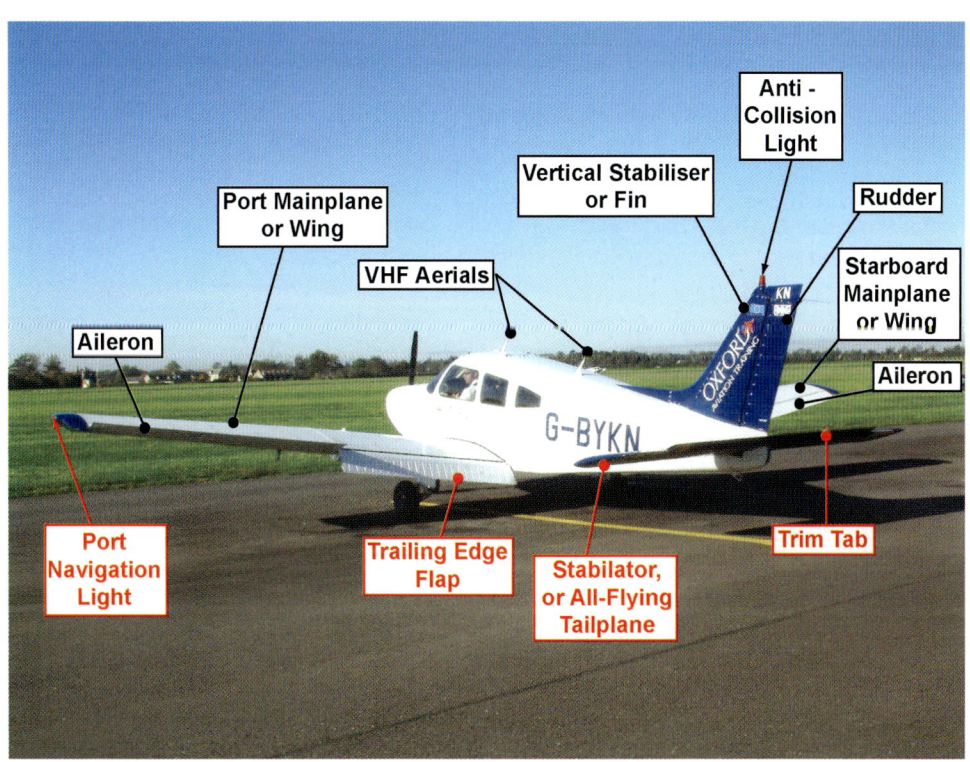

THE AEROPLANE (GENERAL LAYOUT)

THE MAULE M-7.

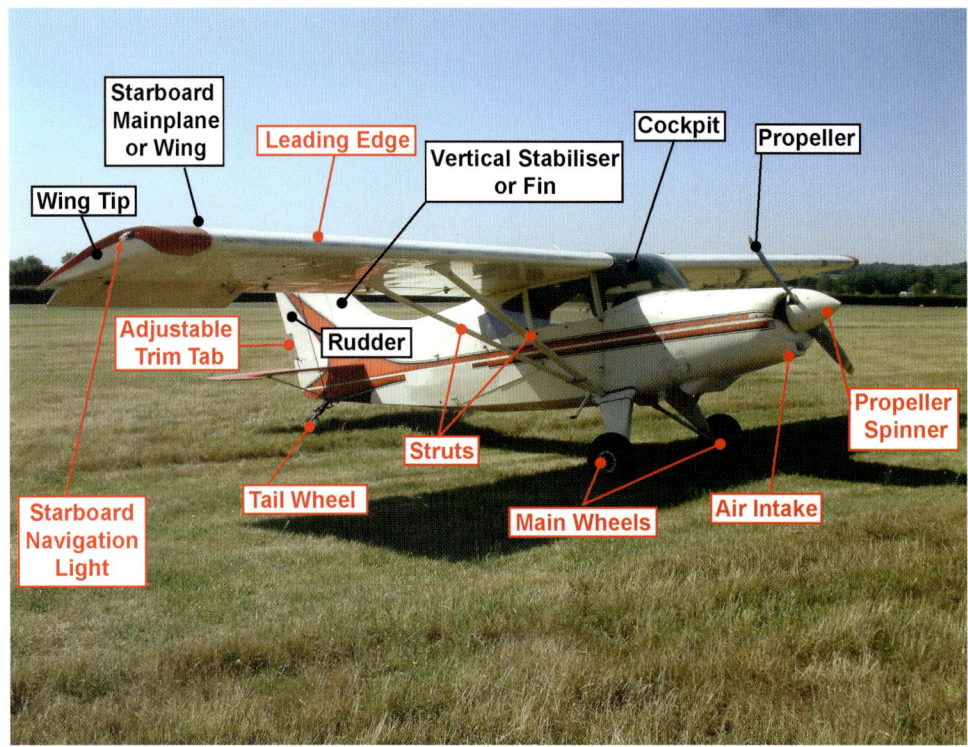

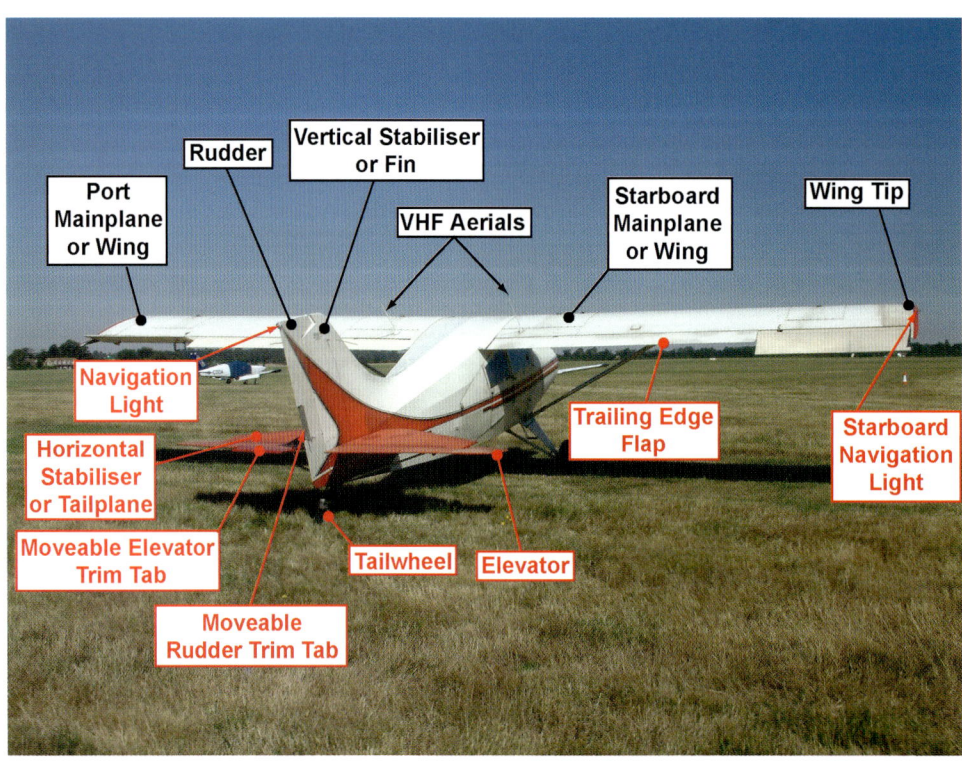

CHAPTER 1
AIRFRAMES

CHAPTER 1: AIRFRAMES

CHAPTER 1: AIRFRAMES

AIRFRAMES.

The **airframe** comprises the main structural elements of the aircraft which support the loads to which the aircraft is subjected in the air and on the ground. The principal components of the airframe are the **fuselage**, the **wings**, the **tail assembly** and the **flying controls**. In this chapter we look not only at the **airframe**, but also at the loads applied to the airframe, the aircraft **emergency equipment** and certain **safety checks** and **emergency drills**.

FUSELAGE.

The **fuselage** is the main structure or body of the aircraft *(see Figure 1.1)*. It carries the **passengers** and **crew** in safe, comfortable conditions.

The **fuselage** also provides space for **controls**, **accessories** and other equipment. It transfers loads to and from the **mainplanes** or **wings**, the **tailplane**, **fin**, **landing gear** and, in certain configurations, the **engines**.

Figure 1.1 Fuselage.

There are three main types of **fuselage** construction. First there is the **truss** or **framework** type *(see Figure 1.2)* which is generally used for light, non-pressurised, aircraft. Then there is **monocoque** construction, which was mostly used during the early twentieth century. Finally, there is the **semi-monocoque fuselage** *(see Figure 1.4)* which is in use on most aircraft other than non-pressurised aircraft. The latter two types of structure - **monocoque** and **semi-monocoque** - are more generally referred to as **stressed skin constructions**.

Truss or Framework Construction.
When **truss** or **framework construction** is used for the fuselage, the framework consists of light steel tubes of minimal wall thickness which are welded together to form a space frame of triangular shape. This gives the most rigid of geometric forms. Each tube carries a specific load, the magnitude of which depends on whether the aircraft is airborne or on the ground. This type of fabrication is strong, easily constructed and gives a relatively trouble free basic arrangement. The framework is normally covered by a lightweight aluminium alloy or fabric skin to form an enclosed, aerodynamically efficient load carrying compartment. Examples of aircraft using this construction are the Auster J6 and Piper Cub.

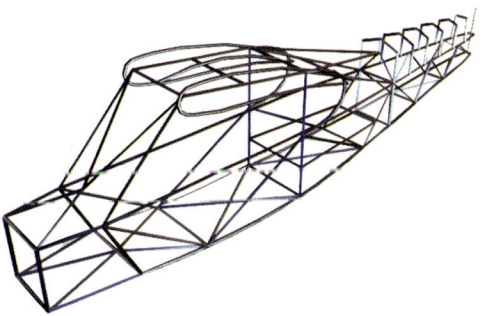

Figure 1.2. Framework Construction.

All self and imposed loads are carried by the skin in a monocoque structure, which contains no openings and no internal support structure.

Stressed Skin Construction: Monocoque Construction.
Monocoque is a French word meaning 'single shell.' In a **monocoque structure** all the loads are absorbed by a **stressed skin** with just light internal frames or formers to give the required shape.

CHAPTER 1: AIRFRAMES

With a **stressed-skin** structure, even slight damage to the skin can seriously weaken the structure.

To be a true **monocoque** the structure would have no apertures in it at all, like an ostrich egg; but for practical purposes, in an aircraft, apertures have to be provided for access and maintenance. The apertures have to be reinforced so that the integrity of the structure is maintained. But, once the aircraft doors are closed and all the hatches and access panels are fitted, the fuselage is to all intents and purposes a **monocoque structure**. Two aircraft constructed in accordance with the **monocoque** principle were the plywood construction Roland CII (1915), and the Ford Trimotor (1926).

Figure 1.3. An Ostrich egg is a monocoque construction.

Stressed Skin Construction: Semi - Monocoque Construction.

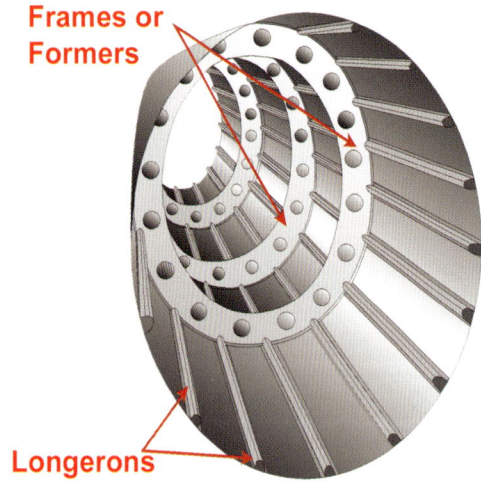

Figure 1.4. Semi - Monocoque Construction.

As aircraft became larger and the air loads greater, the pure monocoque structure was found not to be strong enough. Additional structural members known as **longerons** were added to run lengthwise along the fuselage joining the **frames** together. A light alloy **skin** was then attached to the **frames** and **longerons** by riveting or adhesive bonding. This type of **stressed-skin** fuselage construction is called **semi-monocoque** *(see Figure 1.4)*.

In **semi-monocoque** fuselages, then, **longerons** and **frames** stiffen the **skin**, and flight loads are shared between the **skin** and the **structure** beneath.

Bulkheads *as illustrated in Figure 1.5,* are set in place to separate the different sections of the **semi-monocoque** fuselage; for instance, between the engine compartment and the passenger compartment. The **bulkhead** has the same basic shape as the **frames** or **formers**, but almost completely isolates one compartment from the other. However, holes have to be made in the bulkhead. These allow control fittings, pipework and electrical cables to pass through the length of the fuselage.

Bulkheads are usually much more substantially built than the **frames** because they are subject to greater

Figure 1.5. An Engine Bulkhead.

loads. Additionally, the **bulkhead** which separates the engine from the passenger compartment serves to retard the passage of fire from the engine rearwards, should a fire break out.

MAINPLANES (WINGS).

The **wings** or **mainplanes** generate **lift** and, in steady flight, support the **weight** of the aircraft in the air. When the aircraft is manoeuvring, the **wings** will have to support **loads** which are several times the **weight** of the aircraft. Therefore, the **wings** must have sufficient strength and stiffness to be able to do this. The degree of strength and stiffness is determined by the thickness of the wing, with the thickness and type of construction used being dependent on the speed requirements of the aircraft. Various types of **wing construction** are **bi-plane**, **braced monoplane** and **cantilever monoplane**.

Bi-plane Construction.
Very few **bi-planes** fly at more than 200 knots in level flight, so the air loads are low, which means that a truss type design, which is covered in fabric, is usually satisfactory. The wing spars, interplane struts and bracing wires form a lattice girder of great rigidity which is highly resistant to bending and twisting. Unfortunately the struts and bracing wires also generate a relatively large amount of drag, which accounts for the modest speed of **bi-planes** *(see Figure 1.6).*

Figure 1. 6 Bi-plane Construction.

Braced Monoplane.
This type of design is also used on low speed aircraft.

In the **braced monoplane**, the wings are strengthened or 'braced' by external struts, which help relieve the bending loads applied to the wing spars in flight. One of the most famous **braced monoplanes** was the **'Spirit of St Louis'** *(see Figure 1.7.)* which Charles Lindbergh piloted in his epic, solo transatlantic flight.

Figure 1.7 The Spirit of St. Louis. Picture, courtesy of Peter Chambers.

Cantilever Monoplane.
On a **cantilever monoplane**, the wings are **unbraced**, being supported at one end only. Most modern aircraft are **cantilever monoplanes**. Cantilever wings have to absorb the stresses due to lift and drag in flight and their own weight when on the ground *(see Figure 1.8).*

Figure 1.8 Cantilever Monoplane.

CHAPTER 1: AIRFRAMES

CONSTRUCTION OF THE CANTILEVER WING.

The load bearing ability of a **cantilever wing** is achieved by building the wing around one or more main load bearing members known as **spars** *(Figure 1.9)*, which are constructed so that they will absorb the downwards bending stresses when on the ground, and the upwards, rearwards and twisting stresses when in flight.

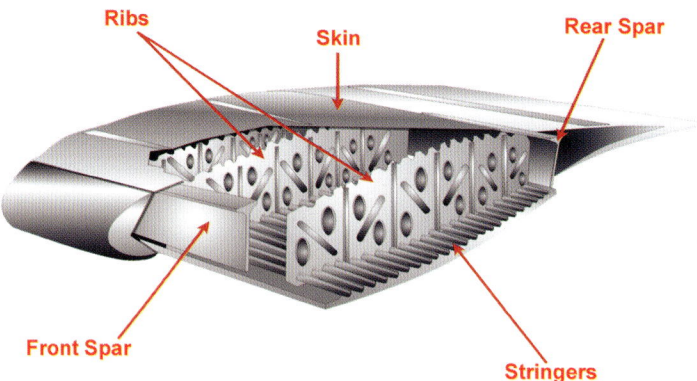

Figure 1.9 Cantilever Wing Construction.

The major structural components of the **cantilever wing** are generally manufactured from aluminium alloys, with composite materials such as glass-reinforced plastic, carbon-reinforced plastic and honeycomb structures being used for fairings, control surfaces and flaps etc.

Relief of bending stress is aided by positioning the major fuel tanks within the wing.

Cantilever wings may be of **single spar**, **twin spar** or **multispar construction**. A conventional mainplane structure would consist of front and rear spars, with metal skin attached to the spar booms to form a torsion box, which counteracts twisting forces.

The Skin.
The **skin** of a cantilever wing *(see Figure 1.9)* helps bear the loads. It generates direct stresses in a spanwise direction as a response to bending moments, and also resists twisting.

The Stringers.
Stringers *(see Figure 1.9)* are **spanwise members** which give the wing rigidity by stiffening the skin in compression.

Ribs.
Ribs *(see Figure 1.9)* maintain the aerofoil shape of the wings, support the spars, stringers and skin against buckling, and pass concentrated loads from the engines, the landing gear and control surfaces into the skin and spars.

CHAPTER 1: AIRFRAMES

STABILISING SURFACES.

The stabilising surfaces are designed to return the aircraft to balanced flight in the pitching and yawing planes when the aircraft has been disturbed from steady, straight flight. On conventional aircraft, the primary stability surfaces are the **tailplane** (or **horizontal stabiliser**), and the **fin** (or **vertical stabiliser**).

Figure 1.10 A T-Tail.

Tail Units.
The **tail unit**, which is sometimes called the **empennage**, comes in many different designs. It can be **conventional**, **T-tail**, **H-tail** or **V-tail**.

Figure 1.11 An H-Tail.

An example of each of the less common of these types of **tail units** is shown in Figures 1.10, 1.11 and 1.12.

The tail unit, as a whole, provides longitudinal and directional stability and control.

Figure 1.12 A V-Tail.

The fin gives an aeroplane directional stability.

However, in some aircraft, longitudinal stability and control is provided by **foreplanes**, called **canards** (see Figure 1.13).

Figure 1.13 A Canard Foreplane.

The Tail Plane.
The horizontal fixed tail surface, which is known as the **tailplane** or **horizontal stabiliser**, provides **longitudinal stability** by generating upwards or downwards forces as required.

Structurally the tail unit components are generally smaller versions of the mainplanes in that they use spars, ribs, stringers and skin in their construction. They also use the same basic materials as are employed in the manufacture of mainplanes; for instance, aluminium alloys or composites with honeycomb structures.

The Fin.
The fixed vertical surface, known as the **vertical stabiliser** or **fin**, generates sideways forces as required to give **directional stability**.

THE AIRCRAFT'S AXES.

To maintain steady flight the aircraft must be in a state of balance about its three main axes (see Figure 1.14). The stabilising surfaces help to maintain this state of balance. The flying controls enable the pilot to manoeuvre the aircraft around its three axes.

CHAPTER 1: AIRFRAMES

The Longitudinal Axis.
The aircraft's **longitudinal axis** is illustrated in *Figure 1.14*. Rotation about the **longitudinal axis** is termed **roll**. **Roll** is controlled by the **ailerons**.

The Lateral Axis.
The aircraft's **lateral axis** is illustrated in *Figure 1.14*. Rotation about the **lateral axis** is termed **pitch**. **Pitch** is controlled by either the **elevators**, or by an **all-moving tailplane** or **stabiliser**.

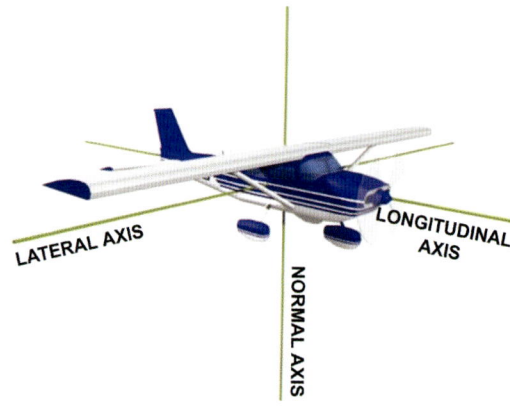

Figure 1.14 The Aircraft Axes.

 *The movement of an aeroplane about its normal (vertical) axis is known as yaw.*

The Normal Axis.
The aircraft's **normal axis** is illustrated in *Figure 1.14*. Rotation about the **normal axis** is termed **yaw**. **Yaw** is controlled by the **rudder**.

THE FLYING CONTROLS.

Primary Flying Controls.
The **primary flying controls** control the aircraft in **pitch**, **roll** and **yaw**. The movement of the flying control surfaces in response to the movement of the cockpit controls in light aircraft is achieved mechanically. This means that the control surfaces are connected directly to the cockpit controls by a system of cables, rods, levers and chains.

Pitch Control.
Pitch control is obtained through the use of either **elevators** *(see Figure 1.15)*, an all moving **stabilator** *(see Figure 1.23)* or canard control *(see Figure 1.13)*. For the purpose of this chapter, we will assume that the aircraft has **elevators** fitted to the **tail plane**. The **elevator** is controlled by fore and aft movement of the control column or control wheel *(see Figure 1.17)*. Rearward movement of the control column causes upward movement of the **elevator** which causes the aircraft to **pitch** nose upwards, and vice versa.

Figure 1.15 Elevators and Rudder.

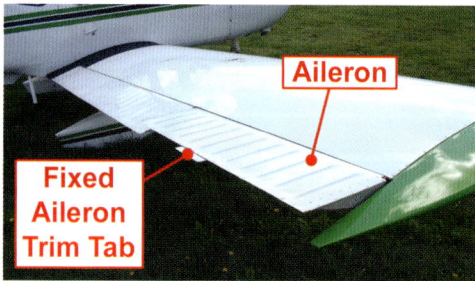

Figure 1.16 An Aileron.

Roll Control.
Control in **roll** is achieved by **ailerons** *(see Figure 1.16)*. Turning the control wheel or moving the control column to the right causes the right **aileron** to move up and the left **aileron** to move down, inducing **roll** to the right and vice versa.

8

CHAPTER 1: AIRFRAMES

Yaw Control.
Control in **yaw** is achieved by the **rudder**, (*Figure 1.15.*) Moving the right **rudder pedal** forward causes the **rudder** to move to the right which, in turn, causes the aircraft to **yaw** to the right, and vice versa.

Range of Control Movement.
The movement of each control surface to either side of its neutral position is laid down by the aircraft designer so that the required control can be achieved over the full range of operating conditions.

The movement is not necessarily the same each side of neutral; for example, an elevator usually has a greater deflection upward than downward. The limit of movement of the control surface is determined by a mechanical stop *(see Figure 1.17)*. The function of mechanical stops is to prevent excessive control surface deflection which may cause the aircraft structure to be over-stressed during normal operations.

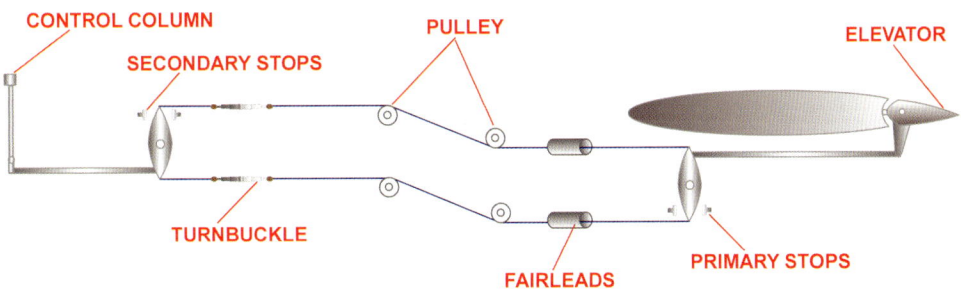

Figure 1.17 A Control Run.

A stop which limits the movement of the control surface is called a primary stop. A stop which limits the movement of the control column or rudder pedals is called a secondary stop. When the primary stop is closed there will be a small clearance at the secondary stop.

Poorly maintained control runs may be a contributory cause to flutter which occurs at speeds below the limiting airspeed.

CONTROL SURFACE FLUTTER

Flutter is the rapid and uncontrolled oscillation of a flight control, (or the surface to which it is attached), which occurs as a result of an unbalanced control surface. **Flutter** is caused by the interaction of aerodynamic forces, inertial forces and the elastic properties of the control surface or structure, and can lead to catastrophic failure of the structure.

Flutter can be prevented by **mass balancing** the control surfaces (*see Figure 1.18*) in order to alter the moment of inertia of the surface and, therefore, the period of vibration. **Mass balancing** is achieved by moving the **centre of gravity** of the flying control surface closer to, or forward of, the hinge of that control surface.

Control surface mass balancing prevents flutter of that control in the higher speed range.

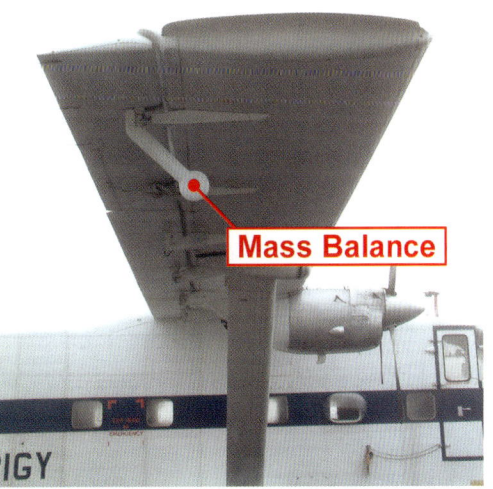

Figure 1.18 A Mass Balance on an aileron.

Flutter must not occur within the normal flight operating envelope of the aircraft. The fact that an aircraft is poorly maintained, particularly in respect of excessive control surface backlash or flexibility, may mean that **flutter** will occur at speeds below the limit airspeed. High density expanding foam is sometimes used within control surfaces, in order to impart greater stiffness to the control surface with a reasonably low weight penalty.

TRIMMING.

An aeroplane is **trimmed** when it will maintain its attitude and speed without the pilot having to apply a force to the cockpit controls. If it is necessary for a control surface to be deflected to maintain balance of the aircraft, the pilot will need to apply a force to the cockpit control to hold the surface in its deflected position. This force may be reduced to zero by operation of the **trim controls** which cause the **trim tabs**, fitted to the rear edges of the main flying control surfaces to move so as to hold the control surfaces in their deflected position.

Figure 1.19 Elevator Trim Mechanism.

The aircraft may need to be **trimmed** in pitch as a result of changes of attitude and speed, changes of power or varying **centre of gravity** positions. An elevator **trim mechanism** and **trim tab** are shown in *Figure 1.19*.

Trimming in yaw will be needed as a result of changes in propeller torque, or if there is an engine failure on a twin engined aircraft. **Trimming** in roll is less likely to be needed, but would be required if there was a lateral displacement of the **centre of gravity**: for example if the contents of the fuel tanks in each wing were allowed to become unequal, or, in the case of a twin engine aircraft, if one engine had failed.

Fixed Tabs.
Some **trimming tabs** are not adjustable in flight, but can be adjusted on the ground by an aircraft technician to correct a permanent out-of-trim condition. **Fixed trimming tabs** are most commonly found on the ailerons *(see Figure 1.16)*.

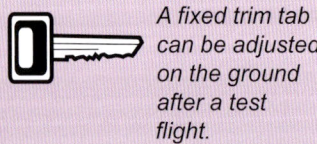

A fixed trim tab can be adjusted on the ground after a test flight.

TRAILING EDGE FLAPS.

Aircraft are fitted with high lift devices to give increased lift at lower airspeeds, to reduce the take-off and landing distances, and to permit suitably steep approach angles on landing. These devices are commonly called **flaps**. A **flap** (*see Figure 1.20*) is a hinged portion of the wing's trailing edge which can be deflected downwards and so produce an increase in wing camber.

There are various types of **flap** design all of which increase both lift and drag in varying amounts. The most common type of **flap** used on light aircraft is the plain **trailing edge flap**.

CHAPTER 1: AIRFRAMES

Figure 1.20 Trailing Edge Flaps.

Effects of Flap.

Lowering **flap** will increase both the lift and the drag of the aircraft but not in the same proportion, the increase in lift being the greater. Selecting **flap** will cause a pitch change. The overall change of pitch will be influenced by the type of **flap**, the position of the wing and the position of the tailplane.

Selecting flap will cause a pitch change.

OTHER METHODS OF CONTROL.

On some aircraft, rotation around two of the axes may be achieved with one control surface. For instance, the **elevon**, which is a combined elevator and aileron, is used on tail-less aircraft to produce both pitching and rolling motion (*see Figure 1.21*).

Figure 1.21 The Elevon.

The **ruddervator** which is the name of the control surfaces on a V-tail aircraft, produces both pitching and yawing motion. A **ruddervator** is shown in *Figure 1.22*.

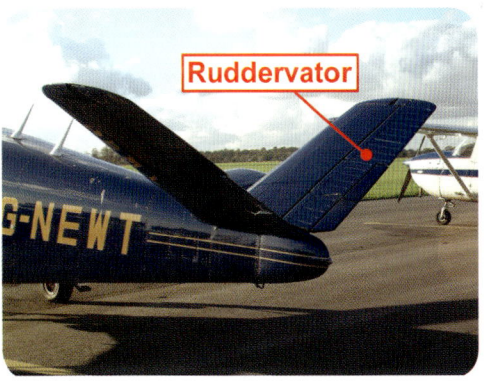

Figure 1.22 Ruddervator.

The **stabilator** (*Figure 1.23*) is an **all-moving tailplane** combining the dual function of horizontal stabiliser and elevator. Consequently, the **stabilator** provides both longitudinal stability and longitudinal control.

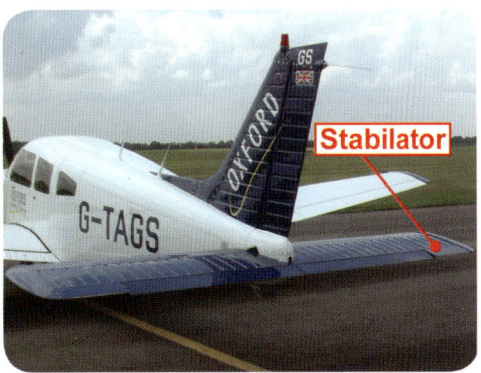

Figure 1.23 The Stabilator.

LOADS APPLIED TO AIRFRAME STRUCTURES.

A **tensile load** is one which tends to **stretch** a structural member. Aircraft components designed to resist tensile loads are known as **ties**.

Compressive loads are the opposite of tensile loads and tend to **shorten** structural members. Aircraft components designed to resist compressive loads are known as **struts**.

A **shear force** is a force which tends to slide one face of a material over an adjacent face. Riveted joints are designed to resist **shear forces**.

Combination Loadings.

Any bending of an aircraft's structure - as occurs in the flexing of a wing in flight, for instance - involves the three basic types of load. In flight, the undersurfaces of the wing will be under **tension**, while the upper surface will be subject to **compressive loading**. **Shear forces** and stresses will be felt across the depth of the wing at the points of maximum bending *(see Figure 1.24a)*.

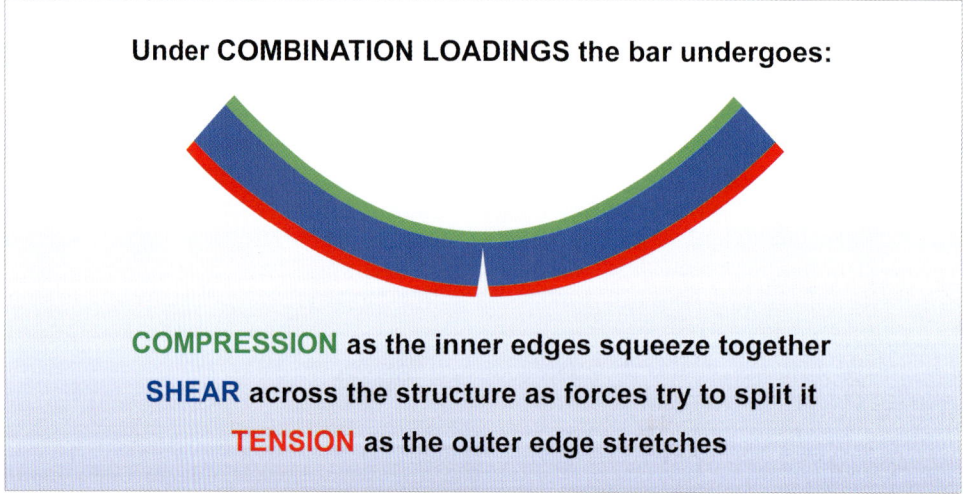

Figure 1.24a Combination Loading.

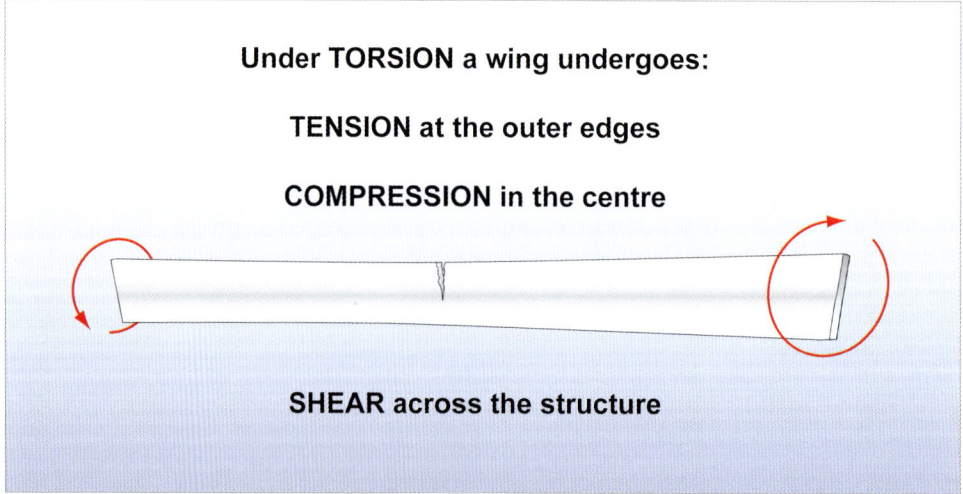

Figure 1.24b Torsion.

Torsion or **twisting forces** produce tension at the outer edge, compression in the centre and shear across the structure *(see Figure 1.24b)*. All parts of the airframe are subject to torsion in flight.

On the ground the different types of load, to which an aircraft's wing are subjected, are reversed. When an aircraft is stationary on the ground, a cantilever wing is subject to **tensile stress** on its upper surface and **compressive stress** on its under surface.

Buckling can occur in the stressed-skin of the aircraft's wing and/or fuselage when subjected to excessive compressive forces. Buckling is a sure sign that an aircraft has been overstressed.

Safety Factor.

The maximum load that the designer would expect an airframe or airframe component to experience in service is termed the **Design Limit Load**. A **safety-factor** is applied to the **Design Limit Load**, to cater for unexpected circumstances which might cause the **Design Limit Load** to be exceeded.

The minimum safety factor specified in design requirements is 1.5. The **Design Limit Load** multiplied by the **safety-factor** is called the **Design Ultimate Load**. The aircraft's structure must be able to withstand the **Design Ultimate Load** without collapse, but the **Design Ultimate Load** may be expected to cause severe deformation of the aircraft's structure. Beyond the **Design Ultimate Load**, the aircraft's structure will almost certainly fail.

A flying control lock is used on the ground to prevent damage to the aircraft controls in windy conditions.

Figure 1.25 Internally Fitted Control Lock.   *Figure 1.26 Externally Fitted Control Lock.*

CONTROL LOCKS.

When an aircraft is parked in the open, strong or gusty winds could blow the controls about against their stops with sufficient force to cause mechanical damage. To prevent this occurring, **control locks** are fitted. These may be fitted internally or externally. If the **control locks** are controlled from the cockpit, they are arranged so that it is impossible to open the throttle until they are removed.

CHAPTER 1: AIRFRAMES

EMERGENCY EQUIPMENT - FIRE EXTINGUISHERS.

Water Or Water Glycol.
Water or water glycol fire extinguishers have red containers, as shown in *Figure 1.27*. Hand held portable Water or Water Glycol fire extinguishers may be found in commercial aircraft. They can be used in passenger cabins for combating fires involving **domestic materials such as paper and furnishing materials**.

Water or Water Glycol fire extinguishers must <u>not</u> be used on fires which involve electrical equipment or liquids.

The glycol is an antifreeze agent which permits operation of the extinguishers at temperatures as low as -20°C. The same type of extinguisher is also used for ground based applications.

Figure 1.27 Water Glycol Extinguisher.

Dry Powder.
Dry Powder extinguishers are blue cylinders or red cylinders with blue labels, *as shown in Figure 1.28*. The use of dry powder in crew or passenger compartments of pressurised aircraft is not permitted.

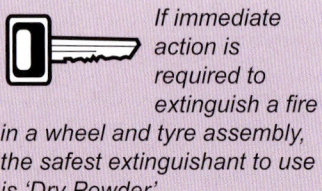

If immediate action is required to extinguish a fire in a wheel and tyre assembly, the safest extinguishant to use is 'Dry Powder'.

The **powder agent**, Potassium Bicarbonate, is a non-toxic powder, similar to talcum powder. It is very effective against fires involving **flammable liquids, wood, fabric and paper**.

Dry Powder is the safest extinguisher to use against **wheel and brake fires** as it is least likely to cause overheated brake discs to explode. **Dry powder** extinguishers are mostly used for ground based applications.

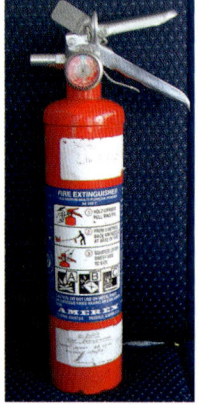

Figure 1.28 Dry Powder Extinguisher.

Bromochlorodifluromethane (BCF).
This extinguishant is stored in signal red, purple, brown or green containers. **BCF** extinguishers are very effective against **electrical and flammable liquid fires**. BCF is only slightly toxic. It is colourless, non-corrosive and evaporates rapidly leaving no residue. It does not freeze or cause cold burns and will not harm fabrics, metals or other materials it comes into contact with. It acts rapidly on fires by producing a heavy blanketing mist, which eliminates air from the fire source. But, more importantly, it interferes chemically with the combustion process. **BCF** has outstanding properties in preventing re-flash after the fire has been extinguished.

It is safe to use a BCF extinguisher in an enclosed cockpit, provided the cockpit is subsequently ventilated.

Hand held containers *(see Figure 1.29)* using **BCF** are used in many aircraft, and although it is slightly toxic, it is quite safe to use provided that the cockpit is **ventilated** after the fire is extinguished. Nevertheless, because of the toxic nature of the fumes produced by a BCF discharge, its use as a fire extinguishant in aircraft is becoming less common.

Figure 1.29 BCF Extinguisher.

CHAPTER 1: AIRFRAMES

Carbon Dioxide (CO_2).

Carbon Dioxide is used on the airfield apron in trolley based extinguishers, like the one shown in *Figure 1.30*. The **Carbon Dioxide extinguishant** is stored in a black cylinder, or in a red cylinder with a black label. It is non-corrosive and extinguishes the flame by dissipating the oxygen in the immediate vicinity.

From the standpoint of toxicity and corrosion, **Carbon Dioxide** is the safest agent to use, and, for many years, was the most widely used in the supervision of aircraft movements on the ground. Nevertheless, if handled improperly it can cause mental confusion and suffocation.

Carbon Dioxide requires a stronger container than most other agents due to its variation in vapour pressure with changes of temperature. The use of this agent inside an aircraft is not permitted.

Figure 1.30
CO_2 Fire Extinguisher.

Carbon Dioxide may be used against most fires. It is particularly useful against **engine fires** as it will extinguish the fire without damaging the engine. Great care must be exercised in handling the discharge nozzle of a Carbon Dioxide Extinguisher. Discharge of the extinguisher is accompanied by a sharp and significant drop in temperature of the nozzle and there is a danger that the skin of the hand can become "cold-welded" to the nozzle. Always handle the discharge nozzle by the grip or handle provided.

Foam.

Foam extinguishers are cream cylinders, or red cylinders with a cream label *(see Figure 1.31)*. **Foam** is the principal extinguishant for use on **flammable liquid fires**, such as **burning paint**, **oil** or **petrol**. It blankets the flames by excluding oxygen. Foam can also be used on combustible material fires as it gives good flame knock down and also prevents re-ignition of the fire.

Foam extinguishers should not be used on electrical fires, as the water base can conduct electricity and may in some cases cause the user of the device to get a severe electrical shock.

> Foam is the principal extinguishant for use on flammable liquid fires, such as burning paint, oil or petrol. Foam can also be used on combustible material fires.

> Foam extinguishers should not be used on electrical fires, as they may cause the user of the device to get a severe electric shock.

Figure 1.31 A Foam Extinguisher.

Foam extinguishers are sometimes called **AFFF** extinguishers; this stands for **Aqueous Film Forming Foam**.

EMERGENCY EQUIPMENT - LIFE JACKETS.

The personal floatation equipment used by the pilot and passengers is the Life Jacket or Life Preserver. There are numerous types of life jacket. The information given here is of a general nature and does not apply to any particular make, model or type.

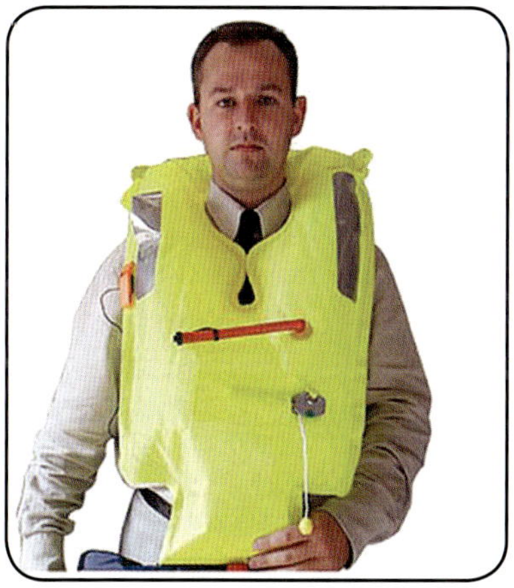

Figure 1.32 The Personal Life Jacket.

> If there is any evidence that life jackets have been mishandled or immersed in sea water, they should not be used operationally.

15

CHAPTER 1: AIRFRAMES

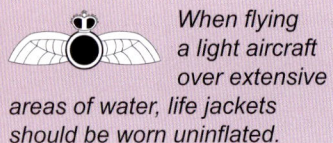

When flying a light aircraft over extensive areas of water, life jackets should be worn uninflated.

Life jackets are designed as lightweight items of equipment and should be treated with care at all times.

Life Jackets are normally stowed in special packs or containers for ease of handling and protection. Stowage in this manner will ensure that the jacket is maintained correctly folded for easy and rapid fitting if required for use.

If there is any evidence of mishandling or immersion in sea water, life jackets should be rejected for operational use. Instructions for fitting are printed on the container and/or the jacket.

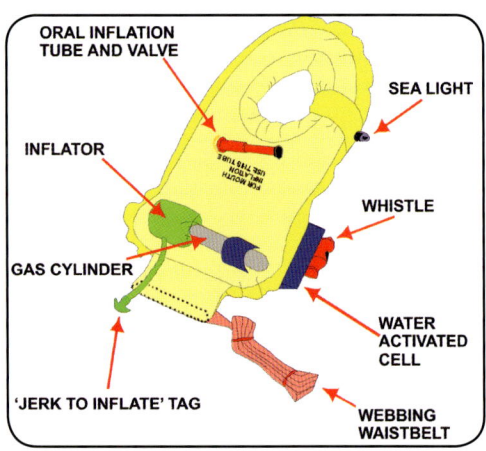

Figure 1.33 The Basic Life Jacket.

All life jackets are basically similar in design *(see Figure 1.33)*. Buoyancy is achieved by inflating the jacket with Carbon Dioxide Gas which is stored under pressure in a small cylinder and released manually by the operation of a toggle or lever. Once it has been released, the gas will pass through a Non Return Valve into the jacket and cannot be stopped.

The life jacket can be inflated or topped up by mouth. The manual inflation tube contains a valve which can be operated to lower or release the pressure in the jacket.

The life jacket is coloured either brilliant yellow or flame red as an aid to location, and may contain equipment to expedite the location of the individual wearing it. If you are flying in a light aircraft over extensive areas of water, the recommended practice in respect of life jackets is that they should be worn uninflated for the flight. In the event of ditching, life jackets should not be inflated until the wearer has left the aircraft.

CHECKS AND EMERGENCY DRILLS.

In the context of normal club flying operations, it is up to the pilot to ensure that the aircraft is safe for flight. To this end, a series of checks is carried out prior to, during, and after the flight.

Initially, student pilots will normally rely on an aircraft's abbreviated Check List to carry out these checks. As students gain experience, checks should become instinctive, and the time taken to do them will decrease, but every so often pilots should compare their actions against the manufacturer's Expanded Check List.

Figure 1.34 Check Lists.

CHAPTER 1: AIRFRAMES

Figure 1.35 Beware of the Propeller.

Carrying out the external pre-flight check will inevitably bring the pilot close to the aircraft's propeller. Propellers should always be treated as being 'live'. No part of the pilot's body or his equipment should be allowed to come within the arc that would be described by a rotating propeller.

Propellers are lethal. They should always be treated as being 'live'. Always remain outside the arc of the propeller.

With experience, student pilots should be able to locate items in the cockpit without looking. Always practise checks thoroughly; but beware of learning them 'parrot fashion'. The Checklist should always be used when carrying out routine checks, but emergency checks should be learnt by heart.

If you drop anything in the cockpit, you must retrieve it. The aircraft should not be allowed to fly again until after the object is found.

Loose Articles.
The danger of loose articles in aircraft cockpits cannot be overstressed. Numerous accidents have been attributed to **foreign objects** left in the aircraft by careless pilots. Personal items such as pens, pencils, keys, combs and coins can all be the cause of accidents if they become lodged in the flying controls.

If you do drop anything in the cockpit, you must retrieve it. If you are unable to locate a misplaced item then you must report this fact to a responsible authority. Only after the lost item is found will the aircraft be allowed to fly again.

Emergency Drills.
Just as the checks must become well practised, so must the initial reactions to emergencies. Emergencies are fortunately rare in modern aircraft, but pilots must be able to deal promptly with any emergency situation that does arise.

Before being sent solo, the student pilot must know how to carry out emergency actions in the event of an engine fire, an engine failure after take off and a forced landing.

The emergency drills should be practised frequently in the air and on the ground. Before being sent solo, the student must know what actions to carry out in the event of a fire, (both on the ground and in the air), an engine failure after take-off, and a forced landing.

CHAPTER 1: AIRFRAMES

Aircraft Operations On The Apron.

On the apron of a busy airfield, apart from your own aircraft, there will be other aircraft and items of ground equipment and personnel, for example refuelling crews. As a consequence of this, all pilots must be conscious of the safety precautions required when starting aircraft engines and when taxying on to, or away from, the apron. Extreme caution must be exercised and the taxying speed must be kept to a minimum. Remember, the pilot is always responsible for the safety of the aircraft.

Figure 1.36 The Apron can be a very busy, and very dangerous place.

CHAPTER 1: AIRFRAMES QUESTIONS

Representative PPL - style questions to test your theoretical knowledge of Airframes.

1. Which of the following correctly describes a semi-monocoque or stressed skin structure?

    a. Containing no openings, but having internal structural members, known as longerons, running lengthwise joining the frames together
    b. Containing openings which are reinforced to maintain the integrity of the load bearing skin
    c. Containing a load bearing structure that transmits loads proportionately to the load bearing skin
    d. Containing no openings and no internal support structure, all loads being carried by the skin

2. A fixed trim tab should:

    a. Never be adjusted
    b. Be adjusted on the ground by an aircraft technician, to correct permanent out-of-trim conditions
    c. Be adjusted to achieve laterally level flight
    d. Only be adjusted if the aircraft pitch trim mechanism is found to be incapable of sufficient movement to trim the aircraft longitudinally

3. Which stabilising surface provides directional stability?

    a. The fin
    b. The rudder
    c. The rudder trim tab
    d. The stabilator

4. Movement about an aircraft's vertical (normal) axis is known as:

    a. Side slipping
    b. Roll
    c. Yaw
    d. Pitch

5. The purpose of a control surface mass balance is to:

    a. Balance the extra mass of the trim tab on the leading edge
    b. Balance the extra mass of the spring tab
    c. Make the control easier to move
    d. Prevent "flutter" at higher speeds

6. The tendency for control surfaces to flutter at high speed can be avoided by:

    a. Adjusting servo tabs on the trailing edge
    b. Fitting a mass balance forward of the leading edge of the control surface
    c. Using balance tabs on the leading edge
    d. Fitting spring tabs to the trailing edge

CHAPTER 1: AIRFRAMES QUESTIONS

7. Ailerons are control surfaces which control an aircraft in:

    a. Roll
    b. Pitch
    c. Yaw
    d. Stall

8. The elevator is a control surface which controls an aircraft in:

    a. Roll
    b. Pitch
    c. Yaw
    d. Stall

9. The rudder is a control surface which controls an aircraft in:

    a. Roll
    b. Pitch
    c. Yaw
    d. Stall

10. The most common type of modern light aircraft fuselage construction is:

    a. Monocoque
    b. Truss or framework construction
    c. Wood and canvas
    d. Semi monocoque/stressed skin

11. Increased lift at lower airspeeds is achieved by deploying:

    a. The elevator
    b. The trailing edge flaps
    c. The rudder
    d. The aileron

12. Rotation of the aircraft about its lateral axis is called:

    a. Side slipping
    b. Roll
    c. Yaw
    d. Pitch

13. Rotation of the aircraft about its longitudinal axis is known as:

    a. Side slipping
    b. Roll
    c. Yaw
    d. Pitch

14. A flying control lock:

   a. Locks controls in flight to neutralize aerodynamic loads and ease the physical load on the pilot
   b. Locks the trim tabs once straight and level flight is established
   c. Locks controls on the ground to prevent damage in windy conditions.
   d. Locks controls on the ground to prevent the pilot damaging them while manoeuvring the aircraft

15. If a fire occurs in a wheel and tyre assembly and immediate action is required to extinguish it, the safest extinguishant to use is:

   a. Dry powder
   b. Carbon dioxide (CO_2)
   c. Bromotrifluoromethane (BTF)
   d. Water acid

16. A BCF fire extinguisher that is used in an enclosed cockpit:

   a. Gives off highly toxic fumes and must never be used.
   b. Is quite safe to use provided the cockpit is subsequently ventilated
   c. May not extinguish wood and fabric fires and may not be suitable for all aircraft
   d. May be refilled with Carbon Dioxide (CO_2) and refitted to the aircraft

Question	1	2	3	4	5	6	7	8	9	10	11	12
Answer												

13	14	15	16

The answers to these questions can be found at the end of this book.

CHAPTER 2
LANDING GEAR, TYRES AND BRAKES

CHAPTER 2: LANDING GEAR, TYRES AND BRAKES

CHAPTER 2: LANDING GEAR, TYRES AND BRAKES

FUNCTIONS OF THE LANDING GEAR.

The functions of the **landing gear** are, firstly, to provide a means of manoeuvring the aircraft on the ground, secondly, to support the aircraft at a convenient height to give clearance for propellers and flaps, etc, and, thirdly, to absorb the kinetic energy of landing.

Figure 2.1 A Warrior aircraft taxying.

Landing Gear Design.
Once airborne, the **landing gear** serves no useful purpose and is dead weight. It would be ideal to replace the landing gear with some ground based equipment for use before the aircraft takes off. But, while it is possible to achieve manoeuvring and support for the aircraft with ground based equipment, no satisfactory alternative exists for absorbing the kinetic energy of landing

Figure 2.2 Once airborne the gear serves no useful purpose.

and providing a means of controlling deceleration. For this reason, a vast amount of research has gone into the design of undercarriage units in order to reduce their weight and their stowed volume when retracted.

LANDING GEAR TYPES - FIXED OR RETRACTABLE.

With slow, light aircraft, and some larger aircraft on which simplicity is of prime importance, a fixed, **non-retractable landing gear** is often fitted. On light, training aircraft, for instance, the reduced performance caused by the drag of the fixed landing gear during flight is offset by its simplicity, its reduced maintenance and also its low initial cost. On high speed aircraft, drag becomes progressively more important, so the landing gear is retracted into the wings or fuselage during flight. There are, however, penalties of increased weight, greater complication and additional maintenance with retractable undercarriages.

The reduced performance caused by the drag of fixed gear during flight is offset by its simplicity, its reduced maintenance and also its low initial cost.

Fixed Landing Gear.
There are three main types of **fixed landing gear**: those which have **spring steel legs**, those which employ **rubber cords** to absorb shocks, and those which have **oleo-pneumatic struts** to absorb shocks.

Spring Steel Legs.
Spring steel legs are usually employed at the main undercarriage positions. The leg consists of a tube, or strip of tapered spring steel, the upper end being attached by bolts to the fuselage and the lower end terminating in an axle on which the wheel and brake are assembled *(see Figure 2.3)*.

Figure 2.3 Spring Steel Legs.

25

CHAPTER 2: LANDING GEAR, TYRES AND BRAKES

Rubber Cord.
When **rubber cord** is used as a shock-absorber, the undercarriage is usually in the form of tubular struts, designed and installed so that the landing force is directed against a number of turns of rubber in the form of a grommet or loop.

Figure 2.4 Rubber Cord.

Oleo-pneumatic Struts.
Some fixed main undercarriages, and most fixed nose undercarriages, are fitted with an **oleo-pneumatic shock absorber strut**. The design of oleo-pneumatic struts varies considerably. Some may be fitted with fairings to reduce drag.

> Some fixed main gear, and most fixed nose gear, are fitted with an oleo-pneumatic shock absorber strut.

Figure 2.5 An Oleo-Pneumatic Strut.

Spats.
Spats may be fitted to the undercarriage in order to reduce drag.

One drawback to their use is that **spats** may pick up mud when landing or taking off from grass airfields. This can add considerably to the weight of the aircraft and may affect take-off performance. To avoid this eventuality, if any mud has been picked up, the **spats** must be removed, cleaned and replaced before the next take-off.

> If the spats have picked up any mud after landing on a grass strip, they must be removed, cleaned and replaced before the next take-off.

Figure 2.6 Spats, fitted to a Pitts S2a.

THE NOSE WHEEL.

The **nose gear** is usually of a lighter structure than the main gear units since it carries less weight and is normally subject only to direct compression loads.

The **nose wheel** must be able to castor freely. Castoring is the ability of the nose wheel to turn to either side in response to differential braking on the main wheels.

Figure 2.7 Nose Gear.

Nose Wheel Steering.
A method of steering is required to enable the pilot to manoeuvre the aircraft safely on the ground.

> The nosewheel steering of most light aircraft is controlled by the operation of the rudder pedals.

Early methods involved the use of differential braking and free castoring nose wheels, but, today, the nose wheel of most light aircraft is steered directly by the rudder pedals.

CHAPTER 2: LANDING GEAR, TYRES AND BRAKES

Wheel Shimmy.

Due to the flexibility of tyre side walls, an unstable, rapid, sinusoidal oscillation or vibration known as **shimmy** can be induced into the steerable parts of the undercarriage. Excessive **shimmy**, especially at high speeds, can set up vibrations throughout the aircraft and can be dangerous.

Worn wheel bearings and uneven tyre pressures can both increase the tendency of the wheels to **shimmy**.

Shimmy can be reduced in several ways; for instance, by fitting a **shimmy damper**, or by having heavy self-centring springs fitted in the nosewheel-steering control-rod run. Some larger aircraft have double nose wheels fitted, while twin contact wheels have also been found to be effective in minimizing tailwheel **shimmy**.

Retractable Landing Gear.

An increasing number of light aircraft are fitted with a **retractable landing gear** for the purpose of reducing drag, thus improving aircraft performance.

Retraction is normally effected by a hydraulic system, but pneumatic or electrical systems are also used.

Figure 2.8 Gear Retracted.

Retractable gear has mechanical locks to ensure that the gear is locked up and down, devices to indicate its position and a means of extending it if the power system fails.

In some instances, power is used for retraction only, extension being effected by gravity and slipstream. Retractable landing gear is also provided with mechanical locks to ensure that each undercarriage leg is locked securely in the retracted or extended positions. Retractable undercarriage systems are also fitted with devices to indicate to the pilot the position of each undercarriage leg, and a means by which the landing gear can be extended in the event of failure of the power source.

In addition, safety systems are provided which prevent retraction of the landing gear when the aircraft is on the ground, and to guard against landing with the landing gear retracted. Undercarriage-wells are normally sealed by doors for aerodynamic reasons.

TYRES.

Introduction.

Aircraft wheels are fitted with pneumatic tyres which usually comprise both a **rubber inner tube** and **outer cover**.

The inner-tube is inflated with compressed air which absorbs shock and supports the weight of the aircraft. The cover restrains and protects the inner-tube from damage, maintains the shape of the tyre, transmits braking effort, and provides a wearing surface.

Figure 2.9 An Aircraft Tyre Outer Cover.

CHAPTER 2: LANDING GEAR, TYRES AND BRAKES

Tyre Covers.

The **tyre cover** consists of a casing made of rubber which is reinforced with **plies** of cotton, rayon or nylon **cords**.

The **cords** are not woven, but arranged parallel in single layers and held together by a thin film of rubber which prevents cords of adjacent plies from cutting one another as the tyre flexes, in use.

During construction of the cover, the plies are fitted in pairs.

Each pair is termed a pocket, which is set so that the cords of adjacent plies are at 90 degrees to one another; this is called **cross-ply**.

The tyre manufacturers give each tyre a **ply rating**. This rating does not relate directly to the number of plies in the tyre, but is instead the index of the strength of the tyre.

To absorb and distribute load shocks, and also to protect the casing from concussion damage, two narrow plies embedded in thick layers of rubber are situated between the casing and the tread, these special plies are termed **breaker strips**.

The casing is retained on the rim of the wheel by interlocking the plies around inextensible steel wire coils to form ply overlaps. This portion of the cover is known as the **bead**.

The Regions Of The Tyre.

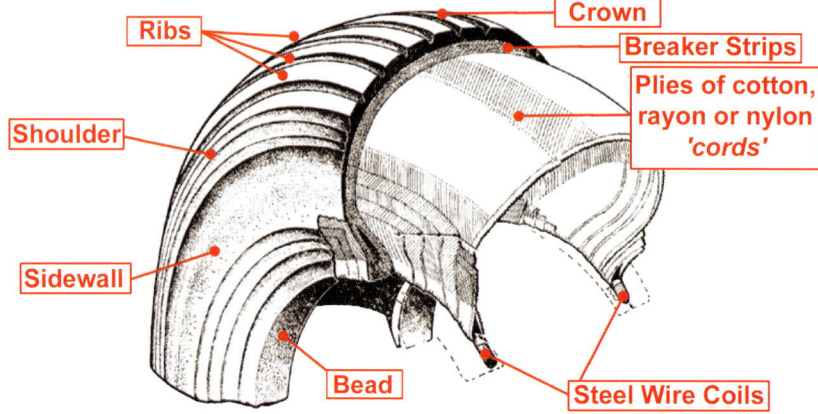

Figure 2.10. The Regions of the Tyre.

The tyre is divided into regions or sections as illustrated here in *Figure 2.10*.

The **tread** of the tyre is situated in the **crown** and **shoulder** section. Note that the term **'tread'** is applied irrespective of whether the rubber is plain and smooth, or moulded on a block pattern.

The most popular tread pattern is that termed **'ribbed'**. This tread pattern is formed from circumferential grooves around the tyre.

Tyre Markings.

The size of a tyre is marked on its sidewall and includes the outside diameter, the inside diameter and the width of the tyre, all in inches.

CHAPTER 2: LANDING GEAR, TYRES AND BRAKES

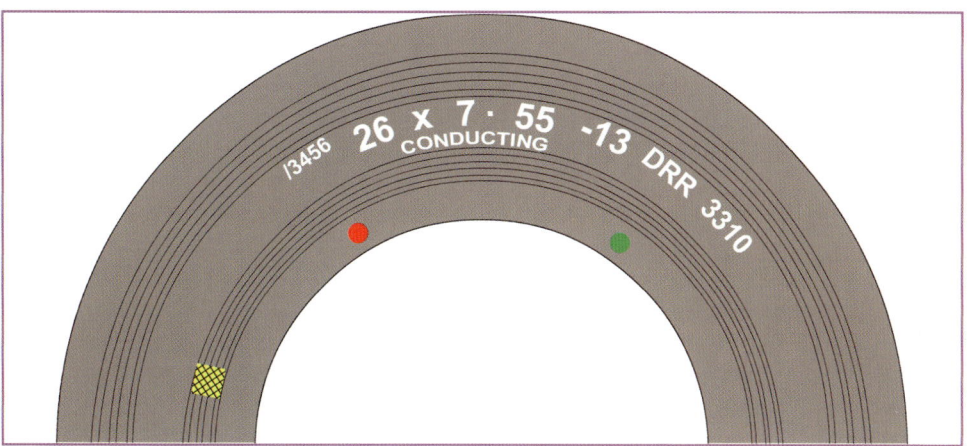

Figure 2.11. Tyre Markings.

A 'ply rating' is the index of the strength of the tyre.

The ply rating, the index of the tyre's strength, is also marked on the sidewall. Normally the ply rating is shown as an abbreviation, i.e. **PR16**, but occasionally it is shown in full as **'16 PLY RATING'**.

The **speed rating** of the tyre, the maximum speed for which the tyre is designed, is imprinted in a panel on the sidewall of some high speed tyres. The rating takes account of pressure altitude, ambient temperature and wind component, enabling the maximum take-off weight that the tyres can sustain to be calculated.

Green or grey dots painted on the sidewall of the tyre indicate the position of the **"awl" vents**. **Awl vents** prevent pressure being trapped between the plies which would cause disruption of the tyre carcass if it was exposed to the low pressures experienced during high altitude flight.

Awl vents prevent pressure being trapped between the plies which would cause damage to the tyre when it is exposed to the low atmospheric pressures of high altitude flight.

A red dot or triangle indicates the lightest part of the tyre. If this is placed adjacent to the **valve** during tyre fitting, it assists in balancing the wheel assembly.

Tyre Contamination.

Tyres must be protected from excessive heat, dampness, bright sunlight, contact with oil, fuel and hydraulic fluid as all of these have a harmful effect on rubber.

Protect tyres from excessive heat, dampness, bright sunlight, contact with oil, fuel and hydraulic fluid. Any hydraulic fluid inadvertently spilt onto a tyre must be wiped off immediately

Covers should be placed over the tyres when the aircraft is to be parked for any length of time or during the periods when oil, fuel, cooling or hydraulic systems are being drained or replenished.

Any fluid inadvertently spilt or allowed to drip onto a tyre must be wiped off immediately.

When tyres are first fitted to a wheel they tend to move slightly around the rim. This phenomenon is called 'creep'.

Creep (Slippage).

When tyres are first fitted to a wheel they tend to move slightly around the rim. This phenomenon is called **'creep'** and at this stage it is considered normal. After the tyres settle down, however, this movement should cease.

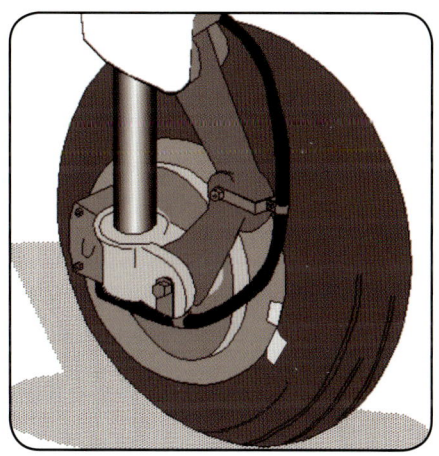

Figure 2.12. Misaligned Creep Marks.

29

CHAPTER 2: LANDING GEAR, TYRES AND BRAKES

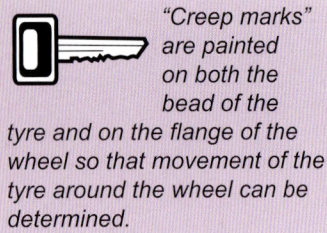

"Creep marks" are painted on both the bead of the tyre and on the flange of the wheel so that movement of the tyre around the wheel can be determined.

In service, the tyre may tend to continue to **creep** around the wheel. If this **creep** is excessive on a tyre fitted with an inner tube, it will tear out the inflation valve and cause the tyre to burst. **Creep** is less of a problem with tubeless tyres, as long as the tyre bead is undamaged and any pressure drop is within limits.

Creep is less likely to occur if the tyre air pressure is correctly maintained. To assist in this, tyre manufacturers specify a rated inflation pressure for each tyre.

Witness marks called '**creep marks**' are painted both on the bead of the tyre and on the flange of the wheel. When the tyre is first fitted to the wheel, the **creep marks** will be aligned with each other. However, for a variety of reasons, including heavy landings, harsh braking and low tyre pressures, the tyre will move around the wheel and the **creep marks** will move in relation to each other.

Movement of the tyre around the wheel must not be such that the **creep marks** become fully misaligned with each other, as illustrated in *Figure 2.12*.

Tyre Damage.

Figure 2.13. Cuts in the Tread of a Tyre.

Any damage to the tyre must be carefully examined to check if the fabric of the tyre has been weakened unduly; if there is any doubt about the serviceability of a tyre, the tyre should be replaced.

During your pre-flight inspection, tyres must be examined for cuts, bulges, embedded stones, metal or glass, signs of wear, creep, etc.

Cuts in the tyre cover penetrating to the cords render the tyre unserviceable. The cords will be recognisable as pieces of white fibrous material embedded in the rubber of the tyre.

Bulges may indicate a partial failure of the casing. If the fabric is fractured, the tyre must be renewed.

Embedded stones, metal, glass etc. must be removed and the cuts examined by a qualified aircraft technician to ascertain their depth.

The decision whether or not the tyre should be repaired or replaced is governed by the depth of the cut. Any flat spots on the tyre tread, especially those caused by skidding or aquaplaning *(see Figure 2.17)*, must be examined with great care to determine whether the fabric of the tyre has been unduly weakened. If there is any doubt about the serviceability of a tyre, it should be replaced.

AQUAPLANING.

Aquaplaning is a phenomenon caused by a wedge of water building up under the tread of the tyre and breaking its contact with the ground.

CHAPTER 2: LANDING GEAR, TYRES AND BRAKES

Figure 2.14 shows a tyre moving slower than **aquaplaning** speed. It can be seen that there is quite a large footprint still in contact with the ground. In this case the tyre is still capable of gripping the runway.

Figure 2.14 Satisfactory contact between tyre and surface.

In *Figure 2.15,* the wedge of water is in the process of lifting the tyre clear of the runway, although at this stage there is still a small footprint which may supply adequate grip.

Figure 2.15 Tyre Footprint Reducing.

Figure 2.16 shows the tyre footprint reduced to zero, at **aquaplaning** speed. The wedge of water has lifted the tyre completely clear of the runway. No grip is being obtained by this tyre in this situation.

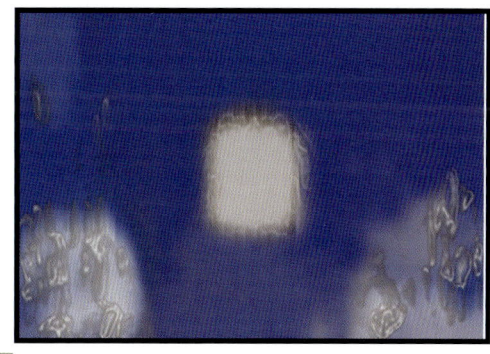

Figure 2.16 Tyre Aquaplaning.

Aquaplaning speed can be calculated, in knots, by multiplying the square root of the tyre pressure, in PSI, by nine.

Figure 2.17. A Tyre Damaged by Aquaplaning.

Aquaplaning speed, measured in nautical miles per hour, is the speed at which the tyre loses contact with the ground. It can be found by applying the formula:-

AQUAPLANING SPEED = $9\sqrt{P}$
(where P = the tyre pressure in lbs/in²)
or
AQUAPLANING SPEED = $34\sqrt{P}$
(where P = the tyre pressure in kg/cm²)

CHAPTER 2: LANDING GEAR, TYRES AND BRAKES

> 🔑 *The amount of heat generated in stopping even a light aircraft is extremely large. The bigger the aircraft, the greater the amount of heat generated.*

> 🔑 *If there is a wheel or brake fire, the best extinguishant to use is dry powder.*

The possibility of **aquaplaning** increases as the depth of the tread is reduced; it is, therefore, important that the amount of tread remaining is accurately assessed.

AIRCRAFT WHEEL BRAKES.

In common with most braking systems, **aircraft wheel brakes** function by using friction between a fixed surface and a moving one to bring an aircraft to rest, converting kinetic energy into heat energy in the process. The amount of heat generated in stopping even a light aircraft is extremely large. The bigger the aircraft, the greater the heat. The problem of dissipating the heat generated by aircraft brakes has been a challenge to aircraft designers and scientists for decades.

Disc Brakes.

Most light aircraft now use hydraulic **disc brakes** as their means of slowing down or stopping *(see Figure 2.18)*. These use a series of fixed friction-pads, bearing on, or gripping, a rotating disc, similar to the **disc brakes** on a car.

The friction-pads are made of an inorganic friction material and the discs are of forged steel with a specially case-hardened surface. This surface and interior structure combination causes the plates to explode if doused with a liquid fire extinguishant when they are red hot. **In the event of a wheel or brake fire, the best extinguishant to use is dry powder.**

Figure 2.18. An Aircraft Disc Brake Assembly.

Brake Operation.

If pressure is applied to the brake pedals or the hand brake lever, hydraulic pressure will build up in the slave cylinder behind the piston. This pressure will cause the piston to move over within the caliper unit, pushing the brake pad against the brake disc *(see Figure 2.20)*.

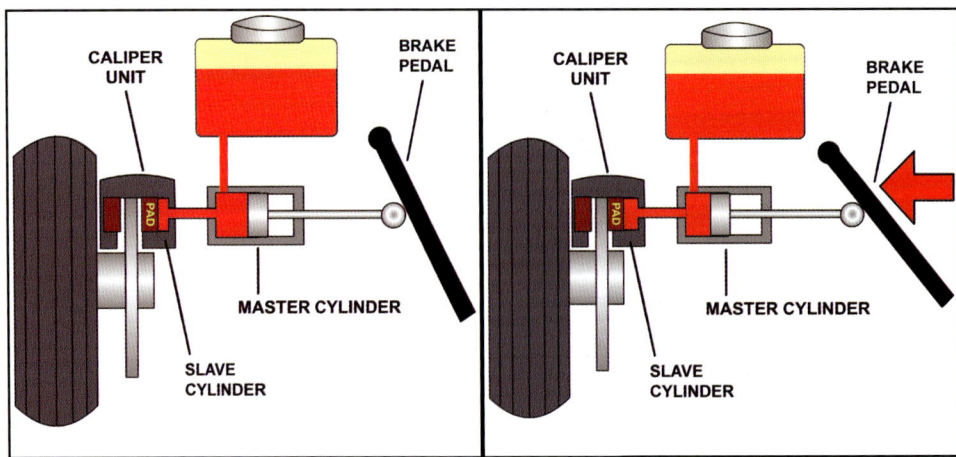

Figure 2.19 No Brake Pressure Applied.   *Figure 2.20 Brake Pressure Applied.*

The reaction of the inner brake pad pushing against the disc will cause the caliper unit to move in the opposite direction to the piston, carrying the outer brake pad with it until the disc is squeezed between the two pads (*see Figure 2.21*).

The force applied to the brake pads will be proportional to the effort applied to the brakes. The brakes can be applied together, or, if differential braking is required for manoeuvring the aircraft within tight spaces, the toe brakes can be used separately.

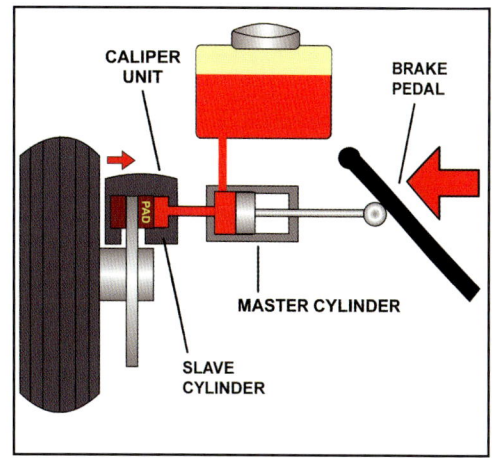

Figure 2.21 Reaction Moving Caliper Unit Over.

Most light aircraft have a hand operated parking brake. When selected, the hand brake will **lock in** the hydraulic pressure applied by the foot brakes.

Pre-Flight Checks.
Before flight, the brake system should be checked for any signs of malfunction. Signs of hydraulic fluid leaks are relatively easy to spot.

Any fluid leaking from the slave cylinders within the caliper units will either drip straight onto the ground, or dribble down the sidewall of the tyre. In either case, it should be fairly easy to see.

Any brake fluid leaking from the slave cylinders within the caliper units will either drip straight onto the ground, or dribble down the sidewall of the tyre where it should be fairly easy to see.

Make sure before you touch the brake assembly that it is not still hot from recent use, and check that the caliper unit is firmly attached to the gear. Also, have a look at the wear on the brake pads. The part of the disc with which the brakes come into contact is bright and shiny. Any rust or pitting on the braking surface of the disc will reduce brake effectiveness, and may be indicative of a malfunction of the system. Any problems associated with the braking system should be rectified before the aircraft is moved.

CHAPTER 2: LANDING GEAR, TYRES AND BRAKES QUESTIONS

Representative PPL - type questions to test your theoretical knowledge of Landing Gear, Tyres and Brakes.

1. Tyre creep:

    a. Can be prevented by painting lines on the tyre and wheel
    b. Refers to the movement of an aircraft against the brakes
    c. Can be recognized by the misalignment of markings painted on the tyre and the wheel
    d. Can be prevented with glue

2. Awl vents in an aircraft tyre:

    a. Prevent damage to the tyre which might be caused at high altitude because of pressure trapped between the tyre plies
    b. Enable tyre creep to be detected
    c. Assist in balancing the wheel assembly
    d. Prevent tyre slippage

3. The principal reason why light training aircraft have fixed undercarriages is that:

    a. Training aircraft need to manoeuvre on the ground
    b. The reduced performance caused by the additional drag of a fixed undercarriage is offset by its simplicity, low cost and easy maintenance
    c. Training aircraft need to be supported at a convenient height
    d. Training aircraft need to ensure that kinetic energy on landing is absorbed

4. Tyre creep may be identified by:

    a. Two yellow diametrically opposed arrows painted on the tyre sidewalls
    b. A tyre pressure check
    c. Alignment marks painted on the tyre sidewall and wheel flange
    d. Two white blocks painted on the wheel flange

5. If a fire occurs in a wheel and tyre assembly and immediate action is required to extinguish it, the safest extinguishant to use is:

    a. Dry powder
    b. Carbon dioxide (CO_2)
    c. Bromotrifluoromethane (BTF)
    d. Water acid

6. Most nose wheel assemblies on modern light aircraft consist of:

    a. Oleo-pneumatic shock-absorber struts
    b. Spring steel struts
    c. Spring coil struts
    d. Compressed rubber struts

7. On a light aircraft fitted with a mechanically-steered nose wheel, steering on the ground is normally effected by:

   a. Cables operated from the aileron control wheel
   b. Use of the differential braking technique, only
   c. Hydraulic jacks which allow self-centreing
   d. Control rods/cables operated by the rudder pedals

8. Aquaplaning speed:

   a. Increases as the depth of tread on the tyres reduces
   b. Can be calculated, in knots, by multiplying the square root of the tyre pressure in PSI by nine
   c. Increases as the depth of water on the ground increases
   d. Is measured in miles per hour

9. The 'Ply Rating' of a tyre:

   a. Indicates the number of rayon or nylon cords
   b. Shows how many breaker strips are embedded in the tyre
   c. Has nothing to do with the strength of the tyre
   d. Is an index of the strength of the tyre

Question	1	2	3	4	5	6	7	8	9
Answer									

The answers to these questions can be found at the end of this book.

CHAPTER 3
ENGINES GENERAL

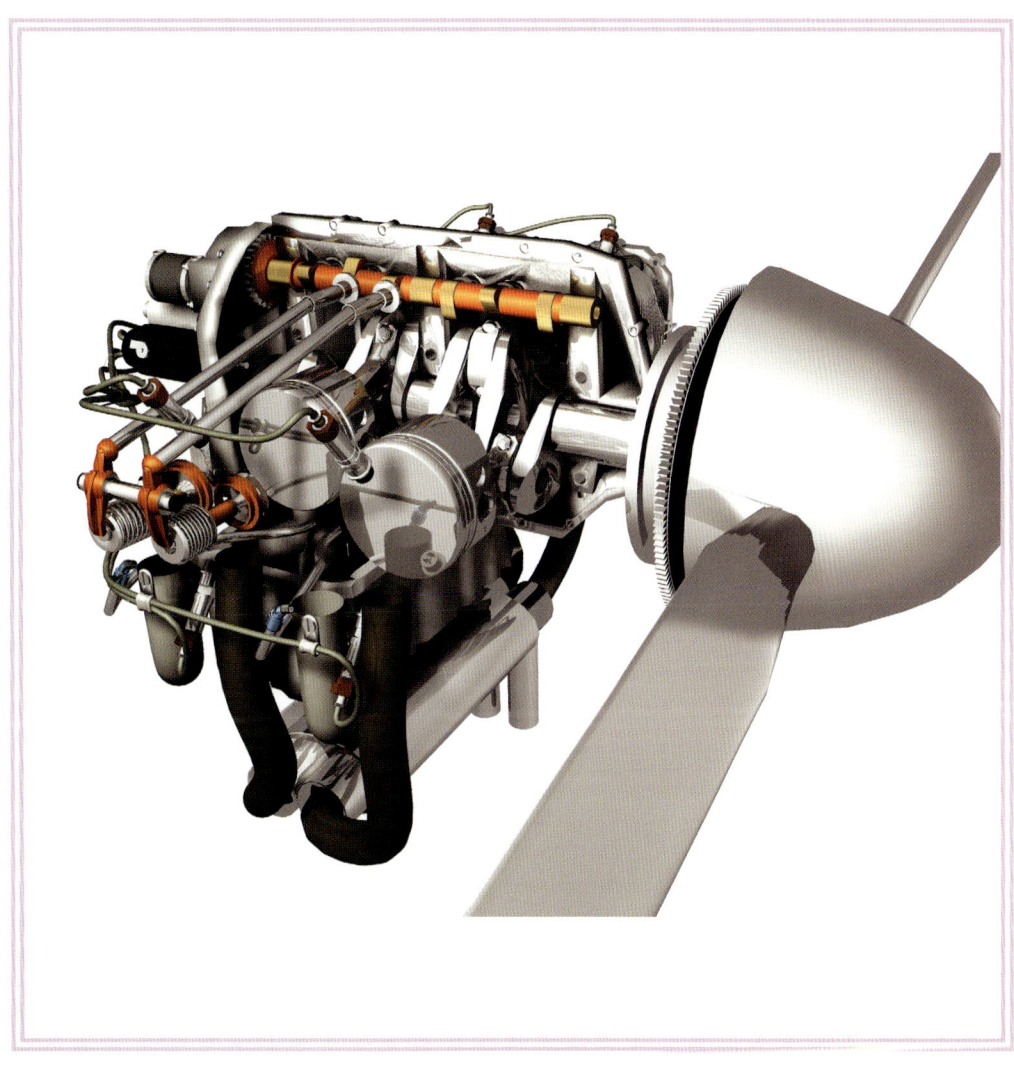

CHAPTER 3: ENGINES GENERAL

CHAPTER 3: ENGINES GENERAL

THE FOUR-STROKE INTERNAL COMBUSTION ENGINE.

The accepted definition of the term 'Piston Engine' is, 'An engine in which the working fluid is expanded in a cylinder against a reciprocating piston.'

This definition could be applied to any reciprocating type of internal combustion engine, but here we will use it to imply the type of engine used in most light aircraft; namely, the four-stroke, gasoline, spark ignition engine.

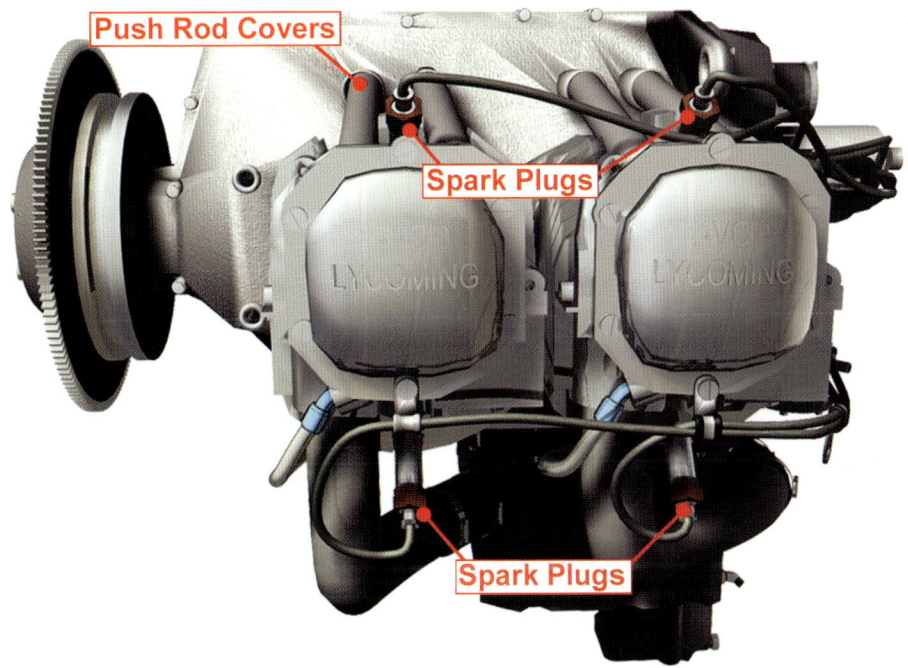

Figure 3.1 A Typical 4 Cylinder Light Aircraft Piston Engine.

The piston engine converts the energy of fuel into heat energy and then into mechanical energy. This conversion is accomplished by introducing an air-fuel mixture into a cylinder which is compressed by a piston.

The mixture is then ignited by an electric spark. The subsequent combustion causes a rapid rise in the temperature and pressure of the gases within the cylinder which forces the piston downwards.

This linear piston movement is converted into rotary motion by the crankshaft. When all of the useful pressure has been used the burnt gases are exhausted to the atmosphere.

The principle of operation of all four-stroke internal combustion engines is based upon the Otto Cycle, originally propounded by Beau de Rochas in 1876. However, Otto was the first to succeed in producing a working engine using this cycle.

CHAPTER 3: ENGINES GENERAL

THE THEORETICAL FOUR-STROKE CYCLE.

The four-stroke cycle involves four strokes of the piston, which produce two revolutions of the crankshaft.

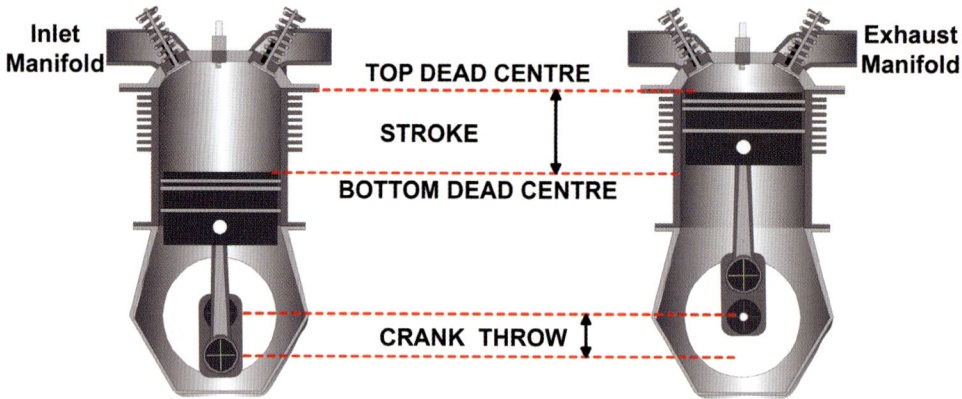

Figure 3.2 The Extent of Piston Travel within the Cylinder.

The **stroke** of the piston is the extent of its travel within the cylinder. The lower limit of travel is called **Bottom Dead Centre**, and the upper limit is called **Top Dead Centre**. These limits are shown in *Figure 3.2*.

The **four strokes** are called:- **Induction, Compression, Power** and **Exhaust**. We will use the example of a simple single-cylinder engine to illustrate the theoretical four-stroke cycle (*see Figures 3.3a, b, c & d*).

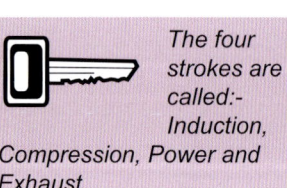
The four strokes are called:- Induction, Compression, Power and Exhaust.

Induction Stroke (Figure 3.3a).
The inlet valve opens at Top Dead Centre, permitting a mixture of fuel and air to be drawn into the cylinder. The piston moves down and the cylinder volume increases. The cylinder pressure decreases to below ambient pressure. The temperature of the air-fuel mixture (called the **charge**) decreases. The mass of the **charge** increases as more and more air-fuel mixture is sucked into the cylinder. The inlet valve closes at Bottom Dead Centre.

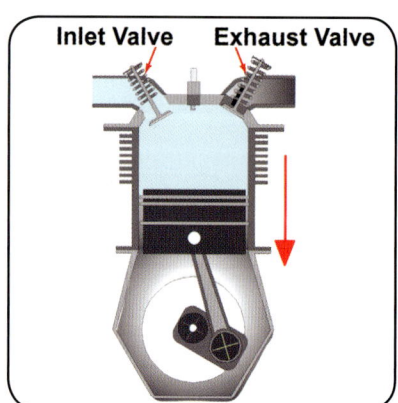

Figure 3.3a Induction.

Compression Stroke (Figure 3.3b).
Both the inlet and exhaust valves are now closed, trapping the **charge** in the combustion chamber. The piston moves up. The cylinder volume decreases. The cylinder pressure increases. The temperature of the charge increases. The mass of the charge is now fixed.

Figure 3.3b Compression.

40

CHAPTER 3: ENGINES GENERAL

Power Stroke (Figure 3.3c).

Both valves are still closed. The piston is stationary at the top of the stroke. A spark plug ignites the mixture to start combustion. The temperature of the **charge** increases rapidly during combustion. Pressure increases rapidly with temperature increase. The piston is forced down by the pressure increase. The cylinder volume therefore increases. This means that pressure decreases, and, as a function of that, the temperature decreases, too.

Exhaust Stroke (Figure 3.3d).

The exhaust valve now opens to the atmosphere. The piston moves up, forcing the exhaust gas past the exhaust valve to the atmosphere. The atmosphere provides resistance to the flow of exhaust gas which is termed '**exhaust back pressure**'. Because of this the pressure in the cylinder increases slightly which causes the temperature to rise also. When the piston reaches **Top Dead Centre**, it once again begins the Induction Stroke to start the cycle again.

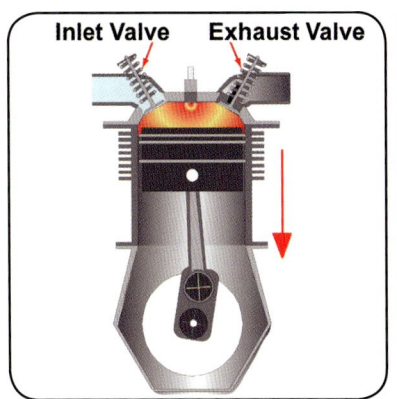
Figure 3.3c Power.

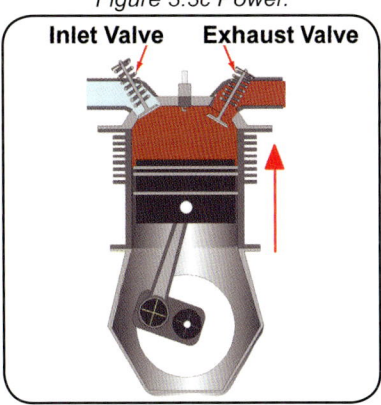
Figure 3.3d Exhaust.

On the power stroke the cylinder volume increases, cylinder pressure decreases, and thus the temperature decreases.

PRACTICAL TIMING.

In practice, the theoretical Otto cycle proved to be inefficient, and so the timing of valve operation and ignition had to be modified. A practical timing diagram, shown in *Figure 3.4*, will help to illustrate the reasons for the modifications.

Opening the **inlet valve before Top Dead Centre** ensures that it is fully open early in the induction stroke. The time lag, which would normally occur between the piston moving down and the mixture flowing into the cylinder, because of the inertia of the mixture, is thereby eliminated. The incoming mixture can, thus, keep up with the descending piston. The momentum of the incoming mixture increases as the induction stroke proceeds, and, towards the end of the stroke, is such that the gases will continue to flow into the cylinder even though the piston has passed **Bottom Dead Centre** and is moving slightly upwards.

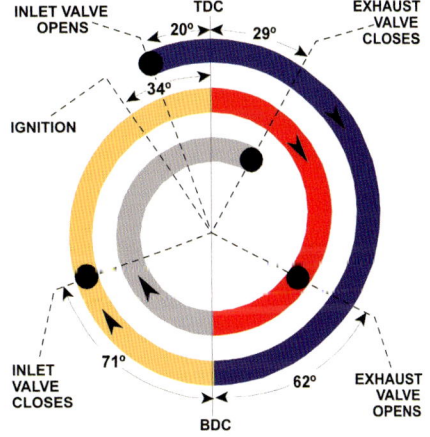
Figure 3.4 A Practical Timing Diagram.

Closure of the **inlet valve** is therefore delayed until **after Bottom Dead Centre**, when the gas pressure in the cylinder approximately equals the gas pressure in the inlet manifold. As the piston continues to move upwards, the inlet valve closes and the **charge** is compressed. By squeezing the **charge** into a smaller space the pressure it will exert when burnt is increased in proportion.

41

CHAPTER 3: ENGINES GENERAL

Just **before** the piston reaches **Top Dead Centre** on the compression stroke, the **charge** is ignited by a spark. The piston is carried past **Top Dead Centre** by the momentum of the moving parts while the flame is spreading through the compressed **charge**. The intense heat raises the pressure rapidly to a peak value which is reached only when combustion is complete.

By timing the ignition to take place **before Top Dead Centre**, complete combustion, and therefore peak pressure, is arranged to coincide with the crankshaft being 10 degrees beyond **Top Dead Centre**. This allows the engine to gain maximum advantage from combustion.

Most of the energy in the **charge** has been converted into mechanical energy by the time the piston has moved halfway down the cylinder. If the exhaust valve opens around this point, any residual gas pressure will start the first phase of exhaust scavenging.

The opening of the exhaust valve **before Bottom Dead Centre** will also ensure that the pressure of gases remaining in the cylinder does not resist the upward movement of the piston during its exhaust stroke.

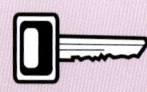
'Valve Lead' is when the inlet valve is open before Top Dead Centre and the exhaust valve is open before Bottom Dead Centre.

In the final part of the four-stroke cycle, the piston moves upwards forcing the remaining gases out of the cylinder. The exhaust valve is left open **after Top Dead Centre** to permit the gases to scavenge the cylinder as completely as possible by virtue of their momentum.

Valve Lead.
The periods during which the inlet valve is open before Top Dead Centre and the exhaust valve is open before Bottom Dead Centre are called 'Valve Lead'.

'Valve Lag' is when the inlet valve remains open after Bottom Dead Centre and the exhaust valve remains open after Top Dead Centre.

Valve Lag.
The periods during which the inlet valve remains open after Bottom Dead Centre and the exhaust valve remains open after Top Dead Centre are called 'Valve Lag'.

Valve Overlap.
The period during which both the inlet and exhaust valves are open at the same time, at the end of the exhaust stroke and the beginning of the induction stroke, is termed 'Valve Overlap'.

'Valve Overlap' occurs when both the inlet and exhaust valves are open at the same time, at the end of the exhaust stroke and the beginning of the induction stroke.

During this period, the action of the exhaust gases flowing out of the cylinder tends to reduce the gas pressure in the induction manifold.

The incoming mixture begins flowing into the area of low pressure, and assists in displacing the remaining burnt gases. This improves the volumetric efficiency of the engine by inducing a greater weight of charge into the cylinder.

BASIC ENGINE CONSTRUCTION.

The core around which the engine is built is called either the **crankcase**, or the **engine block**. It is usually made from aluminium alloy and built in two halves to allow the insertion of the **crankshaft**. If the engine is 'liquid cooled' a large one-piece jacket houses cylinder liners to provide a cooling liquid container around them.

Depending on the manufacturer of the engine, **cylinders** are bored into the engine block, or fitted onto the **crankcase**.

CHAPTER 3: ENGINES GENERAL

Figure 3.5 The Two Halves of the Crankcase Joined Together.

The **cylinders** are made of alloy steel.

The **cylinders** resist the pressure of combustion and provide a working surface for the **piston rings**. If the engine is 'air cooled' the **cylinders** are 'finned' to increase the cooling area.

Pistons, *(see Figure 3.7)* made from light alloy, are fitted within the **cylinders**. Around each **piston** are fitted two, or, in some cases, three **piston rings**.

The **piston rings** are made from cast iron, which contains a large amount of graphite: a substance which allows self lubrication between the rings and the cylinder walls when the engine is first started. The rings ensure that no gases leak from above the piston into the **crankcase**, which, in a wet **sump** engine, constitutes a reservoir for the engine oil. For more information on wet and dry sump engines refer to Chapter 5, Lubrication.

The **connecting-rod** *(see Figure 3.8)* transmits the forces of combustion to the **crankshaft**.

Figure 3.6 A Finned Cylinder.

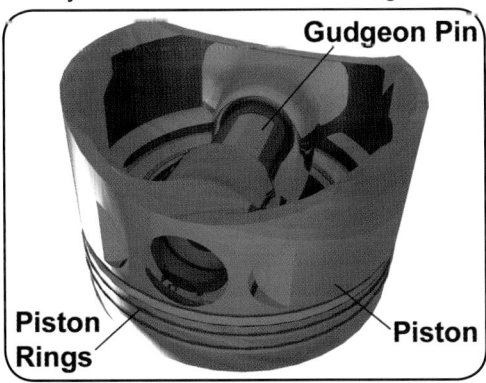

Figure 3.7 The Piston, complete with Gudgeon Pin and Piston Rings.

> The cylinders of an 'air cooled' engine are 'finned' to increase the cooling area.

> Piston rings are made from cast iron, which contains a large amount of graphite, a substance which assists self lubrication when the engine is first started.

43

CHAPTER 3: ENGINES GENERAL

The **connecting-rod** is made from 'H'-section high tensile steel, which combines lightness with the strength necessary to withstand the compressive and tensile loads imposed as the **piston** changes direction.

The **connecting-rod** is joined to the piston by a gudgeon pin *(see Figure 3.7)* which fits through the '**small end**' of the rod. The **connecting-rod** is joined to the **crankshaft**, at the **crank pins** by a large circular bearing called the '**big end**'.

Figure 3.8 The Connecting Rod.

The **crankshaft** converts the linear motion of the **piston** into rotary motion. It transmits torque, the engine's turning moment, to the **propeller** and provides the drive for accessories.

> 🔑 The crankshaft converts the linear motion of the piston into rotary motion.

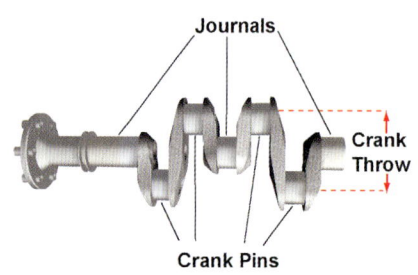

The **journals**, which are the main part of the **crankshaft**, are supported in the '**main**' **bearings** within the **crankcase**.

Figure 3.9 The Crankshaft.

The **crank-pins** are offset from the **journals** by a distance termed the '**crank throw**'. The **crank throw** determines the piston **stroke**, and there are two 'throws' to one **stroke**.

Figure 3.10 shows a plan view of the **pistons** fitted to a **crankshaft** in a horizontally opposed engine, via the **connecting rods**. The view shows the two front **pistons**, those on the left of the picture, both at bottom dead centre, while the two rear **pistons**, those on the right of the picture, are both at top dead centre.

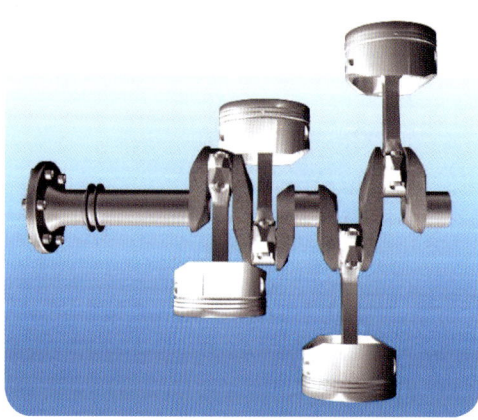

The **cylinder head** *(see Figure 3.11)* is generally made of aluminium alloy and is finned to improve heat dissipation. It seals one end of the cylinder to provide a combustion chamber for the mixture.

Figure 3.10 Crank Assembly.

The **cylinder head** accommodates the **valves** and the **sparking plugs** and supports the valve **rocker arms**. The valve **rocker arms** are operated indirectly by a **camshaft** (or shafts) *(see Figure 3.12)* which is a shaft with eccentric lobes machined on it. The **camshaft** is driven by the **crankshaft** at half the crankshaft speed.

The **camshaft** is driven at half **crankshaft** speed because each **valve** is required to open and close only once per working cycle, that is, once every two revolutions of the **crankshaft**.

CHAPTER 3: ENGINES GENERAL

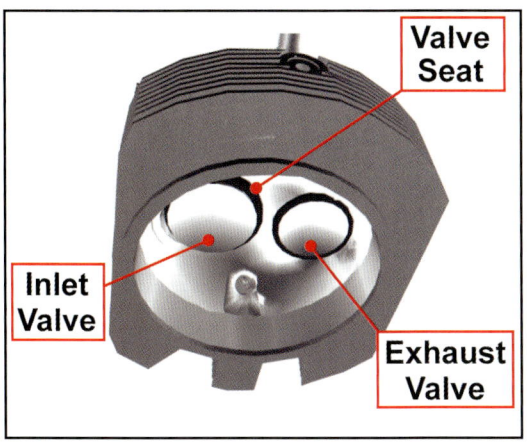

The **valves** are kept concentric to the **valve seats** by **valve guides**. The **valve seat** is ground to form a gas tight seal with the face of the **valve**. The **valves** themselves, both **inlet** and **exhaust**, open and close the passages for the induction and scavenging of the gases.

The face of each **valve** is accurately machined to the same angle as the **valve seat**. The **valve** and the **seat** are then 'lapped' or ground together with an abrasive paste until a full contact is obtained.

Figure 3.11 The Cylinder Head.

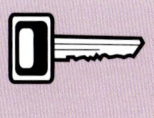

Each valve is only required to open and close once per working cycle.

The **valve springs** are manufactured from special spring steel, and they ensure that the **valves** remain closed except when they are being operated by the **rocker assembly**.

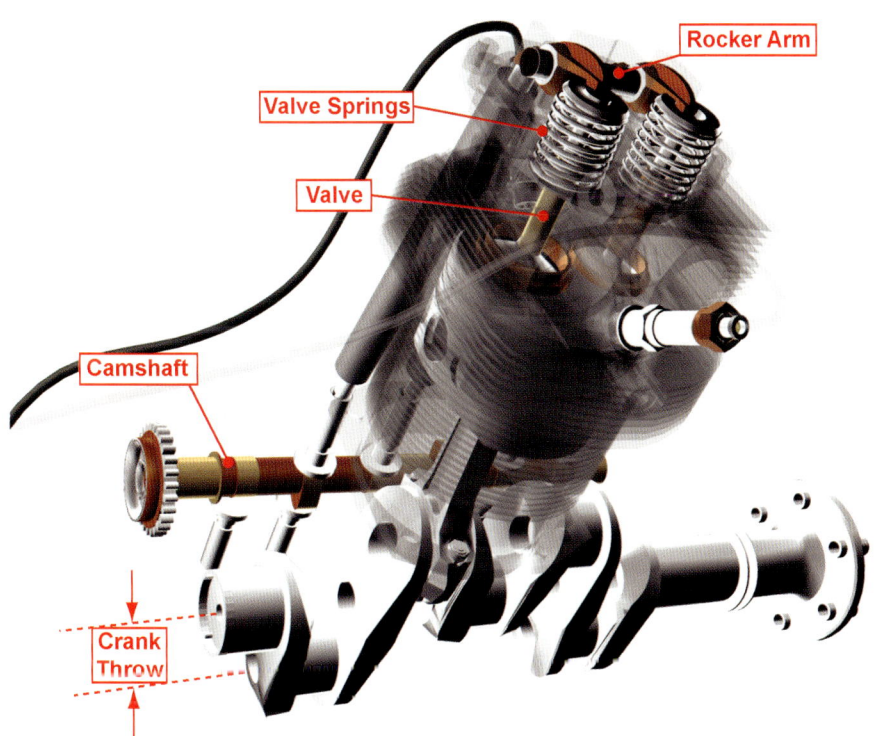

Figure 3.12 Cutaway of Cylinder Head and Crankshaft.

Two springs are fitted to each valve, one inside the other. This provides both a safety factor and eliminates 'valve bounce'.

The **springs** are of the helical coil type, the usual practice being for two springs to be fitted to each **valve**, one inside the other.

This provides a safety factor, and also eliminates 'valve bounce', a condition created by the fact that each valve spring will have a resonant frequency (with the engine RPM) where it will be ineffective at closing the valve on its own.

CHAPTER 3: ENGINES GENERAL

Figure 3.13 The Accessory Housing.

The 'accessory housing', an example of which is shown in *Figure 3.13*, is a casing mounted at the rear of the **block**.

It encloses the **drive gear trains** for the **camshafts**, the fuel, oil, pneumatic and vacuum **pumps**, electric **generator**, **magnetos** and **tachometer**.

POWER OUTPUT AS A FUNCTION OF RPM.

During the four strokes, the changing pressures within the cylinder can be measured and indicated graphically on a device which produces an 'indicator diagram'. This device is only used during the development stage of an engine.

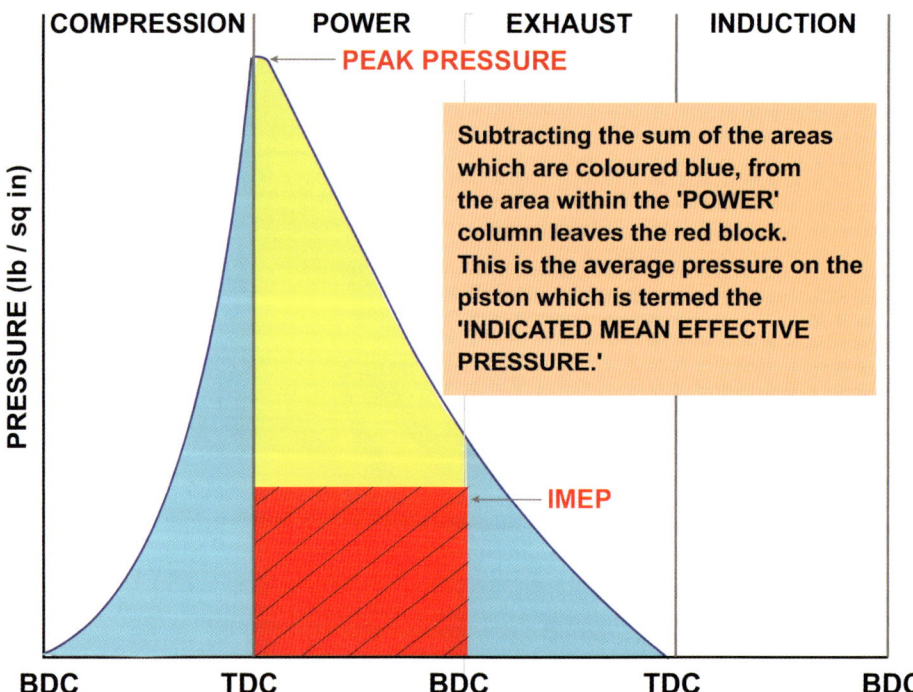

Figure 3.14 An Indicator Diagram.

Figure 3.14 shows an indicator diagram. The area within the power column represents work done on the piston during the power stroke.

The blue areas represent work done by the piston in compressing the gases and exhausting the cylinder against exhaust back pressure; that is, the pressure which the atmosphere exerts against the outflowing gases.

CHAPTER 3: ENGINES GENERAL

Subtracting the sum of the blue coloured areas from the area within the power column leaves the red block.

The red block is indicative of the 'average pressure' during the working cycle. This is termed the 'Indicated Mean Effective Pressure' or IMEP.

We can use the Indicated Mean Effective Pressure in the formula, shown below, which allows us to determine the Indicated Horse Power (IHP) of our particular engine.

$$IHP = \frac{P \times L \times A \times N \times E}{33,000}$$

In the formula, the 'P' represents the Indicated Mean Effective Pressure in pounds per square inch. However we are still required to determine several other values.

The 'L' represents the length of the stroke in feet, the length of the stroke being the distance the piston moves between Top Dead Centre and Bottom Dead Centre.

'A' is cross-sectional the area of the cylinder in square inches.

'N' is the number of cylinders that the engine possesses.

'E' is the effective working strokes per minute or the RPM of the engine.

33,000 is a constant used to change foot pounds of work per minute into horse power. One Horse Power equals 33,000 foot pounds per minute.

Bearing in mind that, for a given engine, only one function of the formula is variable, that is the RPM of the engine, it is logical to assume that engine power output is directly proportional to RPM: increase the engine speed and the power output increases; decrease the engine speed and the power output falls.

Increase the engine speed and the power output increases. Decrease the engine speed and the power output falls.

Compression Ratio.

The compression ratio of an engine is the ratio of the total volume enclosed in a cylinder with the piston at Bottom Dead Centre, to the volume remaining at the end of the compression stroke with the piston at Top Dead Centre. This ratio is shown as a formula overleaf.

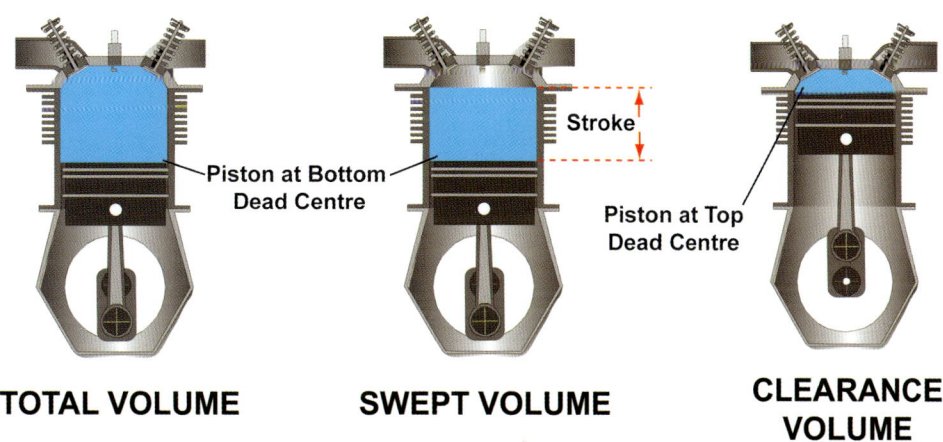

TOTAL VOLUME **SWEPT VOLUME** **CLEARANCE VOLUME**

Figure 3.15 Diagram showing the Total, Swept and Clearance Volumes of a Simple Engine.

CHAPTER 3: ENGINES GENERAL

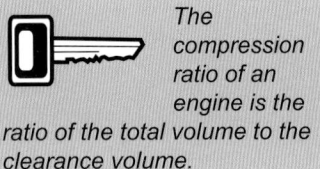
The compression ratio of an engine is the ratio of the total volume to the clearance volume.

The Total Volume of the engine is the sum of the Swept Volume and the Clearance Volume.

$$\text{Compression Ratio} = \frac{\text{Total Volume}}{\text{Clearance Volume}}$$

An example will help to clarify the term. If the Swept Volume of an engine is 1800 cubic centimetres, and its Clearance Volume is 300 cubic centimetres, what is the compression ratio of the engine?

First we must add the Swept and Clearance Volumes to obtain the Total Volume. So 1800 plus 300 is 2,100.

Then we must divide the Total Volume by the Clearance Volume. 2,100 divided by 300 is 7.

Thus, the compression ratio of the engine is 7 to 1.

CHAPTER 3: ENGINES GENERAL QUESTIONS

Representative PPL - type questions to test your theoretical knowledge of Engines General.

1. In a piston engine aircraft the crankshaft:

   a. Converts reciprocating movement into rotary motion
   b. Controls the clearance of the valves
   c. Converts rotary motion into reciprocating movement
   d. Rotates at half the speed of the camshaft

2. During one complete cycle of a four stroke internal combustion engine how many times will each valve open and close?

   a. Four times
   b. Twice
   c. Three times
   d. Once

3. If the crankshaft rotates twice in a piston engine, the camshaft rotates:

   a. Once, because the camshaft operates at 50% of the engine speed
   b. Twice, because the camshaft operates at twice engine speed
   c. Four times, because the camshaft operates at twice engine speed
   d. Once, because the camshaft operates at twice engine speed

4. In one complete Otto cycle, each piston moves:

   a. Up once and down once
   b. Up once and down twice
   c. Up four times and down four times
   d. Up twice and down twice

5. At sea level, the power developed by a four-stroke piston engine:

   a. Decreases proportional to RPM.
   b. Increases along with RPM
   c. Remains constant to RPM
   d. Is proportional to the volume of mixture in the cylinder

6. The power output of an internal combustion engine can be increased by:

   a. Decreasing the area of the cylinder
   b. Decreasing the length of the stroke
   c. Increasing the engine RPM
   d. Increasing the size of the fuel tank

CHAPTER 3: ENGINES GENERAL QUESTIONS

7. The correct working cycle of a four stroke engine is:

    a. exhaust, power, induction, compression
    b. induction, compression, power, exhaust
    c. induction, power, compression, exhaust
    d. exhaust, induction, power, compression

8. The temperature of the gases within the cylinder of a four stroke engine during the power stroke, after completion of combustion:

    a. Decrease
    b. Increase
    c. Follow Charles's Law
    d. Remain constant

9. Engine compression ratio is the ratio of the:

    a. Swept volume to the clearance volume
    b. Clearance volume to the swept volume
    c. Swept volume to the total volume
    d. Total volume to the clearance volume

Question	1	2	3	4	5	6	7	8	9
Answer									

The answers to these questions can be found at the end of this book.

CHAPTER 3A
AERO DIESEL ENGINES

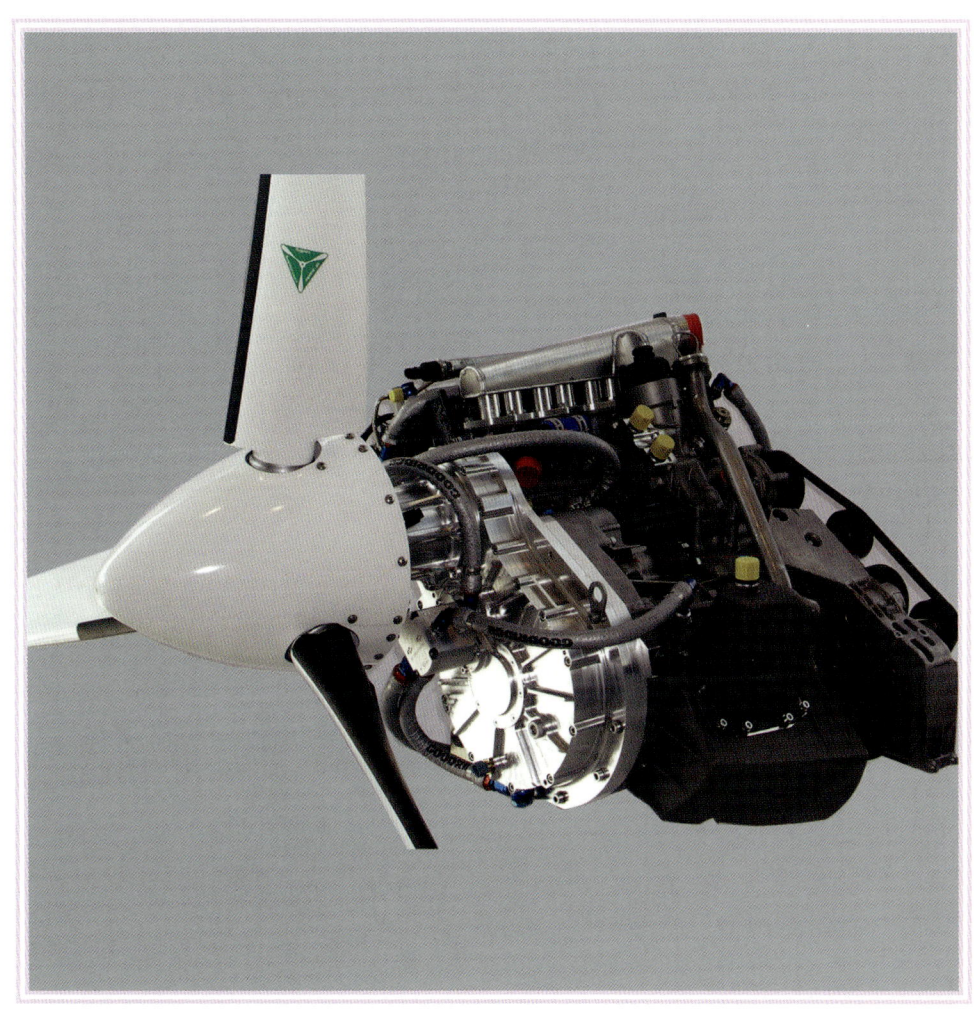

CHAPTER 3A: AERO DIESEL ENGINES

CHAPTER 3A: AERO DIESEL ENGINES

THE BEGINNINGS OF AERO DIESEL ENGINES.

Despite their excellent specific fuel consumption, diesel engines have not been widely used as aircraft engines due to their poor power to weight ratio. However, as early as 1929 the Packard Motor Company of America developed a diesel engine especially intended to power an aircraft. The inaugural flight of the aircraft engine combination, called the 'Stinson Detroiter', shown in *Figure 3a.1*, was from Detroit in Michigan State, to Langley Field in the State of Virginia.

Figure 3a.1 The Stinson Detroiter.

The aircraft accomplished the trip at an average speed of eighty-five miles an hour, through adverse weather. The straight line distance is 560 miles, but this aircraft, in fighting its way around and through extremely bad weather, travelled approximately 650 miles. The cost of the fuel for the flight, in 1929 terms, was $4.68.

But until recently diesel engines were less powerful than aircraft petrol engines, and much heavier. Since the 1980s, however, there has been a great step forward in the development and production of aviation diesel engines. The common-rail fuel injection principle *(see page 57)* enables the relationship between the engine's mass and its power to become far more acceptable for aviation usage. As a consequence, because of the adoption of common-rail technology and direct fuel injection, and also the use of lighter materials and turbo-charger technology, diesel engines offer more advantages to the aviation industry now than they previously could.

The Advantages of Aircraft Diesel Engines.

Aircraft diesel engines are cheaper to operate from two points of view. First of all they use Aviation Turbine Fuel, also known as AVTUR or Jet A1 fuel, which is substantially less expensive than aviation gasoline, and they use considerably less of it. A light aircraft powered by two of these diesel engines can carry four passengers at speeds up to 231 mph while consuming only one gallon for every 19 miles travelled in still air. If the engines are set to give maximum economy, then 42 miles to each gallon of fuel can be obtained. This gives diesel-engined aircraft an excellent specific fuel consumption substantially increased range for a comparable volume of tankage, compared to a petrol driven engine.

Figure 3a.2 A Modern Diesel Engine Aircraft. Picture courtesy of Thielert Aircraft Engines.

The principal advantages of the diesel engine over the petrol engine are that Jet A1 (AVTUR) is cheaper than gasoline, fuel consumption is lower, and diesel engines are more durable.

As mentioned, aircraft diesel engines use the more widely available AVTUR fuel, which is a light-cut of diesel fuel, as opposed to aviation gasoline, about which there are growing global concerns reference that fuel's future availability, as more and more refineries turn to producing aviation turbine fuel.

Aircraft diesel engines are more durable than gasoline aircraft engines, and are safer in operation, because of the reduced fire and explosion risk from using AVTUR fuel and the compression-ignition principle.

CHAPTER 3A: AERO DIESEL ENGINES

THE DIESEL ENGINE.

Rudolf Diesel obtained the German patent for developing the idea for the diesel engine in 1892. His objective was to create a highly efficient engine. Gasoline engines had been invented earlier, in 1876, but were very inefficient at that time.

The Differences Between the Petrol Engine and the Diesel Engine.
There are two main differences between the petrol engine and the diesel engine:

Firstly, while the petrol engine takes in a mixture of gas and air, compresses it and ignites the mixture with a spark, the diesel engine takes in just air, compresses it and then injects a fine mist of diesel fuel into the compressed air just before the piston reaches Top Dead Centre. The injected fuel mist mixing with the compressed air ignites almost simultaneously because of the high temperature of the compressed air and relatively low ignition temperature of the diesel fuel. Thus, it is the heat of the compressed air which ignites the fuel spontaneously rather than a spark plug. The absence of the spark ignition system is a big factor in increasing the reliability of the diesel engine.

In a diesel engine, the piston compresses the air in the cylinder causing the temperature of the air to rise to a level high enough to ignite the air-fuel gas as diesel fuel injected into the cylinder mixes with the compressed air.

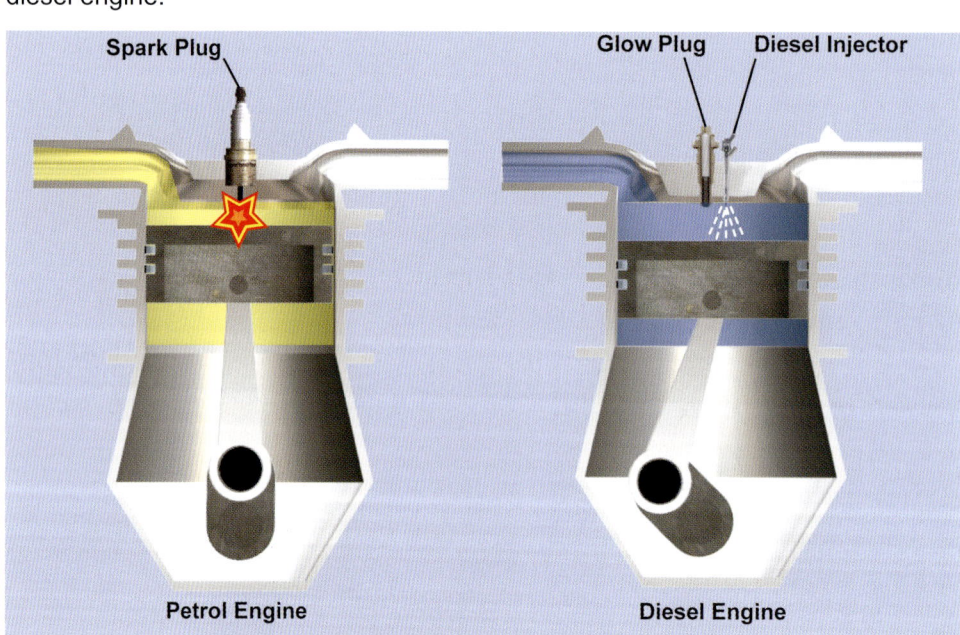

Figure 3a.3 Differences between a petrol and a diesel engine.

Gasoline engines generally use either carburettors, in which the air and fuel is mixed long before the air enters the cylinder, or fuel injection, in which the fuel is injected into the inlet port of each cylinder just prior to the induction stroke. Modern diesel engines, especially those used to power aircraft, use direct fuel injection, which means that the diesel fuel is injected directly into the cylinder, as opposed to the inlet port, as is the case with most fuel injected gasoline engines. *Figure 3a.3* illustrates these differences.

The injector on a diesel engine has to be able to withstand the much higher temperatures and pressures than it experiences inside the cylinder, and yet still deliver the fuel in a fine mist exactly when it is required.

CHAPTER 3A: AERO DIESEL ENGINES

The second big difference between a diesel engine and a gasoline engine is in the injection process. As previously stated, most automobile gasoline engines use a fuel injection system or a carburettor rather than direct injection. In an automobile engine all of the air/fuel mixture is fed into the cylinder during the induction stroke and then compressed during the compression stroke.

It is this compression of the fuel/air mixture which limits the compression ratio of a gasoline engine, because if the engine compresses the mixture too much, it spontaneously detonates, which is grossly inefficient, and can seriously damage the health of the engine.

The compression ratio of a diesel engine can range from 14:1 to about 25:1.

A diesel engine compresses only the air, thus the compression ratio can be much higher. The higher the compression ratio, the greater the power that is generated from a given quantity of fuel, and the higher the thermal efficiency of the engine.

Whereas a gasoline engine compresses the air/fuel mixture at ratios of between 8:1 to 10:1, a diesel engine, which compresses just the air, works at ratios which can range in different engines from 14:1 to as high as 25:1. The higher compression ratio of the diesel engine leads to much better efficiency.

Starting the Diesel Engine - The Glow Plug.

There are problems associated with starting diesel engines from cold, and because of this some of them utilize glow plugs. Glow plugs are required because in a cold engine the compression process may not raise the temperature of the air high enough to ignite the fuel. When the glow plug is energised, its heated ports rise to a temperature of around 1000°C. This aids the compression-ignition process when the engine is cold. Once the engine is warm, the glow plugs are no longer needed.

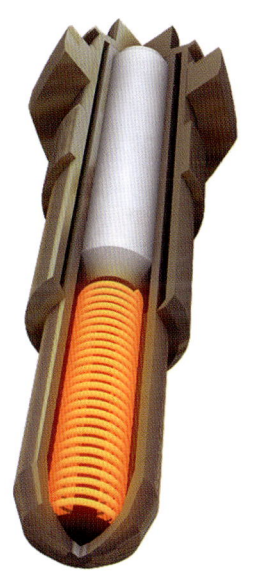

The function of the glow plug is to raise the temperature of the air in the cylinder of a cold engine in order to aid compression-ignition on starting.

There are two types of glow plug in use, the metal type and the ceramic type. Metal type glow plugs have their heating coils mounted in a heat-resistant alloy tube, but ceramic-type glow plugs, which have been employed in diesel engines since 1985, have their heater elements contained in a ceramic material, which is made of silicon nitride. Because of this fact, ceramic-type glow plugs have a greater heat resistance and durability

Figure 3a.4. A Glowplug.

TWO TYPES OF FUEL INJECTION SYSTEM.

There are two types of fuel injection systems used in modern light-duty and medium power diesel engines, they are the direct fuel injection and the common-rail fuel injection systems. We will look at the direct fuel injection system first.

Direct Injection.
Most light-duty diesel engines use an engine-driven in-line pump to distribute fuel under high pressure to each of the injectors. The injectors are situated in each cylinder head. The injectors are mechanical and have spring-loaded poppet valves,

55

CHAPTER 3A: AERO DIESEL ENGINES

so they pop open and spray fuel when the fuel line pressure exceeds a certain limit (typically 4,500 pounds per square inch). Electronic controls on late model injection pumps regulate injection timing, fuel mixture and idle speed.

The purpose of the fuel injection pump is to deliver an exactly metered amount of fuel, under high pressure, at the right time to the injector. The injector, unlike those fitted in a gasoline engine, injects the fuel directly into the cylinder, or in some cases a pre-chamber which is connected to the cylinder.

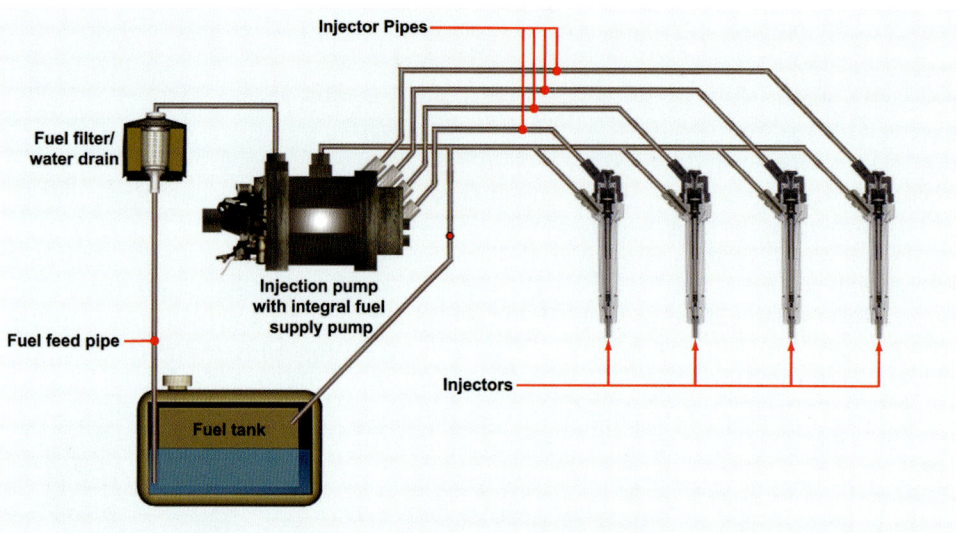

Figure 3a.5 Direct Injection System.

The injection system that delivers fuel to a diesel engine operates at much higher pressure than a gasoline injection system. It can be as high as 17,400 pounds per square inch (psi) for a direct injection system and up to 23,500 psi for common rail systems, compared to 35 to 90 psi for most **gasoline** fuel injection systems. The fuel is also sprayed directly into the combustion chamber, rather than into each cylinder's intake port, as is the case with most **gasoline** injected engines. Some other functions of the fuel injection pump are:

Timing.

The timing of the fuel pulses is adjusted in response to engine RPM. At higher engine RPM, because the vane transfer pump, or feed pump, (which pulls fuel from the tank to the input of the high pressure section of the pump), is driven by the engine, the fuel pressure from the pump is higher.

These fuel pressure changes are used to either advance or retard the timing. There is also a cold start device which advances the idle timing manually.

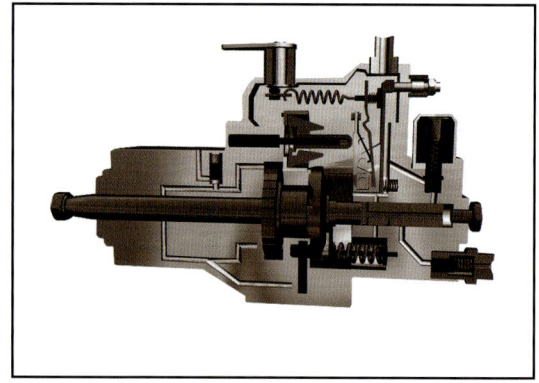

Figure 3a.6 The Injector Pump.

CHAPTER 3A: AERO DIESEL ENGINES

Governor.
A mechanical governor limits the maximum speed of the engine.

Stop.
A magnet valve or solenoid opens and shuts off the fuel channel between the feed pump and the metering pump.

Pressure Sensor.
An air inlet pressure sensor is used to determine the maximum amount of fuel delivered by the injection pumps for turbo-charged engines. On newer, normally aspirated, engines a similar arrangement is used for altitude compensation.

Common-Rail Fuel Injection Systems.
A common-rail engine is designed to supply constant fuel pressure to electronically controlled injectors from a shared fuel reservoir. This means that the fuel supply is not dependent on engine rotational speed. A common-rail system is built around four basic components:

- A high-pressure pump with a pressure regulator and an inlet metering valve

- A rail, or fuel feed, which contains a pressurized reserve of fuel

- Injectors which inject precise amounts of fuel into the combustion chamber as required

- A Diesel Control Unit — the 'brain' of the system, which precisely controls injector flow and timing, as well as rail pressure, while continuously monitoring the operating conditions of the engine

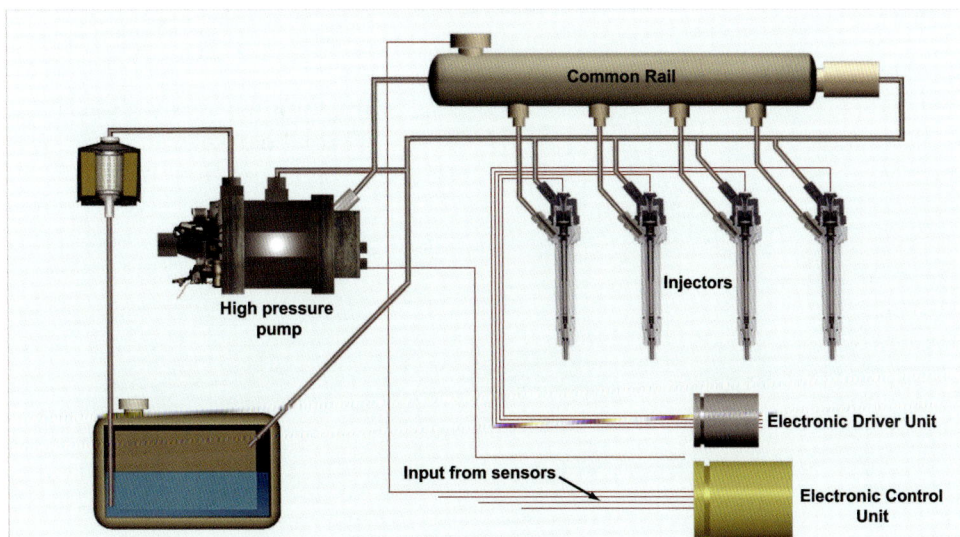

Figure 3a.7 Common-Rail Engine.

Simply explained, the term 'common-rail' refers to the single fuel feed line from which the individual feeds for each injector are taken, on the common-rail direct-injection (CDI) engine. Whereas conventional direct-injection diesel engines must repeatedly generate fuel pressure for each injection, in the CDI engines the pressure is built up independently of the injection sequence in a high pressure pump with pressure regulator and inlet metering valve. This pressure remains permanently available in the fuel line.

CHAPTER 3A: AERO DIESEL ENGINES

The common-rail, which contains a pressurized reserve of fuel, is upstream of the cylinders. It acts as an accumulator, distributing the fuel to the injectors at a constant pressure of up to 1600 bar.

Mounted in the cylinder heads, fuel injectors, which are really high-speed solenoid valves, inject precise amounts of fuel into the combustion chamber as required. A microcomputer controls each injector's opening and closing. This procedure is regulated by an electronic engine management device, the 'brain' of the system, which separately and precisely controls the injection timing, rail pressure and the amount of fuel injected for each cylinder. It does this by using information obtained by continuously monitoring the operating conditions of the engine. Sensor data from the camshaft and crankshaft provide the foundation for the electronic control unit to adapt the injection pressure precisely to demand.

Fuel 'pressure generation' and fuel 'injection' are managed totally independently of each other. This factor is in itself an important advantage of common-rail injection over conventional fuel injection systems.

Common-Rail Direct Injection also offers distinct environmental advantages, with enhanced combustion efficiency leading to reduced exhaust emissions. The system produces quieter, smoother operation compared to engines with either direct or indirect fuel injection.

PRODUCTION DIESEL ENGINES FOR AIRCRAFT.

There are several different types of aircraft diesel engine presently in production.

The Thielert Centurion 1.7.

The 'Centurion 1.7', shown in *Figure 3a.8*, is developed by Thielert Aircraft Engines, who are based in Lichtenstein. They took a four-cylinder engine, which was first used by Mercedes, and totally re-engineered it for use in aircraft. All of the critical parts of the engine were redesigned by Thielert and are now manufactured by them.

Figure 3a.8. The 'Centurion 1.7'. Picture courtesy of Thielert Aircraft Engines.

It is the first modern diesel engine which is fitted to a certified airframe and scheduled for production with solid orders on the books. The manufacturers say that the engine reduces the costs of flying by 70% compared to petrol powered aircraft (based on fuel prices in Germany). Total operating costs for a diesel engine over its lifetime are projected to be an order of magnitude less than that of comparative gasoline powered engines.

The Centurion 1.7 is a liquid cooled, turbocharged four-cylinder, four-valve, in-line engine with common-rail fuel injection. It develops 135 hp and 302.4 lb-ft of torque. Displacement is 1.68 litres, and it has a compression ratio of 18:1. It is presently fitted in the Diamond Star DA40 aircraft, manufactured by Diamond Aircraft Industries.

Although rated at only 135 hp, the Centurion 1.7 can replace more powerful petrol engines because it provides more static thrust. Static thrust is the thrust developed when the throttle is fully opened with the aircraft stationary and the brakes applied. Cruise fuel consumption for the Centurion 1.7 is 15 - 20 litres per hour.

The SMA 305.
SMA, a French engine manufacturer, have produced the SR 305 which was first certified for the Cessna 182 in 2003. The SMA 305 is also currently certified for a range of light aircraft, including the Maule M7, the Vulcanair range, the SOCATA TB20 and the Piper PA28. This horizontally-opposed air-cooled four cylinder engine develops 200 hp at altitudes of up to 10 000 ft, and is aimed at replacing gasoline engines in the 180 - 250 hp range.

The DeltaHawk DH160 and 200.
DeltaHawk Inc. have developed two-stroke turbo and supercharged, inter-cooled four-cylinder diesel engines developing 160 and 200 hp. Again, pitched to compete with the Lycoming gasoline engines of similar power, they are undergoing testing with a view for type certification for a range of different aircraft manufacturers.

Other Aero Diesel engines.
Other manufacturers currently developing Aero Diesel engines for certification include UK manufacturers Wilksch, American manufacturers Textron-Lycoming and Teledyne Continental, and German manufacturers Zoche.

PRINCIPLE OF OPERATION OF THE DIESEL ENGINE.

Basic diesel engine operation is as follows: Air is compressed in the combustion chamber before the fuel is injected. The compression ratio of the diesel engine is much higher than that of its gasoline equivalent, (between 14 and 25 to 1, as opposed to about 12 to 1 in high performance gasoline engines). This high compression ratio causes the air temperature to rise above the flashpoint of the fuel. When the fuel is then introduced into the combustion chamber, it mixes with the air and combusts spontaneously.

The pressure generated by the expansion of the gases as the mixture burns pushes the piston down. The connecting rod transfers the linear motion thus induced to the crankshaft, which translates it into rotary motion.

In contrast to the petrol engine, the power of the diesel engine is actually controlled by the amount of fuel that is introduced into the combustion chamber, while the amount of air remains constant.

CHAPTER 3A: AERO DIESEL ENGINES

In the petrol engine, both the amount of air and the amount of fuel are changed in response to throttle position, the amount of fuel being further altered by the position of the mixture control lever. The mixture control lever of the petrol engine is required to maintain a balance between the amount of fuel and air being allowed into the combustion chamber in order that a reasonable fuel consumption can be maintained while still keeping the spectre of detonation at bay.

Because the fuel is not injected into a diesel engine until the actual required moment of combustion, detonation in this type of engine is not a problem. Diesel engines do not usually operate at the stoichiometric ratio. (The stoichiometric ratio is the air-fuel ratio in an engine where all of the fuel and all of the oxygen is burnt completely.) If there is more air than is required, a gasoline engine will run weak. If there is more fuel than is required, then the gasoline engine will run rich. Diesel engines always run on a weak mixture, the actual mixture strength depending on the power setting.

In the petrol engine, the engine is choked by the throttle valve at all times when it is not operating at full throttle, which limits its efficiency. With no throttle valve the diesel engine's intake is fully open all the time resulting in a much higher efficiency.

DIESEL ENGINE FUELS.

Diesel fuel is a form of light fuel oil, very similar to kerosene. Most aircraft diesel engines will use regular AVTUR, otherwise known as Jet A1, as well as commercial diesel fuel.

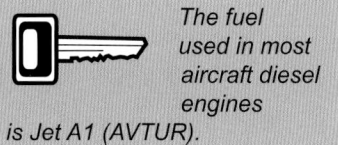
The fuel used in most aircraft diesel engines is Jet A1 (AVTUR).

AVTUR is not a very good lubricant, a problem which has to be especially addressed in the fuel pumps used on gas turbine engines. The fuel pumps used on aircraft diesel engines are no exception; they have to be specially developed for use with AVTUR.

Although anti-icing additives are used in AVTUR, they may not be included in some of the other fuels which can be used in the aviation diesel engine. There is a question, which is still unresolved at the time of writing, as to whether or not to allow anti-icing additives to be used in these other fuels. Anti-icing additives would overcome a tendency which kerosene-like fuels have to absorb more water than does aviation gasoline, but the use of these additives is being curtailed in some countries for environmental reasons. The ability of the fuel to flow in extremely low temperature conditions must also be ensured, and new requirements regarding 'Cetane Number' must be specified for kerosene-jet fuel which is currently unspecified.

The 'Cetane Number' is a measure of the ignition quality of a diesel fuel. It is often mistaken as a measure of fuel quality. The 'Cetane Number' is actually a measure of a fuel's ignition delay. This is the time period between the start of injection and start of combustion of the fuel. In a particular diesel engine, higher cetane fuels will have shorter ignition delay periods than lower cetane fuels. Using the appropriate cetane rated fuel in a diesel engine is critical to developing the power of that engine.

CONCLUSION.

Historically diesel engines were not widely used as powerplants for aircraft, because although their specific fuel consumption was much lower than that of equivalent petrol engines, they were simply too heavy for the power developed. However, the rapid improvement in automobile diesel technology has meant that higher power-weight ratios are now being achieved and, so, the modern diesel engine is much more suitable for use in aircraft.

This fact, coupled with the increasing cost of aviation gasoline (AVGAS) has led to increasing interest in diesel-powered light aircraft by private owners and flying training organisations.

CHAPTER 3A: AERO DIESEL ENGINES QUESTIONS

Representative PPL - type questions to test your theoretical knowledge of Pressure Instruments.

1. The purpose of the glow plug in the cylinder of a diesel engine is to:

    a. Heat up the diesel fuel in the fuel tank in order to aid compression-ignition on starting
    b. Raise the temperature of the air in the cylinder in order to aid compression-ignition on starting
    c. To warm the air in the induction manifold in order to aid compression-ignition on starting
    d. To ignite the diesel fuel in the cylinder.

2. The principle of operation of a diesel engine is that:

    a. The piston compresses the air in the cylinder causing the temperature of the air to rise to a level high enough to ignite the air-fuel gas as diesel fuel injected into the cylinder mixes with the compressed air
    b. The diesel fuel is injected into the cylinder and the piston compresses the air-fuel mixture in the causing the temperature of the mixture to rise to a point where ignition occurs
    c. The piston compresses the air in the cylinder and the diesel fuel is ignited by the glow plug as it is injected into the engine
    d. The mixture of air and diesel fuel is drawn into the cylinder on the induction stroke, compressed on the compression stroke and the mixture is ignited by the glow plug just before Top Dead Centre

3. The compression ratio of a diesel engine can be as high as:

    a. 45:1
    b. 5:1
    c. 8:1
    d. 25:1

4. The advantages of diesel engines over petrol (gasoline) engines are:

    a. Diesel fuel is cheaper than gasoline
    b. Fuel consumption is lower
    c. Diesel engines are more durable
    d. All of the above

5. Which of the following fuel is used to power aircraft diesel engines:

    a. AVGAS
    b. MOGAS
    c. Jet A1
    d. Paraffin

Question	1	2	3	4	5
Answer					

The answers to these questions can be found at the end of this book.

CHAPTER 4
ENGINE COOLING

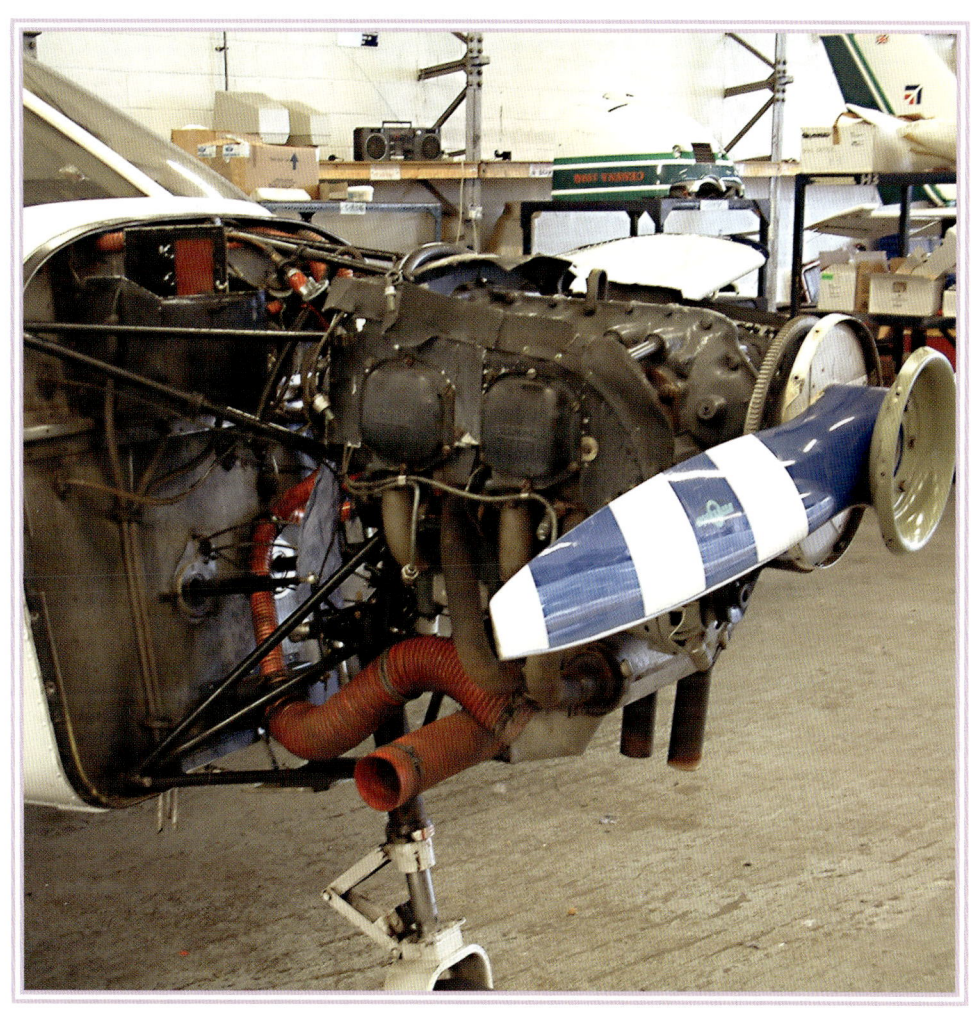

CHAPTER 4: ENGINE COOLING

CHAPTER 4: ENGINE COOLING

AIR COOLING.

The piston engine is a heat engine. Its purpose is to convert the energy released from burning fuel into mechanical energy, and, by so doing, generate usable power. The thermal efficiency of a light aircraft piston petrol engine may reach 30 percent. This, however, means that 70 percent of the heat energy released by the fuel is wasted. Around 40 percent will leave with the exhaust gas, but 30 percent stays behind to raise the temperature of the engine components and the oil.

Figure 4.1 A Light Aircraft Engine.

Overheating.

If nothing were done to alleviate the rising temperature of the engine, several problems could occur:-

- Engine components could start to fail structurally.

- The oil could break down and lose its lubricating properties. (You will learn more about this in the chapter on lubrication.)

- The fuel could ignite as soon as it enters the cylinder, before the spark plug fires; this is called pre-ignition. Pre-ignition causes loss of power and may exacerbate the overheating problem. The incoming mixture may get too hot, which will cause unstable combustion, usually called detonation, or knocking. (You will learn more about this in the chapter on carburation.) Detonation will also cause loss of power and further overheating, and possible damage to the engine.

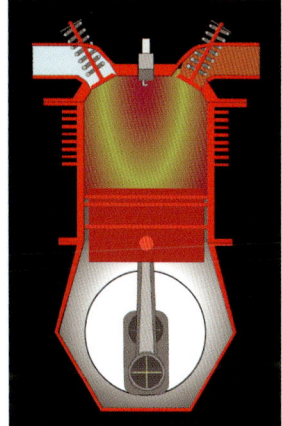

Figure 4.2 Engine Overheating.

Detonation will cause loss of power, overheating, and possible damage to the engine.

Overcooling.

The problems associated with overheating are perhaps obvious, but what problems can be caused by overcooling? We have first to remember that maximum thermal efficiency is only achieved at high engine temperatures, so the engine needs to be kept as hot as possible without causing the problems mentioned in the paragraph on 'Overheating'.

A low engine temperature also increases the viscosity (the internal friction) of the oil which will reduce the Brake Horse Power. A pilot must, therefore, keep the engine temperature, and thus the oil temperature, fairly high, but not so high that the oil breaks down.

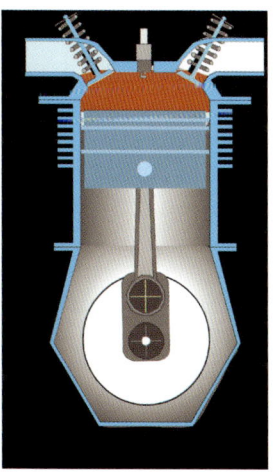

Figure 4.3 Engine Overcooling.

In order to burn, the fuel must vaporize. Very low engine temperatures would prevent complete fuel vaporization. Some fuel would not be burnt, reducing the power output of the engine.

COOLING SYSTEMS.

In order to work efficiently, the engine needs to be at the highest temperature consistent with safe operation.

To maintain the engine temperature within a range which will satisfy its working requirements a cooling system is required. Most light aircraft engines are air-cooled. The simplicity of an air-cooled cooling system makes it virtually maintenance free and it is much lighter than the alternative, the liquid cooling system. However, the liquid cooling system is more efficient, gives more precise control of engine temperature and generates less drag. Many high performance piston engines, therefore, especially those which powered military aircraft during and after World War 2, employed liquid cooling systems.

FACTORS AFFECTING COOLING.

Ambient Air Temperature.
One of the major factors governing the efficiency of an air-cooled system is the ambient air temperature. Although the ambient air temperature can vary widely with changes in climate and altitude, it must be borne in mind that dissipation of the heat will be more rapid as air temperature decreases.

Airspeed.
The speed of the airflow is the other major factor affecting the efficiency of the air cooling system. Uncontrolled, the speed of the airflow over the cylinders will vary with the speed of the aircraft and cause the temperature of the cylinders to fluctuate accordingly. Obviously, air-cooling is least effective at high power settings and low airspeed. Consequently, engine temperatures have to be monitored closely in the climb, especially if the climb is prolonged.

Engine Materials.
Several methods of improving the efficiency of cooling systems can be employed. Firstly, the engine components are made of materials with a high conductivity, for instance cylinder heads are sometimes made from aluminium alloys, aluminium being a good conductor of heat.

Fins.
The walls of the cylinders are finned to increase the cooling area *(see Figure 4.4)*. The fins are thin in section and may be extended at local hotspots, such as the exhaust ports, to increase their area, in order to achieve an even temperature.

Figure 4.4 The cylinder is finned to increase the cooling area.

CHAPTER 4: ENGINE COOLING

Oil.
The oil used to lubricate the engine is also a cooling medium, so the amount of oil in the engine must be within limits.

The Engine Cowling.
The engine is streamlined by surrounding it with a cowling. This encloses the engine within a controllable environment and also reduces drag.

Baffles.
Baffles *(see Figure 4.5)* are directional air guides which direct the airflow in an efficient manner around the cylinders. Baffles must be close-fitting and are sealed against the cowling to ensure that all of the airflow is over the cylinders and that each part of the cylinder is supplied with equal amounts of cooling air.

Cowl Flaps Or Gills.

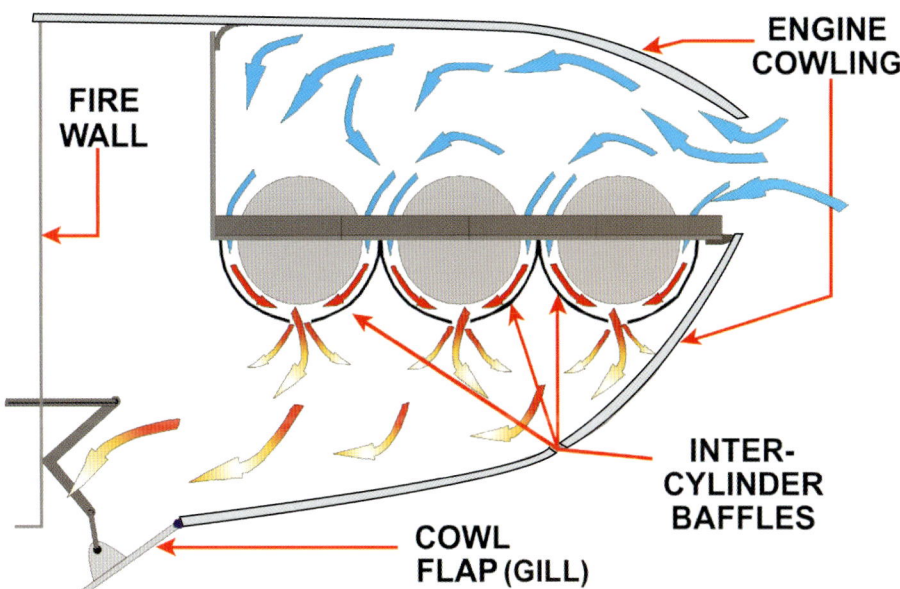

Figure 4.5 Cowl Flaps.

As well as lubricating the engine, oil plays an important part in cooling the engine.

Cowl flaps and Gills *(see Figure 4.5)* can be fitted to the cowlings to ensure control of the temperature. They are usually manually controlled on light aircraft, and, when open, the airflow over them causes a pressure drop which accelerates the airflow within the cowlings.

PROCEDURES TO ENSURE ADEQUATE COOLING.

Prior to flight, the air inlet and outlet to the cowlings must be checked to ensure that they are clear of obstruction.
The condition of baffles and cowling must be checked.

The operation of the cowl flap or gill, if fitted, must be checked.

CHAPTER 4: ENGINE COOLING

Check the engine oil level. Remember that as well as lubricating the engine, oil plays an important part in engine cooling.

At high power settings and low airspeeds, such as those occurring at take off, the cowl flaps (gills) should be selected open in order to increase the flow rate over the cylinders, and so increase cooling.

In the climb and cruise the cowl flaps or gills can be adjusted to maintain the engine temperature at the optimum.

In descent, engine power is reduced and less heat is generated. A very rapid descent will overcool the engine, and this can lead to what is known as Thermal Shock. Thermal Shock is the name given to cracking as a result of rapid temperature change. Overcooling in the descent can cause engine components to contract at different rates, and, thus, can result in their failure. Therefore the cowl flaps (gills) should be closed during descent to reduce the cooling effect. The cowl flaps (gills) should be opened on final approach in case the pilot is required to go around. If no cowl flaps (gills) are fitted, the pilot should increase engine RPM for a brief period, at regular intervals during the descent, in order to avoid overcooling of the engine.

During ground running, engine oil temperatures and cylinder head temperatures should be closely monitored to ensure the limitations are not exceeded. Although initially after engine start the cowl flaps (gills) should be closed to encourage quick engine warm up, they should subsequently be opened to prevent overheating.

During flight, especially during a long climb at full power, monitor the oil temperature and cylinder head temperature closely. If the cylinder head temperature becomes excessive, there are several methods of cooling the engine. Obviously, as has just been stated, the cowl flaps (gills) can be opened. Perhaps less obviously, the mixture can be made richer. With a rich mixture, the excess fuel will evaporate and cool the charge. A reduction in engine power will tend to lower engine temperatures. An increase in forward speed will have the same effect.

CHAPTER 4: ENGINE COOLING QUESTIONS

Representative PPL - type questions to test your theoretical knowledge of Engine Cooling.

1. Which of the following actions would help to improve engine cooling during the climb in an aircraft fitted with an air cooled engine?

    a. Leaning the air/fuel mixture
    b. Closing the cowl flaps
    c. Increasing power and reducing speed
    d. Decreasing power and increasing speed

2. Which of the following design features would not increase the effectiveness of the air-cooling of an aircraft piston engine?

    a. The fitting of baffles and directional air ducts
    b. "Finning" the cylinders
    c. Manufacturing major engine components using low conductivity materials
    d. Fitting cowl flaps and gills

Question	1	2
Answer		

The answers to these questions can be found at the end of this book.

CHAPTER 5
ENGINE LUBRICATION

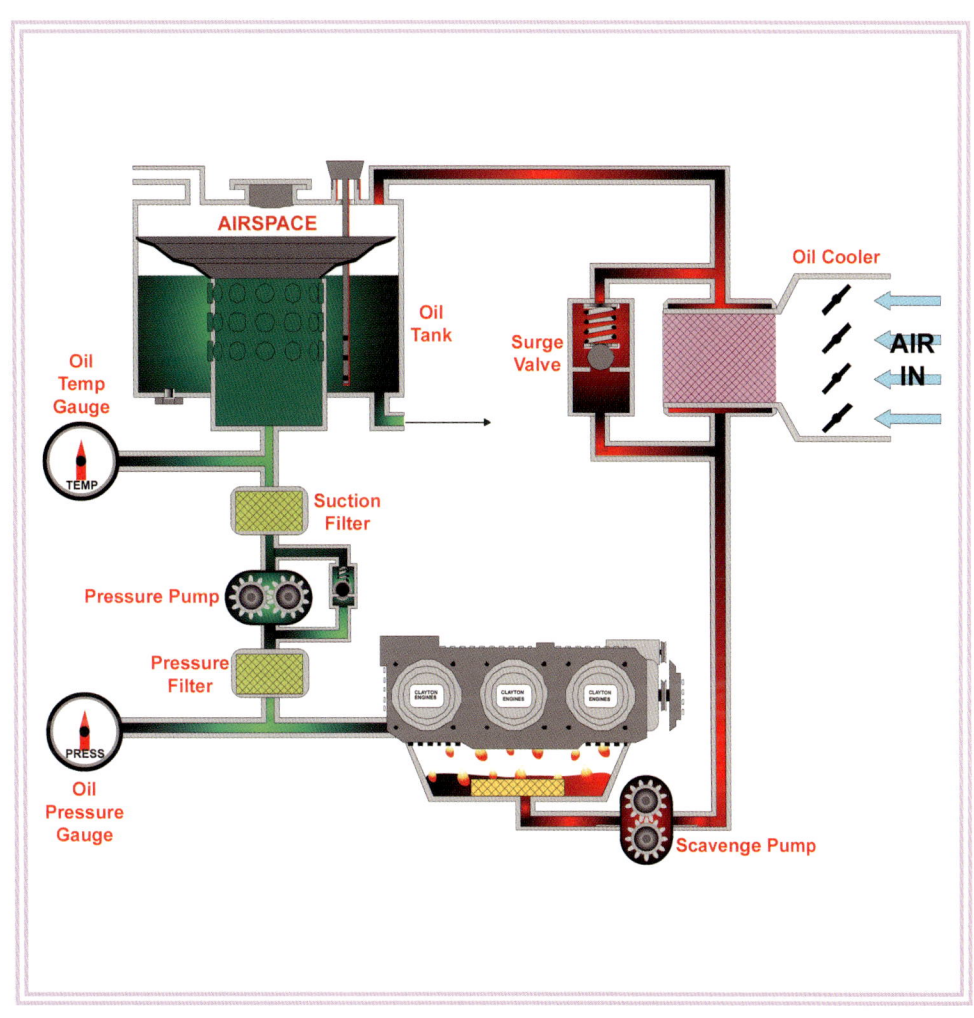

CHAPTER 5: ENGINE LUBRICATION

CHAPTER 5: ENGINE LUBRICATION

PRIMARY TASK OF THE LUBRICATION SYSTEM.

Reducing Friction.
Engine components which move against each other are subject to friction. Friction of this kind causes engine power to be wasted, and leads to wear of the engine components.

Friction can be reduced by introducing a lubricant between the moving surfaces. In the case of aviation engines the lubricant is oil. An engine that relies on 'Pressure Lubrication' requires the oil to be forced between the moving parts at relatively high pressure. Alternatively the components can be 'Splash Lubricated': in a system whereby the moving parts are splashed by oil which has been thrown around the crankcase of the engine by the moving parts themselves.

The primary task of the oil in an engine lubrication system is to reduce friction and wear. But the oil also has a number of secondary functions which are extremely important.

SECONDARY TASKS OF THE LUBRICATION SYSTEM.

Cooling.
Perhaps the most important of the secondary tasks is that of cooling. Oil flowing through the engine absorbs heat which is then dissipated through an oil cooler, one of which is shown in *Figure 5.1*. Without the oil cooler, the temperature of the oil would rise uncontrollably until the oil broke down and lost its lubricating ability.

Figure 5.1 An Oil Cooler.

Cleaning.
As the oil flows through the engine it carries away the by-products of combustion and thus cleans the engine too. A filter like the one shown in *Figure 5.2* will remove contaminants from the oil. In this way the oil acts as a detergent. Most of the components of the engine are ferrous in nature and will, if left alone in a damp oxygenated atmosphere, corrode, or oxidise. The oil prevents this corrosion by excluding the oxygen from the surface of the metal.

Figure 5.2 An Oil Filter.

CHAPTER 5: ENGINE LUBRICATION

The Oils as a Hydraulic Medium.
The oil can act as a hydraulic medium, for instance, when used as the hydraulic fluid in a variable pitch propeller mechanism, or within hydraulic tappets.

The Oil as an Indicating Medium.
Oil can also act as an indicating medium, giving information to the pilot about engine condition and power output, by, for instance, showing the oil pressure and temperature on gauges in the cockpit.

TYPE OF LUBRICATION SYSTEMS.

There are two types of lubrication system in common use. They are the **wet-sump system** and the **dry-sump system**.

Most light 'non-aerobatic' aircraft, like the one shown in *Figure 5.3*, use the wet-sump system, where the oil is stored in the bottom of the engine, in an engine component which is usually called the **sump**. It is from the word "sump" that we get the names of the two lubrication systems.

Figure 5.3 A Wet-Sump Engine.

THE WET-SUMP SYSTEM.

The use of a wet-sump simplifies the construction of the engine, but leads to a number of disadvantages which we will discuss later. In the wet-sump engine the oil is circulated by the pressure pump. The oil then passes through a high pressure filter into internal drillings in the crankcase. These internal drillings are called the 'oil gallery'.

Ducts in the oil gallery transfer the pressure oil to provide lubrication for the various drives in the accessory casing and also the main crankshaft bearings.

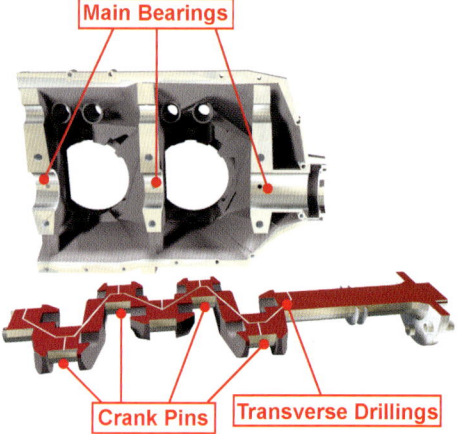

Figure 5.4 Oil grooves in the crank case main bearings and crankshaft.

Annular grooves *(see Figure 5.4)* are cut in the main bearings and these are aligned with transverse drillings in the crankshaft itself. The annular grooves fill with pressure oil, which is forced through the transverse drillings in the crankshaft, via the crank pins, into the big end bearings *(see Figure 5.5)*.

Oil droplets which are squeezed from between the bearing surfaces will collide with the crankshaft as it rotates, causing the inside of the crankcase to be filled with a fine oil mist. This oil mist will provide splash lubrication for the cylinder walls, the pistons, the small end bearings, gear teeth and valve mechanisms et cetera.
Lubrication for the valve gear rocker arms is fed through external oil pipelines.

CHAPTER 5: ENGINE LUBRICATION

Disadvantages of The Wet-Sump System.

The first disadvantage of the wet-sump system is that there are lubrication difficulties during some aerobatic manoeuvres, such as stall turns and inverted flight. During extreme manoeuvres, oil is thrown around inside the engine sump. This causes parts of the engine to be under-lubricated, which can damage components. Likewise, parts of the engine can be over-lubricated, which can be equally hazardous, potentially causing a damaging build up of oil pressure.

The second disadvantage of the wet-sump system is that the temperature of the oil is more difficult to control, because it is stored within the engine in the sump, which itself is hot.

Figure 5.5 Annular grooves in the Big End bearings.

Inverted flight can be particularly dangerous to a wet-sump engine.

The third disadvantage of the wet-sump system is that the oil becomes oxidised and blackened by the continual stirring action of the crankshaft and connecting rods. This means that the oil and the oil filter have to be changed much more often than would be the case in a dry-sump engine.

Finally, the amount of oil available is limited by the sump capacity. The sump of a wet-sump engine is the container for the oil supply, and its size is determined by the original engine design, which in practical terms cannot be changed.

THE DRY-SUMP SYSTEM.

The dry-sump system overcomes all of the problems of a wet-sump system by storing the oil in a remotely mounted tank.

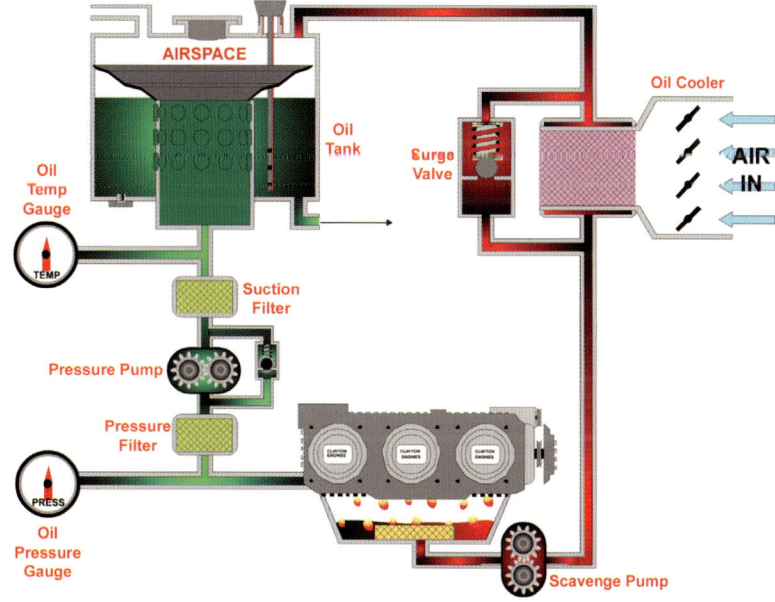

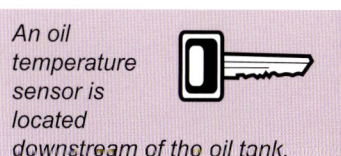

An oil temperature sensor is located downstream of the oil tank.

Figure 5.6 A Dry Sump Lubrication System.

CHAPTER 5: ENGINE LUBRICATION

System Components.
The oil tank is made of sheet metal, suitably baffled internally in order to stop the oil surging around while the aircraft is manoeuvring.

The Tank.

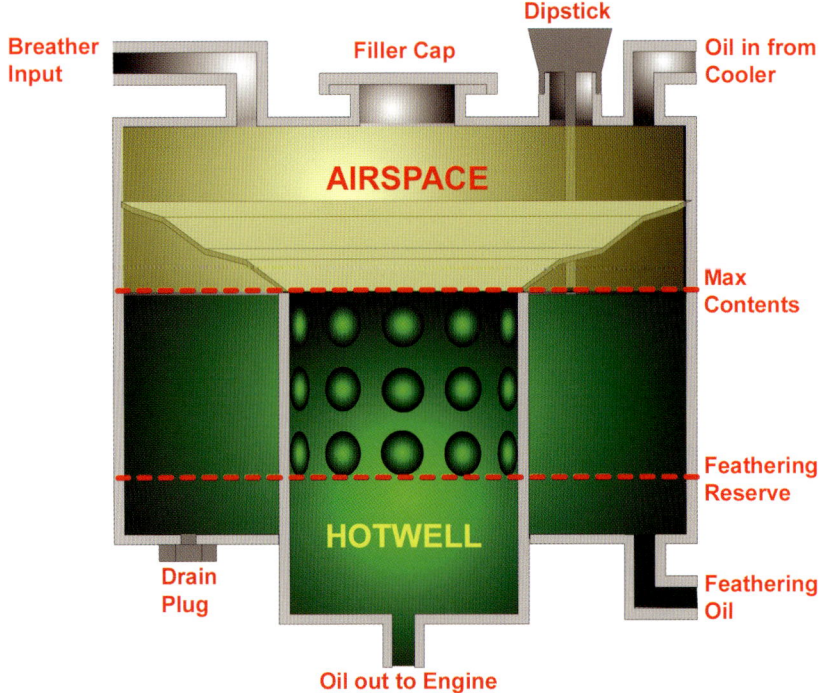

Figure 5.7 An Oil Tank.

Whenever possible the tank is placed above the level of the engine to ensure a gravity feed into the engine. The tank forms a reservoir of oil large enough for the engine's requirements, plus an air space.

The air space is very important, allowing for several potentially hazardous lubrication situations. For instance, the airspace permits the expansion of the oil when it gets hot, as it inevitably will. Also frothing of the oil due to aeration as it flows around the engine will occur, requiring a greater volume of space in the tank.

Another situation which requires the air space arises every time the engine is shut down. After engine shutdown, the walls of the crankcase are saturated with oil that drains into the sump. The oil will remain there until the engine is restarted, when the scavenge pump, which is fitted at the bottom of the sump, will return the oil to the oil tank. There has to be sufficient room in the tank to accommodate the returned oil. Finally, if the engine has any oil operated devices fitted to it, such as a variable pitch propeller, the displaced oil caused by these mechanisms has to go somewhere, and the tank serves as the receptacle for it.

 *An oil pressure pump must be able to supply a minimum specified oil pressure when the engine is running slowly and the oil temperature is very high.*

The Pressure Pump.
The pressure pump *(see Figure 5.8)* consists of two deep-toothed spur gears rotating in a close fitting pump casing. It is fitted on the accessory casing and is driven from the crankshaft by gears.

Oil pressure is sensed at the outlet of the pressure pump *(see Figure 5.6)*.

CHAPTER 5: ENGINE LUBRICATION

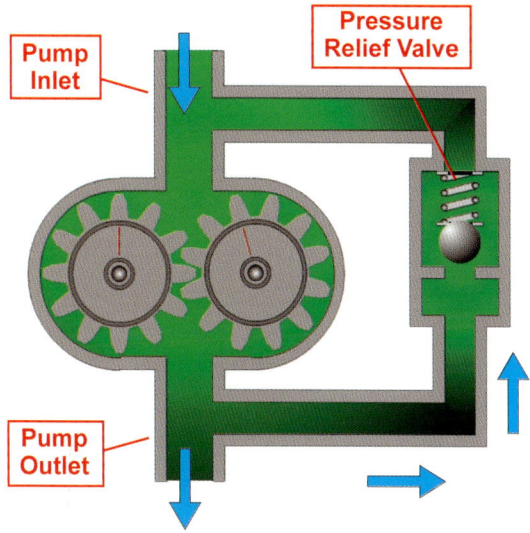

Figure 5.8 A Pressure Pump.

Unless it is controlled, the oil pressure will vary depending on the speed of the pump, the temperature of the oil and the resistance offered by the engine components.

The pump must be able to supply a minimum oil pressure under the most adverse running conditions; that is, when the engine is running slowly and the oil inlet temperature is very high. Consequently, there is an inherent danger that under normal running conditions, oil pressure may be too high and damage the engine or its components.

> *In order to maintain the oil pressure constant during normal engine running conditions, and to prevent excessive oil pressure in the system, an oil pressure relief valve is fitted.*

Therefore, to maintain the oil pressure constant during normal engine running conditions, and also to prevent excessive oil pressure in the system, a pressure relief valve is fitted across the inlet and the outlet pipes of the pump.

When the pressure reaches a predetermined figure, the valve opens and sufficient oil is returned to the inlet side of the pump to limit the maximum oil pressure. A coarse wire mesh suction filter is fitted between the tank and the pressure pump. It is designed to remove large solid particles from the oil before it enters the pressure pump, and thus prevent damage to the pump.

The pressure filter is fitted downstream of the pressure pump, before the oil enters the engine. The pressure filter is designed to remove very small solid particles before the oil passes to the bearing surfaces, again preventing damage to the engine.

The scavenge pump returns the oil which has passed through the engine into the sump back to the oil tank. Essentially the scavenge pump is the same design as the pressure pump, but larger. This is because in order to maintain a dry-sump, the scavenge pump needs to be of a larger capacity than the pressure pump.

> *The scavenge pump has the same design as the pressure pump but has a larger capacity.*

The Oil Cooler.

Oil is used as a cooling medium in the engine. If the oil gets too hot then it will fail as a lubricant and, as a consequence, the engine will also fail. To prevent the oil temperature becoming too high, an oil cooler is introduced into the system *(see Figure 5.1)*. The oil cooler consists of a matrix block which forces the oil into a thin film as it passes through it. The cooler matrix is exposed to the flow of cold slipstream air which is directed through the cowlings.

Engines with a high power output may have shutters fitted to the oil cooler. The shutters are used to control the flow of air through the cooler. They can be manual or automatic in operation.

Prior to engine start, the engine oil will normally be cold and viscous. The cooler matrix is fairly delicately constructed and can easily be damaged by high internal pressures. To prevent damage to the cooler matrix, an anti-surge valve, which is sensitive to oil pressure, is placed in parallel with the oil cooler *(see Figure 5.6)*. The anti-surge valve allows cold thick oil to by-pass the cooler and return directly to the tank.

> *In order to prevent damage to the oil cooler matrix, an anti-surge valve, which is sensitive to oil pressure, is placed in parallel with the oil cooler.*

CHAPTER 5: ENGINE LUBRICATION

QUALITIES AND GRADES OF OIL.

> *Viscosity is defined as the measure of the internal friction of a fluid.*

Different engines operating in different ambient conditions will need different grades of oil. The grade of an oil is mainly dictated by its viscosity.

Viscosity is defined as the measure of the internal friction of a fluid. A liquid that flows freely has a low viscosity, and a fluid that flows sluggishly has a high viscosity.

There are various standards employed to determine the viscosity of oils in order that different oils may be compared.

COMMERCIAL S.A.E No	SAYBOLT UNIVERSAL
30	60
40	80
50	100
60	120

Figure 5.9 A Viscosity Table.

The two standards which are generally employed in aviation are the 'Society of Automobile Engineers' or SAE; and the 'Saybolt Universal'. Both systems use numbers to denote the viscosity, the lower the number, the thinner the oil.

Figure 5.10 Oil 80 and Oil W80.

Some oils have two viscosity values. For example, SAE 15/50. Oils with two viscosity values are called 'Multigrade Oils'. Multigrade oils have the characteristics of low viscosity at low temperatures, and high viscosity at high temperatures.

The type of oil normally used in aircraft piston engines is mineral based. However, some engine manufacturers have trialed and approved the use of 'Semi-Synthetic' oils.

If an oil contains no additives it is called a 'Straight' oil. A straight oil can be recognised by the fact that it only has an identification number. For instance, the bottle with the blue label marked 'Oil 80' in *Figure 5.10* contains a straight oil. Note that the oil has a viscosity rating of SAE 40. Generally speaking, a straight oil is used only when running in new engines. However, there are certain requirements of some engines that straight oils cannot meet.

To satisfy such requirements, additives must be mixed with the oil. These additives can take the form of anti-oxidants, detergents and oiliness agents.

Oils with additives are called 'Compound' oils. A compound oil of the same viscosity as the straight oil shown previously, SAE 40, would be kept in a container marked W80, like the one with the red label in *Figure 5.10*. This particular oil is used where specific cleaning qualities are required.

CHAPTER 5: ENGINE LUBRICATION

OIL PRESSURE AND TEMPERATURE.

Oil pressure and temperature readings, when interpreted correctly, are indicative of the mechanical integrity of engine operation. A scan of the aircraft instruments must always include these vital items. The information they give may enable the pilot to take action which will prevent a bad situation getting much worse.

The oil contents must be verified during the pre-flight check to ensure there is sufficient oil for the flight.

Figure 5.11 Engine Instruments.

As part of the pre-flight check, the pilot must verify that the oil contents are sufficient for the flight that is to be undertaken. The oil filler cap must be secure and a thorough check made to ensure that there are no oil leaks.

After engine start the oil pressure guage must indicate the correct oil pressure within a specified time. If the engine is started from cold, the oil pressure may initially seem excessively high. However, as long as the oil pressure drops to normal as the engine warms up, the initial high pressure reading can be considered acceptable.

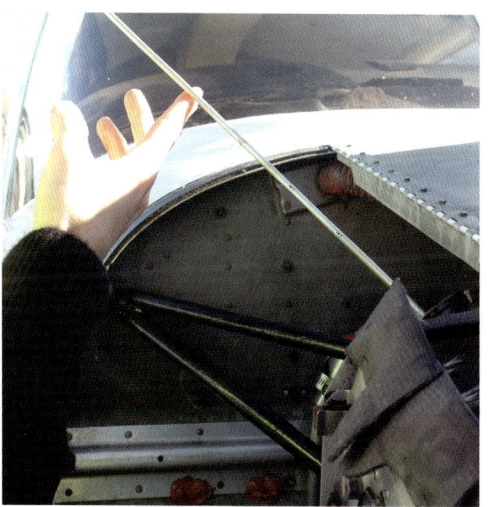

Figure 5.12 Oil Contents Check.

If the aircraft has a dry-sump engine, its oil contents must be checked immediately after the engine has stopped: realistically within a few minutes of shut down. This ensures that the tank contents are recorded accurately before the oil migrates into the sump under the influence of gravity. If, on the other hand, the engine has a wet-sump, a period of 15 to 20 minutes must elapse before the contents are checked, to allow all oil to return to the sump.

After a wet sump engine is shut down, 15 to 20 minutes must elapse before the oil contents are checked.

HYDRAULICING.

Radial and inverted engines can suffer from a condition known as 'hydraulicing'. Hydraulicing happens if oil accumulates between the piston and the cylinder head in the cylinders at the bottom of the engine.

CHAPTER 5: ENGINE LUBRICATION

Because oil is incompressible, if it is trapped between the piston and the cylinder head on the compression stroke, a hydraulic lock will be formed. If this happens, severe damage may occur when the starter motor is being used to start the engine. The piston might break, the connecting rod might bend, the cylinder may be torn from the crankcase, or the crankshaft may break.

To prevent hydraulicing, the engine must be rotated by turning the propeller, after confirming that the magnetos are OFF before the propeller is touched.

> To prevent 'hydraulicing' on some radial and inverted engines, the engine must be rotated by pulling through on the propeller, after confirming that the magnetos are 'OFF' before the propeller is touched.

OIL SYSTEM MALFUNCTIONS.

There are four main indications associated with a failure of the lubrication system:-

- Oil pressure too high
- Oil pressure too low
- Fluctuating oil pressure
- Oil pressure falling to zero

Oil Pressure Too High.

Too high an oil pressure, with normal oil temperature, may be caused by the pressure relief valve being set incorrectly. But this is unlikely unless the component has been worked on just prior to the flight. If, on the other hand, the oil temperature is low, the high oil pressure may be caused by the relatively high viscosity of the oil at low temperatures making it difficult for the oil to pass through the engine. The oil pressure relief valve may be unable to control the situation completely until the oil temperature rises. But, as long as

Figure 5.13 High Oil Pressure.

the oil pressure drops to normal as the engine warms up, the initial high pressure can be considered acceptable. However, if the pressure indication is very high, and remains high even after the oil temperature gauge has indicated a significant temperature rise the engine must be shut down to prevent damage.

Oil Pressure Too Low.

Too low an oil pressure, with normal or even low oil temperature, could once again mean that the oil pressure relief valve has been set incorrectly. But again this is unlikely unless the component has been worked on just prior to the flight. The problem here is more likely to be excessive clearance in the bearings due to wear. Potentially even worse is an oil leak from the output side of the pressure pump.

Figure 5.14 Low Oil Pressure.

80

CHAPTER 5: ENGINE LUBRICATION

If the minimum oil pressure cannot be maintained, the engine must be shut down in order to prevent damage.

If the oil pressure is too low, with an associated high oil temperature, then this is probably due to the temperature causing the viscosity of the oil to drop below the viscosity value at which the oil pressure relief valve can cope. Remember, the task of the relief valve is to maintain constant engine oil pressure, regardless of engine R.P.M. or oil temperature.

If the engine is fitted with oil cooler shutters, they can be opened in an attempt to lower the oil temperature. If oil cooler shutters are not fitted, the pilot should consider either reducing engine power, or lowering the nose to increase airspeed. The mixture may also be enriched. Any or all of these actions can be taken to cool the engine and, thus, cool the oil, bringing its viscosity back up to the value where the lubrication system can function normally. Once again though, if the minimum oil pressure cannot be maintained, then the engine must be shut down to prevent damage.

Fluctuating Oil Pressure.
Small fluctuations of the oil pressure gauge needle, either side of the correct pressure, indication may be symptomatic of a sticking pressure relief valve.

A sticking pressure relief valve would initially cause the pressure to build up beyond the optimum level. Subsequently, when the pressure reached a value high enough to overcome the "stiction" of the valve, the valve would open, causing the pressure to fall momentarily below the correct level. Then the cycle would start again.

Figure 5.15 Fluctuating Oil Pressure.

Large fluctuations of the oil pressure gauge needle, will probably be caused by insufficient oil in the system. If the engine has been leaking oil, the oil level will eventually drop to a point where the pressure pump cannot sustain its output. In such a situation pressure will drop momentarily until the pump draws in more oil. At this point the pressure will rise again, if only for a moment. Again, if the minimum oil pressure cannot be maintained, the engine must be shut down to prevent damage.

Figure 5.16 Zero Oil Pressure.

Oil Pressure Falling to Zero.
If the oil pressure falls suddenly to zero, the pilot needs to quickly work out what has happened. If the minimum oil pressure cannot be maintained, the engine must be shut down immediately to prevent damage. The probable cause of a zero pressure indication is either failure of the pressure pump or a catastrophic loss of oil from the system.

CHAPTER 5: ENGINE LUBRICATION QUESTIONS

Representative PPL - style questions to test your theoretical knowledge of the Lubrication System.

1. By what activation method does the valve which allows oil to either flow through or by-pass a serviceable engine oil cooler work?

    a. Temperature activated
    b. Pressure activated
    c. Manually activated
    d. Electrically activated

2. Excessive oil pressure can be resolved by using:

    a. An oil pressure relief valve
    b. A thermal cut-out
    c. A filter by-pass valve
    d. An oil tank overflow

3. The prevention of excessive oil pressure in an aircraft engine is assured by:

    a. Ensuring that the engine does not exceed the red-line RPM value.
    b. The engine's high capacity pressure pump.
    c. The engine's oil pressure relief valve.
    d. The engine's filter by-pass valve.

4. Where is the sensor of the engine oil temperature gauge located?

    a. Within the exhaust sections of the engine
    b. Before the oil cooler
    c. After passing through the oil cooler, but before reaching the hot sections of the engine
    d. In the same position as the pressure sensor for the oil pressure gauge

5. The scavenge pump:

    a. Is of a similar design as the pressure pump but has a smaller capacity
    b. Is located at the exit of the oil cooler
    c. Has a fine mesh filter at its outlet to protect the oil cooler matrix
    d. Is of the same design as the pressure pump but has a larger capacity

Question	1	2	3	4	5
Answer					

The answers to these questions can be found at the end of this book.

CHAPTER 6
IGNITION SYSTEMS

CHAPTER 6: IGNITION SYSTEMS

CHAPTER 6: IGNITION SYSTEMS

IGNITION SYSTEMS.

All aircraft piston engines are fitted with dual-ignition; that is, they have two electrically independent ignition systems. Each cylinder, therefore, has two spark plugs, and each spark plug is fed by a separate magneto, as shown in *Figure 6.1*.

Spark plugs receive their high tension supply from a magneto which is independent of the aircraft electrical system.

Figure 6.1 The Rear of an Engine showing the Two Magnetos.

Dual-ignition systems serve two purposes. Firstly they reduce the risk of engine failure due to faulty ignition. Secondly, by igniting the mixture within the cylinder at two points, the combustion time is reduced, thus reducing the chance of detonation. (Detonation is a phenomenon which is covered in the Chapter 7, 'Carburation'.)

In an aircraft engine ignition system, the high tension supply to the spark plugs comes from the magneto's primary and secondary self generation and distribution system.

MAGNETOS.

Magnetos are self-contained, engine driven electrical generators which produce high voltage sparks. Magnetos are completely independent of the aircraft electrical system.

Low voltage pulses are generated in the primary coil of the magneto *(see Figure 6.2)* and these are transformed into high tension pulses by a secondary coil. Within the magneto, a rotary switch called a distributor directs the sparks to the plugs in the correct firing sequence.

The magneto combines two basic principles: that of the permanent magnet generator, and that of the step-up transformer.

Magnetos are self-contained, engine driven, electrical generators which produce high voltage sparks.

85

CHAPTER 6: IGNITION SYSTEMS

The contact breaker in the primary circuit of a magneto assists in the collapse of the magnetic field created by the permanent magnet generator.

Principles of the Magneto.

Figure 6.2 illustrates the first basic principle of the magneto: that of the permanent magnet generator. The only modification to the standard permanent magnet generator is the addition of a contact breaker which collapses the magnetic field in the primary circuit more quickly than would normally happen in a generator of this type.

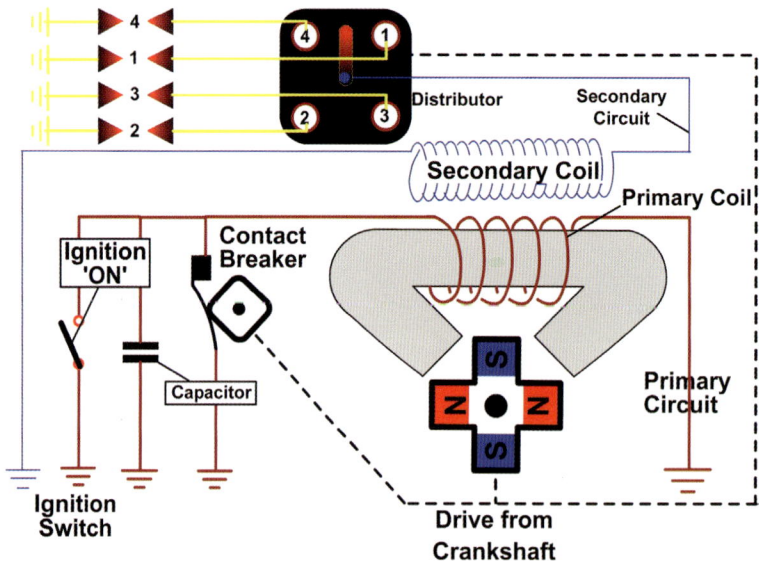

Figure 6.2 A Diagram of a Simplified Magneto Circuit.

The second basic principle of the magneto, that of the step-up transformer, is utilised in the magneto's secondary circuit. The secondary coil is a step-up transformer which consists of thousands of turns of very thin wire. A very high voltage is induced in the secondary windings by the rapid collapse of the magnetic lines of force in the primary circuit.

The capacitor in the primary circuit of a magneto assists in collapsing the magnetic field, helps prevent erosion of the contact breaker points and prevents sparking at the contact breaker points.

The Capacitor.

The faster the magnetic lines of force collapse the greater is the voltage induced in the secondary windings.

To ensure that the primary field collapses as fast as possible, and also to prevent the contact breaker points being eroded by the sparks which would occur when the points opened, a capacitor is placed in parallel with the points. This can be seen in the diagram shown in *Figure 6.2*.

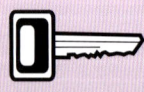
The distributor arm rotates at half engine speed.

The Distributor.

Once the high voltage sparks have been produced, they are passed to the spark plugs in the correct firing sequence. This is achieved by the distributor, illustrated in *Figure 6.2*. The distributor rotor arm rotates at half the engine speed.

Ignition Control.

When a magneto is selected OFF, the ignition switch is closed and the circuit is earthed.

To give the pilot control of the magneto, an ignition switch is fitted in the magneto's primary circuit. When the ignition switch is placed to the OFF position, both ends of the primary coil are earthed, which makes it impossible for current to be generated. In *Figure 6.2*, the ignition switch is shown in the ON position.

CHAPTER 6: IGNITION SYSTEMS

With the ignition switch in the OFF position, the primary circuit is earthed. The secondary circuit is not now cut by the magnetic lines of force which would otherwise enable it to generate the sparks. Therefore, the ignition system is dead.

If the magneto becomes electrically disconnected from the ignition circuit, a potentially lethal situation arises. The magneto is now permanently live, and the engine will continue running even if both magnetos are selected OFF.

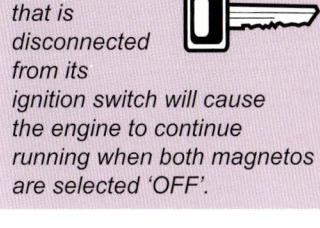

A magneto that is disconnected from its ignition switch will cause the engine to continue running when both magnetos are selected 'OFF'.

After engine start, the magnetos' operation must be checked in several ways, one of which is the Dead Cut check. This, essentially, is a check to ascertain whether or not the pilot has full control of the magnetos. The check requires that each of the magnetos be selected OFF in turn, to check that there is a drop in engine RPM, but that the engine does not stop. If, during this check, it appears that the engine may stop, the pilot must allow it to do so. To do otherwise may cause the engine to suffer damage.

If, while carrying out the Dead Cut Check, you suspect that the engine is going to stop running, you should allow it to stop completely.

Starting the Engine - Spark Augmentation.

During start-up, the engine is cranked at about 120 rpm. At this speed, the magneto is not capable of producing sparks with sufficient energy to ignite the mixture. This makes it necessary to employ various methods of spark augmentation. There are three methods of spark augmentation. They are the **high tension booster coil**, the **low tension booster coil** and, the most common in small aircraft engines, the **impulse coupling**.

Because the speed of rotation of the engine during starting is too low for the magneto to produce sufficient energy to ignite the air-fuel mixture, aircraft ignition systems use a means of spark augmentation.

The high tension booster coil supplies a stream of high voltage impulses to a trailing brush on the distributor rotor. This ensures that a fat retarded spark is generated in the cylinder. The retardation of the spark is necessary only during engine start, because of the low rotational speed. Once the engine has started, the magnetos will produce sparks of sufficient strength, which allow the high tension booster coil to be switched OFF. As a consequence of this, the high tension booster Coil is switched ON only for engine start.

The low tension booster coil supplies the primary coil of the magneto with a low voltage during the engine start. Once again, as soon as the engine has started, the low tension booster coil is switched OFF.

Impulse Coupling.

The impulse coupling, a diagram of which is shown in *Figure 6.3*, is a mechanical device which uses a spring to temporarily increase the speed of rotation of the magneto. This gives a fat retarded spark during the starting cycle.

The diagram shows a cutaway view of the impulse coupling within the magneto.

The cam is driven anticlockwise by gears from the crankshaft at half the crankshaft speed, and drives the hub through the spring.

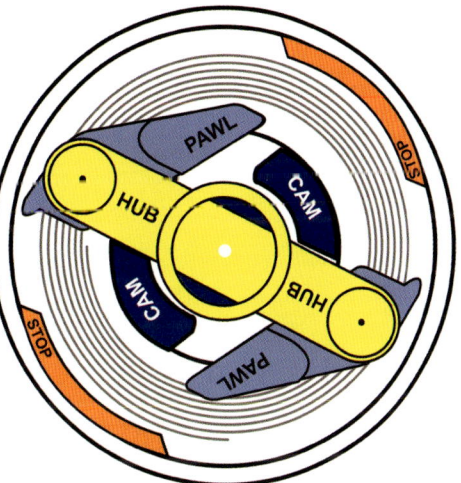

Figure 6.3. The Impulse Coupling Mechanism.

An impulse coupling is a mechanical device which uses a spring to temporarily increase the speed of rotation of the magneto.

87

The permanent magnet of the magneto is attached to the hub, which also carries the pawls.

Initially the cam rotates, turning the spring which carries the hub round until the pawls come into contact with the stops. The cam continues to rotate, tensioning the spring, until the leading edges of the cams contact the pawls, pushing them out of contact with the stops. The hub, under the impulse of the spring, rotates very quickly, carrying its attached magnet.

Rotating the magnet this quickly enables it to generate the high voltage spark required to ignite the mixture. The spark is also retarded, which ensures that the engine is driven in the correct direction. Once the engine has started, the pawls are rotating at such a speed that centrifugal force holds them out at an angle which prevents them contacting the stops. Thus the spring has no further effect.

CHAPTER 6: IGNITION SYSTEMS QUESTIONS

Representative PPL - type questions to test your theoretical knowledge of Ignition Systems.

1. The high tension supply connected to the spark plugs comes from:

   a. The magneto's primary and secondary self-generation and distribution system
   b. The battery during start up and low idle
   c. The battery, and is transformed by the magneto
   d. The battery and the high tension coil

2. When a magneto is selected OFF, the switch located in the primary circuit:

   a. Is closed and the circuit is earthed
   b. Is opened, breaking circuit continuity
   c. Is opened and the circuit is earthed
   d. Is closed, earthing the plug leads

3. If a magneto becomes inadvertently disconnected from its ignition switch, it will:

   a. Stop the engine if the other magneto is "OFF"
   b. Cause a high mag drop indication
   c. Cause the engine to continue running when both magnetos are selected to "OFF"
   d. Cause the failure of one plug in each cylinder

4. The high tension supply to the spark plugs is supplied from:

   a. The alternator
   b. The magneto and is independent of the aircraft electrical system
   c. The magneto, supplied from the aircraft electrical system
   d. The battery on engine start-up and low idle, and the magneto once the engine is running at fast idle

5. Magnetos are:

   a. Generators, driven by the cam-shaft, used to supply electrical equipment
   b. Used to generate low voltage sparks for the spark plugs
   c. Fitted within the distributor, and fire in the same sequence as the spark plugs
   d. Self-contained, engine-driven, electrical generators which produce high voltage sparks

CHAPTER 6: IGNITION SYSTEMS QUESTIONS

6. The function of the contact breaker in the primary circuit of a magneto is to:

    a. Allow the magneto to be switched on and off
    b. Time the sparks to the spark plugs
    c. Assist in the collapse of the magnetic field created by the permanent magnet generator
    d. Prevent the build up of excess static charge

7. Of the following, which are functions of the capacitor in the primary circuit of a magneto?

    (i) Assists in collapsing the magnetic field
    (ii) Smooths the output of the magnetic field
    (iii) Helps prevent erosion of the contact breaker points
    (iv) Prevents sparking at the contact breaker points

    a. (i) and (ii) only.
    b. (iii) and (iv) only.
    c. (i) and (iv) only
    d. (i), (iii) and (iv).

8. The distributor arm rotates at:

    a. One quarter engine speed
    b. A half engine speed
    c. Engine speed
    d. Twice engine speed

9. Of the following statements, which relates factually to an Impulse Coupling?

    a. It supplies a stream of high voltage impulses to a trailing brush on the distributor rotor
    b. It supplies the primary coil of the magneto with a low voltage during engine start
    c. It is a mechanical device which uses a spring to temporarily increase the speed of rotation of the magneto
    d. All of the above

10. Aircraft engine ignition systems incorporate a means of spark augmentation:

    a. Because, at high engine speeds, a fat spark is needed to extract maximum power from the air-fuel mixture
    b. Because the speed of rotation of the engine, during starting, is too low for the magneto to produce sufficient energy to ignite the air-fuel mixture
    c. In order to overcome the problem of spark-retard during starting
    d. All of the above

CHAPTER 6: IGNITION SYSTEMS QUESTIONS

11. While carrying out the Dead Cut Check, with the right magneto selected, you notice that the engine falters, and you suspect it will stop running. You should:

    a. Allow the engine to stop completely
    b. Quickly switch to the left magneto
    c. Quickly switch to both magnetos.
    d. Open the throttle to keep the engine running, then select both magneto

Question	1	2	3	4	5	6	7	8	9	10	11
Answer											

The answers to these questions can be found at the end of this book.

CHAPTER 7
CARBURATION

CHAPTER 7: CARBURATION

CHAPTER 7: CARBURATION

MIXTURE RANGE.

The Chemically Correct Ratio.

Although air and fuel vapour will burn when mixed in proportions ranging from between 8 : 1 (which is rich) to 20 : 1 (which is weak), complete combustion occurs only with an air / fuel ratio of 15 : 1 by weight. This is called the chemically correct ratio. At this ratio all of the oxygen in the air combines with all of the hydrogen and carbon in the fuel.

The chemically correct mixture does not, however, give the best results, because the temperature of combustion is so high that power can be lost through detonation.

Figure 7.1 The Chemically Correct Ratio

An air/fuel ratio of 15:1 by weight is called the chemically correct ratio.

Detonation.

Detonation is a phenomenon usually associated with weak mixtures and high cylinder head temperatures. Detonation is unstable combustion or, put more simply, an explosion which occurs after the normal ignition point.

In normal conditions, when the air-fuel mixture is ignited by the spark plug, the flame travels smoothly through the mixture as the advancing flame front heats the gases immediately ahead of it, so that they, in turn, burn. Progressively, more and more heat is concentrated in the flame front which is brought to bear on the remaining unburnt portion of the mixture, termed the end gas, raising the temperature of the end gas.

Detonation of the air/fuel mixture in a piston engine is usually associated with weak mixtures and high cylinder head temperatures.

The end gas is also subjected to increasing pressure, partly from the fact that the piston is reducing the remaining space available, and partly because the burnt gases themselves are expanding.

However, if the mixture is too weak, and the temperature too high, there may be sufficient pressure and heat available to bring all the end gas to the point of combustion at the same instant, and it will explode.

The flame rate increases from its normal 60 to 80 feet per second to 1 000 ft per second, with a degree of violence that depends on the amount of end gas that remains.

Because of the ringing nature of the noise produced by the explosion or detonation, the noise is sometimes called pinking, or knocking. Detonation can be extremely harmful to the engine, particularly to the piston crown, which may eventually burn away, with inevitable consequences.

Detonation is damaging to the pistons.

Preventing Detonation.

Reducing the temperature of the mixture, for instance by deselecting carburettor heat, or reducing cylinder head temperature by selecting a rich mixture, will assist in preventing detonation.

95

CHAPTER 7: CARBURATION

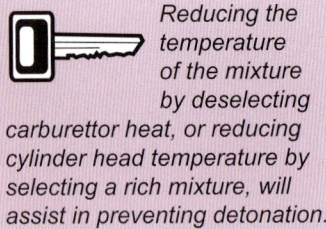
Reducing the temperature of the mixture by deselecting carburettor heat, or reducing cylinder head temperature by selecting a rich mixture, will assist in preventing detonation.

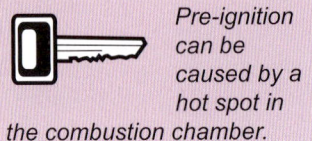
Pre-ignition can be caused by a hot spot in the combustion chamber.

With a supercharged or turbocharged engine, reducing the boost pressure and increasing propeller RPM will also assist in preventing detonation.

Pre-ignition.
Pre-ignition is often confused with detonation, but is, in fact, quite different. Whereas detonation occurs after the normal ignition point, pre-ignition, as inferred by its very name, occurs before the spark is generated at the plug. Pre-ignition is usually caused by a local hot spot in the combustion chamber, either a piece of incandescent accumulated carbon *(see Figure 7.2)*, or perhaps very hot spark plug points.

Pre-ignition will cause rough running and an inevitable loss of power, and may cause the engine to continue running (running on), after the ignition has been turned off.

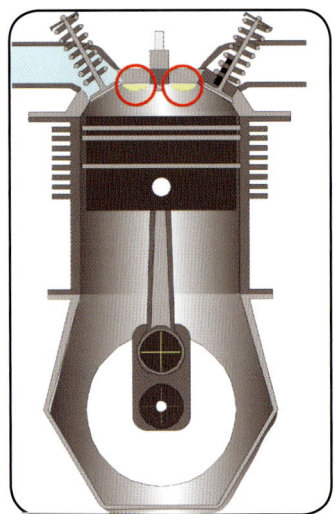
Figure 7.2 Incandescent Carbon in the Cylinder.

Practical Mixture Strengths.
Although the chemically correct mixture strength would theoretically produce the highest temperature and, therefore, engine power, in practice mixing and distribution are less than perfect. This situation results in the mixture in some parts of the engine being richer, and in other parts, being weaker than the optimum strength. This variation in mixture strength may also exist between one cylinder and another.

The Result of Having a Slightly Rich Mixture.
A slightly rich mixture does not have much effect on power since all the oxygen is still consumed and the excess of fuel simply serves to slightly reduce the effective volumetric efficiency. In fact, the cooling effect of a slightly rich mixture can be to some extent beneficial.

The Result of Having a Weak Mixture.
Weak mixtures, however, rapidly reduce power since some of the inspired oxygen is not being utilized. This power reduction is much greater than that resulting from a slight richness of the mixture. It is, therefore, quite common to run engines (when maximum power rather than best fuel economy is the objective) at somewhat richer than chemically-correct mixtures (e.g. about 12.5 : 1), in order to ensure that no cylinder is left running at severely reduced power from drawing in an unduly weak mixture.

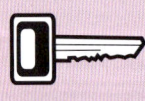
The ideal air/fuel mixture ratio of a piston engine should be in the region of 1:12, by weight.

Mixture Control Setting.
However, mixture requirement is ultimately dependent upon engine speed and power output. *Figure 7.3* shows typical air/fuel mixture curves for different phases of engine operation. The following sections on Engine Starting, Take-Off Power, Climbing and Cruising refer to *Figure 7.3*.

Engine Starting.
Notice that a rich mixture is required for starting and slow running; this is because fuel will burn only when it has vaporized and is mixed with air.

When starting an engine from cold, there is little heat to assist the vaporizing process; therefore only the lightest fractions of the fuel will vaporize.

CHAPTER 7: CARBURATION

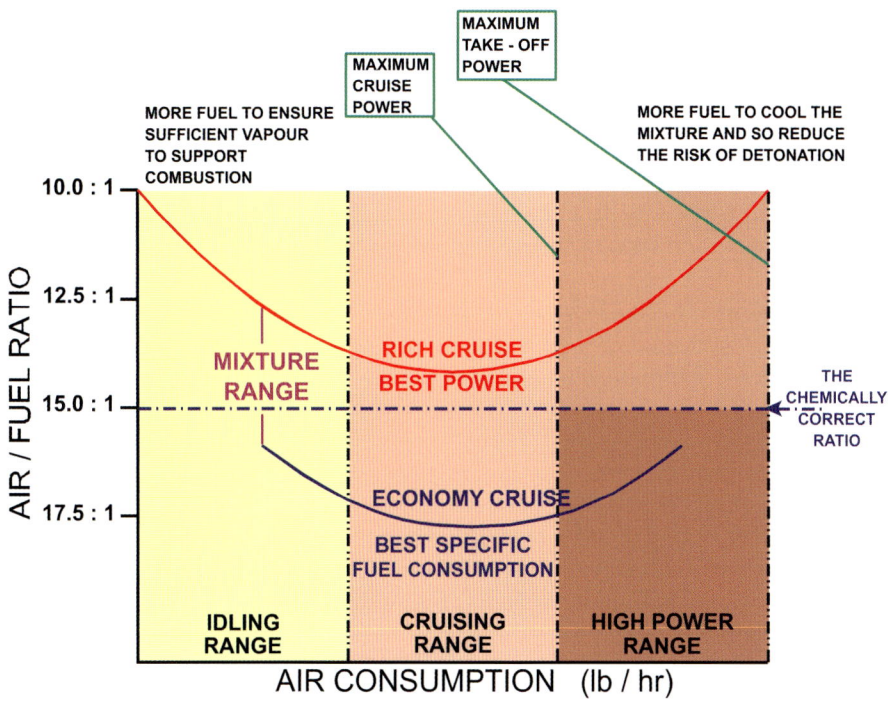

Figure 7.3 Typical Air/Fuel Mixture Curves.

Because the surplus fuel helps cool the engine, it is best to run the engine with the mixture slightly rich.

To make sure that there is sufficient fuel vapour in the cylinders to support combustion, a rich mixture is therefore required.

Take-off Power.
When full power is selected for take-off, the mixture is set to fully rich; that is about 10 : 1.

This maximum charge induced into the cylinders in a given time delivers full power. The fully rich mixture protects against detonation and pre-ignition, and also contributes to engine cooling.

But if taking off from an airfield at very high elevations, say in the United States or Africa, the mixture may need to be leaner than fully rich.

Climbing.
Most light aircraft climb under full power. Again the mixture should be selected fully rich for climbs up to about 5 000 ft above sea level. At higher altitudes, the less dense air can cause the mixture to become too rich for the engine to develop full power.

Cruising.
The cruise portion of the diagram in *Figure 7.3* shows that the cruise phase of flight is that in which the pilot needs to think about what strength of mixture to set.

If time is no object, then during cruising flight only moderate power is required from the engine. Thus an economy cruise setting can be used. Fuel consumption will decrease accordingly. If a high "cruise climb" speed is desired, then performance cruise power can be selected, which requires a richer mixture. Once cruising altitude has been reached and cruise power set, the pilot may wish to think about leaning the mixture, to choose the correct air/fuel ratio for best fuel economy.

CHAPTER 7: CARBURATION

 *As the aircraft climbs and air density decreases, the weight of air entering the engine also decreases. Therefore, the mixture will become richer.*

Density Change and Mixture Adjustment.
Because the density of the air decreases with increasing altitude, as the aircraft climbs, the weight of air drawn into the cylinder decreases. For a given intake velocity, the pressure drop in the carburettor venturi will decrease as ambient density decreases. However, the fuel flow due to this pressure drop will not decrease by the same proportion, and so the mixture will become richer. Therefore, if we are not to use too much fuel when flying at altitude, it becomes imperative that we have some method of defining and regulating the mixture strength.

Setting the Mixture Control Using Engine RPM as a Guide.
There are two approved methods of setting the desired mixture strength. The first method presumes some knowledge of the effects that mixture change will have on the engine.

Bear in mind that as the mixture control is moved from fully rich to a weaker setting, the air/fuel ratio approaches the chemically correct value of approximately 15:1. At this ratio all of the air and fuel are consumed and the heat released by combustion is at its maximum. More heat means more power. With a fixed pitch propeller, the RPM will rise, and airspeed will increase as more power is produced.

If the mixture is weakened even more, the RPM will drop. Pushing the mixture control back to where the chemically correct mixture was found will bring the engine speed back up, but this cannot be maintained without risking the generation of detonation. To prevent this happening, the mixture control should be moved to a slightly richer position, at which point the RPM will fall slightly. This setting can be considered the optimum mixture setting for a rich cruise.

Using the Exhaust Gas Temperature Gauge to Set the Mixture Control.
The Exhaust Gas Temperature (EGT) gauge consists of a thermocouple fitted into the exhaust pipe of the hottest cylinder on the engine. The thermocouple produces a voltage directly proportional to its temperature. The voltage is indicated on a gauge calibrated to show exhaust gas temperature.

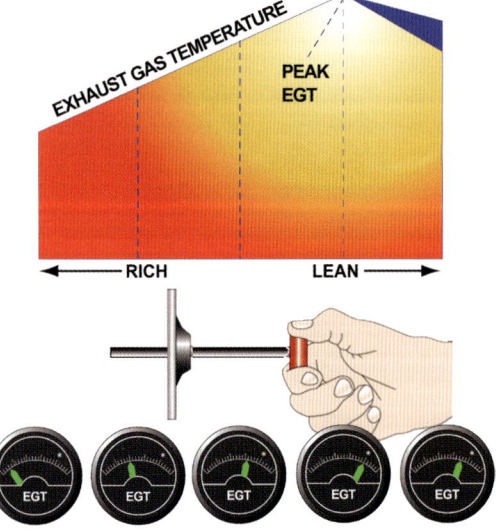

Figure 7.4 E.G.T. Changes with Weakening Mixture.

If the mixture control is moved toward lean, the temperature will peak at the ratio of 15 : 1. It should be remembered that this ratio should not be used, as detonation can occur. On reaching the peak EGT, the mixture control should then be moved towards rich and the exhaust gas temperature will drop. The aircraft's flight manual will specify a temperature drop which will give the rich cruise setting.

CHAPTER 7: CARBURATION

PRINCIPLES OF THE FLOAT CHAMBER CARBURETTOR.

The simplest solution to the problem of maintaining the correct air-fuel ratio in response to throttle settings at all operating altitudes is the float chamber carburettor.

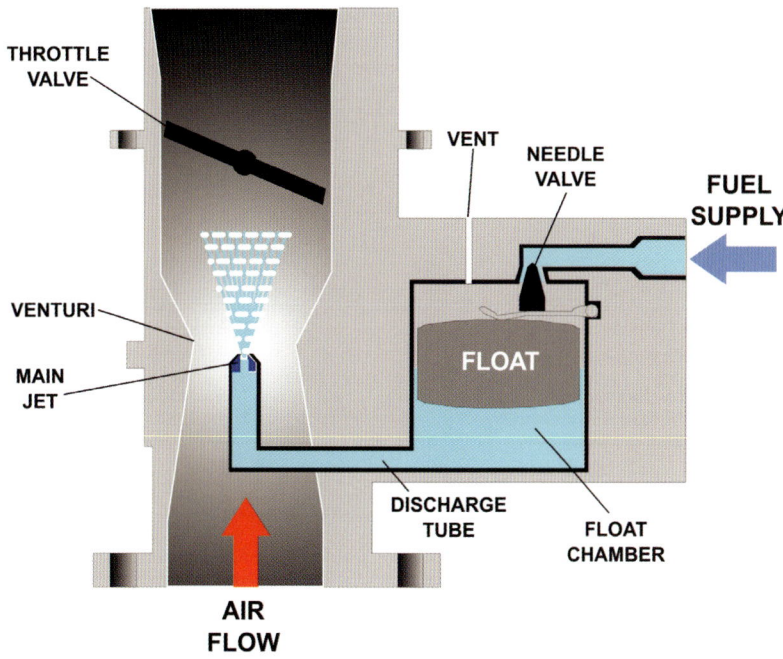

Figure 7.5 A Simple Float Chamber Carburettor.

Principles of the Float Chamber Carburettor, the 'U' Tube and the Venturi.

The float chamber carburettor employs two basic principles. They are: the 'U tube' Principle and the Venturi Principle.

The 'U tube' Principle states that if a tube is bent into the shape of a 'U', as in the discharge tube in *Figure 7.5*, and then filled with liquid, the level in the two legs of the 'U' tube will be the same, provided that the pressure acting on each end of the tube is the same.

If, however, a pressure difference is created across the 'U' tube, the level of the liquid will rise in one of the legs. In the carburettor, this principle will cause fuel to flow through the discharge tube.

The 'U' tube in the carburettor, then, is the discharge tube. In the float chamber carburettor, one leg of the 'U' tube is opened out to form the float chamber, itself, and a constant fuel level in the chamber is maintained by a float and valve mechanism regulating the flow of fuel from a fuel pump (or pumps) delivering a supply from the main aircraft tanks. The other leg of the discharge tube is located within the Venturi tube section of the carburettor, sometimes referred to as the Choke Tube.

The float chamber carburettor employs two basic principles. They are the 'U tube' principle and the Venturi principle.

Bernoulli's Theorem.

Bernoulli's Theorem states that the total energy per unit mass along any one streamline in a moving fluid is constant.

Bernoulli's Theorem states that the total energy per unit mass along any one streamline in a moving fluid is constant.

CHAPTER 7: CARBURATION

The moving fluid possesses energy because of its pressure, temperature and velocity. If one of these changes, one or both of the others must also change to maintain the same overall energy.

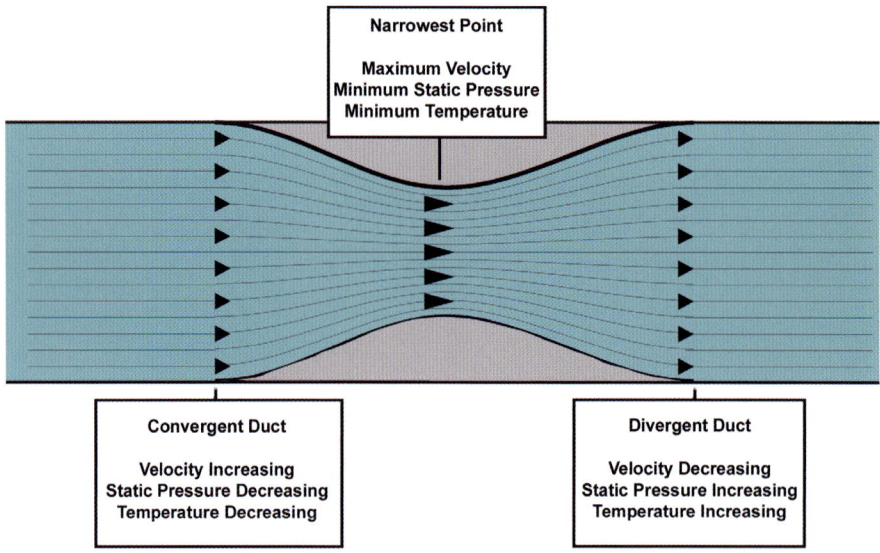

Figure 7.6 A Venturi.

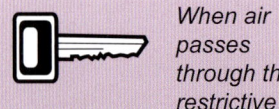 *When air passes through the restrictive throat of a carburettor venturi there is a static pressure decrease, a velocity increase and a temperature decrease.*

As the air passes through the restriction of the venturi its velocity increases, causing a drop in the static pressure and temperature of the air. In the carburettor, the pressure drop at the throat of the venturi is proportional to the mass of the airflow, and is used to make fuel flow from the float chamber by placing one leg of the discharge tube within the venturi.

Engine suction provides a flow of air from the air intake through the venturi in the carburettor to the induction manifold. This air speeds up as it passes through the venturi, and a drop in static pressure occurs at that point.

Atmospheric air pressure acts on the fuel in the float chamber which is connected to the fuel discharge tube located in the throat of the venturi. Atmospheric pressure is, of course, higher than the reduced static pressure in the carburettor's venturi.

The difference in pressure between the float chamber and the throat of the venturi provides the force necessary to discharge fuel into the airstream. As airflow through the venturi increases so the static pressure drops further, and a higher pressure differential acts on the fuel to increase its flow in proportion to the airflow.

In this simple carburettor, the airflow to the engine is controlled by a throttle valve, and the fuel flow is controlled by a metering jet.

Although this simple carburettor contains all the components necessary to provide a suitable air fuel mixture over a limited range, modifications are required if it is to give anything more than this basic service.

CHAPTER 7: CARBURATION

IMPROVEMENTS TO THE BASIC FLOAT CHAMBER CARBURETTOR.

The Pressure Balance Duct.

To maintain the correct rate of discharge of fuel through the main jet, the pressure in the float chamber and in the air intake section of the engine induction system must be equal.

Equalized pressure conditions can be obtained only by connecting the float chamber directly to the air intake by a duct which is called the pressure balance duct *(see Figure 7.7)*.

As engine speed and airflow through the venturi increase, the proportion of fuel to air rises as a result of the different flow characteristics of the two fluids.

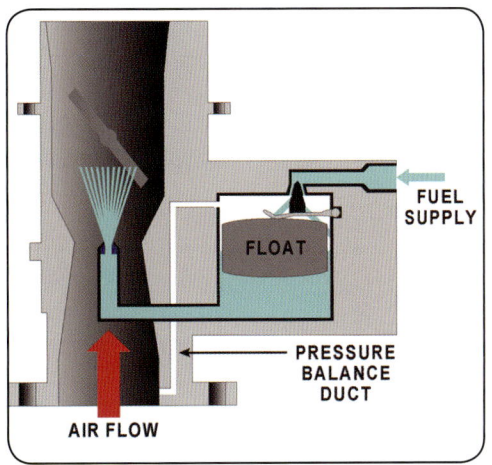

Figure 7.7 The Pressure Balance Duct.

This causes the mixture to become richer as the engine RPM increases. In some ways this may be looked upon as a virtuous combination of events, because at high engine power a rich mixture is needed. However, a method for setting the mixture accurately is still required.

The Diffuser.

To overcome the effect of the air/fuel mixture becoming richer with increasing engine RPM, some carburettors are fitted with a diffuser, *Figure 7.8*.

As engine speed is progressively increased above idling, the fuel level in the diffuser well drops, and progressively uncovers more air holes in the diffuser. These holes allow more air into the discharge tube, and, by reducing the pressure differential, prevent enrichment of the air/fuel mixture.

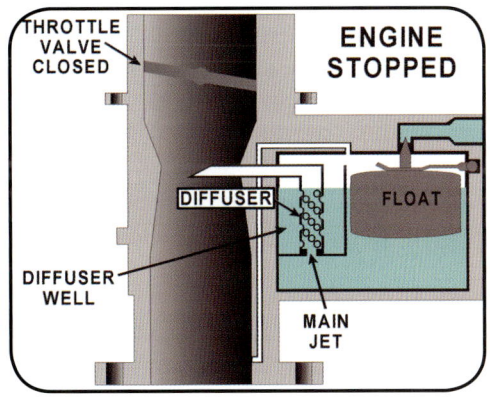

Figure 7.8 A Diffuser Well.

Some carburettors are fitted with a diffuser which prevents the mixture becoming too rich as the RPM increases.

The process of drawing both air and fuel through the discharge tube also has the effect of vaporizing the fuel more readily, particularly at low engine speeds. This effect assists the complete combustion of the fuel in the cylinders.

Slow Running Systems.

At low engine speeds, the volume of air passing into the engine is so small that the depression in the choke tube (Venturi) may be insufficient to draw fuel through the main jet. A considerable depression exists above the throttle-valve, and this is utilised to effect a second source of fuel supply for slow-running conditions.

A slow running fuel passage with its own jet, (called the slow running jet or idle jet) leads from the float chamber to an outlet at the lip of the throttle-valve, as shown over the page in *Figure 7.9*.

CHAPTER 7: CARBURATION

The strong depression between the lip of the throttle-valve and the slow-running passage gives the necessary pressure difference to create a fuel flow.

The size of the slow-running, or idle jet is such that it will provide the rich mixture required for slow-running conditions. An air bleed, opening into the choke-tube below the throttle-valve, assists atomization.

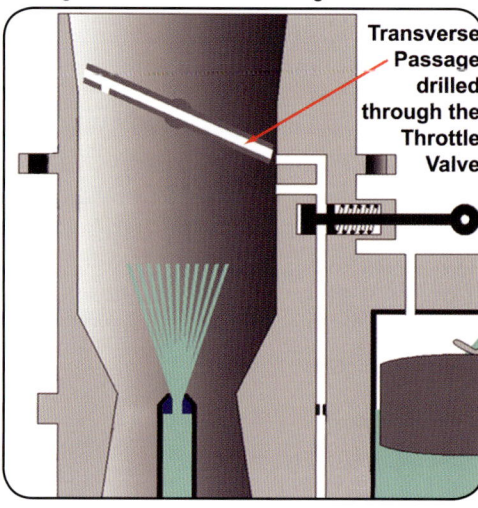

Figure 7.9 A Slow Running or Idle Jet.

The purpose of the transverse passage drilled through the throttle-valve (see Figure 7.10) is to evenly distribute the mixture over the area of the induction manifold.

A small hole is drilled into the transverse passage from the choke-tube side, and acts as an air bleed to draw some of the fuel through the throttle valve to mix with the air passing to the engine.

As the throttle is opened, the depression at the lip of the throttle-valve decreases and the depression in the choke-tube increases to the point where the main jet starts to deliver fuel and the flow through the slow-running system slows down. Carburettors must be carefully tuned in order to obtain a smooth progressive change-over between the slow-running system and the main system to prevent flat spots.

Figure 7.10 The transverse passage through the throttle valve.

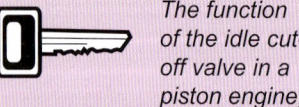 *A flat spot occurs when the throttle is opened quickly and the mixture becomes temporarily too weak to support combustion.*

Flat Spot.
A flat spot is a period of poor response to throttle opening caused by a temporary weak mixture; it normally makes itself felt as a hesitation during engine acceleration.

Idle Cut-Off Valve.
An idle cut-off valve (see Figure 7.9) is usually incorporated in the slow-running passage, and is used when stopping the engine. When the idle cut-off is operated, the valve moves over to block the passage to the slow-running delivery. The mixture being delivered to the engine becomes progressively weaker until it will not support combustion and the engine stops.

The function of the idle cut-off valve in a piston engine, when selected, is to inhibit fuel flow from the discharge nozzle.

Using the idle cut-off valve to shut down the engine, rather than simply switching off the ignition, prevents any possibility of the engine continuing to run erratically due to pre-ignition, and also prevents fuel condensing in the cylinders which would tend to wash the oil from the cylinder walls, leading to insufficient lubrication of the cylinders when the engine is next started.

The idle cut-off may be a separate control, or it may be incorporated in the mixture control lever.

CHAPTER 7: CARBURATION

MIXTURE CONTROL.

As we stated earlier, as altitude increases, the weight of air drawn into the cylinder decreases because the air density decreases. For a given intake velocity, the pressure drop in the venturi or choke tube will decrease as ambient density decreases. However, the fuel flow due to the pressure drop does not decrease by the same amount and so the mixture will become richer.

This progressive richness with increased altitude is unacceptable for economic operation of the engine.

Needle-Type Mixture Control.

With a needle-type mixture control, such as the one shown here in *Figure 7.11*, a pilot-operated lever is connected to a needle valve in the float chamber. Operation of the pilot's lever moves the needle in the jet, and varies the rate of fuel flow through the main jet.

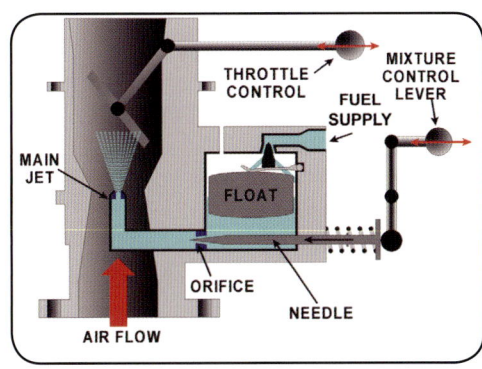

The position of the needle, therefore, controls the mixture strength. In the fully-in position the needle will block fuel flow to the main jet completely, causing the engine to shut down.

Figure 7.11 A Needle-Type Mixture Control.

Fuel Strainer.

The mixture control jets in the carburettor are the smallest orifices in the whole fuel system. To prevent any blockage of the jets by dirt or debris, a fuel strainer is normally fitted between the aircraft's fuel tanks and the carburettor *(Figure 8.8)*.

Air Bleed Mixture Control.

The air bleed type of mixture control, shown in *Figure 7.12*, operates by controlling the air pressure in the float chamber, thus varying the pressure differential acting on the fuel.

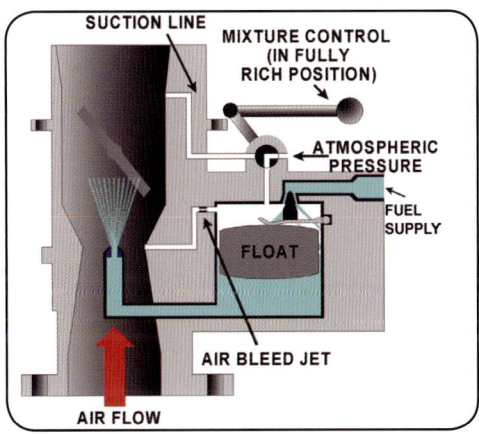

A narrow air bleed between the float chamber and the venturi tends to reduce air pressure in the float chamber. A valve connected to a pilot-operated lever controls the flow of air into the float chamber. When this valve is fully open, the atmospheric pressure acting on the fuel in the float chamber is greatest, and the mixture is fully rich. As the valve is closed the air pressure decreases, thus

Figure 7.12. An Air Bleed Mixture Control.

reducing the flow of fuel and weakening the mixture. In the carburettor shown here in *Figure 7.12*, the valve also includes a passage connecting the float chamber to the engine side of the throttle-valve. When this connection is opened by the pilot moving the cockpit control to the idle cut-off position, float chamber air pressure is reduced and fuel ceases to flow, thus stopping the engine.

CHAPTER 7: CARBURATION

ACCELERATOR PUMP.

If the throttle-valve is opened quickly, airflow responds almost immediately and a larger volume of air flows through the carburettor.

The fuel metering system, however, responds less quickly to the changing conditions because fuel is more dense than air. Consequently, a flat spot (or weak cut) will occur before fuel flow again matches airflow.

This weak cut or flat spot is prevented by fitting an accelerator pump which is linked directly to the throttle. The

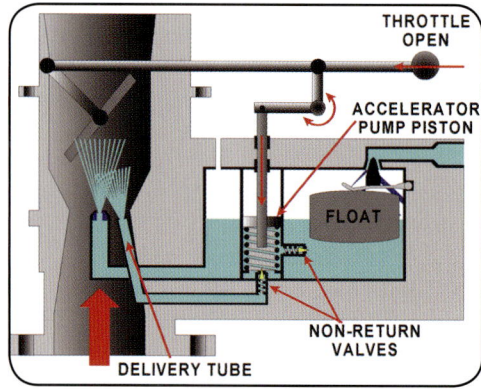

Figure 7.13. An Accelerator Pump.

accelerator pump forces fuel into the venturi whenever the throttle is opened, as shown here in *Figure 7.13*.

In some accelerator pumps a controlled bleed past the pump piston allows the throttle to be opened slowly without passing fuel to the engine. In other pumps, a delayed-action plunger is incorporated to supply an additional quantity of fuel to the engine for a few seconds after throttle movement has ceased.

THE INDUCTION SYSTEM.

The Air Intake.
The induction system takes air from a forward facing air intake, which provides a small positive boost as a result of the aircraft's forward speed. This dynamic pressure boost is sensed at the carburettor and the inlet manifold.

Figure 7.14. A Warrior Air Intake.

Air Filter.
An air filter prevents debris getting through to the carburettor and the engine.

CHAPTER 7: CARBURATION

ENGINE ICING.

The problems of engine icing, particularly in engines fitted with carburettors, are well known.

At descent power, serious carburettor icing is likely to occur while operating at an ambient temperature of +25°C and a relative humidity of 50%.

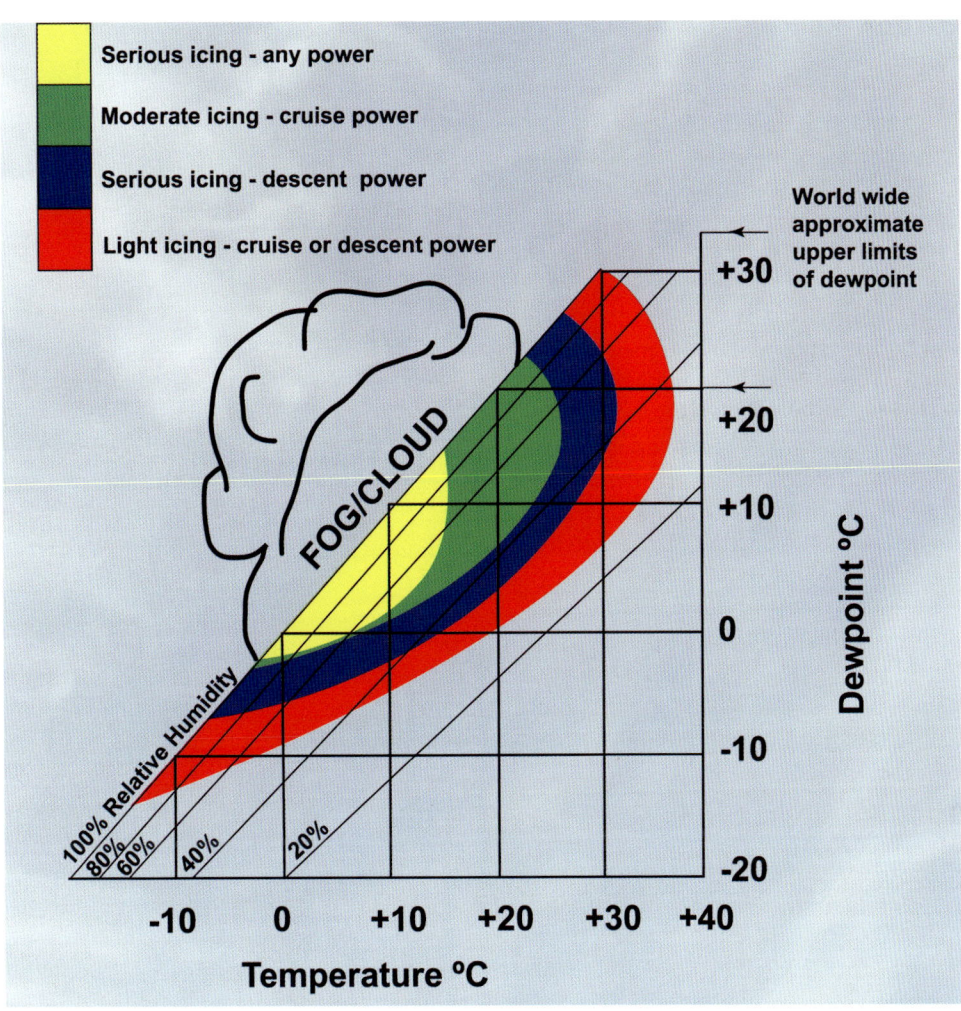

Figure 7.15 Graph indicating risk of Carburettor Icing.

Atmospheric conditions, particularly of high humidity, and temperatures ranging from -17°C (0°F) to as high as +37°C (98°F), may cause carburettor icing.

Atmospheric conditions, particularly of high humidity and temperatures ranging from -17°C (0°F) to as high as +37°C (98°F), may cause carburettor icing.

Figure 7.15 illustrates graphically these types of conditions. The temperature and humidity range indicated on the graph are likely to occur throughout the year in all areas of the United Kingdom and Europe.

Pilots should be constantly aware of the possibilities of icing and take the corrective action necessary to prevent or counter carburettor icing before icing becomes a problem and threatens the safety of the aircraft.

Basically, there are three forms of icing which affect the induction systems of piston engines fitted with carburettors. They are:- Impact Icing, Refrigeration Icing and Fuel Icing.

CHAPTER 7: CARBURATION

Impact Ice.
Impact ice forms on the air intake air filter and on bends in the induction system *(see Figure 7.16)*.

Refrigeration Ice (Carburettor Icing).
Refrigeration ice or carburettor icing, illustrated in *Figure 7.16*, forms in float type carburettors as a result of the low temperatures caused by both fuel vaporization and low pressure acting on the moisture in the atmosphere.

Fuel Icing.
Fuel icing is caused by moisture in the fuel coming out of suspension and being frozen by the low temperatures in the carburettor. This ice tends to stick to the inlet manifold around its corners, as shown in *Figure 7.16*, and this reduces the flow of the mixture into the engine.

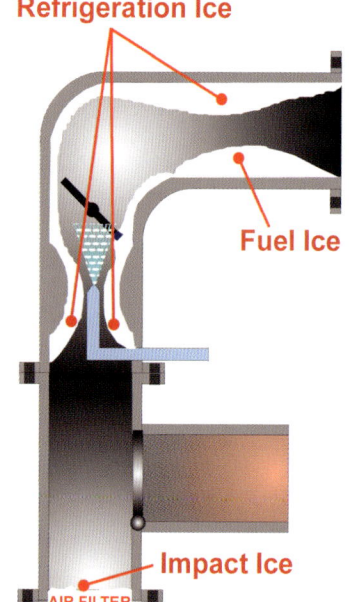

Figure 7.16 Types of Engine Icing.

Recognition and correction of induction system icing is vital. Once an engine stops due to induction icing it is most unlikely that it can be restarted in time to prevent an accident.

Recognition of Induction System Icing.
Once an engine stops due to induction or carburettor icing, it is most unlikely that a pilot will be able to restart in time to prevent the necessity of an emergency landing. Therefore, early recognition and correction of the onset of icing is vital.

The Indications of Induction System Icing.
The indications of induction system icing to the pilot of an aircraft fitted with a carburettor and a fixed pitch propeller would be a gradual drop in RPM which may be accompanied by engine rough-running and vibration.

The indications of induction system icing in an aircraft fitted with a carburettor and a fixed pitch propeller would be a gradual drop in RPM, possibly accompanied by engine rough running and vibration.

If the aircraft is fitted with a constant speed propeller, induction system icing would be indicated by a drop in manifold pressure or reduction in airspeed in level flight.

When icing is suspected, the carburettor heat control should be selected to fully hot and left in the hot position for a sufficient length of time to clear the ice. This could take up to 1 minute, or even longer, depending on the severity of the situation.

Full carburettor heat must always be used unless the aircraft is equipped with a carburettor air temperature gauge.

Figure 7.17. Carburettor Heat Control.

106

CHAPTER 7: CARBURATION

Full carburettor heat must always be used unless the aircraft is equipped with a carburettor air temperature gauge. The carburettor heat control directs heated air from around the exhaust pipe into the induction system. The hot air melts the ice which then passes through the engine as water.

Icing is more likely to occur during prolonged periods of flight at reduced power, such as during a glide descent or let-down for approach and landing. Heat is derived from the engine, so during long descents at low power or idle power the engine temperatures will gradually cool, thus reducing the effectiveness of the hot air system.

Whenever there is a risk of icing, the pilot should select full hot air before reducing power, so that benefit is gained from the hot engine before its temperature starts to lower.

To help maintain engine temperatures and provide a sufficiently great heat source during a prolonged descent to melt any ice, a pilot should increase power periodically at intervals of between 500 and 1 000 feet. This action also prevents fouling of the spark plugs.

Under no circumstances should carburettor heat be used during take-off.

Carburettor icing can occur during taxying at small throttle settings or when the engine is at idle RPM. In these circumstances ensure that hot air is used during taxying to clear any ice, but remember to select cold air before opening the throttle to full power on take-off, and check that the correct take-off RPM and manifold pressure is obtained.

Under no circumstances should carburettor heat be selected "hot" during take off.

When selecting carburettor heat "hot" there are a number of factors that a pilot should understand.

- The application of hot air reduces engine power output by approximately 15% and also creates a richer mixture which may cause rough running.

- Carburettor heat should not be selected "hot" at power settings greater than 80% as there is a danger of detonation and engine damage. Intake icing should not occur at high power settings.

- The continuous use of carburettor heat should be avoided because to do so modifies mixture strength, and increases engine temperatures.

Ground Operation.

The following two points should be understood when using the carburettor heat control.

- Use of the heat control on the ground should be kept to a minimum as the intake air is not filtered when carburettor heat is selected "hot" and consequently dust and dirt may be fed into the induction system causing additional wear on pistons and cylinders.

- A functional check of the carburettor heat control should be made before take-off. Engine rotational speed should drop by approximately 100 RPM when carburettor heat is selected "hot" and return to the original RPM level when selected cold.

A functional check of the heater control should be made before take-off.

CHAPTER 7: CARBURATION

Take-Off.
If icing is evident on the ground before take-off, use carburettor heat to clear the ice but return the control to cold before applying take-off power. Check that normal take-off power is available.

Climb.
Do not use carburettor heat during the climb or at power settings above 80%.

Operation of the System in Flight.
Be aware of conditions likely to cause carburettor icing. Carburettor icing is most likely to occur in conditions of high humidity; for example on damp, cloudy, foggy or hazy days, or when flying close to cloud or in rain or drizzle.

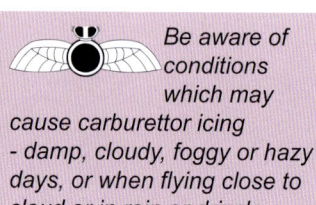
Be aware of conditions which may cause carburettor icing - damp, cloudy, foggy or hazy days, or when flying close to cloud or in rain or drizzle.

In cruising flight, monitor the engine instruments for an unaccountable loss of RPM or manifold pressure. Make frequent checks for icing by applying heat for a period of between 15 to 30 seconds, noting first the selected RPM then the drop of RPM as heat is applied.

Listen to the engine noise and check the outside air temperature. Should RPM increase when carburettor heat is applied, or the RPM return to a higher level than original when re-selected to cold, then ice is present.

Continue to use carburettor heat while icing conditions persist.

Descent.
During glide descents or long periods of flight at reduced power, select carburettor heat to "hot", remembering to warm the engine for short periods, say every 500 - 1 000 ft, in the descent.

Approach and Landing.
During approach and landing, carburettor heat should remain at cold, except for a glide approach, but if icing conditions are known to exist, or even suspected, full heat should be applied.

Remember, though, that the carburettor heat selector must be returned to cold before applying power for either a "touch and go" or a "go-around".

Ice and Fuel-Injection Engines.
Engines fitted with fuel-injection do not, of course, have the problems of ice forming at the venturi (choke tube) of a carburettor, but other parts of the system may accumulate ice, leading to a similar loss of power.

Fuel icing may gather at the bends in the system. Impact icing may form at the impact sensing tubes or on the intake air filters, particularly when flying in cloud at low temperatures. If such icing problems arise, the alternate air system fitted to fuel-injection engines should be selected and the icing drill followed in accordance with the aircraft check list.

PRINCIPLE OF OPERATION OF A FUEL-INJECTION ENGINE

A typical fuel-injection system is shown in *Figure 7.18*.

CHAPTER 7: CARBURATION

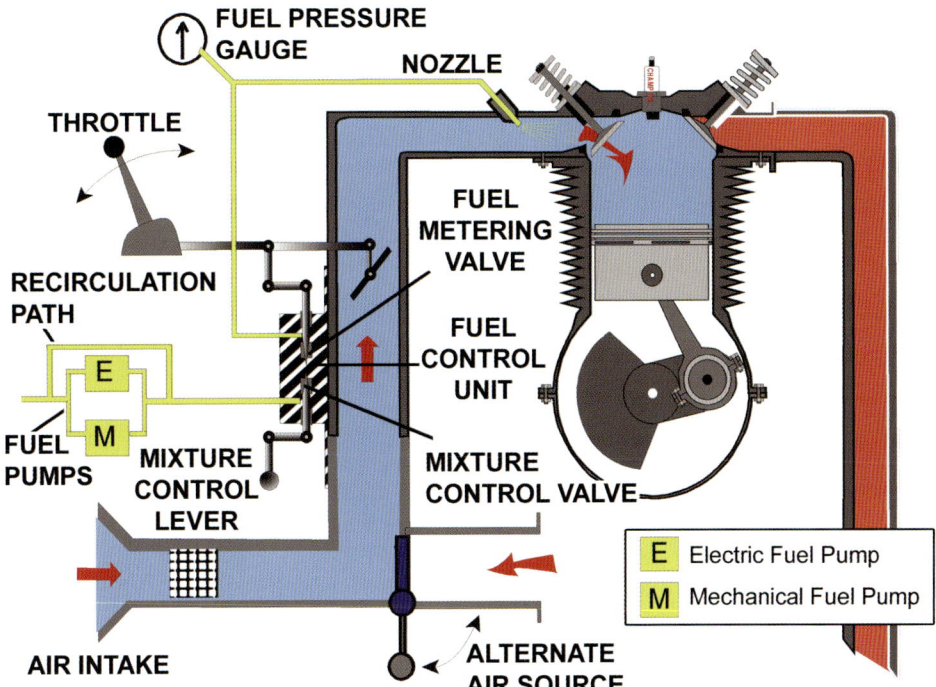

Figure 7.18 A Fuel Injection System.

In the low-pressure, continuous-flow fuel-injection system, which is illustrated here and which is used in many aircraft piston engines, fuel is sprayed continuously into the induction pipe as close to the inlet valve as possible.

The advantages claimed for fuel-injection are low operating pressure, good fuel distribution, freedom from icing problems and the incorporation of a pump which does not have to be timed to the operating cycle.

Mixture strength is varied by a manually operated mixture control valve which adjusts the fuel pressure for altitude and operating conditions as necessary. Because of the method of operation of the injector, no special idling arrangements are required and a separate priming system for engine starting is unnecessary.

The main components of the system are: fuel pumps, a fuel control unit and, of course, the discharge nozzles themselves, one for each cylinder. In addition, a fuel pressure gauge is fitted to enable any mixture adjustments to be checked accurately.

SYSTEM COMPONENTS OF A TYPICAL FUEL-INJECTION SYSTEM.

Fuel Pumps.
The fuel pumps supply more fuel than is required by the engine, and a recirculation path is provided.

Two pumps are provided, arranged in parallel, so that when the mechanical pump is not operating, fuel under positive pressure from the electrical pump can by-pass the mechanical pump, so allowing the electrical pump to be used for engine priming, starting and for emergency situations

Discharge Nozzles.

A fuel discharge nozzle is located in each cylinder head, with its outlet directed into the inlet port. Nozzles are fitted to individual engines as a set, each nozzle in a set being calibrated for that set only.

Fuel Control Unit.

The fuel control unit is mounted on the intake manifold. It contains three control elements: the throttle-valve, the fuel metering valve and the mixture control valve.
The air-throttle assembly contains the air-throttle valve, which is connected to the pilot's throttle lever and controls airflow to the engine.

Notice that the intake manifold has no venturi or other restrictions to airflow.

The fuel metering valve is connected to the air-throttle and controls fuel flow to the fuel manifold valve according to the position of the air-throttle. Thus, fuel flow is proportioned to air flow and provides the correct air/fuel ratio.

The mixture control valve is connected to the pilot's mixture control lever, and bleeds off fuel pressure applied to the fuel metering valve. Thus the air/fuel ratio can be varied as required by operating conditions.

CHAPTER 7: CARBURATION QUESTIONS

Representative PPL - type questions to test your theoretical knowledge of Carburation.

1. At what power setting is serious carburettor icing likely to occur if operating at an ambient temperature of +30°C and a relative humidity of 50%?

    a. Climb power
    b. Cruise power
    c. Take-off power
    d. Descent power

2. What is the ideal fuel/air mixture ratio in a piston engine?

    a. 1 : 15 by weight
    b. 1 : 9 by volume
    c. 1 : 12 by weight
    d. 1 : 7 by weight

3. The idle cut-off valve in a piston engined aeroplane:

    a. Inhibits fuel flow from the discharge nozzle when selected
    b. Controls engine slow running via the carburettor idle jet
    c. Changes fuel flow to the main jet from the idle jet when power is increased
    d. Allows instant response to throttle opening

4. How does the venturi throat of a carburettor change the characteristic of the air?

    a. A dynamic pressure increase and a velocity decrease
    b. A dynamic pressure decrease and a velocity increase
    c. A drop in local static pressure and velocity increase
    d. A dynamic pressure increase and a temperature increase

5. Detonation could result from:

    a. Weak mixtures and high cylinder head temperatures
    b. A designed interrupted ignition sequence during start-up when backfiring occurs
    c. Rich mixtures and low cylinder head temperatures
    d. High engine RPM when using high octane fuel

6. Pre-ignition, in a four stroke piston engine, is:

    a. An uncontrolled explosion of the fuel/air mixture
    b. A hot spot in the combustion chamber causing premature ignition of the fuel/air mixture
    c. Slow burning of a rich mixture in a hot engine
    d. The generation of fulminates in the combustion chamber which explode spontaneously under conditions of great pressure and temperature

CHAPTER 7: CARBURATION QUESTIONS

7. The "chemically correct ratio" for air to fuel is 15:1 by weight. What, however, is the approximate air-fuel ratio for the optimum mixture strength for use in a piston engine?

   a. 15 : 1 by volume
   b. 8 : 1 by volume
   c. 9 : 1 by weight
   d. 12 : 1 by weight

8. Detonation:

   a. Is harmful to the pistons
   b. Is also known as 'piston slap'
   c. Is part of normal engine running
   d. Cannot be identified externally

9. It is best to run the engine with the mixture:

   a. Slightly rich, as the surplus fuel helps cool the engine
   b. Chemically correct, as this is most efficient
   c. Slightly rich, as the surplus air helps cool the engine
   d. Slightly weak, as the surplus air helps cool the engine

10. As the aircraft climbs, density _____ and the weight of air entering the engine _____ . Therefore, the mixture will become _____ :

    a. decreases   increases   richer
    b. increases   decreases   weaker
    c. decreases   decreases   richer
    d. decreases   decreases   weaker

11. As air enters the restriction of a Venturi, its velocity _____ , static or ambient pressure _____ and temperature _____ .

    a. increases   increases   increases
    b. increases   decreases   decreases
    c. decreases   increases   decreases
    d. decreases   decreases   increases

12. Some carburettors are fitted with a diffuser which:

    a. Prevents the mixture becoming too lean as the rpm increases
    b. Prevents the mixture becoming too lean as the rpm decreases
    c. Prevents the mixture becoming too rich as the rpm increases
    d. Prevents the mixture becoming too rich as the rpm decreases

CHAPTER 7: CARBURATION QUESTIONS

13. An accelerator pump is used to prevent a flat spot. A flat spot arises:

    a. When the throttle is opened quickly and the mixture becomes temporarily too rich
    b. When the throttle is closed quickly and the engine is starved of fuel
    c. When the throttle is closed and the mixture becomes temporarily too rich
    d. When the throttle is opened quickly and the mixture becomes temporarily too weak to support combustion

Question	1	2	3	4	5	6	7	8	9	10	11	12	13
Answer													

The correct answers to these questions can be found at the end of this book.

CHAPTER 8
AERO ENGINE FUELS AND FUEL SYSTEMS

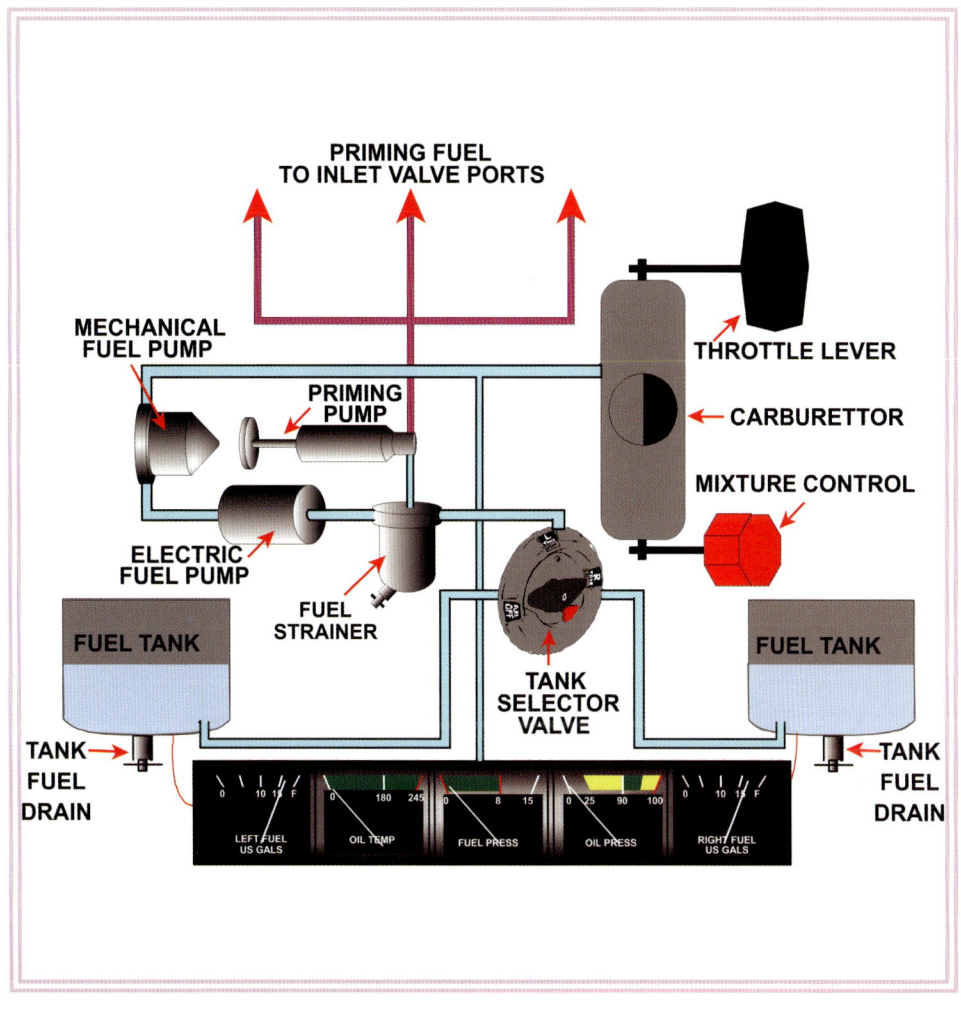

CHAPTER 8: AERO ENGINE FUELS AND FUEL SYSTEMS

CHAPTER 8: AERO ENGINE FUELS AND FUEL SYSTEMS

AERO ENGINE FUELS AND FUEL SYSTEMS.

This chapter on Aircraft Engine Fuels and Fuel Systems confines itself to systems and fuels of gasoline (petrol) engines, though brief mention is made of Jet A1 fuel. For technical reasons, the term 'gasoline' has been preferred to 'petrol', but the reader should note that these two terms are synonymous. Gasoline or petrol, which was originally a by-product of the petroleum industry (kerosene being the main product) became the most common piston engine fuel because of its ability to mix readily with air in a carburettor.

Figure 8.1 A Fuel Tanker.

The fuel used in diesel aero engines, Jet A1 (AVTUR) is given greater mention in Chapter 3a: Aero Diesel Engines.

Classification of Fuels by Specification Number.
Fuel specifications are the means by which producers and users of aviation fuel identify and control the properties necessary for satisfactory performance.

All aviation fuels have a specification number. For instance, Jet A1, the fuel normally used in jet engines, has a specification number DERD 2494. Other jet fuels have different specification numbers.

Gasoline, the fuel used in petrol-driven piston engines, has a specification number (Directorate of Engine Research and Development) DERD 2485. Contained within that blanket specification number are grades of aviation gasoline such as AVGAS 100, AVGAS 100 LL and AVGAS 80.

Quality Control.
Many tests are carried out on the fuel when it is manufactured. One of those tests is used to determine the fuel's octane rating. To do this, the particular blend of fuel that is the subject of the test is compared with two reference fuels under standardised conditions in a special test engine *(see Figure 8.2.)*.

Figure 8.2 A Co-operative Fuel Research Engine. Picture Courtesy Waukesha -Dresser Inc.

The two reference fuels are Iso-octane and Normal Heptane.

117

CHAPTER 8: AERO ENGINE FUELS AND FUEL SYSTEMS

Iso-octane.
Iso-octane has very good combustion characteristics and shows little tendency to detonate when mixed with air and ignited at high temperatures. It is given an octane rating of 100.

Normal Heptane.
Normal heptane on the other hand detonates very readily and has an octane rating of zero.

Comparing the Fuel on Test with Two Reference Fuels.
The particular fuel which is to be tested is compared with a blend of the two reference fuels. This is done by first running the test fuel in the special test engine and then trying to produce the same degree of detonation in the engine while using a blend of the two reference fuels.

If the blend of the two reference fuels which gives the same detonation characteristics is say 95% iso-octane and 5% normal heptane, the fuel under test would be given an octane rating of 95. The octane rating is considered to be a measure of how well the fuel resists detonation. So, in other words, the fuel's octane rating is known as its anti-knock value.

Originally, tests were based on an air/fuel ratio which gave maximum detonation, but a situation which gives maximum detonation is not truly representative of the working range of the engine. Maximum detonation occurs with economical mixtures which are normally used for cruising, but for take-off and climb rich mixtures are used.

Performance Number.
It is important to know how the fuel will behave under these varying mixture strengths, and so aviation fuel has two ratings. The 'two rating' figure is sometimes referred to as the performance number or performance index.

As an example, AVGAS 100 is a 100 octane fuel with a performance number of 100 / 130. The lower figure is the weak mixture detonation point and the higher figure the rich mixture detonation point. It follows that if an engine is designed to use a certain grade of fuel, then a lower grade should never be used, as this would cause detonation. If at any time the correct octane rating is not available, a higher octane rating must be used.

ADDITIVES.

Tetraethyl lead.
In the past, in order to increase the octane rating of a fuel, Tetraethyl Lead, or TEL, used to be added. For instance, 2 millilitres of lead were added to each gallon of fuel to take its octane rating to 100 / 130. The action of TEL is to reduce the formation of peroxides which can cause the end gas to explode, but it has to be used with care as, during combustion, lead oxide is formed. Lead oxide is not volatile at these temperatures, and it has a corrosive effect on the exhaust valve, its seat, and the sparking plug electrodes.

Ethylene Dibromide.
To prevent this corrosion, it is necessary to add ethylene dibromide to the fuel to change the reaction during combustion and to allow lead bromide to form.

CHAPTER 8: AERO ENGINE FUELS AND FUEL SYSTEMS

Lead bromide is volatile and, thus, is easily ejected with the exhaust gases.

The Medical Hazards of Lead

Lead in the atmosphere is absorbed into the bloodstream, and can harm the brain. Because of the threat to the health of anyone who breathes in exhaust fumes, fuel companies now use additives other than lead in the fuel to raise its octane rating. Thus we have fuels such as AVGAS 100 LL, the LL standing for low lead.

IDENTIFICATION OF FUELS BY COLOUR.

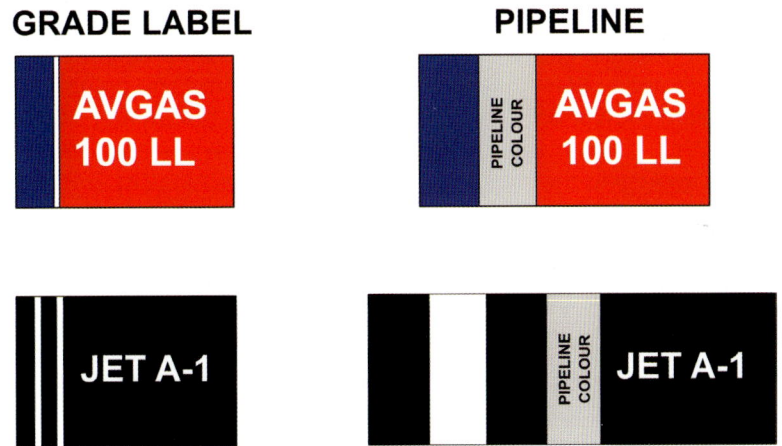

The primary colour for all labels relating to 100LL is red and the colour of the fuel itself should be blue.

Figure 8.3 Identifying labels.

To make it easy to identify the fuels, they are coloured differently. For instance, AVGAS 100 LL is coloured blue, while AVGAS 100 is coloured green. AVTUR, which is aviation turbine fuel, is either clear or is of a straw colour.

To assist in differentiating between the fuels when refuelling an aircraft, all refuelling equipment is marked in such a way as to make it easy to identify which fuel may be dispensed from a particular device. The colours of the labels on the equipment and the pipelines are shown here in *Figure 8.3*.

MOGAS.

Some aviation authorities allow the use of automobile gasoline, or MOGAS, in some aircraft. Within the United Kingdom, the rules governing the use of MOGAS are laid down in Airworthiness Notices, Numbers 98 and 98a. Further information on the use of MOGAS can be found in the CAA Safety Sense Leaflet Number 4a. Great caution should be taken when using MOGAS.

MOGAS has a much higher volatility than AVGAS and, consequently, will evaporate much more quickly. This means that the possibility of vapour locks and carburettor icing occurring is much greater than if AVGAS was being used.

Information regarding aircraft that may legally be fuelled with MOGAS may be found in CAA Airworthiness Notices.

Figure 8.4 Safety Sense Leaflet Number 4a.

CHAPTER 8: AERO ENGINE FUELS AND FUEL SYSTEMS

FUEL CONTAMINATION.

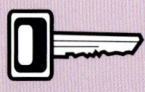
The presence of water in the fuel will cause fuel system contamination resulting in the loss of engine power.

The most common contaminant in fuel is water, the presence of which may cause loss of engine power. Water is always present in the fuel in varying amounts despite the manufacturers stringent quality control and preventative measures taken during storage and transfer. However, further measures can be taken to minimize water accretion once the fuel has been transferred to the aircraft tanks. Once the fuel is in the aircraft fuel tanks, the main source of water contamination is atmospheric air which remains within the partially filled tank.

Fuel In the aircraft tanks is most likely to be contaminated by water from atmospheric air in the tanks.

If the tanks are topped-up to full, air, of course, is excluded, together with the moisture it contains, thus minimising the likelihood that the fuel will be contaminated. If the fuel is allowed to settle after replenishment, the water droplets, being heavier than the fuel, will fall to the bottom of the tank and can then be drained off through the water drain valve. If water is allowed to stay in the fuel system, however, it will eventually find its way to the engine where it could cause loss of engine power, or even a dead cut.

Inspection for Contamination.

The wing tank quick-drains should be used to obtain a sample of the fuel in a suitable container. The sample should be examined for water, and then discarded.

Each fuel tank is equipped with a drain valve. This is located at the lowest part of the tank, sometimes within a sump which will collect any water as it settles. These wing tank drains should be used first, to drain the sumps. Sufficient fuel should be allowed to flow to ensure removal of contaminants including water. This fuel should be collected in a suitable container, examined for contaminant, and then discarded. After having drained any amount of fuel, always ensure that no fire hazard exists before starting the engine. If a large quantity of water is found in the tanks, the aircraft should be declared unserviceable.

Figure 8.5 Fuel Check.

After using each drain, always ensure that it has been closed completely and is not leaking.

Fuel Tank Vents.

Ensure the fuel tank vents are not damaged or blocked up, otherwise it will be difficult getting fuel to the engine from that tank.

While checking the fuel tank drains, the pilot should also check the fuel tank vents *(see Figure 8.6)*. Each tank is fitted with a forward facing vent pipe which allows atmospheric pressure to be maintained inside. They are usually fitted in the lower surface of the wing.

Make sure that the fuel vents are not damaged or that they are not blocked up in any way; otherwise a depression will form in the tank which will adversely affect fuel flow to the engine.

Figure 8.6 Fuel Tank Vent.

120

CHAPTER 8: AERO ENGINE FUELS AND FUEL SYSTEMS

Fuel Strainer.

The fuel strainer *(see Figure 8.7)* is also equipped with a quick-drain facility. The fuel strainer itself is located at the lowest point of the fuel system, usually somewhere in the engine compartment. The fuel strainer should be drained once for each of the tanks which can be selected on the aircraft's fuel selector valve. Once again, sufficient fuel should be allowed to flow to ensure complete removal of any water.

Figure 8.7 Fuel Strainer.

THE FUEL SYSTEM.

A simple light aircraft fuel system is shown in *Figure 8.8*. The fuel is contained in two wing tanks, each of which has a quick-drain fitted at its lowest point.

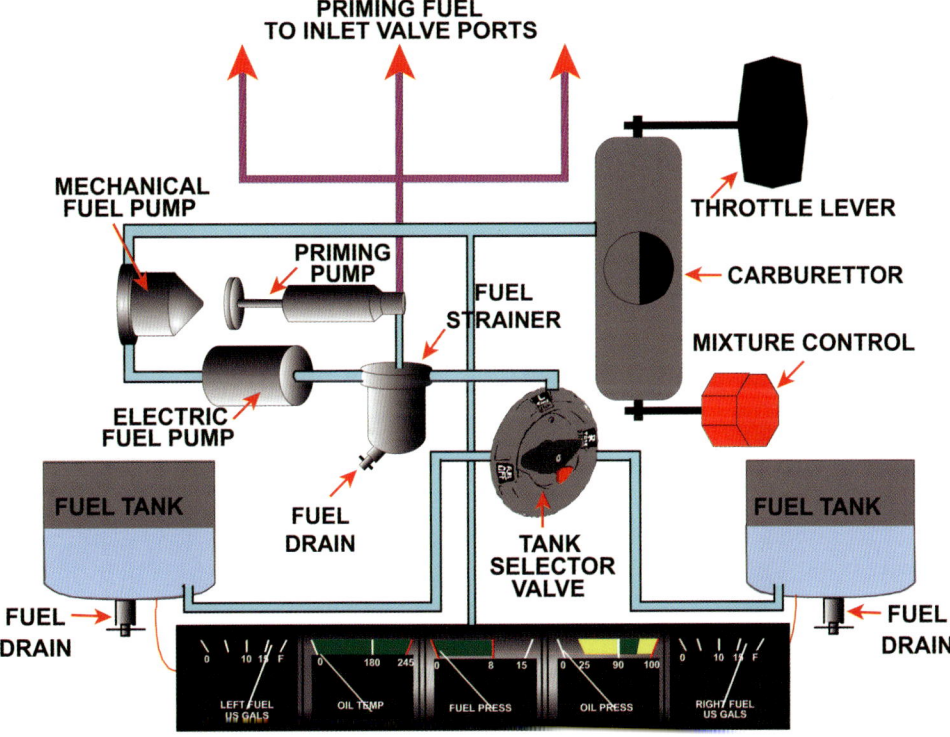

Figure 8.8 A Simple Fuel System.

Fuel quantity is measured by simple float-type sensors in the tanks and is indicated to the pilot in the cockpit on fuel guages. Float-type sensors are fairly unreliable, except when the aircraft is on the ground or in prolonged straight and level flight. So, before flight, a pilot must always visually check the fuel contents, by removing the tank filler caps and looking into the tanks to make his own assessment of the quantity.

Float-type sensors are fairly unreliable, except on the ground or in prolonged straight and level flight. So before flight always visually check the contents of the fuel tanks.

The fuel passes to the engine system via a tank selector valve. This allows the pilot to control fuel flow from each tank in turn and, thus, keep the aircraft balanced laterally.

CHAPTER 8: AERO ENGINE FUELS AND FUEL SYSTEMS

In most light aircraft the electrical fuel pump should be switched on for take-off, flight below 1,000 feet, landing and when changing over the fuel tank selector.

Next in line is the fuel strainer, at the lowest point in the system. Remember, during the pre-flight check the fuel strainer should be drained twice via its drain, with each tank selected in turn.

Mechanical and Electrical Pumps.

After the fuel strainer comes the electrical fuel pump. It is sometimes called the booster pump, or the auxiliary pump. It is fitted to the system in case of failure of the mechanical fuel pump. Some fuel systems have their fuel pumps in parallel.

The normal location of an electrically driven auxiliary fuel pump on a piston engine is upstream of the engine-driven pump.

Figure 8.9 Mechanical Fuel Pump.

The Pilot's Operating Handbook for most light aircraft advises that the electrical fuel pump should be switched on for take-off, flight below 1 000 feet, and for landing. It is also advisable to select this pump to 'on' when using the tank selector valve to change tanks.

A fuel pressure gauge may be included in the system *(see Figure 8.8.)* This can be used to check the output of the electrical pump when the engine is not running.

Downstream of the electrical pump is the engine-driven mechanical pump *(see Figure 8.9)*. The fuel pressure gauge will sense the output pressure of the mechanical pump whenever the electrical pump is switched off.

High wing aircraft, with tanks in the wings only, may not require a fuel pump, relying on gravity as the prime mover of the fuel to the engine system.

Carburettor and Priming Pump.

The final item in the system is the carburettor. This meters the fuel to the engine in response to the pilot's operation of the authority of the throttle and the mixture control.

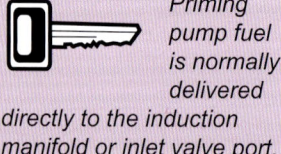
Priming pump fuel is normally delivered directly to the induction manifold or inlet valve port.

The priming pump is a hand operated device which is used to pump fuel to the inlet valve ports of the cylinders prior to engine start. The priming pump takes its fuel from the top of the fuel strainer *(see Figure 8.8)*.

122

CHAPTER 8: AERO ENGINE FUELS AND FUEL SYSTEMS

Great care must be taken to ensure that the priming pump plunger is locked in after use. If it inadvertently becomes unlocked, it may vibrate open. This will create a risk of fuel being sucked from the top of the fuel strainer into the inlet manifold of the engine, thereby making the mixture extremely rich and perhaps stopping the engine.

If the priming pump is left unlocked after use, it may allow fuel to be sucked from the fuel strainer into the inlet manifold, causing an extremely rich mixture.

FUEL SYSTEM MANAGEMENT.

It is essential that a pilot understands the fuel system of the aircraft he is about to fly. A pilot should therefore study the Pilot's Operating Handbook (POH) and follow the recommended fuel management procedures.

The basic principles of fuel system management are as follows:

- Ensure that the aircraft has sufficient fuel for the flight being undertaken, including all necessary reserves.

- If the aircraft requires refuelling, ensure that the correct grade of fuel is used. Check that fuel caps are replaced and are tightly closed. Fuel caps situated on the top of wing surfaces are in the low pressure area of the airflow. If a cap in this location becomes loose, fuel can be syphoned out of the tanks in flight.

- Before the first flight of the day, carry out fuel contamination checks.

- Ensure that there are no leaks in the fuel system during the pre-flight check.

- Switch on the electric fuel pump before switching tanks in flight. Switch tanks according to the procedure detailed in the POH.

Refuelling.

- No one must remain in the aircraft during refuelling.

- The engine must be shut down.

- Ignition switches must be off.

- Appropriate extinguishers and fire-fighting equipment must be at hand.

- No one must smoke in the vicinity of an aircraft being refuelled.

- All earth wires fitted to the refuelling equipment must be employed in accordance with operation procedures to eliminate the risk of static electricity generating a spark which might ignite fuel vapour.

CHAPTER 8: AERO ENGINE FUELS AND FUEL SYSTEMS QUESTIONS

Representative PPL - type questions to test your theoretical knowledge of Engine Fuels & Fuel Systems.

1. During preflight checks, water in the fuel system is monitored. This is because water will cause:

    a. Icing
    b. The fuel to freeze
    c. Fuel system contamination resulting in the loss of engine power
    d. Emulsification of the fuel in the fuel lines which could cause them to become blocked

2. The type of aeroplane which may legally be fuelled with MOGAS may be found in:

    a. CAA Airworthiness Notices and Safety Sense leaflets
    b. AICs
    c. Notams.
    d. Flight Information Handbook

3. The fuel and the tank labels of refuelling installations are colour coded. The colour for all labels relating to 100LL is....(i)...., and the colour of the fuel itself is....(ii)....:

	(i)	(ii)
a.	black	red
b.	red	blue
c.	blue	straw
d.	red	straw

4. The electrically driven auxiliary fuel pump on a piston engine is located:

    a. At the lowest point of the fuel tank
    b. Upstream of the tank selector valve
    c. In the tank-to-tank fuel transfer line
    d. Upstream of the engine driven pump

5. A fuel priming pump normally delivers fuel directly to:

    a. The induction manifold or inlet valve port
    b. The carburettor float chamber
    c. The combustion chamber
    d. The accelerator pump outlet

6. In the aircraft tanks, fuel is most likely to be contaminated by water from:

    a. Poorly fitting fuel caps
    b. Contamination during refuelling
    c. Leaks in the tanks that have let in rain
    d. Atmospheric air remaining in partially-filled tanks

CHAPTER 8: AERO ENGINE FUELS AND FUEL SYSTEMS QUESTIONS

7. It is important to ensure that the priming pump is locked after use because:

    a. It may cause a fuel leak, resulting in an increased fire risk
    b. It may cause fuel to be sucked from the fuel tank into the carburettor, causing an extremely rich mixture
    c. It may allow fuel to be sucked from the fuel strainer into the inlet manifold, causing an extremely rich mixture
    d. If it vibrates closed, it will cause the engine to stop

Question	1	2	3	4	5	6	7
Answer							

The answers to these questions can be found at the end of this book.

CHAPTER 9
PROPELLERS

CHAPTER 9: PROPELLERS

CHAPTER 9: PROPELLERS

PURPOSE OF A PROPELLER.

Most general aviation aircraft are powered by propellers. The purpose of a propeller (*Figure 9.1*) is to convert the power delivered by an engine into propulsive thrust.

The detailed theory of how thrust is produced is complex, but expressed simply, there are two principles which explain the nature of thrust:

- The propeller accelerates a mass of air rearwards and, in accordance with Newton's 3rd law, experiences a force acting on itself in the opposite direction. This force is called thrust.

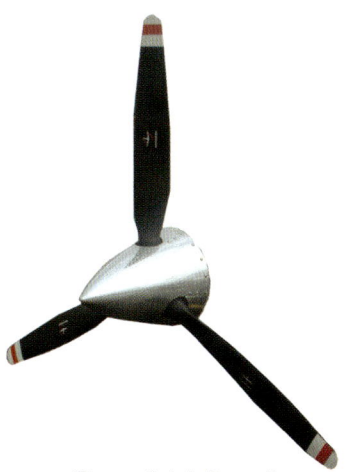

- The propeller blades are aerofoils which act like rotating wings causing a difference in static pressure across the blades.

Figure 9.1 A Propeller.

Just as a wing generates a lifting force acting upwards, the propeller generates a forward horizontal force called thrust. Airflow over a propeller is more complex than over a wing because the propeller is not only rotating, but moving forwards. Some aerodynamicists believe that both of the above principles of propeller thrust are connected, and are explained by Newton's Second Law, in the sense that rotating propeller blades impart a rate of change of momentum to the air flowing over the blades, thus applying a force to the air, changing its velocity and pressure distribution.

The 'Principles of Flight' volume of this series discusses propeller aerodynamics in detail. In this chapter we will deal primarily with the technical and mechanical aspects of propellers and their operation.

BLADE GEOMETRY.

The propeller consists of two or more aerodynamically shaped blades attached to a central hub. This hub is mounted onto a propeller shaft driven by the engine.

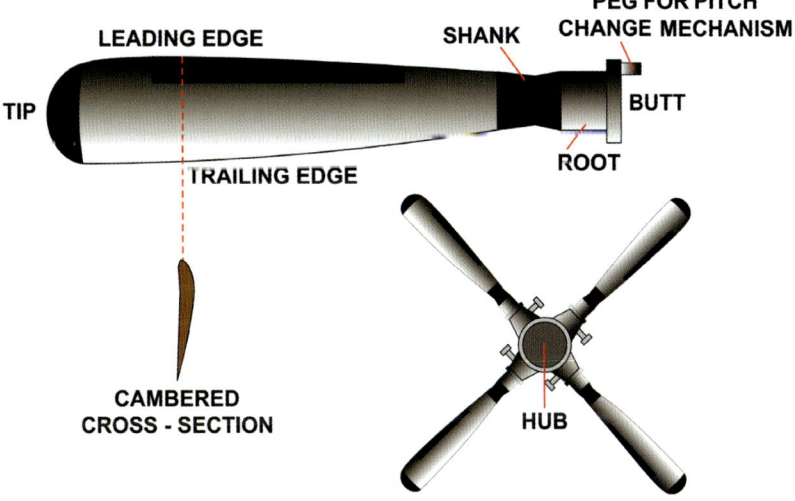

Figure 9.2 Propeller Nomenclature.

CHAPTER 9: PROPELLERS

The whole assembly is rotated by the propeller shaft, rather like rotating wings.

Like a wing, a propeller blade has a root and a tip, a leading and trailing edge and a cambered cross-section whose chord line passes from the centre of the leading edge radius to the trailing edge. At the root area, where the section of the blade becomes round, is the blade shank. The base of the blade, where any pitch change mechanism would have to be attached, is called the blade 'butt'.

Chord Line.
The chord line of the propeller blade is a straight line joining the centres of curvature of the leading and trailing edges of the blade.

Chord.
The chord of the propeller blade is the distance between its leading edge and its trailing edge, measured along the chord line.

Blade Angle Or Pitch.
The blade angle or pitch is the angle between the blade chord line and the plane of rotation.

Blade angle decreases from the root to the tip of the blade *(see Figure 9.5)* because the rotational velocity of the blade increases from root to tip. This twist along the length of the blade ensures an optimum angle of attack throughout the blade length. For reference purposes, the blade angle is measured at a point 75% of the blade length from the root.

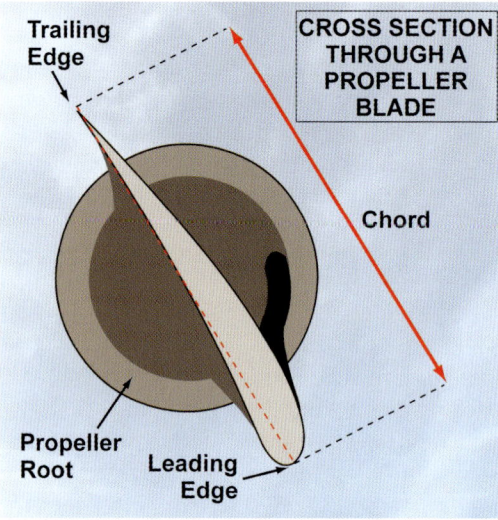

Figure 9.3 Propeller Definitions.

Blade Twist.
Blade sections near the tip of the propeller are at a greater distance from the propeller shaft and travel through a greater distance for each rotation. Therefore, for any given engine speed (measured in revolutions per minute or RPM), the rotational speed of the tip of the propeller is greater than that of blade elements near the hub.

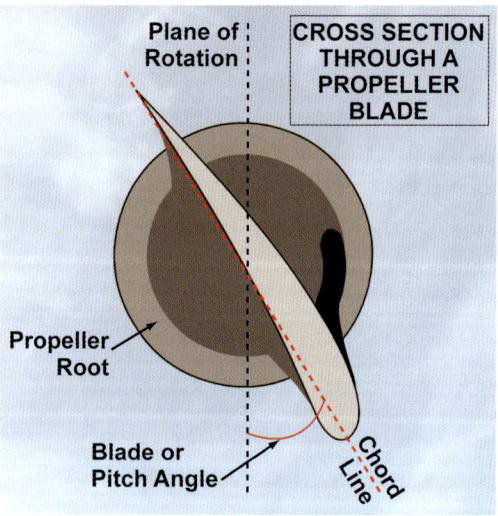

Figure 9.4 Blade Angle.

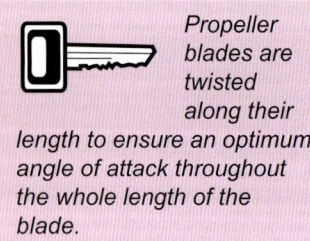
Propeller blades are twisted along their length to ensure an optimum angle of attack throughout the whole length of the blade.

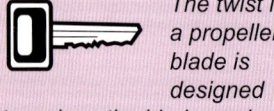
The twist in a propeller blade is designed to reduce the blade angle towards the tip.

The blade angle must be decreased towards the tip across the whole length of the blade to ensure an optimum angle of attack. This aspect of a propeller's operation is discussed fully in the Principles of Flight volume in this series.

The blade angle determines the geometric pitch of the propeller. A small blade angle is called fine pitch while a large blade angle is called coarse pitch.

CHAPTER 9: PROPELLERS

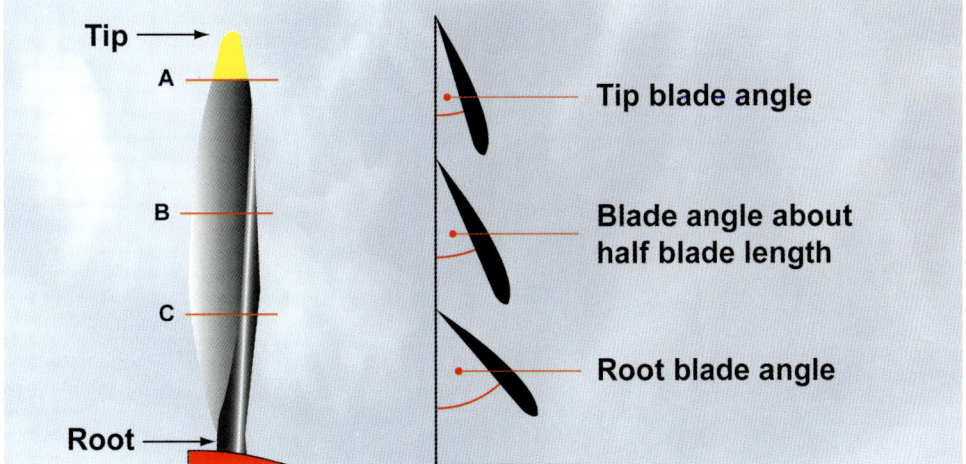

Figure 9.5 Blade Angle decreases from root to tip.

Geometric Pitch.

The geometric pitch, (*Figure 9.6*), is the distance the propeller would travel forward in one complete revolution if it were moving through the air at the blade angle, just as a wood screw advances through wood as it is twisted by the screwdriver.

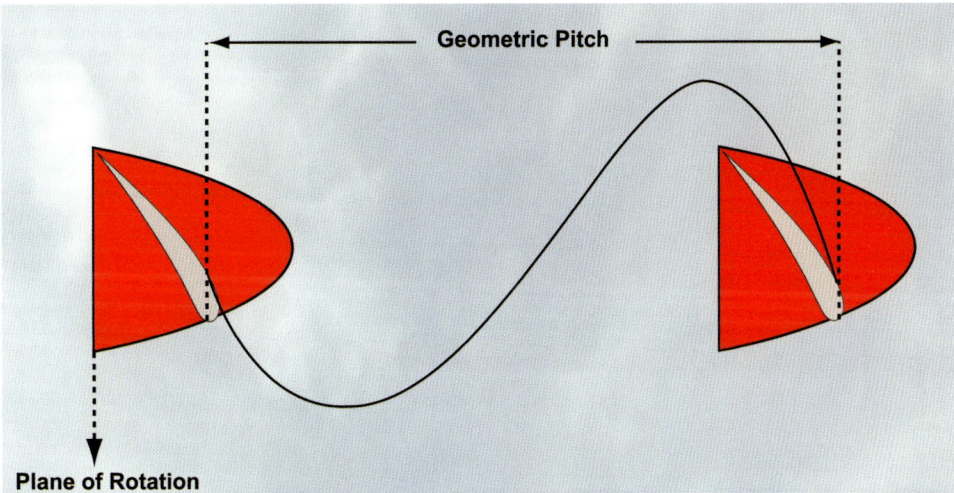

Figure 9.6 Geometric Pitch.

Effective Pitch.

In flight, the propeller does not move through the air at the geometric pitch, because as air is a fluid, and not a solid medium, slippage always occurs

The distance which it actually moves forward in each revolution is called the 'effective pitch' or 'advance per revolution' (*Figure 9.7, overleaf.*)

Propeller Slip.

The difference between the geometric pitch and the effective pitch is called propeller slip, this is shown in *Figure 9.7, overleaf*.

The Helix Angle.

The helix angle is the angle that the actual path of the propeller makes to the plane of rotation as shown in *Figure 9.8, overleaf*.

CHAPTER 9: PROPELLERS

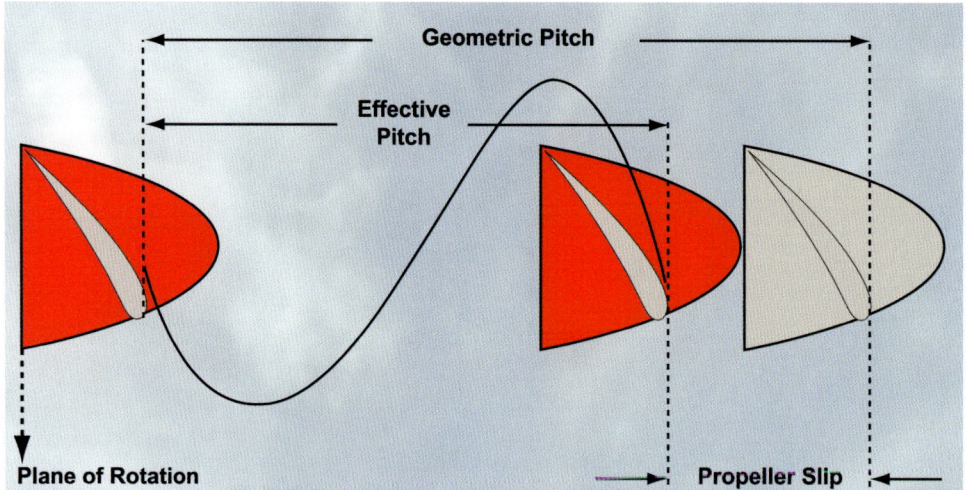

Figure 9.7 Effective Pitch and Propeller Slip.

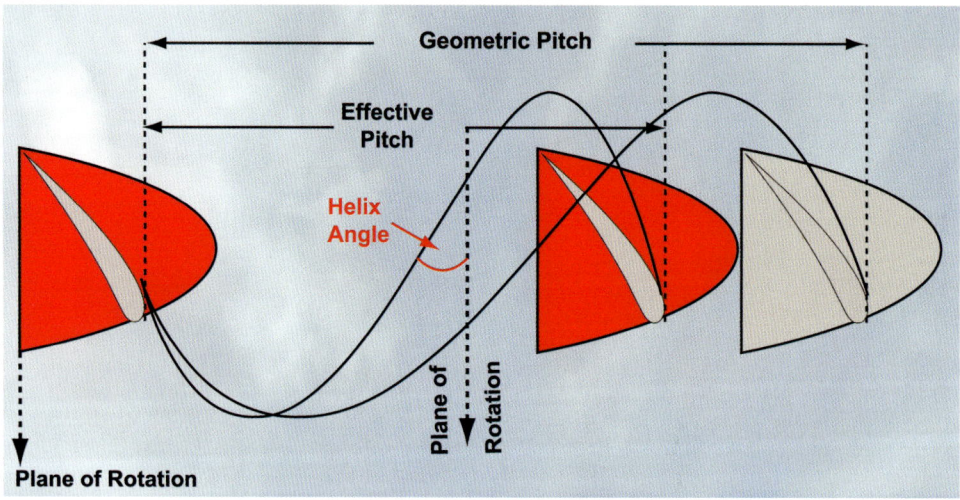

Figure 9.8 The Helix Angle.

Blade Aspect Ratio
Blade aspect ratio is the ratio of blade length to the blade's mean chord.

Angle of Attack.
The angle between the blade chord and the relative airflow during propeller rotation is the angle of attack, shown in the diagram as alpha (α) *(Figure 9.9)*.

The angle of attack of a fixed-pitch propeller depends on the propeller's RPM and aircraft's forward speed.

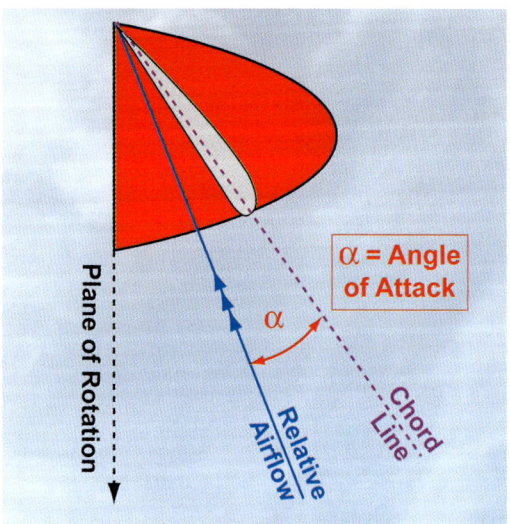

Figure 9.9 Angle of Attack.

CHAPTER 9: PROPELLERS

POWER ABSORPTION AND EFFICIENCY.

Propeller Diameter.

A propeller must be able to absorb all the shaft horse power developed by the engine and it also must operate with maximum efficiency throughout the required performance envelope of the aircraft.

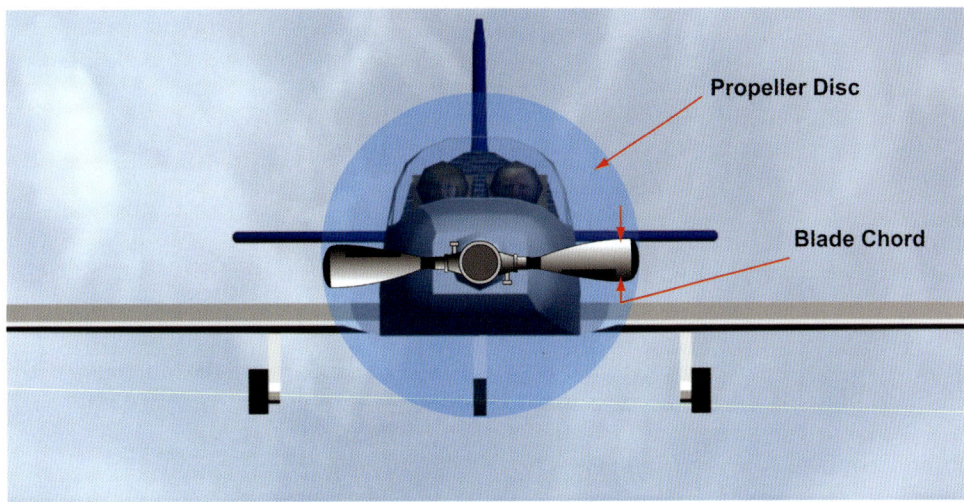

Figure 9.10a Use of a thick blade chord will increase propeller solidity.

At any given engine speed, measured in Revolutions Per Minute (RPM), the larger the diameter, the greater would be the tip velocity. For instance, at 2 600 RPM, an 8ft diameter propeller would have a tip velocity of 653 miles per hour, approaching the speed of sound at sea level.

A large diameter propeller would be a good "absorber" of engine power. But a critical factor in terms of propeller efficiency is tip velocity. If tip velocity is too high, the blade tips will approach the local speed of sound and compressibility effects will decrease thrust and increase rotational drag.

Supersonic tip speed will considerably reduce the efficiency of a propeller and greatly increase the noise it generates. This factor imposes a limit on propeller diameter and RPM, and the speed at which it can be achieved by propeller-driven aircraft. Another limitation on propeller diameter is the need to maintain adequate ground clearance.

Solidity.

To increase power absorption, several characteristics of the propeller, other than diameter, can be considered. The usual method is to increase the 'solidity' of the propeller. Propeller solidity is the ratio of the total frontal area of the blades to the area of the propeller disc.

One way of achieving an increase in solidity is to increase the chord of each blade. This increases the solidity, but blade aspect ratio is reduced, making the propeller less efficient.

Secondly, the number of blades can be increased. Power absorption is thus increased without increasing the tip speed or reducing the aspect ratio. This is the method normally used to increase propeller solidity. However, increasing the number of blades beyond a certain number (five or six) will reduce overall efficiency.

CHAPTER 9: PROPELLERS

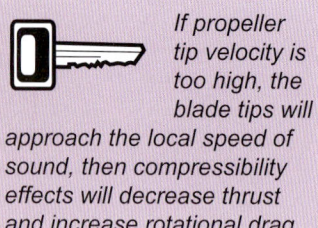

If propeller tip velocity is too high, the blade tips will approach the local speed of sound, then compressibility effects will decrease thrust and increase rotational drag.

Figure 9.10b An increase in the number of blades will increase propeller solidity.

However, as we have learnt, thrust is generated by accelerating air rearwards. So, making the disk too solid will reduce the mass of air that can be drawn through the propeller and accelerated. To increase the number of blades efficiently, contra-rotating propellers could be used; that is, two propellers rotating in opposite directions on the same shaft. However, contra-rotating propellers are practicable only on very powerful propeller driven aircraft.

MOMENTS AND FORCES GENERATED BY A PROPELLER.

Because of its rotation, a propeller generates yawing, rolling and pitching moments. These are due to several different causes such as torque reaction, gyroscopic precession, spiral slipstream effect and asymmetric blade effect.

Torque Reaction.

Propeller torque reaction will be greatest during high power, low indicated airspeed flight conditions. Low IAS will reduce the power of the controls to counter the turning moment due to torque.

If the propeller rotates clockwise, the equal and opposite reaction or torque will give the aircraft an anticlockwise rolling moment about the longitudinal axis. During take-off this will apply a greater download to the left main wheel, causing more rolling resistance on the left wheel making the aircraft want to yaw to the left. This is illustrated in *Figure 9.11*, where the left wheel is shown as having more pressure applied to it than the right wheel. In flight, torque reaction will also make the aircraft want to roll to the left with a clockwise rotating propeller. This effect is particularly noticeable when full power is applied to initiate a climb. Obviously, for a propeller rotating anti-clockwise, all the effects described in this section will be in the opposite direction.

The torque reaction generated by the clockwise turning propeller of a single engined aircraft on take-off will tend to cause it to roll, left wing down.

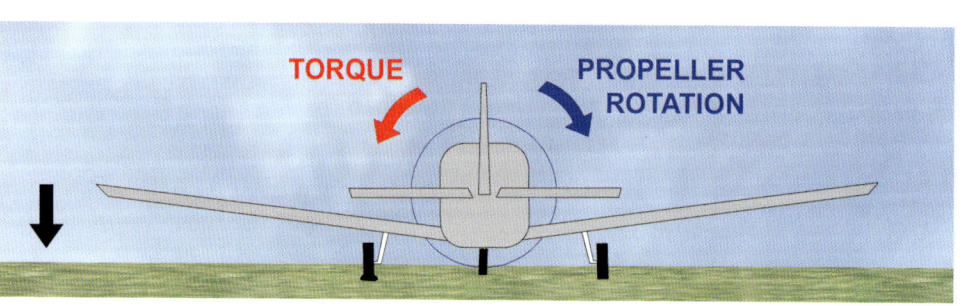

Figure 9.11 Torque Effect.

Torque reaction will be greatest during high power, low Indicated Airspeed (IAS) flight conditions.

Low IAS will reduce the effectiveness of the controls to counter the turning moment due to torque. Torque reaction could be eliminated by fitting contra-rotating propellers. Torque from the two propellers, rotating in opposite directions on the same shaft, will cancel each other out. The cost of such a solution could, however, be high, and it would, in any case, be suitable only for very high powered engines.

Gyroscopic Effect.

A rotating propeller has the properties of a gyroscope: rigidity in space and precession. The property which produces what is known as the gyroscopic effect is precession.

Gyroscopic precession is the name given to the effect that occurs when a force is applied to the rim of a rotating disc. This phenomenon is demonstrated in *Figure 9.12*. When a force is applied to the edge of the spinning propeller disc, the action of the force is felt at a point at 90° in the direction of rotation, and in the same direction as the applied force.

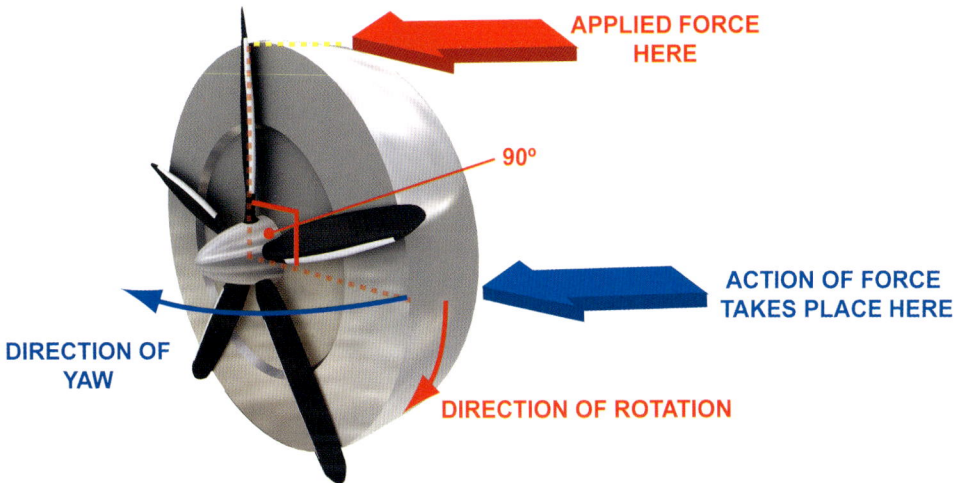

Figure 9.12 The Gyroscopic Action of a Propeller.

As the aircraft is pitched up or down or yawed left or right, a force is applied to the edge of the spinning propeller disc.

For example, if an aircraft with an anticlockwise rotating propeller (as viewed from the cockpit) is pitched nose down, as shown in *Figure 9.12*, the aircraft acts as if a forward force has been applied to the top of the propeller disc. But the effective line of action of this force acts at 90° in the direction of rotation, causing the aircraft to yaw to the right.

Gyroscopic effect can be easily determined when the point of application of the force on the propeller disc is considered. The following situations apply for a propeller rotating anti-clockwise, as seen by the pilot.

PITCH UP   Forward force on the bottom, reaction occurs at 90° anti-clockwise, result left yaw.

LEFT YAW   Forward force on the right, reaction occurs at 90° anti-clockwise, result pitch down.

RIGHT YAW   Forward force on the left, reaction occurs at 90° anti-clockwise, result pitch up.

The effect of gyroscopic precession is felt only when the aircraft pitches and/or yaws.

Slipstream Effect.

As the propeller rotates it produces a backward flow of air, or slipstream, which rotates around the aircraft, as illustrated in *Figure 9.13*. This spiral slipstream causes a change in airflow around the fin.

In the case shown here, due to the clockwise direction of propeller rotation, the spiral slipstream meets the fin at an angle from the left, producing a sideways force on the fin to the right, thus inducing yaw to the left.

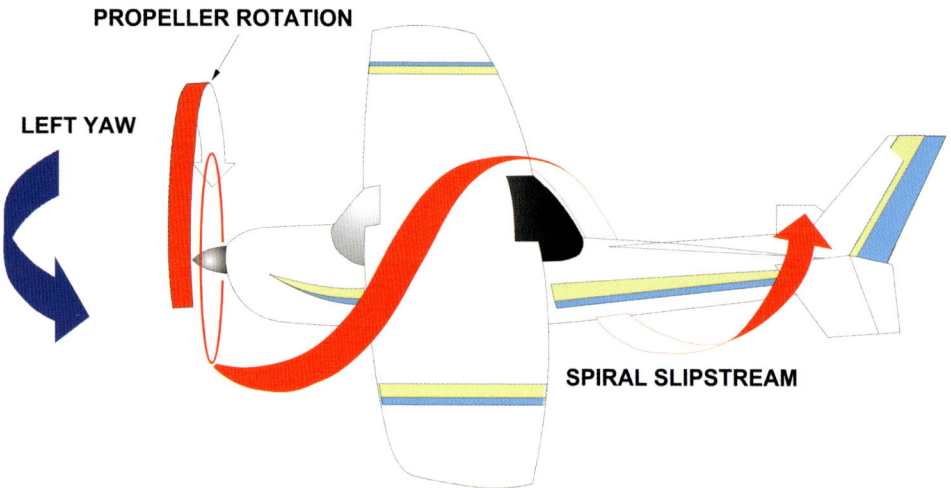

Figure 9.13 Slipstream Effect.

The amount of rotation given to the air will depend on the power setting. Spiral slipstream effect can be reduced by any or all of the following:- a small fixed tab on the rudder, the engine thrust line being inclined slightly to the right, or offsetting the fin slightly.

Asymmetric Blade Effect.

During take-off or landing in a tail-wheel aircraft, the propeller shaft will be inclined upwards with respect to the horizontal. Consequently, as the aircraft moves forward, the down-going blade of the rotating propeller covers a larger path than the up-going blade, for each rotation. This fact means that the linear velocity of the down-going blade is higher than that of the up-going blade, and its angle of attack is also greater.

Therefore the downgoing blade will generate more thrust than the up-going blade. The difference in thrust on the two sides of the propeller disc will generate a yawing moment to the left for a clockwise rotating propeller.

Asymmetric blade effect will be greatest at full power and low airspeed with high angle of attack.

N.B. Torque Reaction, Gyroscopic Effect and Assymetric Blade Effect will all cause the aircraft to swing in the same direction: to the right for a propeller rotating anti-clockwise, as seen by the pilot, and to the left for a clockwise rotating propeller. Gyroscopic Effect and Assymetric Blade Effect are most marked on tailwheel aircraft on take-off. During take-off, all effects will either be exacerbated or countered by a cross wind.

CHAPTER 9: PROPELLERS

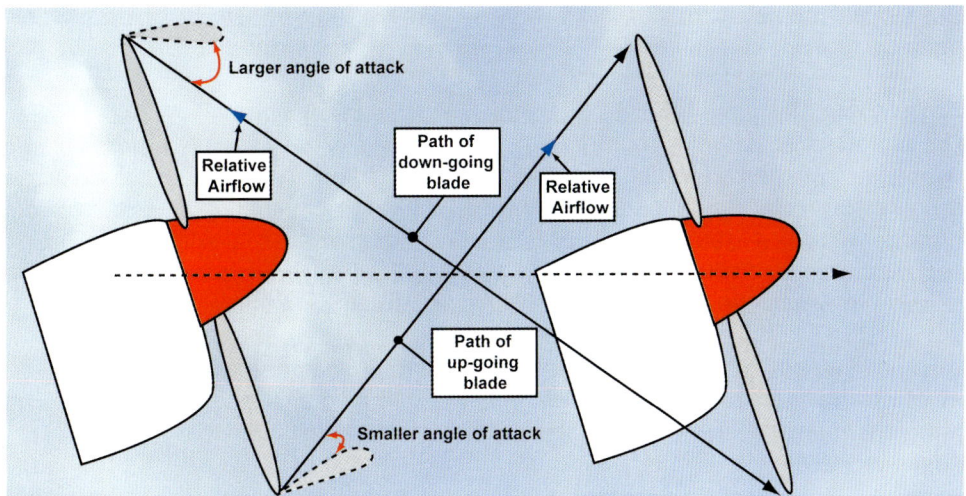

Figure 9.14 Asymetric Blade Effect.

FIXED PITCH PROPELLERS.

Disadvantages.

A fixed pitch propeller receives its relative airflow from a direction governed by the aircraft's true airspeed and the speed of the propeller rotation in RPM.

It can be seen from *Figure 9.15* that an increase in True Air Speed (TAS), i.e an increase in the length of the TAS vector arrow, will reduce the angle of attack, causing the engine RPM to increase. On the other hand, an increase in RPM, i.e. an increase in the RPM vector arrow, will increase the angle of attack.

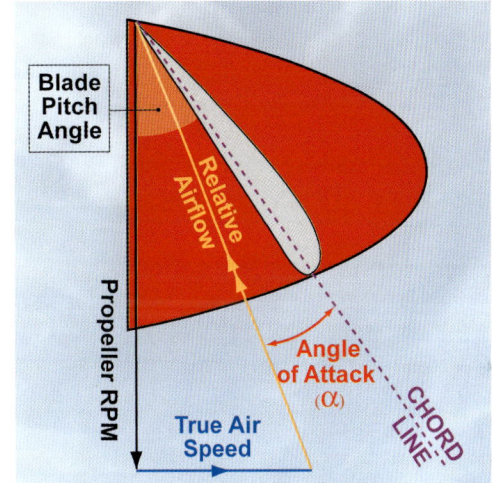

Figure 9.15 Angle of Attack.

Both decreased TAS and increased RPM will increase the angle of attack of a fixed pitch propeller blade.

Propeller Efficiency.

At high forward speed, for instance in a power off dive, it is possible to reduce the angle of attack of a fixed pitch propeller to zero and overspeed the engine, while at low TAS with a high RPM, for instance in a climb, propeller angle of attack is large and it is possible to stall the propeller blade.

Both extremes are obviously inefficient, and therefore, undesirable. The conclusion that must be drawn is that a fixed pitch propeller will only function efficiently at one combination of true air speed (TAS) and RPM (that is, at an efficient angle of attack.) This limitation is the major disadvantage of the fixed pitch propeller. The maximum efficiency of a fixed pitch propeller is in the region of 70%.

$$\text{Propeller Efficiency \%} = \frac{\text{Propulsive Power}}{\text{Engine Power}} = \frac{\text{Thrust} \times \text{Velocity of Incoming Airflow}}{\text{Engine Power}}$$

The Propeller Efficiency Equation confirms what you have just learned about efficiency. With a fixed pitch propeller, the largest increase in velocity imparted to the air flow by the rotating propeller occurs when the aircraft is stationary under full power.

CHAPTER 9: PROPELLERS

But though thrust is high at the start of the take-off run, propeller efficiency is low because of the low velocity of the airflow entering the propeller disc.

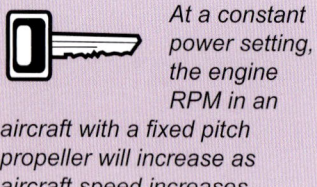

At a constant power setting, the engine RPM in an aircraft with a fixed pitch propeller will increase as aircraft speed increases.

As flight speed increases, the velocity of the air flowing into the propeller disc increases. But the increase in velocity imparted by the propeller decreases with increasing airspeed. Thus, as shown by the equation, at very high speed the efficiency of the propeller is again low. Only at the desired cruising combination of airspeed and propeller RPM is a fixed pitch propeller efficient. If the aircraft's airspeed is increased to a maximum by diving, the propeller acts like a windmill, driving the engine instead of being driven by the engine. Engine damage can occur in these conditions.

Because there is only one given combination of forward speed and rotational speed at which the fixed pitch propeller will operate at its optimal angle of attack - and therefore optimal efficiency - advanced aircraft are fitted with variable pitch, constant speed propellers.

VARIABLE PITCH PROPELLERS.

On an aircraft fitted with a fixed-pitch propeller, the pilot has only one method of increasing or decreasing thrust and propulsive power; that is by varying engine RPM. With variable pitch propellers both engine RPM and propeller blade angle (pitch) can be varied in order to control thrust.

There are several different types of variable pitch propellers; here are some which the private pilot may come across.

Adjustable-Pitch Propellers.
Adjustable-pitch propellers, like the one shown in *Figure 9.16*, are propellers which can have their pitch adjusted on the ground by mechanically resetting the blades in the hub. In flight, they act as fixed-pitch propellers.

Two-Pitch Propellers.
Two-pitch propellers, similar to the one fitted to the Grob 109b in *Figure 9.17*, are propellers which have fine and coarse-pitch settings that can be selected in flight.

Fine pitch can be selected for take-off, climb and landing and coarse-pitch for cruise. Two-pitch propellers will usually also have a feathered position.

Figure 9.16 Adjustable-Pitch Propeller.   *Figure 9.17 A Two-Pitch Propeller.*

CHAPTER 9: PROPELLERS

CONSTANT-SPEED PROPELLERS.

Modern aircraft have propellers which are controlled automatically to vary their pitch (blade angle) so as to maintain a selected RPM. The control mechanism is called the Constant Speed Unit (CSU). The operation of the CSU is beyond the scope of PPL studies. A constant-speed, variable pitch propeller permits high efficiency to be obtained over a wider range of airspeeds, giving improved take-off and climb performance and cruising fuel consumption.

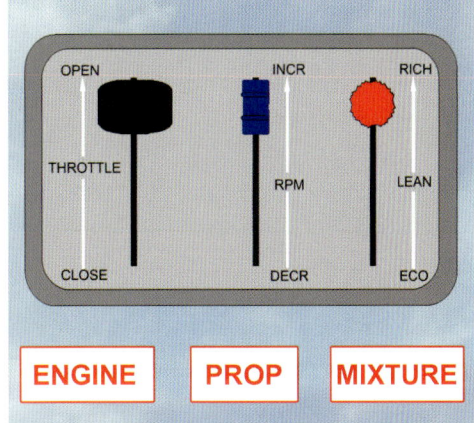

Figure 9.18 Constant-Speed Propeller.   *Figure 9.19 Engine and Propeller Controls.*

Constant-Speed Propeller Controls.
Figure 9.19 illustrates a typical set of engine and propeller controls for a small piston engine aircraft with a constant speed propeller. Throttle, propeller and mixture controls are shown in the take-off (all forward) position.

At any given throttle setting, coarsening propeller pitch and pulling back on the RPM control will decrease RPM.

Pushing forward on the RPM control will fine off propeller pitch and increase RPM.

A reasonable analogy is to think of the propeller control as an infinitely variable gear change; forward movement (increase RPM) is first gear, backwards movement (decrease RPM) is fifth gear

Fine-Pitch.
Figure 9.20 shows conditions during the early stages of take-off roll. At low air speeds, at the start of the take-off run, the blade angle needs to be small (fine pitch) for the angle of attack to be optimum. Therefore, the RPM is set to maximum and the true air speed is low.

As the aircraft accelerates, air speed will increase, causing a decrease in the angle of attack of the blades. Less thrust and less propeller torque will be generated.

Thus there is less resistance for the engine to overcome and RPM will tend to increase. The constant speed unit (CSU) senses the RPM increase and will increase blade pitch angle to maintain a constant blade angle-of-attack throughout the aircraft's acceleration.

CHAPTER 9: PROPELLERS

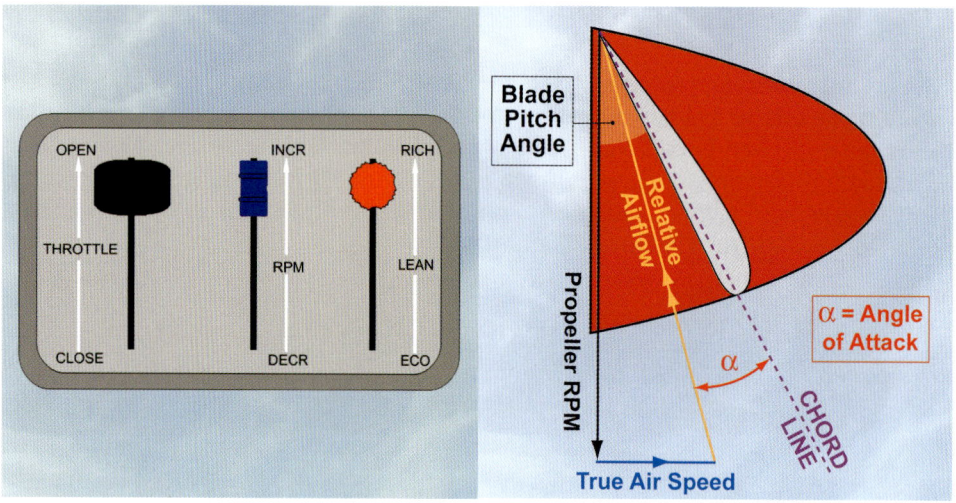

Figure 9.20a Prop controls - Take-Off.   Figure 9.20b Prop Take Off Conditions.

Coarse-Pitch (High Speed Flight).

Figures 9.21a and 9.21b show the conditions at high forward speed in level flight. As the airspeed increased, the CSU would have continually increased the blade angle (coarsened the pitch) to maintain a constant blade angle of attack, and, thus, constant Propeller RPM.

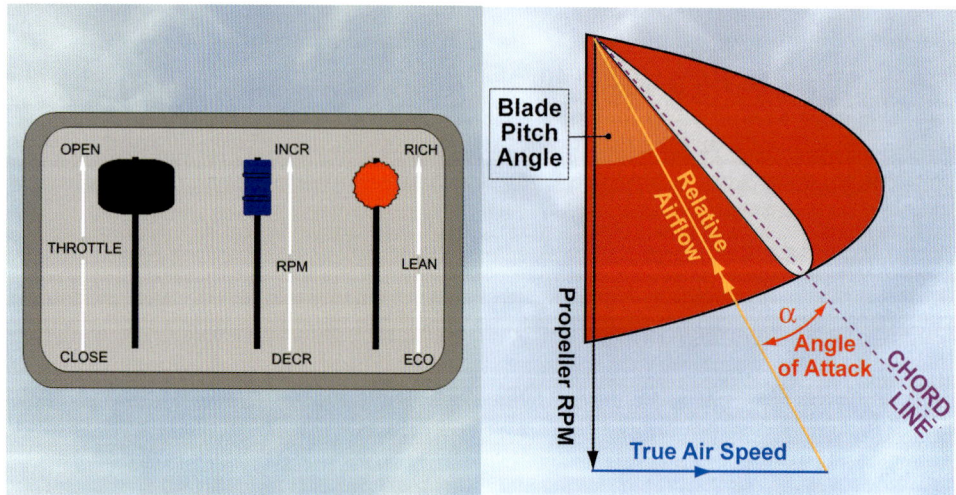

Figure 9.21a Conditions of high forward speed in level flight.   Figure 9.21b Conditions of high forward speed in level flight.

Cruising Flight.

Figure 9.22a shows the constant speed propeller controls set for cruising flight, and the associated blade pitch angle and True Air Speed vector. The throttle and RPM settings are no longer at maximum. Optimum settings for RPM and manifold pressure (throttle settings) during cruising flight will be found in the aircraft's Pilot Operating Handbook. The recommended procedure for transiting from the climb to cruising flight is to reduce throttle first, then RPM.

Once cruising configuration has been established, the Constant Speed Unit (CSU) will adjust the blade pitch angle to maintain the selected RPM whatever the subsequent flight conditions, unless the pilot selects a different RPM.

CHAPTER 9: PROPELLERS

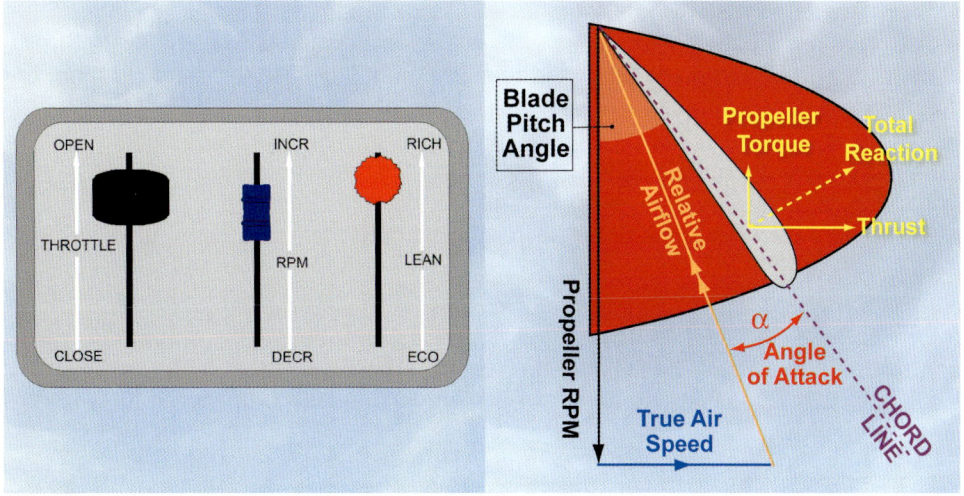

Figure 9.22a Conditions of cruising speed in level flight.

Figure 9.22b Conditions of cruising speed in level flight.

If, for instance, the pilot lowered the nose slightly to commence a shallow dive, the load on the propeller would decrease, and RPM would tend to increase. The CSU, however, will sense this tendency and increase the pitch angle of the propeller blade to slow the RPM down to the value selected by the pilot.

If the pilot entered a shallow climb the reverse would happen. The load on the propeller would increase and the propeller RPM would begin to decrease. However the CSU would sense this and fine-off the propeller blade in order to maintain the original RPM.

Windmilling.

If there is no engine torque (for instance, the throttle is closed or the engine fails), the propeller will fine-off in an attempt to maintain the set RPM.

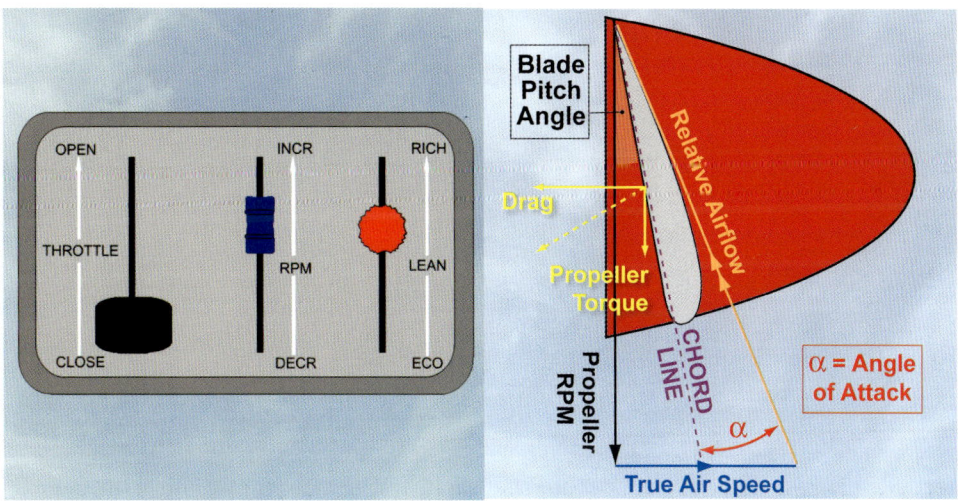

Figure 9.23a Throttle closed in a descent.

Figure 9.23b Throttle closed in a descent.

As shown in *Figure 9.23b*, the relative airflow will impinge on the front surface of the blade and generate drag, and consequently negative propeller torque. The propeller will now drive the engine. This is called windmilling.

141

CHAPTER 9: PROPELLERS

The drag generated by a windmilling propeller is very high. To prevent this undesirable condition arising, constant-speed propeller blades are able to be feathered; that is, the blades can be turned edge-on to the direction of flight. In this configuration, the propeller will cease rotating.

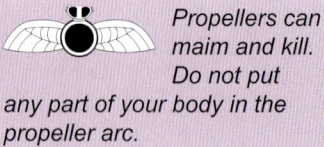
Propellers can maim and kill. Do not put any part of your body in the propeller arc.

A single engine aeroplane fitted with a constant speed propeller may not have a feathering capability, as such. However, following engine failure, drag can be reduced to a minimum by moving the propeller pitch control to the fully coarse position.

Flight Safety.

A rotating propeller blade is lethal. Always give the propeller arc a wide berth when approaching an aircraft, or carrying out checks or pilot maintenance tasks. Always treat the propeller as live. An electrical fault may cause the propeller to turn, when least expected.

Figure 9.24 A multi-bladed propeller.

CHAPTER 9: PROPELLERS QUESTIONS

Representative PPL - type questions to test your theoretical knowledge of Propellers.

1. The purpose of a twist along the length of a propeller blade is to:

   a. Prevent aerodynamic interference with the engine cowling
   b. Reduce drag at the propeller tips, thereby reducing torque
   c. Ensure an optimum angle of attack over the whole length of the blade
   d. Increase drag at the propeller tips, thereby reducing torque

2. The twist in a propeller blade is designed to do what to the blade angle?:

   a. Maintain the same blade angle from hub to tip
   b. Increase the blade angle towards the tip
   c. Reduce the blade angle towards the hub
   d. Reduce the blade angle towards the tip

3. With a constant throttle setting and a fixed pitch propeller, during acceleration the engine RPM will:

   a. Increase
   b. Remain unchanged
   c. Decrease
   d. Initially increase, but then decrease

4. As viewed from the cockpit, a clockwise turning propeller, the torque reaction will cause:

   a. The tail to rise
   b. A roll to the left
   c. A roll to the right
   d. The tail to drop

5. Of the following, which will increase the angle of attack of a fixed-pitch propeller blade?

   a. Increased TAS and increased RPM
   b. Increased TAS and decreased RPM
   c. Decreased TAS and increased RPM
   d. Decreased TAS and decreased RPM

6. For an aircraft with a fixed pitch propeller, propeller efficiency will be:

   a. Low at low True Air Speed (TAS) and high at high TAS
   b. High at low TAS and low at high TAS
   c. Constant at all airspeeds
   d. Low at both very low TAS and very high TAS and optimal at cruising TAS

CHAPTER 9: PROPELLERS QUESTIONS

7. The purpose of a constant-speed propeller is:

    a. To improve performance during take-off
    b. To improve performance in cruising flight
    c. To adopt the most efficient blade pitch angle for all phases of flight
    d. To prevent windmilling

Question	1	2	3	4	5	6	7
Answer							

The answers to these questions can be found at the end of this book.

CHAPTER 10
ENGINE HANDLING

CHAPTER 10: ENGINE HANDLING

CHAPTER 10: ENGINE HANDLING

PRECAUTIONS BEFORE STARTING.

In the interests of the safety of the aircraft, that of people on the ground, and of the pilot, a number of precautions have to be taken before and after flight. The following paragraphs expand on a few of these precautions.

Engine Preparation.

The engine oil contents should be checked to ensure that there is sufficient oil for the planned flight. Some aircraft have the oil dipstick integral with the oil filler cap, as is shown in *Figure 10.1,* so make sure that the filler cap is secure after either checking the contents, or replenishing the oil.

Figure 10.1 Checking the Oil Contents.

Look for signs of oil, fuel or hydraulic fluid leaks; remember that leaks will always get worse when the engine is running, especially oil leaks.

Check that plug leads are firmly attached to the plugs and that the priming lines are secure. Once the check inside the cowlings is finished, ensure that the cowlings are closed and the catches are secure.

The propeller should be checked for damage. Make sure that there are no nicks or cuts on the blades. Check that the spinner is secure and undamaged. Treat the propeller with a great deal of respect at all times. The results of the engine firing just once could be fatal if you are in the way of the propeller blade, so stay out of its arc and do not touch it or move it unnecessarily.

Positioning the Aircraft.

The aircraft should be sited on firm level ground, free from loose stones or litter which might damage servicing equipment or injure ground crew if thrown up by the slipstream *(Figure 10.2)*.

When starting the engine, the aircraft should be sited on firm level ground free from loose stones, litter, servicing equipment and persons.

Where practicable, the aircraft should be facing nose into wind, and so positioned that the slipstream is directed away from other aircraft, persons and buildings. There must also be room to taxy away

Figure 10.2 Before Engine Start.

CHAPTER 10: ENGINE HANDLING

 *When starting the engine, the parking brake should be applied or the main wheels should be securely chocked.*

Preparing for Engine Start.
The parking brake should be applied, as in *Figure 10.3*, or alternatively, the main wheels should be securely chocked, as is shown in *Figure 10.4,* before starting the engine.

Figure 10.3 Parking Brake.

Figure 10.4 A Chock.

All covers (e.g. pitot tube covers) and blanking plugs must be removed before starting the engine, and all access panels and hatches must be securely closed.

Ground Crew.
If you need any assistance to start the aircraft, make sure that those individuals involved are thoroughly conversant with the procedures used.

Also ensure that they are not wearing loose clothing that may get tangled in the propeller or blown about the airfield in the slipstream.

If you need assistance to start the aircraft, make sure that the individuals involved are thoroughly briefed in the procedures to be used.

Figure 10.5 Ground Crew.

Engine Starting.
Bear in mind that the advice given in these chapters is general. The advice does not apply to any particular aircraft type. Initially, prime the engine, using the priming pump, *(Figure 10.6)*, with the recommended amount of fuel for the prevailing engine temperature.

Overpriming an engine may flood the engine and wet the plugs and it will also put excess fuel into the induction system which may start a carburettor fire.

Being too generous with the priming may cause trouble for you later. Firstly, it may flood the engine and wet the plugs and, secondly, it could also put fuel into the induction system which may start a carburettor fire if the engine backfires. This is potentially a very dangerous situation.

 *If you have a carburettor fire on start-up, keep the engine turning over on the starter motor. Select the mixture control to Idle Cut Off and open the throttle.*

If you are unfortunate enough to have a carburettor fire, keep the engine turning over on the starter motor; put the mixture control to the idle cut-off position and open the throttle. Turning the engine over will tend to suck the flames into the cylinders, where they will not do any harm.

Figure 10.6 The Priming Pump.

148

CHAPTER 10: ENGINE HANDLING

Selecting idle cut-off will starve the fire of fuel, and opening the throttle will make it easier for the engine to suck the flames into the cylinders. If the fire does not go out, follow the actions detailed in the checklist for your aircraft

Assuming that you have primed the engine correctly, set the mixture control to the rich position and set the throttle just open.

Check that the area around the propeller is clear of persons and obstacles. Making sure that all in the vicinity can hear you, shout "Clear prop!"

Turn the magneto/starter switch through to the start position. Most aircraft starter motors have a limitation on how long they can remain energised. Make sure you know the limitation on your particular engine, and do not exceed it.

If the starter warning light remains illuminated after engine start, you should shut down the engine immediately.

As soon as the engine is running, release the starter switch and immediately check that the "starter-engaged" warning light is out. If the warning light is still illuminated, stop the engine immediately.

Figure 10.7 Starter Engaged Warning Light.

Now check the engine oil pressure gauge. If the oil pressure does not register within 30 seconds, stop the engine immediately.

The engine should now be allowed to warm up. Wait until minimum temperatures and pressures are obtained before opening the throttle further. This warming up is done at the recommended RPM as stated in the operator's handbook.

If the oil pressure gauge does not register within 30 seconds after starting a cold aircraft engine, shut down the engine.

This is a convenient time to check that the aircraft systems are functioning satisfactorily. Check that the fuel pressure is within limits and that the alternator is on line. Make sure that the suction system is providing the correct amount of vacuum and that the hydraulic system is providing the correct pressures.

Magneto Dead-Cut Check.
With the throttle still set at the prescribed slow running RPM (this would be 1 200 RPM in the Piper PA28 Warrior), the dead-cut check can be carried out. This check endeavours to ascertain whether the two magnetos are both working under your control.

If, during the dead-cut check, the engine does stop, do not be tempted to re-select the magneto switch back to the 'BOTH' position. This could possibly cause mechanical damage to the engine.

Each magneto must be selected "off" in turn. Check in each case that there is a drop in RPM but that the engine does not stop. If the engine does stop, do not be tempted to re-select the magneto switch back to the BOTH position; this could possibly cause mechanical damage to the engine.

Engine Systems Check.
Now check that the engine pressures and temperatures are within the green arcs, or, at the very least, the yellow sectors of the gauges. Change the fuel tank selector to the other tank and set the throttle to the correct RPM for the magneto check: usually around 2 000 RPM.

149

CHAPTER 10: ENGINE HANDLING

Check the correct operation of the carburettor heat selector now. You should note a drop in engine speed as carburettor heat is selected ON because the engine is receiving hot, less dense air, as the mixture has been made weaker. The RPM drop should be regained after carburettor heat has been reselected "cold" and once more cold air is being fed into the carburettor. Ensure that the suction system is providing the correct amount of vacuum.

Magneto Check.

The magneto check is carried out to make sure that both magnetos are functioning correctly.

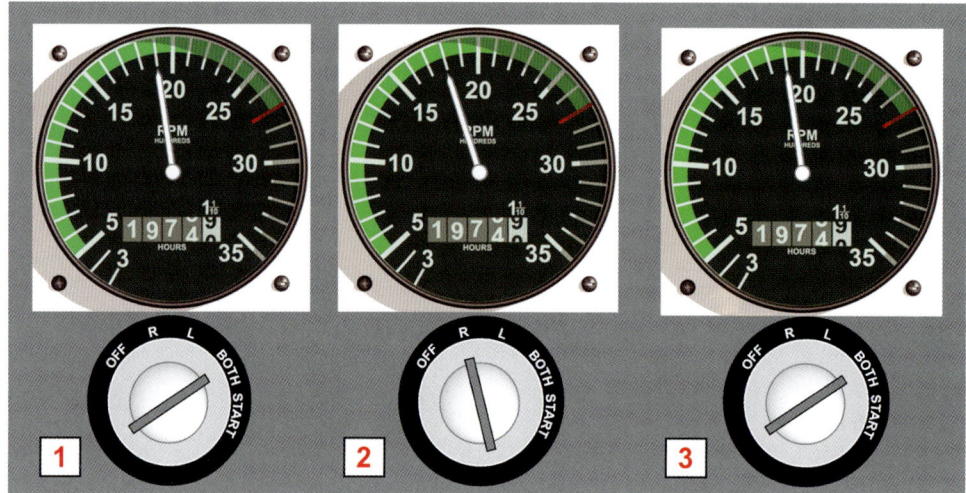

Figure 10.8 Checking the right-hand magneto; 1 = both on, 2 = right on only, 3 = back to both.

As each magneto is selected in turn, check for a drop in RPM. This drop must be within the limits laid down by the manufacturers, and the difference between the RPM drop of each magneto must also be within a tolerance figure given by the manufacturers. The fall in engine speed is due to the fact that as you switch off a magneto, you are essentially switching off a plug in each cylinder, thus increasing the time it takes for the mixture to be fully consumed within the cylinder.

If no drop in RPM occurs, this may indicate that the deselected magneto has not been switched off or that it was not working in the first place. However, such a situation should really have been noticed during the dead-cut check.

An excessive RPM drop when a magneto is switched off may be indicative of one of several problems. For instance, the plugs of the remaining magneto may be defective or just fouled. If fouled plugs are suspected, then it may be worth leaning the mixture off for about 10 or 20 seconds to clear them, and then resetting the mixture to the rich position, preparatory to trying the check again.

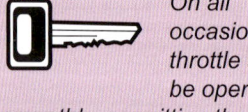 *On all occasions, the throttle should be operated smoothly, permitting the mixture-strength and charge quantity to change in line with the engine requirements.*

After completing the magneto check, check the aircraft systems once again. Note the engine oil temperature and pressure gauges, and the low oil pressure warning light. Ensure also that the fuel pressure is within tolerances and that the suction vacuum level is sufficient.

After checking that the alternator is still on line, and that the ammeter reading is normal for the loads selected, close the throttle and note that the engine idles at about 600 RPM.

Then set the RPM to the recommended idle speed, usually about 1 200 RPM. Setting the throttle to this level prevents the plugs becoming fouled during prolonged idling.

OPERATION OF THE THROTTLE.

Get used to operating the throttle lever smoothly. Jerky or rapid movement of the throttle lever will not make the engine respond any more quickly. In fact, it may cause the engine to hesitate or stutter because of an overweak mixture.

Engines have been known to stop because of a weak-cut caused by a rapidly opened throttle. This could be hazardous at the start of an attempted go-around. Count slowly up to three while opening the throttle from idle to full power. You should then find that the engine will accelerate at about the same rate as that at which the throttle lever moves.

The same practice should be followed when reducing power, especially when throttling back from take-off power settings. Smooth operation of the engine controls will allow time for mixture strength and charge quantity to change in line with the engine's requirements.

CYLINDER HEAD AND EXHAUST GAS TEMPERATURE.

The exhaust gas temperature gauge and the cylinder head temperature gauge are often confused with each other. They do, however, perform different functions.

The exhaust gas temperature gauge is primarily a fuel management instrument.

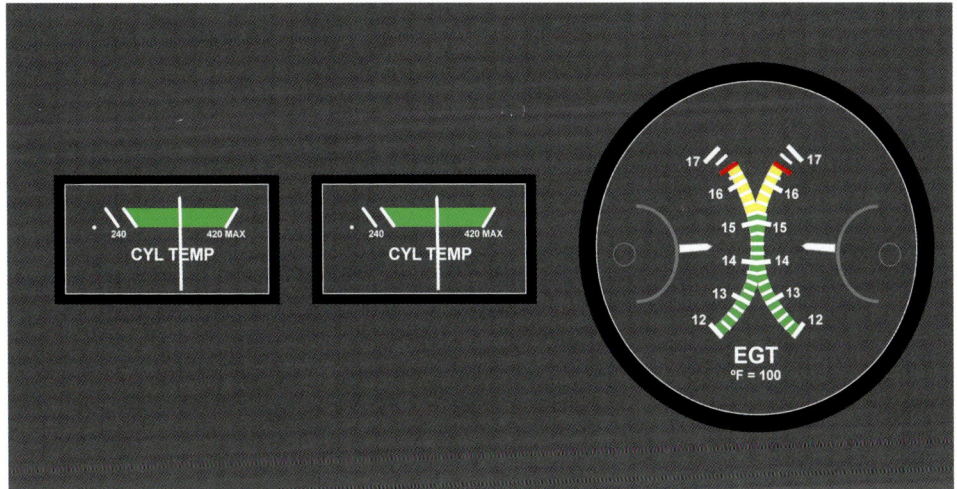

Figure 10.9 Exhaust Gas and Cylinder Head Temperature Gauges.

The exhaust gas temperature probe is installed about four inches from the cylinder head in the exhaust system. Although the exhaust gas temperature gauge can help in troubleshooting a problem on the engine, it is primarily a fuel management instrument. On the other hand, the cylinder head temperature gauge is an engine instrument designed to protect the engine against excessive heat.

Most general aviation aircraft engines take the cylinder head temperature from the hottest single cylinder. The hottest cylinder is determined by extensive flight tests carried out by the engine manufacturers.

CHAPTER 10: ENGINE HANDLING

Minimum in-flight cylinder head temperature should be 65° Celsius. Maximum in most direct drive normally aspirated engines is 260° Celsius. Some of the higher powered, more complex engines have a maximum limit of 245° Celsius.

Although these figures are minimum and maximum limits, the pilot should operate his engine at more reasonable temperatures in order to enable it to achieve its expected overhaul life.

In practice, it has been found that engines have benefited greatly during continuous operation by keeping Cylinder Head Temperatures below 205° Celsius in order to achieve the best life and wear.

In general, it would be normal during all year operations, in climb and cruise, to maintain the cylinder head temperatures within the range of 175° to 225° Centigrade.

THE MIXTURE CONTROL.

The way the mixture control works has been described in the chapter on carburation. We will now describe its operation during the take-off and landing phases, the climb and the cruise, and also its use in the idle cut-off (ICO) operation.

Use of the Mixture Control During Take-off and Landing.

We know that detonation is most likely to occur under conditions where charge temperatures and pressures are high. The take-off is a phase of flight when these conditions occur. Also, because a pilot may have to go-around from the landing phase, once again generating the same conditions as on take-off, he must select the mixture to fully rich, in this circumstance, too.

The addition of extra fuel into the cylinders reduces the volumetric efficiency of the engine, which also reduces the potential of the engine to produce power. On the other hand, the cooling effect that the evaporation of the fuel has on the charge, prevents detonation, and therefore allows the engine to deliver its maximum rated output.

Use of the Mixture Control During the Climb.

We already know from the carburation chapter that, because of the air's decreasing density with increasing altitude, the fuel-air mixture gets richer as the aircraft climbs. This is because the weight of fuel being fed into the cylinders does not reduce by the same proportion as the air being fed into the cylinders.

As long as the climb does not continue above, say, 5 000 feet, this is not really a problem. The rich mixture does the same job it did during the take off phase; it stops detonation by cooling the charge temperature. So the mixture control can be left at fully rich in the climb.

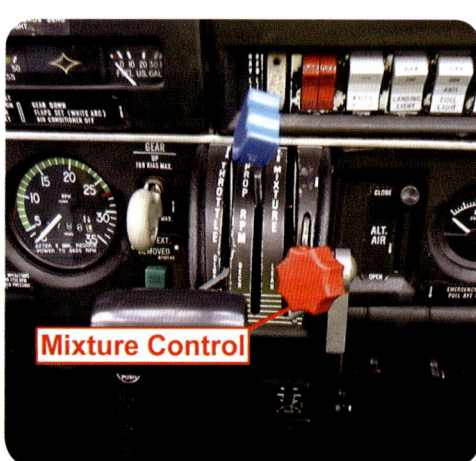

Figure 10.10 The Mixture Control.

CHAPTER 10: ENGINE HANDLING

Use of the Mixture Control at Altitude.

During the cruise phase of flight, the mixture can be leaned off to give better fuel economy. If your aircraft has an exhaust gas temperature (EGT) gauge, this can be used to give an indication of the correct mixture setting. If the mixture control is moved towards lean, the EGT will peak when the air-fuel ratio is 15:1.

It should be remembered, though, that this ratio should not be used, as detonation can occur. On reaching the peak EGT, the mixture control should be moved towards rich. The cylinder head temperature should then reduce. The aircraft's flight manual will specify a temperature drop which will give the rich cruise setting.

If an EGT gauge is not fitted, the following alternative method of setting the correct mixture strength for the cruise, by using the engine RPM as a guide, may be utilized.

Moving the mixture control from the fully rich position to a weaker setting brings the air-fuel ratio closer to the chemically correct value of approximately 15:1. Remember, at this ratio all of the air and fuel are consumed and the heat released by combustion is at its maximum. More heat means more power, so with a fixed pitch propeller the RPM will rise. But continuing to weaken the mixture from this point will cause the RPM to reduce.

Move the mixture control to a position a little richer than the chemically correct position, and note that the RPM decreases slightly. This setting can be assumed to be the optimum for economical cruising flight.

When leaning the fuel/air mixture at altitude, to obtain the most efficient mixture setting, the control is first moved towards the LEAN position until the engine RPM decreases then the mixture control is moved slightly to the RICH side of peak RPM.

Idle Cut-Off.

The normal method of shutting down an aircraft engine is by cutting off the fuel supply. This has several advantages over the method used in automobile engines where the ignition is switched off.

Cutting off the fuel ensures that the engine cannot 'run on', a phenomenon which can occur if the engine has any incandescent carbon deposits in the combustion chamber. It also means that no fuel is allowed to be sucked into the cylinders during those few last revolutions before the engine stops. Any fuel brought into the cylinder after combustion ceases will tend to wash the lubricating oil from the cylinder walls, and, as a consequence, the next time it starts, the engine suffers wear.

In the chapter on carburation, the idle cut-off section of the carburettor was described in some detail.

The idle cut-off may be a separate control, or it may be incorporated in the mixture control lever. By closing the throttle and pulling the mixture control lever to the idle cut-off position, the fuel flow between the float chamber and the venturi is cut off.

The normal method of shutting down an aircraft engine is to close the throttle and move the mixture lever to the idle cut-off position.

CHAPTER 10: ENGINE HANDLING QUESTIONS

Representative PPL - type questions to test your theoretical knowledge of Engine Handling.

1. To correctly set the fuel/air mixture whilst in flight, the control is moved to the lean position until engine RPM:

    a. Drops and then the mixture control is then moved slightly to the RICH side of peak RPM
    b. Rises and then the mixture control is left in that position
    c. Decreases by approximately 150 RPM. The mixture control is then moved slightly more towards the LEAN position
    d. Decreases. The mixture control is then left in that position

2. What is an appropriate action to take if you have a carburettor fire on start-up?

    a. Deselect carburettor heat
    b. Select mixture control to Idle Cut-Off
    c. Turn the starter switch to "Off"
    d. All of the above

3. Immediately after starting an aircraft engine, you must check the starter warning light. If it is still illuminated you should:

    a. Monitor it for 30 seconds. If it remains illuminated shut down the engine
    b. Do nothing. The starter warning light is designed to stay on while the engine is running
    c. Shut down the engine immediately
    d. Shut down the engine, count to 30, then attempt a re-start

4. After starting a cold aircraft engine the oil pressure gauge should register:

    a. Immediately; otherwise shut down the engine
    b. Within 30 seconds; otherwise shut down the engine
    c. By the time pre-flight checks are complete; otherwise shut down the engine
    d. Immediately, otherwise, as long as the oil levels were at an adequate level before start-up, and RPM is within limits, it is probable that the oil pressure gauge is faulty and this should be reported after the flight

5. The normal method for shutting down an aircraft engine is to:

    a. Switch the starter switch to off
    b. Move the mixture to idle cut-off (ICO)
    c. Close the throttle
    d. Close the throttle and move the mixture to ICO

CHAPTER 10: ENGINE HANDLING QUESTIONS

6. On take-off, the throttle should be operated:

   a. Smoothly, to avoid a weak cut, allowing the engine to respond as fast as it is able, and permitting the mixture-strength and charge quantity to change in line with the engine requirements
   b. Smoothly, but it may be opened abruptly if several aircraft are waiting to take off
   c. Smoothly, following a count of three
   d. As required by the air traffic situation

Question	1	2	3	4	5	6
Answer						

The answers to these questions can be found at the end of this book.

CHAPTER 11
ELECTRICAL SYSTEMS

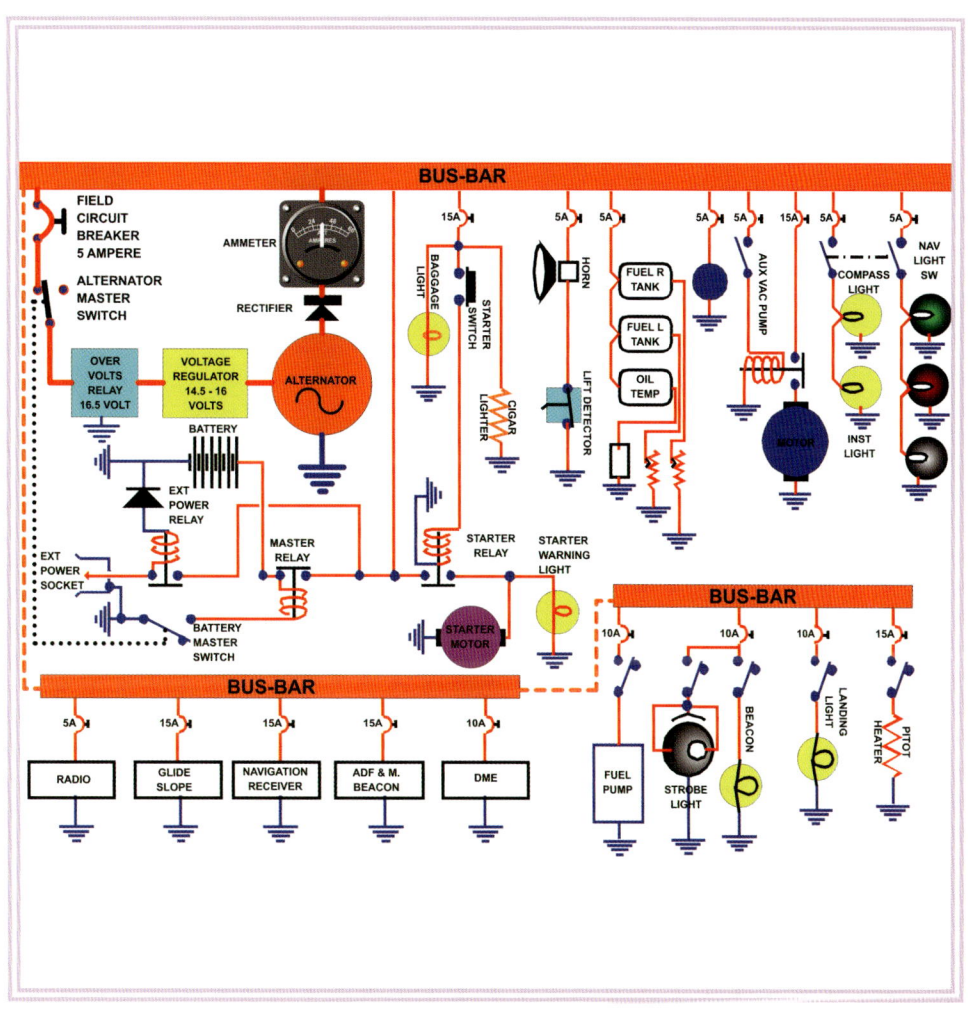

CHAPTER 11: ELECTRICAL SYSTEMS

CHAPTER 11: ELECTRICAL SYSTEMS

INTRODUCTION.

The **electrical system** in a light aircraft operates components and services such as the **landing light**, **radios**, **turn co-ordinator**, **starter motor**, **transponder**, **navigation equipment**, **pitot heater**, **electric fuel pump** and so on.

ELECTRICAL CURRENT.

Direct Current.
Most light aircraft use a **direct current (DC)** supply to drive the electrical services.

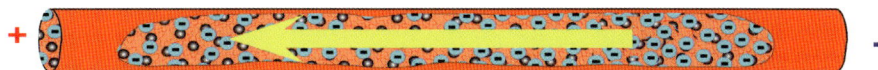

Figure 11.1 Direct Current - Actual Electron Flow.

The term **direct current** implies that the electrons which make up the flow of current are travelling in one direction only. Convention, used by electricians and electrical engineers, states that the electrons flow from a positive terminal to a negative terminal, but the scientific explanation of electric current shows that actual electron flow is from the negative pole to the positive pole as depicted in *Figure 11.1*. The difference between the directions of "**conventional flow**" and "**actual flow**" will not concern you for your PPL studies.

Alternating Current.
In an **alternating current (AC)** the electrons in the circuit **oscillate** backwards and forwards about a mean point. This might seem at first glance as if it would be rather ineffective, one movement cancelling out the other, but this is not the case. Any movement of electrons generates **electrical energy**.

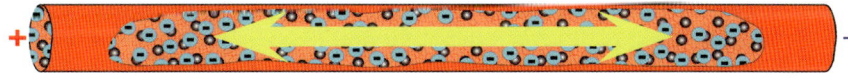

Figure 11.2. Electrons Move Backwards and Forwards in an Alternating Current Circuit.

Although **alternating current** is used in light aircraft only for power generation, it is used much more than **direct current** in commercial airliners where relatively light, powerful, reliable and efficient machinery is required.

159

CHAPTER 11: ELECTRICAL SYSTEMS

Current Flow.

The strength of **current** flowing through a conductor, such as an aircraft electrical cable, is measured in **Amperes**, commonly known as Amps, by an instrument called an **Ammeter**.

The strength of current flowing through a conductor, such as an aircraft electrical cable, is measured in Amperes, commonly known as Amps, by an instrument called an Ammeter.

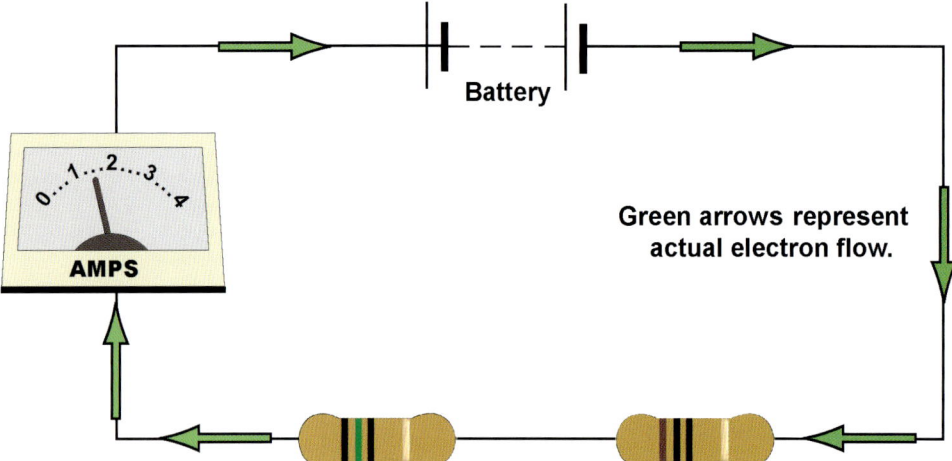

Figure 11.3 An Ammeter Measuring Current Flow.

Water Analogy.

Imagine the current flowing through a cable as being similar to water flowing in a pipeline.

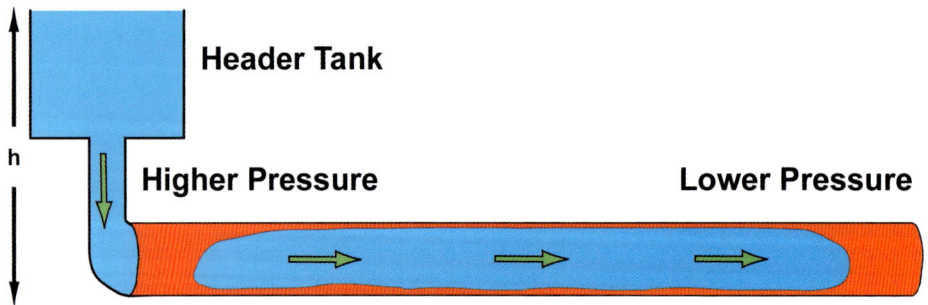

Figure 11.4 The Water Analogy of the electric current flow.

This analogy, pictured in *Figure 11.4*, is called the 'water analogy'. For people not too well acquainted with electricity, the water analogy can come in very handy in almost all situations when dealing with simple direct current circuits.

For water to flow through the pipe, a pressure difference must exist across the pipe. The pressure at one end of the pipe must be greater than the pressure at the other end. Pressure difference is usually obtained by placing a header tank above the level of the whole water system and thus the force of gravity causes the water to flow.

Voltage.

In an electrical circuit, the "pressure difference" required to move electrons along a wire is termed the **"electromotive force" (EMF)**, or simply **"voltage"**, which is measured in **volts** on an instrument called a **voltmeter**.

The pressure required to cause current to flow along a conductor is termed the voltage or electromotive force, which is measured in volts on a voltmeter.

160

CHAPTER 11: ELECTRICAL SYSTEMS

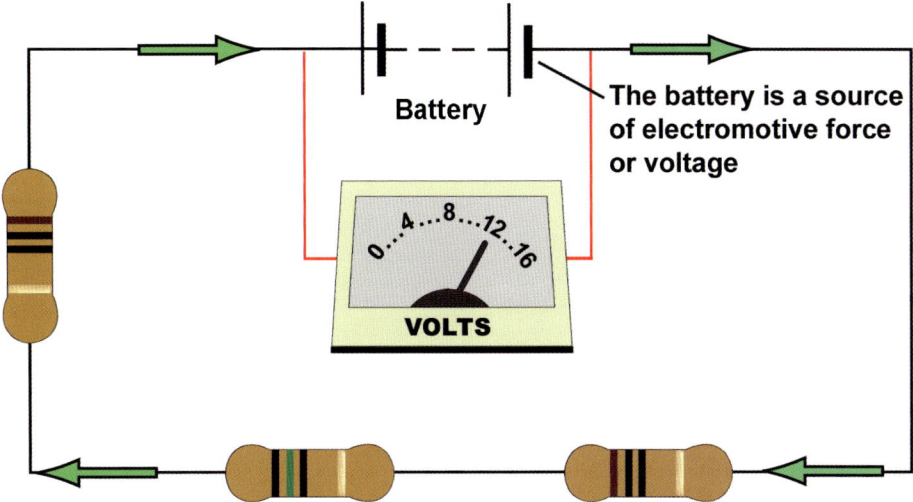

Figure 11.5 A Voltmeter Measuring Voltage, or Electromotive Force.

This electromotive force, or voltage, can be generated in several ways. In a light aircraft, the main source of EMF or voltage is the generator or alternator, with the battery serving as a back-up. The battery can run the aircraft's essential services for about 30 minutes, if an aircraft's generator or alternator fails. The battery also supplies power for engine starting.

Resistance and Resistors.

Any component or characteristic of a circuit which opposes electron flow is called a **resistor**. Components which are designed specifically to provide **resistance** are called **resistors**. **Resistors** are used in the construction of all practical circuits.

Any component or characteristic of a circuit which opposes electron flow is called a resistor.

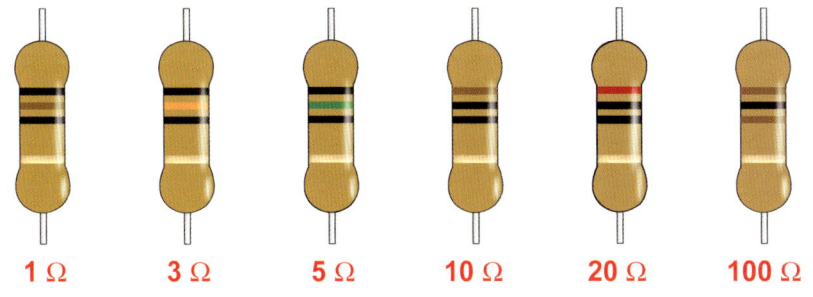

Figure 11.6 A range of resistors of differing values. Resistance is measured in Ohms (Ω).

POWER DISTRIBUTION.

Electric current is fed by a generator or alternator to the individual electrical components of any aircraft electrical system via busbars, which are merely convenient collection and distribution points for current flow.

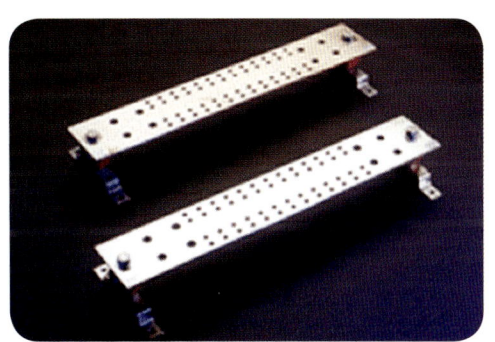

Figure 11.7 Busbars.

The busbars are usually solid copper bars which are drilled and tapped so that supply and distribution cables can be attached to them.

161

CHAPTER 11: ELECTRICAL SYSTEMS

Single-Pole.
Most light aircraft which utilise metal construction are single-pole or earth-return electrical systems. This means that the individual components are supplied via the busbars and cables, and to complete the circuit, the return current flows back through the metal of the airframe.

Double-Pole.
Aircraft which are made of non-conductive materials, like the Diamond Star shown in *Figure 11.8*, require a double-pole or two wire system. This means that as well as having a cable taking the current flow to each individual component, another cable is required to complete the electrical circuit back to the negative side of the generator or alternator.

🔑 *A double-pole electrical system requires one cable to take the current to the component and a second cable to complete the circuit.*

Figure 11.8 The Airframe of this Diamond Star is made of non-conductive materials.

Alternators and Generators.
Alternators and generators produce the electricity needed to charge the battery and to operate the aircraft's electrical equipment. Put simply, while a generator produces direct current, an alternator produces alternating current internally, and uses a device called a diode rectifier to turn the alternating current into direct current, which is then fed to the aircraft circuit.

Alternators are commonly used in aircraft because of their dependability.

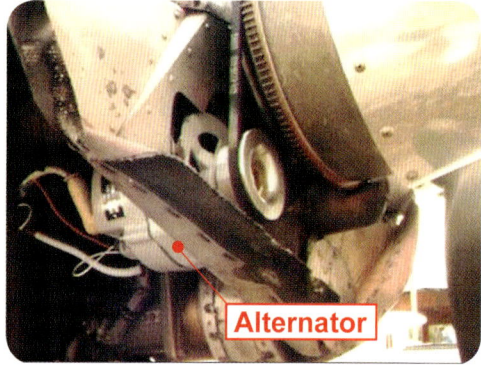

Figure 11.9 An Alternator.

While a generator will generally require the engine to run at approximately half speed before it will deliver its full output, an alternator will give almost full power even at engine idling speed.

BATTERIES.

In a light aircraft, a lead-acid battery provides a store of electrical energy enabling the engine to be started. The battery is also a source of emergency electrical power, in the event of alternator or generator failure.

A battery is made up of a number of cells connected in series which convert chemical energy into electrical energy

Figure 11.10a An aeroplane battery.

CHAPTER 11: ELECTRICAL SYSTEMS

Primary Cells.
There are two types of cell: the primary and the secondary.

The primary cell is the type normally used in hand-held equipment, such as torches and transistor radios etc. It consists of two electrodes in contact with a chemical called an electrolyte. The electrolyte encourages electron transfer between the electrodes until an electron imbalance between them exists, giving rise to a potential difference or voltage. A potential difference of approximately 1.5 Volts exists between the electrodes of an unused primary cell.

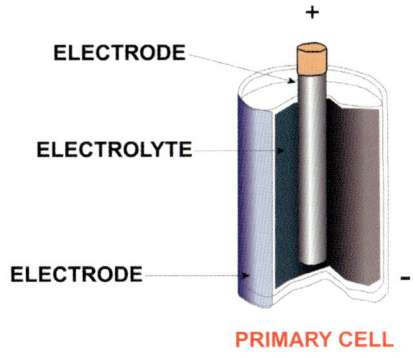

Figure 11.10b A Primary Cell.

For convenience, one of the electrodes is the case of the cell and contains the electrolyte. The other electrode is placed within this case, as shown in *Figure 11.10b*. When the two electrodes, which we may call positive and the negative poles, are connected within a circuit, electrons will flow through the circuit.

This flow of electrons in the circuit is matched by an internal transfer of electrons from the positive to the negative electrode of the primary cell. As the flow of electrons continues, the negative electrons slowly dissolve into the electrolyte until no further electron imbalance exists. At this point the cell is dead. Once discharged, primary cells cannot be recharged.

Secondary Cells.
Secondary cells work on the same principle as primary cells, but in the case of the secondary cell, the chemical energy in the cell can be restored when the cell has been discharged, by passing a charging current through the cell in the reverse direction to that of the discharge current. In this way, the secondary cell can be charged and discharged many times over a long period of time.

When a battery is recharged, electrical energy is converted into chemical energy which is retained within the battery until it is once again discharged. The lead-acid battery is the most common type of secondary-cell battery used in light aircraft. The electrodes in a lead-acid battery are called plates. Plates are illustrated in *Figure 11.11*.

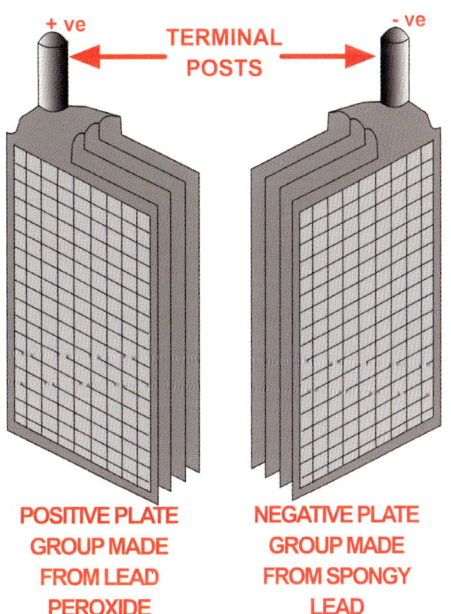

The chemical energy in a secondary cell can be restored after discharge by passing a charging current through the cell.

Figure 11.11 The Plates of a Secondary Cell.

There is a positive plate, which is made of lead peroxide, and a negative plate which is made of spongy lead. Both of the plates are immersed in an electrolyte of dilute sulphuric acid.

CHAPTER 11: ELECTRICAL SYSTEMS

The state of charge of a lead-acid cell can be determined by measuring the specific gravity of the electrolyte solution with a hydrometer, an example of which is shown in *Figure 11.12*. The electrolyte of a fully charged cell will have a specific gravity of 1.275, whereas the electrolyte of a discharged cell will have much more dilute acid, with a specific gravity somewhere in the region of 1.17.

Voltage.
The voltage of a lead-acid battery cell when it is off load, that is, not generating current, is 2.2 Volts. If a load is applied to the terminals of the cell, the output voltage will fall to just 2.0 Volts.

Capacity.
The capacity of a cell is a measure of how much current it can provide over a certain period of time. The capacity of a cell is determined by the area of the electrodes, or plates as they are called in a secondary cell. Capacity is measured in Ampere-hours.

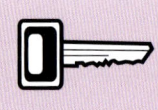 *A 60 amp/hour battery will, in theory, supply 20 Amps for up to 3 hours.*

Aircraft batteries are usually 12 or 24 Volt lead-acid batteries consisting of a number of individual cells connected in series. Batteries are classified by their voltage and their capacity to provide a current for a given amount of time.

Figure 11.12 An Hydrometer.

A cell with a capacity of 80 Ampere-hours should provide a current of 8 Amperes for 10 hours, or alternatively, 80 Amperes for 1 hour. However, because the ability of a battery to retain its output voltage diminishes as the discharge rate increases, capacity is normally tested at the 10 hour rate. A typical light aircraft battery would be rated at around 30 Ampere-hours.

Cells Connected in Series.
The circuit diagram in *Figure 11.13* shows cells connected in series, as in a 12 Volt aircraft battery. Each cell is rated at 2 Volts, and has a capacity of 80 Ampere-hours. Notice how the voltage of the circuit increases with the addition of each cell. Note also, however, that the capacity of the complete battery remains the same as the capacity of one cell, regardless of how many cells there are connected in series.

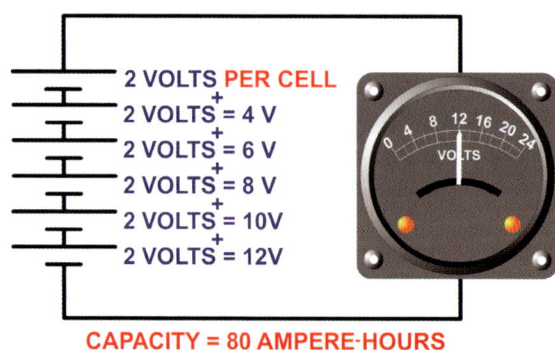

Figure 11.13 Cells Connected in Series.

CHAPTER 11: ELECTRICAL SYSTEMS

Cells Connected in Parallel.

The circuit diagram in *Figure 11.14* shows five cells joined together in parallel. Each cell is rated at 2 Volts, and, in this case, has a capacity of 20 Ampere-hours. The output voltage of the circuit is that of just one cell, 2 Volts, but the total capacity is the sum of the individual cell capacities, that is, 100 Ampere-hours.

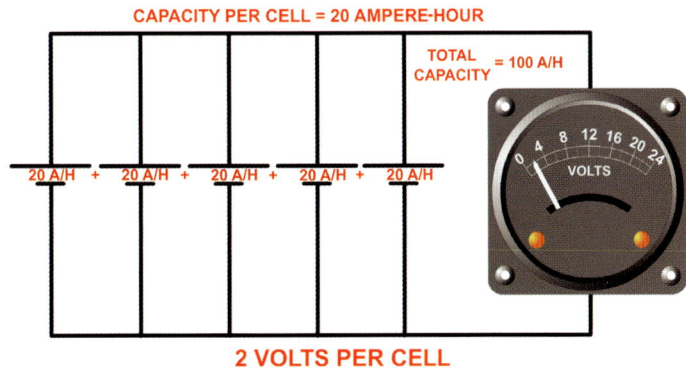

Figure 11.14 Cells Connected in Parallel.

Charging A Battery.

To charge a battery, it must be connected to an electrical supply which has a slightly higher voltage than that of the battery itself.

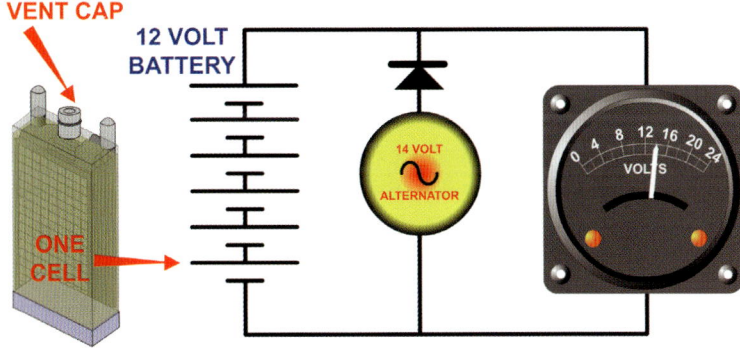

Figure 11.15 Charging a 12 Volt Aircraft Battery.

> Great care must be taken during battery charging to ensure that the hydrogen gas produced is allowed time to escape through the battery vent cap. There is a danger that a build up of gas pressure could cause the battery to explode.

When the battery is being charged, great care must be taken regarding the rate of charge. If the rate of charge is too high, then 'gassing' will take place.

Gassing is the formation of hydrogen gas on the plates. The gas must be allowed time to escape through the vent cap of the battery; if too much gas is produced in too short a time then there is a danger that a build up of gas pressure could cause the battery to explode, with the subsequent release of the sulphuric acid within.

Under normal circumstances, the output voltage of the alternator or generator charging a 12 Volt battery on an aircraft would be maintained constant at 14 Volts, as is shown in *Figure 11.15*, whereas the output of an alternator on an aircraft with a 24 Volt system would be maintained constant at 28 Volts.

CHAPTER 11: ELECTRICAL SYSTEMS

AMMETERS.

Ammeters have a low internal resistance and are placed in series with an electrical circuit to measure the current flowing into or out of the battery. There are two types of ammeter used in light aircraft;

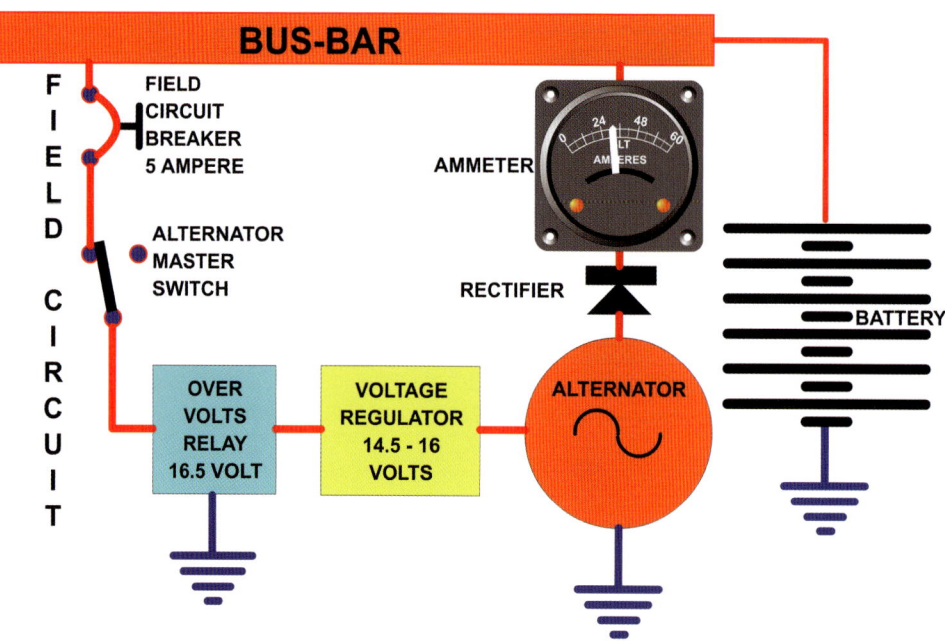

Figure 11.16a. The Loadmeter-type Ammeter.

The Loadmeter.

The first type of ammeter, shown in Figure *11.16a*, has its zero position on the dial over to the extreme left of the scale. This type of ammeter indicates the actual load on the alternator, in other words the alternator's output, and is, therefore, commonly called a loadmeter.

A high battery charge rate after engine start could result in a battery overheating and suffering damage.

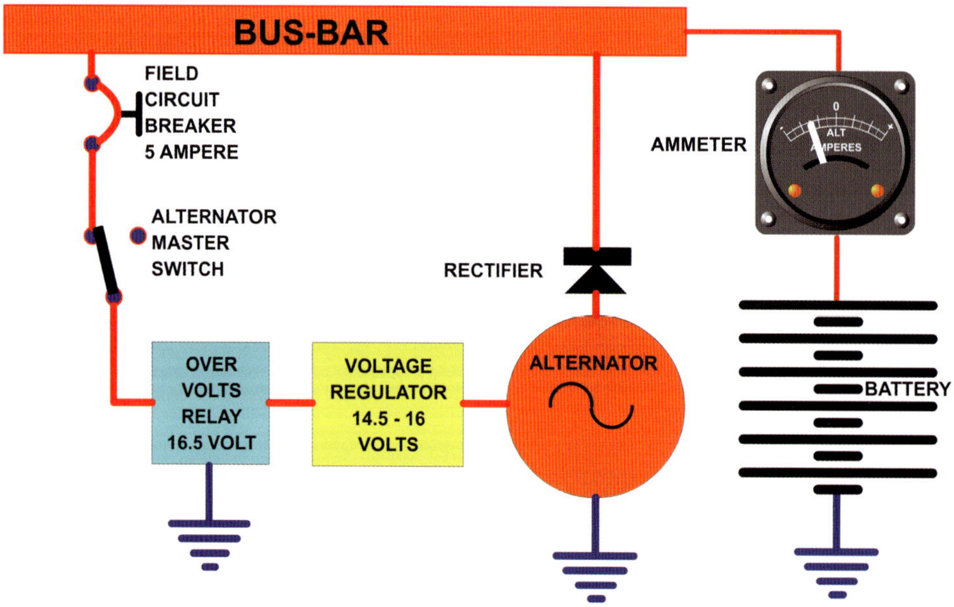

Figure 11.16b. The Centre Zero Ammeter.

166

The Centre-Zero Ammeter.

The second type of ammeter, shown in *Figure 11.16b*, has its zero position in the centre of the scale. This type of ammeter indicates the current flow, both in and out of the battery. When the battery is being charged, the needle is deflected to the right of the centre position. When the battery is discharging, the needle is displaced left of centre.

VOLTMETERS.

Voltmeters have a high internal resistance. They are connected in parallel with an electrical circuit or component to measure the voltage drop, or potential difference between two points in a circuit *(see Figures 11.5 and 11.15)*. In a light aircraft, the voltmeter indicates the condition of the battery and its ability to deliver the current required to power the aircraft systems.

LOAD INDICATIONS AND FAULTS.

After starting an engine using the aircraft battery, the generator or alternator continually recharges the battery.

Recharging is indicated on both the centre-zero ammeter or loadmeter as a load. Initially the indication of charge will be quite high, but it should quickly reduce as the battery is recharged.

Pilots should be aware that, if the load increases or remains high, this could be an indication of a faulty battery. Remember, a high charge rate could result in a battery overheating and suffering damage.

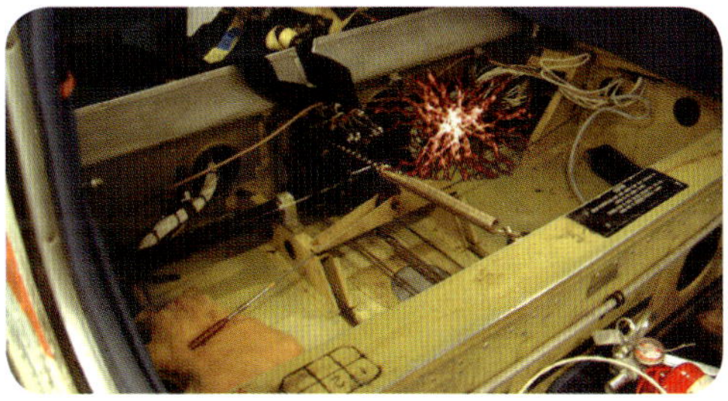

Electrical Faults.

Abnormal conditions may arise in an electrical circuit for a variety of reasons. For instance, a breakdown of the

Figure 11.17 Electrical Faults May Cause Fires.

insulation on one of the cables carrying the supply to a component will cause a dramatic rise in the current flowing in that cable if the cable comes into contact with the metal of the airframe.

There are several serious problems inherent in this situation. Firstly, and probably least serious, is the fact that the component being fed by the faulty cable will cease to operate.

Secondly, if the circuit was not protected, the current which would flow through this short circuit, caused by contact between an exposed cable and the airframe, would be so great that it could cause the power generation circuit, (the alternator or generator and the battery), to fail. This would leave the aircraft without electrical power.

Thirdly, and potentially the most serious, there is the risk of fire. At the point where the unprotected cable contacts the airframe metal, there will undoubtedly be sparks which will ignite anything in the vicinity, and the cable itself will get so hot that more insulation will be melted from the cable, making the situation worse.

CHAPTER 11: ELECTRICAL SYSTEMS

TYPES OF CIRCUIT PROTECTION.

Although there are a number of protection devices used in aircraft electrical systems, we will only look at only two of them. These are circuit-breakers *(Figure 11.18)*, and fuses *(Figure 11.19)*.

Figure 11.18. An Aircraft Circuit-Breaker Panel.

The fundamental difference between fuses and circuit-breakers is the time it takes for each of them to operate from the moment maximum fault-current flows in the circuit.

A fuse normally breaks the circuit before full fault-current is reached, whereas the circuit-breaker operates to break the circuit after full fault-current is reached.

The circuit-breaker can also function in certain circumstances as a switch, opening and closing a circuit as required.

Fuses.

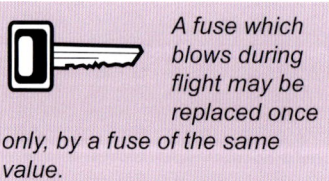 *A fuse which blows during flight may be replaced once only, by a fuse of the same value.*

The most common type of fuse in use on light aircraft is the cartridge fuse, illustrated in *Figure 11.19*. It consists of a tubular glass or ceramic body with the fuse element running through the centre, connected to two brass end caps.

The wire fuses, or blows, when the current flowing through it is sufficient to melt the fuse element. The time this takes varies inversely with the current. All fuses are rated at a specific current value: that current being the current the element will carry continuously without unduly heating up or deteriorating.

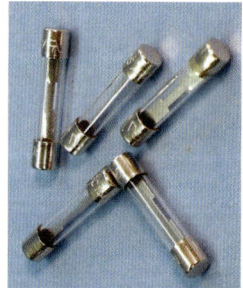

Figure 11.19. Fuses.

The current rating of a fuse (e.g 5 Amp or 15 Amp) in a particular circuit is such that it is not less than the normal current flowing in that circuit, but will blow at a current level below the safety limit of the equipment or cable used. For this reason, only the specified fuse rating should be used in a particular circuit.

A fuse which has blown may be replaced with another fuse of the correct rating, but only once. If the replacement fuse blows when the circuit is reactivated, then there is obviously a defect in the system, and the fuse must not be changed again until the circuit has been fully investigated.

Fuses which have a greater rating than that specified for a particular circuit must never be used. The consequences of doing so will most probably include greater damage being caused, and maybe an electrical fire if the circuit does develop a fault.

CHAPTER 11: ELECTRICAL SYSTEMS

Circuit-Breakers.

Circuit-breakers are fitted, as are fuses, to protect equipment from overload or fault conditions. They incorporate a heat sensitive tripping device and a manually operated trip / reset switch.

The type of circuit breaker shown in *Figures 11.18* and *11.20* can be rated from between 5 to 45 Amps. The button is shown in the "popped" position, indicating that the circuit is broken.

Figure 11.20. A Circuit Breaker.

Do not be tempted to reset a circuit breaker a second time. A circuit breaker which has operated twice is a definite indication that an electrical fault is present.

A circuit-breaker which has operated, or popped, may be reset once only. Do not be tempted to reset it a second time. If it has popped twice, you may be sure that an electrical fault is present. Resetting the circuit-breaker twice will only exacerbate the fault.

THE ALTERNATOR CIRCUIT.

When the engine is running, the alternator produces the electric current to charge the battery and operate the aircraft's electrical equipment. *Figure 11.21* shows a simplified alternator control circuit. *Figure 11.27*, at the end of this chapter, shows the construction of the rotating field alternator of the type fitted to most light aircraft.

Some aircraft, such as motor-gliders, have a generator instead of an alternator. From the point of view of the pilot, generator and alternator control circuits are very similar, the only difference worth noting is that the alternator circuit incorporates a diode rectifier as shown in *Figure 11.21*. The diode rectifier changes the alternating current output of the alternator to direct current, a procedure which is unnecessary with a generator because its output is direct current.

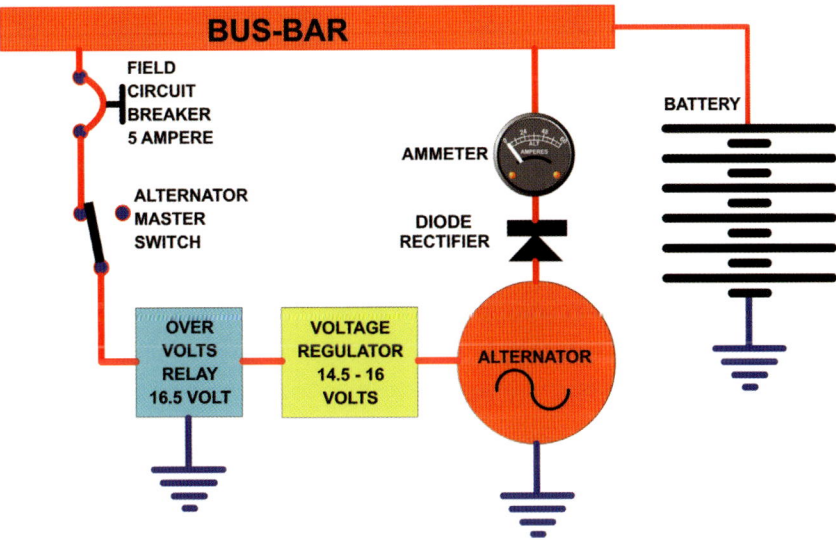

Figure 11.21 A Simplified Alternator Control Circuit.

At the top of the diagram you can see the busbar, which, as we previously explained is a distribution point for the output of the alternator. On the left of the circuit diagram is the field circuit and to the right is the power circuit, both of which we will now describe in more detail.

169

CHAPTER 11: ELECTRICAL SYSTEMS

Field Circuit.

The field circuit is the circuit which excites or powers the magnetic coil inside the alternator, and which controls the alternator output. The greater the current through the field circuit, the greater the strength of the current produced by the alternator. Consequently, the circuit breaker in the cockpit is the 5 Amp alternator field circuit breaker. The power circuit of the alternator carries up to 50 Amps. There could be no circuit breaker in the cockpit big enough to carry that size of current.

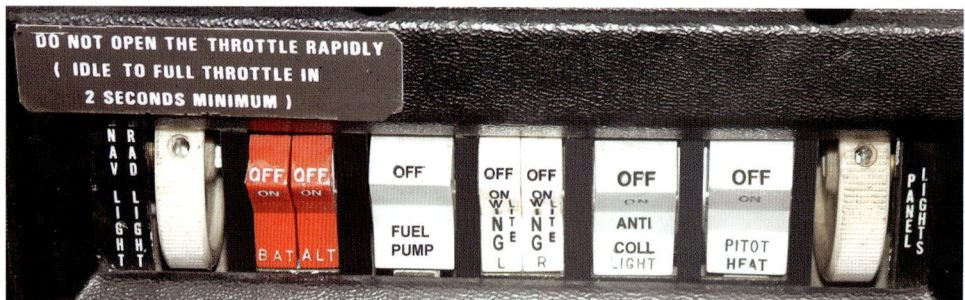

Figure 11.22. Power Switches in a PA 28 Aircraft.

Alternator output is controlled by the field circuit. The field circuit of the alternator shown in *Figure 11.21* is protected by a 5 Ampere circuit-breaker. Also in the field circuit is the alternator master switch *(see Figure 11.22.)* The alternator master switch is the right-hand switch of the pair of red switches. Immediately to the left of the alternator master switch is the battery master switch, also red. These two switches control all aircraft electrical systems except the ignition system.

The battery master and alternator master switches can be switched on individually, but only the alternator switch can be switched off on its own. Switching the battery master switch off, will also switch the alternator off. If either the field circuit-breaker or alternator master switch is opened, then the alternator field becomes inoperative and the alternator will not produce any output.

Also shown in *Figure 11.21,* in the field circuit, is the overvolts relay. A relay is just an electrically operated switch. This relay will operate to open the field-circuit if the alternator output voltage rises above 16.5 Volts. The effect will be the same as if the field circuit-breaker or alternator master switch had been opened, that is, that the alternator will cease producing output. In the type of circuit shown, the overvoltage relay can be reset by switching off the alternator master switch for about two seconds and then switching it back on again.

Adjacent to the alternator in *Figure 11.21* is the voltage regulator. As its name implies, it controls the voltage output of the alternator, in this case maintaining output at between 14.5 to 16 Volts.

Power Circuit.

The power circuit shown in *Figure 11.21*, conducts the output of the alternator to the busbar, where current is then distributed to the individual aircraft electrical components. The diode-rectifier is necessary, to convert the alternating current output of the alternator to direct current. The ammeter measures the total current flowing from the alternator to the busbar.

CHAPTER 11: ELECTRICAL SYSTEMS

ELECTRICALLY OPERATED SERVICES.

Figure 11.23 shows a simplified electrical wiring diagram of a typical light aircraft. It is worth studying the circuit closely and noting that in the type of aircraft electrical circuit illustrated, all of the loads but two are protected by circuit-breakers of varying amperage. The exceptions are the power side of the starter circuit and the battery.

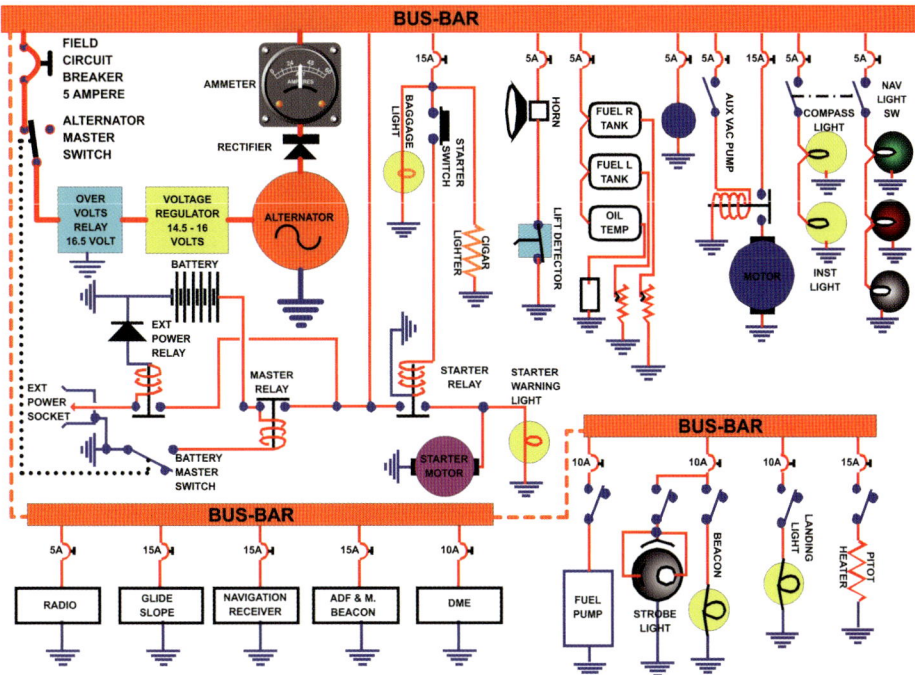

Figure 11.23 A Simplified Electrical Circuit of a Light Aircraft.

The Starter Circuit.

Although the power side of the starter motor circuit shown in *Figure 11.23* is not protected, the control part of that circuit is. Note that the starter switch gets its supply from the busbar via a 15 Amp circuit-breaker.

A starter motor will take considerably more than 15 Amps when it is first selected upon engine start. In fact, the initial load on the battery will exceed this figure by more than a factor of four. This strength of current flow would cause the circuit-breaker to pop open in an instant, and, if such a current were to flow through the starter switch, it would either melt its contacts or weld them together.

To prevent either of these occurrences, the starting current is taken from the battery and passed through a starter relay.

The starter relay is remotely controlled by the starter switch. When the starter switch is operated, it sends a supply of current to energize the coil of the starter relay. The starter relay has large contacts which are capable of passing the very high current required by the starter motor. So, using this relay method, the small current flowing through the starter switch circuit is able to generate a more powerful current, causing the starter motor to rotate the engine.

When the starter is operated, the current flowing through the switch is much lower than the current flowing throught the starter-motor circuit.

CHAPTER 11: ELECTRICAL SYSTEMS

The Battery Circuit.

Once the engine has started, the current that has been drained from the battery must be replaced by the alternator. We have already stated that initially this current flow, which will be indicated on the ammeter, will be quite high. However the current flow should quickly reduce as the battery becomes recharged. If no loads at all are selected, then the only current flowing through the ammeter will be the battery charging current. Even when the battery is fully recharged, the residual charging current will still be about 2 Amps. During night flying, the pilot should add this to the other loads placed on the alternator and you would expect a reading of approximately 32 Amps.

Operating an aircraft which has a 'flat' battery is not recommended, as the alternator may not be able to fully charge the battery during normal operations.

If the ammeter reading drops to zero in flight, this probably indicates that the alternator has failed.

In *Figure 11.16* we showed two ways in which ammeters can be wired into the electrical system. One type of ammeter has the zero position on the left side of the dial and is called a loadmeter. The other type of ammeter has the zero in the centre of the dial and is referred to as a centre-zero ammeter.

Prior to engine start, with perhaps the navigation lights, instrument panel lights and the electrical fuel pump selected on, a centre-zero ammeter will show, by the fact that the needle is indicating in the negative portion of the dial, that the battery is discharging.

Just after start, when the battery is some way towards having recovered its charge, the ammeter needle should indicate in the positive portion of the dial. This tells the pilot that the alternator is capable of supplying all the electrical loads as well as the battery charging current.

If, on the other hand, with the engine running, the ammeter needle is in the negative side of the scale, it is telling the pilot that the alternator is unable to supply demand and that the battery is discharging. In this situation, the pilot should switch off unnecessary electrical loads until the ammeter needle is once again in the positive portion of the dial. This will then indicate that there is a flow of charge-current into the battery.

An aircraft with a flat battery should not be flown. The alternator may not fully charge the battery during the flight. If an alternator or generator failure should occur, the battery needs be fully charged if the battery is to be able to power essential electrical equipment for a reasonable minimum amount of time.

RECOGNITION OF MALFUNCTIONS IN THE ELECTRICAL SYSTEM.

Most malfunctions of the aircraft electrical system will be indicated to the pilot by either the illumination of warning lights or by the readings on the ammeter.

If the aircraft has an annunciator (warning light) system, it is likely that this includes an alternator failure warning light. A test button will be incorporated into the annunciator system to check the light bulb filaments.

The ammeter readings have already been covered, but we will cover them once more from the point of view of the indications of malfunctions.

CHAPTER 11: ELECTRICAL SYSTEMS

Malfunctions Indicated on the 'Loadmeter'.

The loadmeter, the type of ammeter which has the zero on the left side of the dial, will indicate alternator failure by the needle dropping to zero.

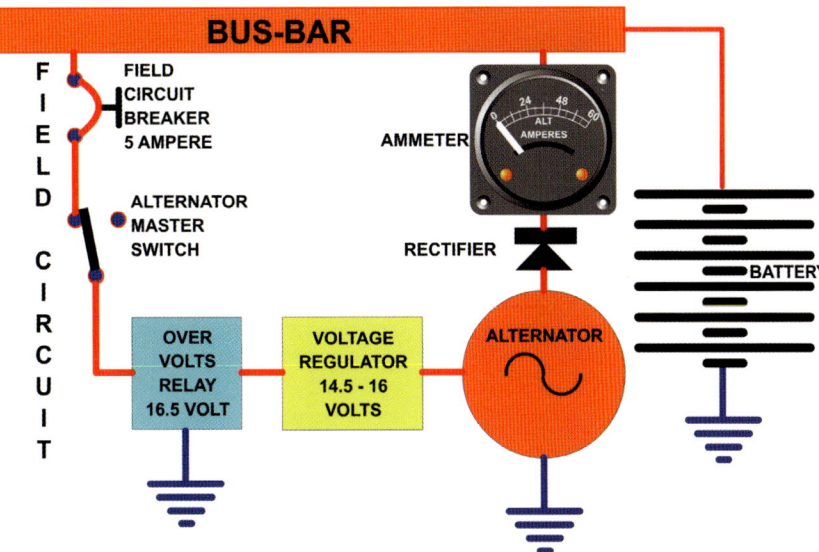

Figure 11.24. Indication of Alternator Failure on the Loadmeter.

The loadmeter, the type of ammeter having the zero on the left side of the dial, indicates alternator failure by the needle dropping to zero.

On the other hand, if the loadmeter reading remains excessively high, beyond the time period during which the battery would normally have recharged itself, this reading may indicate that the battery has an excessive charge-rate.

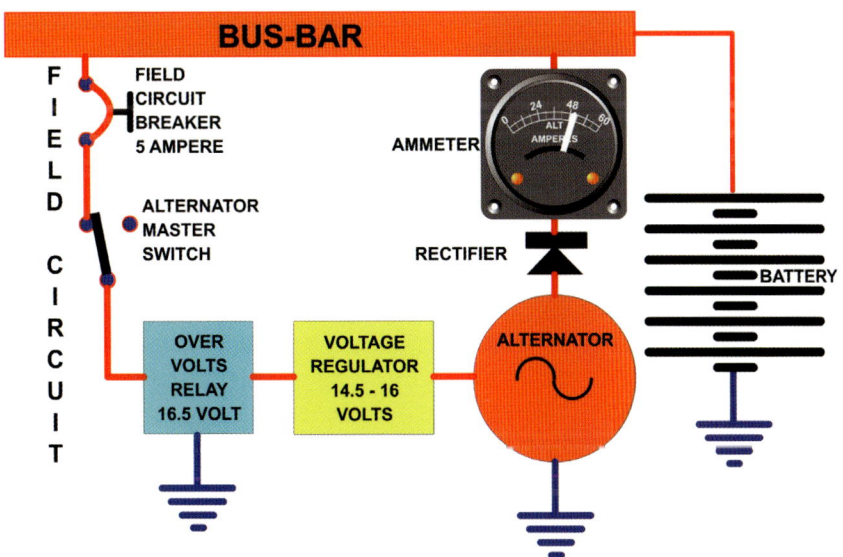

Figure 11.25. Indication of High Charge on a Loadmeter.

The needle staying central, or just right of centre of the gauge on the centre-zero ammeter is an indication that the battery is charged.

An excessive charge-rate will cause the battery to start losing some of the material from its plates. This will cause lasting and serious damage to the battery. The high charge will also cause the battery to get very hot, possibly so much so that the electrolyte will evaporate, exposing the plates to the air and once again causing them damage.

173

CHAPTER 11: ELECTRICAL SYSTEMS

The pilot, however, should bear in mind that the high charge rate could perhaps be brought about by a faulty voltage regulator. If this is the case, all of the aircraft equipment will be at risk of becoming overheated and impaired, especially heat sensitive components like the radio and navigation equipment.

Indications on the Centre-Zero Ammeter.

The indication on the centre-zero ammeter that the battery is charged, and the system is functioning normally, is given by the needle staying central, or just right of centre of the gauge.

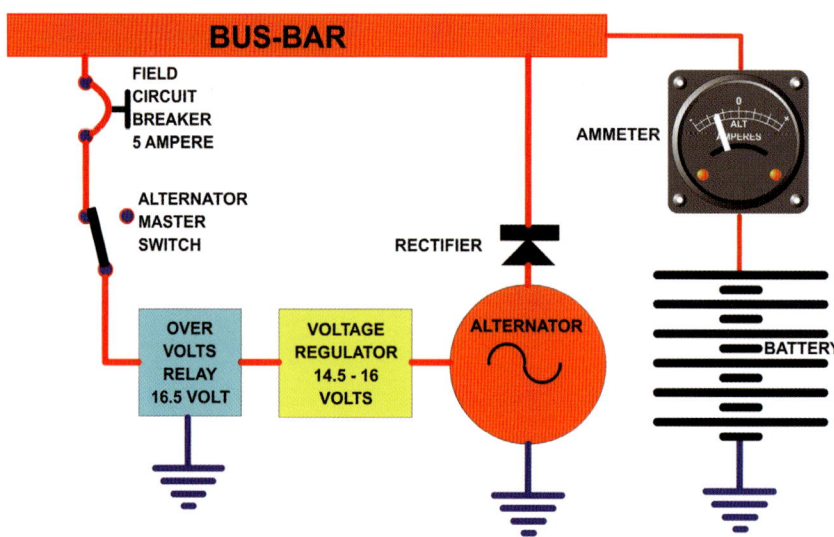

Figure 11.26. Constant Heavy Discharge on a 'Centre Zero Ammeter'.

The centre-zero ammeter will indicate alternator failure by the needle showing a constant heavy discharge; that is, far into the left side of the scale.

If the needle stays just in the negative portion of the scale for any length of time, this may indicate that the alternator is incapable of supplying all the loads as well as re-charging the battery at the same time. This situation will require some of the electrical equipment to be switched off, otherwise the battery will eventually become completely discharged.

Alternator Failure Drill.

The following practices are not to be considered as being representative of emergency drills for any particular aircraft type. They are purely general recommendations which should be considered if an alternator should fail.

If the alternator warning light illuminates at normal engine speed, and either the loadmeter shows zero or the centre-zero ammeter indicates a heavy discharge, the following actions should be considered.

Initially, judiciously select off any electrical, radio and navigation services not vital to the safe operation of the aircraft.

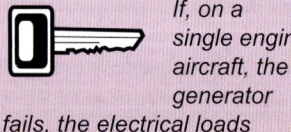

If, on a single engine aircraft, the generator fails, the electrical loads should be reduced to a minimum and a landing made as soon as is practicable.

CHAPTER 11: ELECTRICAL SYSTEMS

Next, check the field circuit-breaker to see if it has tripped. If it looks normal, consider tripping and resetting it anyway. If your aircraft system has overvoltage protection and the field circuit-breaker has not tripped, these indications may be evidence that the over-voltage relay has tripped.

Switch off the alternator master switch, shown in *Figure 11.22*, and leave it off for about two seconds. Then switch it back on again. Now check the loadmeter or centre-zero ammeter and the alternator failure warning light. If the indications are that the alternator output has been restored, switch on the services singly in order of their importance to the safe operation of the aircraft. Do this relatively slowly and deliberately, allowing sufficient time between each service selection for the load to be taken up by the alternator. Should the alternator fail again, the drill should be repeated, but this time without selecting the faulty service.

If, after carrying out the initial drill for an alternator failure, the indications are that the alternator output has been restored, restore the services singly, relatively slowly and deliberately, in order of their importance to the safe operation of the aircraft, allowing time between each selection for the load to be taken up by the alternator.

If the pilot's attempt at restoring the alternator is unsuccessful, it is advisable to reduce the electrical load as much as possible, and land as soon as is practicable. The battery will continue powering electrical equipment for a short while, but all unnecessary equipment should be shut down.

Remember that for some electrical equipment, such as the turn co-ordinator, the only way to switch off is to pull the circuit breaker. If the alternator has failed, you should turn off the alternator-half of the master switch because the field circuit of the inoperative alternator will still be drawing electric current and, if not isolated from the battery, will use up battery power unnecessarily.

Remember, too, that any radio transmissions you make will also use up battery power.

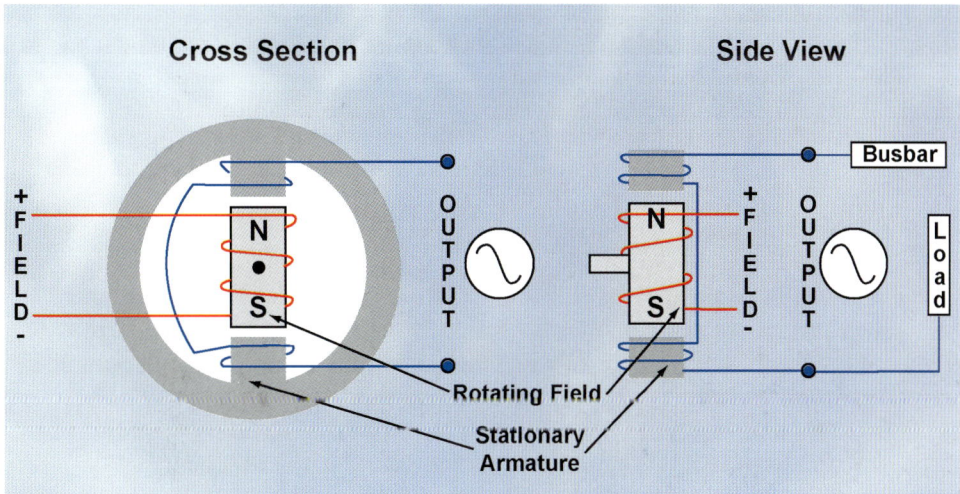

Figure 11.27 A Rotating Field Alternator.

175

CHAPTER 11: ELECTRICAL SYSTEMS QUESTIONS

Representative PPL - type questions to test your theoretical knowledge of the Electrical System.

1. If the only alternator or generator fails during flight:

    a. No action need to be taken
    b. The master switch should be turned off and the flight aborted
    c. The electrical loads should be reduced to a minimum and the flight aborted
    d. An emergency landing should be carried out as soon as possible, because the engine ignition system gets its supply from the aircraft battery

2. Continuing the flight with a 'flat' battery:

    a. Is not a concern, because the alternator will charge the battery during flight
    b. Is not recommended, because the dilute battery acid may freeze during high altitude flight
    c. Is not a concern because the battery is not essential
    d. Is not recommended, as the alternator may not fully charge the battery during normal operations

3. If a fuse blows during flight then it:

    a. Should be replaced, once only, by one of the same value
    b. May not be replaced
    c. Should not be replaced until after landing
    d. May be replaced by fuses of greater and greater value until one is found that does not blow

4. A 100 Amp/hour battery theoretically will supply 20 Amps for up to:

    a. 2 hours
    b. 3 hours
    c. 5 hours
    d. 30 minutes

5. Compared with the current flow through the starter motor, the current flow through the starter switch in the start position:

    a. Is lower
    b. Is higher
    c. Is the same
    d. Leads the voltage because of the inductive nature of the starter motor circuit

6. Connecting two 12 Volt 40 Ampere hour capacity batteries in series will provide a battery with a total capacity of:

    a. 12 Volts and 80 Ampere hours
    b. 24 Volts and 40 Ampere hours
    c. 24 Volts and 20 Ampere hours
    d. 12 Volts and 40 Ampere hours

7. Below is a schematic diagram of a light aircraft DC electrical system using a centre-zero reading ammeter. The most probable cause of the needle of the ammeter being in the centre-zero position would be that:

    a. The battery is fully charged
    b. The alternator has failed
    c. The battery is flat
    d. All electrical loads have been switched off

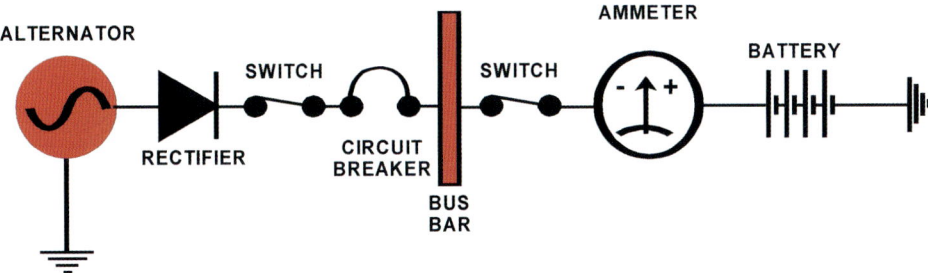

8. Below is a schematic diagram of a light aircraft DC electrical system. The most probable cause of the needle of the loadmeter being in the position shown would be that:

    a. The battery is fully charged
    b. The alternator has failed
    c. The battery is flat
    d. All electrical loads have been switched off

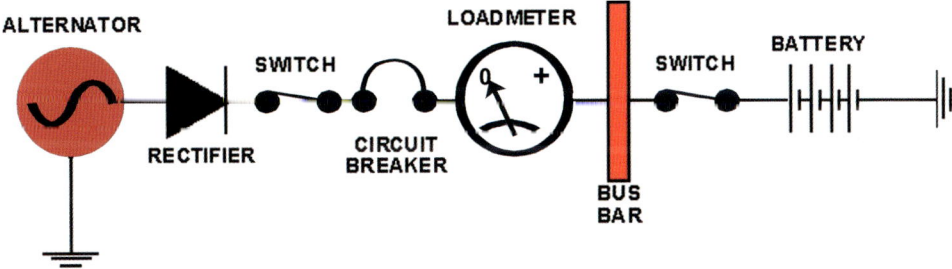

9. Secondary cells:

    a. Cannot be recharged
    b. Have an off-load voltage of 1.5 Volts when fully charged
    c. Are used in hand-held equipment like radios and torches
    d. Can be charged and discharged many times

CHAPTER 11: ELECTRICAL SYSTEMS QUESTIONS

10. A double-pole electrical system:

    a. Is not required in aircraft which are made of non-conductive materials
    b. Requires one cable taking the current from the generator or alternator to the component and another to complete the circuit back to the of the generator or alternator
    c. Has the return current flowing back through the metal of the airframe to complete the circuit
    d. Is fail-safe, and so does not require a battery

Question	1	2	3	4	5	6	7	8	9	10
Answer										

The answers to these questions can be found at the end of this book.

CHAPTER 12
VACUUM SYSTEMS

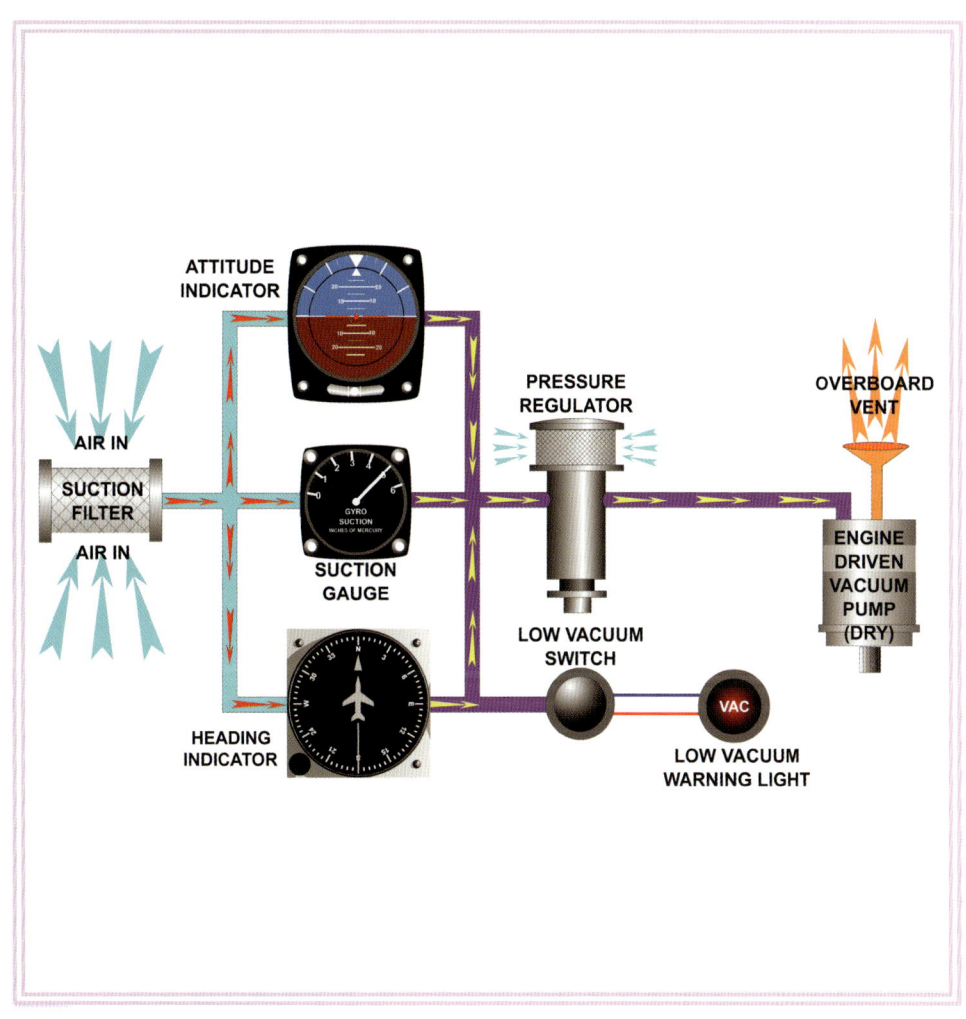

CHAPTER 12: VACUUM SYSTEM

CHAPTER 12: VACUUM SYSTEM

INTRODUCTION.

Most modern light aircraft use engine-driven suction pumps, like the one shown in *Figure 12.1*, to generate a vacuum, or, more accurately, a low pressure area which induces an airflow into the main gyro operated instruments. (There is usually at least one electrically-driven gyro instrument, usually the turn co-ordinator or turn indicator, in case of vacuum system failure.)

Figure 12.1 An Engine Driven Vacuum Pump.

A vacuum pump directs sufficient airflow onto buckets on the gyro rotor rim to drive it round.

The airflow is directed over buckets formed in the rim of the rotor of the instrument gyros and this spins them round at very high speed.

The instruments which are usually powered by the vacuum system are the Attitude Indicator, or Artificial Horizon, and the Heading Indicator, often called the Direction Indicator (DI), shown in *Figure 12.2*.

Figure 12.2 The Direction Indicator and the Attitude Indicator.

The instruments usually powered by a vacuum system are the Direction Indicator and the Attitude Indicator.

COMPONENTS.

The vacuum system consists of a means of generating a vacuum, a method of controlling the vacuum, a filter to clean the air being sucked through the instruments and the necessary pipework to join all the components together. The components forming a simplified vacuum system are shown in *Figure 12.3*.

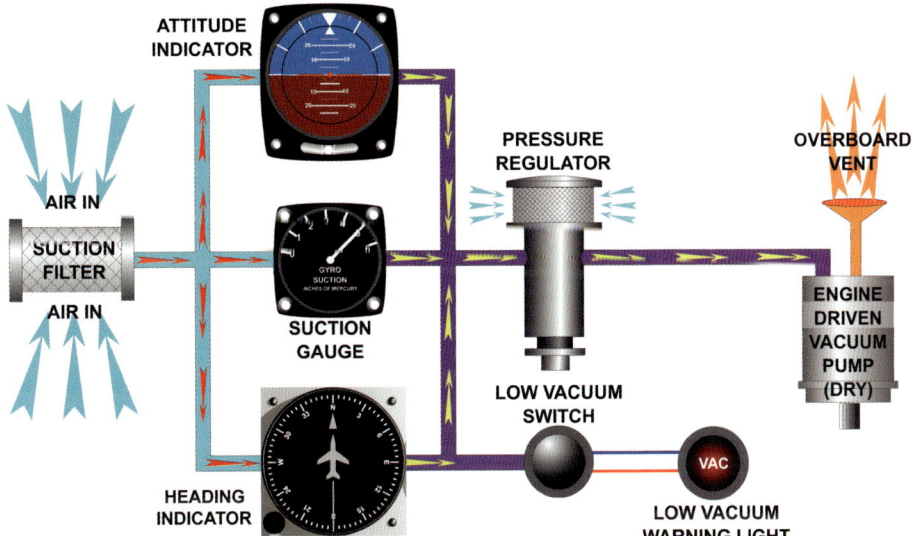

Figure 12.3 Components of a Vacuum System.

181

CHAPTER 12: VACUUM SYSTEM

Because a dry vacuum system is vulnerable to contamination by liquids, a system lubrication device is not used.

The vacuum system usually generates vacuum in one of the following ways:

- An engine driven vacuum pump
- A venturi tube placed in the airstream
- Connection to the inlet manifold of a normally aspirated engine

Venturi Tubes.

A system powered by a Venturi Tube will only work reliably when sufficient air is flowing through the venturi. This may not happen for some time after the aircraft has become airborne.

Older aircraft such as the Auster Mark 6, and the De Havilland Hornet Moth, may have a venturi tube fitted to the outside of the airframe to generate the vacuum, like the one shown in *Figure 12.4.*

The venturi tube works on the principle that when it is placed in the airstream, its effect is to accelerate the air passing through the tube. When the air accelerates its static pressure drops. At the narrowest point of the venturi the speed of the air is greatest and its static pressure lowest. Once through the narrowest point, the air decelerates and its static pressure rises once more. Placing the suction tube at the point of lowest pressure makes use of the partial vacuum thus generated.

Figure 12.4 A Venturi Tube and suction tube on an Auster Mk6.

The pilot should be aware that the system will work reliably only when sufficient air is flowing through the venturi. This may not happen for some time after the aircraft has become airborne. A certain elapsed time is required to allow the partial vacuum to become effective in driving the gyros fast enough to give the correct indications on the instruments.

Inlet Manifold Suction.

A few aircraft are fitted with an inlet manifold suction system similar to the one depicted in *Figure 12.5.*

This type of system works on the principle that whenever a normally aspirated piston engine is running, there is a depression created in the inlet manifold. This depression is greatest when the engine is just ticking over with the throttle almost fully closed, and gets less as the throttle is opened. The partial vacuum thus created at low to medium engine speeds is sufficient to drive the instrument gyros.

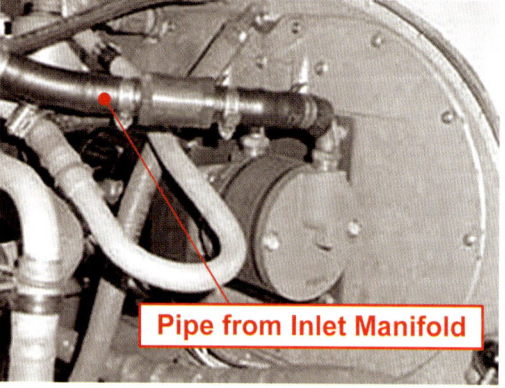

Figure 12.5 An Inlet Manifold Suction Fitting.

CHAPTER 12: VACUUM SYSTEM

Vacuum Pumps.
Some early light aircraft (those built in the 1960's) were fitted with 'wet' vacuum pumps like the one shown in *Figure 12.6*. Wet pumps used metal vanes which were lubricated with engine oil. Wet vacuum pumps wore out slowly and gradually and were very reliable.

Most modern light aircraft, since about 1970, have used what are termed 'dry' vacuum pumps to power their suction system. They are called dry because they use self-lubricating graphite vanes which rotate within an eccentric aluminium cavity.

Figure 12.6. A 'Wet' Vacuum Pump.

> One disadvantage of a dry vacuum pump is that it can fail catastrophically, and with no warning.

Dry vacuum pumps are generally very reliable. However, when they fail they do so catastrophically and without warning. To ensure that a failure cannot damage the engine's accessory drive, the pump drive incorporates a shear-coupling which will break if the pump's input torque exceeds its normal operating figure by any significant amount.

If the drive does shear, then, of course, the gyro driven instruments will cease to function. To cover for this eventuality, some aircraft have an electrically driven auxiliary vacuum pump which will provide an independent back-up in the event of engine driven pump failure.

Pressure Regulator.
Air driven gyro instruments are designed to operate with a pressure differential of about 5 inches of Mercury. Modern engine-driven vacuum pumps are designed to produce a large surplus of airflow through the instruments even when the engine is running slowly on the ground. At engine cruise RPM the pumps increase their capacity by a factor of 8 or more, and, as a consequence, if the suction were uncontrolled the gyros would be driven far too fast.

A constant airflow through the gyros is maintained by the pressure regulator, which admits sufficient air to leak into the system downstream of the gyros to limit the pressure differential across them to about 5 inches of Mercury. The pressure regulator in most systems is adjustable.

Vacuum Gauge.
The vacuum or suction gauge *(Figure 12.8)* is connected to read the pressure differential across the gyro instruments. Most suction gyro instruments require a pressure differential of 5 inches of Mercury to ensure that they operate correctly.

Filter.
Ambient air enters the system through a vacuum filter. A representative inlet filter is illustrated in *Figure 12.7*. This ensures that the gyros are fed with only clean air that has had dirt and other contaminants removed from it.

When the filter is first fitted to the system there is almost no pressure drop across it.

Figure 12.7 An Inlet Filter.

CHAPTER 12: VACUUM SYSTEM

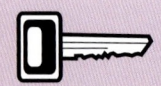

If a dry vacuum pump system is not meticulously cleaned after pump failure there is a danger that carbon fragments will re-enter it. If this happens the replacement pump will quickly fail.

SYSTEM MALFUNCTIONS.

Dry vacuum pumps are very vulnerable to contamination by liquids. The graphite vanes are designed to operate in an absolutely dry environment. If any form of liquid, for instance water, oil or engine cleaning fluid, gets into the pump, the vanes may be destroyed.

Figure 12.8 Two Types of Malfunction Warning.

If, with the gyro-driven instruments apparently functioning normally and no low vacuum warning light, the suction gauge is showing system failure, the suction gauge is probably faulty.

Another form of contamination which will quickly destroy a dry pump is carbon. When a pump fails it will do so suddenly, generating a cloud of carbon fragments which can lodge in the outlet pipes of the pump. If the system is not meticulously cleaned when a replacement pump is being fitted, there is a danger that these fragments will fall back into it. If this is the case then the replacement pump will not last long.

Pump failure can also be brought on through overheating because the pump is having to work too hard to produce the required suction level. This can be the result of a partially blocked filter, or perhaps a hose in the system collapsing or having a kink in it. If the pressure regulator is adjusted to bring the system pressure back to its normal operating level then the pump will be working harder to produce the same results in the cockpit. A pump that is working too hard will run hot and will fail prematurely.

If there is a system malfunction, there are two indications in most aircraft cockpits to warn the pilot of vacuum system failure. They are the suction gauge and the low vacuum warning light, which are illustrated in *Figure 12.8*. A further clue to system malfunction may be the erratic operation of the gyro driven instruments.

If the Direction Indicator indicates to the pilot that the aircraft is not maintaining a steady heading, while the Attitude Indicator, at the same time, shows wings level then there may be a vacuum system malfunction.

If both instruments appear to be giving erroneous indications, then it is a fair assumption that the suction system has failed. System malfunction, of course, should already have been indicated to the pilot by the suction gauge and the low vacuum warning light.

CHAPTER 12: VACUUM SYSTEM

Procedures in the event of Malfunctions.

If the pilot determines that his engine-driven vacuum pump has failed, and his aircraft is fitted with an auxiliary vacuum pump *(see Figure 12.9)*, it should be selected 'ON'. A couple of words of caution however:

Firstly, be aware that the electrical load that these pumps place on the aircraft's electrical system is quite substantial. It may be that the pilot will have to consider switching-off unnecessary electrical services if he is obliged to select the auxiliary vacuum pump.

Secondly, the strength of the magnetic field generated by the electric motor in the pump is such that it can cause compass errors.

Some aircraft may have 'inlet manifold suction' fitted as a back-up to the normal vacuum system. It should be selected as a back up as soon as the pilot determines that the engine-driven vacuum pump has failed. If there is no back-up vacuum system fitted to the aircraft, the pilot will have to revert to the limited-panel flying technique.

Figure 12.9. An Auxiliary Vacuum Pump.

> The electrical load and the strength of the magnetic field generated by the auxiliary vacuum pump electric motor are quite high. You may have to switch-off unnecessary electrical services.

CHAPTER 12: VACUUM SYSTEM QUESTIONS

Representative PPL - type questions to test your theoretical knowledge of the Vacuum System.

1. The engine driven vacuum pump is designed to produce and direct sufficient airflow:

   a. Across a turbine that, in turn, drives the gyros
   b. Through a helical impeller which drives the gyros
   c. Onto gyro rotors to drive them round
   d. Over the instrument case to move the gyro

2. The instruments usually powered by a vacuum pump system are:

   (i) Direction Indicator
   (ii) Turn Coordinator
   (iii) Attitude Indicator or Artificial Horizon
   (iv) Altimeter
   (v) Magnetic Compass

   a. (i) and (ii)
   b. (i) and (iii)
   c. (i) (iii) and (iv)
   d. (i) (iii) and (v)

3. Which of the following is not a component of a dry vacuum system?

   a. A vacuum generator
   b. A vacuum controller
   c. A filter to clean the air
   d. A system lubrication device

4. One disadvantage of a dry vacuum pump when compared to a wet vacuum pump is that:

   a. Dry pumps tend to be less reliable
   b. Dry pumps fail catastrophically with no warning
   c. Dry pumps require regular lubricating
   d. Dry pumps are tolerant of contamination

5. On your instrument panel, the suction gauge is showing system failure. However, the gyro-driven instruments appear to be functioning normally, and the low vacuum warning light is out. The fault probably lies:

   a. In the suction gauge
   b. In the suction system
   c. With the low vacuum warning light
   d. In the gyro driven instruments

Questions	1	2	3	4	5
Answer					

The answers to these questions can be found at the end of this book.

CHAPTER 13
ENGINE INSTRUMENTS

CHAPTER 13: ENGINE INSTRUMENTS

CHAPTER 13: ENGINE INSTRUMENTS

INTRODUCTION.

It would be very difficult to fly a modern light aircraft safely if there were no engine instruments to indicate to the pilot the state of the engine.

Some engine instruments, like those shown in *Figure 13.1*, are termed **engine condition indicators**. These include the Cylinder Temperature and Oil Temperature gauges and the Exhaust Gas Temperature gauge.

Engine condition indicators include the Oil Pressure and Oil Temperature gauges and the Exhaust Gas Temperature gauge.

Figure 13.1 Engine Condition Indicators.

Other engine instruments are called **performance indicators**. Within this group are placed the Engine RPM Gauge and the Manifold Pressure Gauge, examples of which are shown in *Figure 13.2*. As their name suggests, these instruments are intended to show how well the engine is performing.

Performance indicators include the engine RPM Gauge and the Manifold Pressure Gauge.

Figure 13.2 Performance Indicators.

Furthermore, without engine instruments, effective management of the engine would be impossible; the engine would not give long and efficient service and faulty operation would be commonplace.

It is, thus, essential that the engine instruments function correctly. The pilot must also be assiduous in monitoring the engine instruments.

TEMPERATURE SENSING EQUIPMENT.

Piston engines are heat engines. The power they produce is directly proportional to the heat released during the combustion of the fuel. Engine components and systems are designed to withstand certain temperatures. If the temperature limits are exceeded, the components may fail.

CHAPTER 13: ENGINE INSTRUMENTS

For safe operation, the engine temperatures must be monitored. The following temperatures are monitored on piston engines: oil, exhaust gas, and cylinder head.

Oil Temperature Gauge.

Monitoring the engine oil temperature is important from at least two points of view.

Firstly, the oil itself will retain its lubricating properties up to a certain maximum temperature. Above that temperature, the oil breaks down and the moving parts of the engine begin rubbing against each other, generating excessive heat. Engine failure quickly follows.

Figure 13.3 Oil Temperature Gauge - graduated in Degrees Fahrenheit.

Secondly, the engine expends a percentage of its power forcing the oil into the bearings. The colder the oil, the larger that percentage of power will be. If the aircraft is to perform safely, the engine oil temperature must reach a certain level before the pilot can be sure that his engine is delivering the power to the propeller that the manufacturers intended.

In a wet-sump system, oil temperature is normally sensed where the oil enters the engine, after the oil has passed through the oil cooler.

In a wet-sump lubrication system, oil temperature is normally sensed at the point where the oil enters the engine, after it has exited the oil cooler. In a dry-sump lubrication system, the oil temperature is sensed between the oil cooler and the oil tank. In a typical engine oil temperature indicating system, the indicator is powered by the aircraft electrical system. An electrical resistance-type thermo-bulb, installed in the engine oil pump housing measures the temperature of oil entering that unit. The temperature reading is usually in degrees Celsius, although the example shown in *Figure 13.3*, from a Piper Warrior, is displaying the temperature in degrees Fahrenheit. The pilot must take particular care to ensure that the oil temperature remains within limits during a prolonged climb or glide descent.

Exhaust Gas Temperature Gauge.

An exhaust gas temperature gauge, like the one shown in *Figure 13.4*, can show you whether your engine is running too lean or too rich.

The exhaust gas temperature gauge can be used to indicate mixture strength.

An exhaust-gas temperature probe is installed about four inches from the cylinder head on the exhaust system. The probe is the junction of two dissimilar metals called a thermocouple. When a thermocouple is heated, a voltage is produced which is proportional to the temperature at the junction. The gauge, itself, is a millivolt-meter which is calibrated in degrees Celsius or Fahrenheit. Fahrenheit is still common in American-made light aircraft. Although the exhaust gas temperature gauge can help in troubleshooting a problem

Figure 13.4 An EGT Guage - graduated in degrees Fahrenheit.

on the engine, it is primarily a fuel management instrument.

CHAPTER 13: ENGINE INSTRUMENTS

Cylinder Head Temperature Gauge.

The Cylinder Head Temperature Gauge, of which an example is shown in *Figure 13.5*, is an engine instrument designed to protect the engine against excessive heat.

The principle of operation of the Cylinder Head Temperature Gauge system is similar to that of the exhaust gas temperature gauge. A probe consisting of two dissimilar metals, joined together to form a thermocouple, is mounted on the engine cylinder head. The probe transmits a voltage to the gauge in the cockpit which is proportional to the temperature sensed.

The cylinder head temperature gauge obtains its temperature information from a thermocouple probe, which consists of the junction of two dissimilar metals.

Most general aviation aircraft engines sample the cylinder head temperature of the hottest cylinder. The hottest cylinder is determined by extensive flight tests carried out by the engine manufacturers. Again, the pilot must ensure that the cylinder head temperature remains within limits in a prolonged climb (risk of overheating), or a prolonged descent (risk of overcooling).

Figure 13.5 A Cylinder Head Temperature Gauge.

PRESSURE-SENSING EQUIPMENT.

Direct Reading and Remote Indicating Instruments.

The function of many aircraft engine systems relies on the action of liquids and gases whose pressure must be measured and indicated to the pilot. The gauges and indicating systems fall into two categories: Direct Reading and Remote Indicating. Both of these systems are illustrated in *Figure 13.6*.

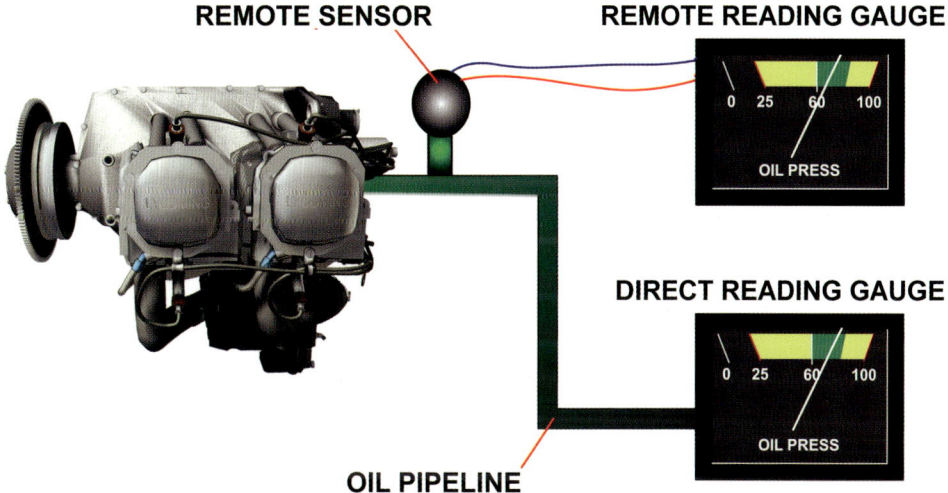

Figure 13.6 Direct and Remote Reading Gauges.

"Direct reading" describes the type of instrument used when the fluid that is being sampled is fed directly to the interior of the instrument positioned in the cockpit.

"Remote indicating" is where a separate sensing element is connected to a pressure source at some remote point and the information required is transmitted electrically to the instrument in the cockpit.

PRINCIPLE OF OPERATION OF PRESSURE SENSING INSTRUMENTS.

Pressure is defined as force per unit area. In light aircraft engine instrument terms, it is normally indicated in either pounds per square inch (PSI), bars, or inches of mercury (in. Hg).

In engine pressure measurement, we are concerned with the following terms: **Absolute Pressure** and **Gauge Pressure**. Most pressure gauges measure the difference between the absolute pressure and the atmospheric pressure. This is **Gauge Pressure**. To actually measure pressure in a system, elastic pressure sensing elements are used, in which forces can be produced by applied pressures and converted into mechanical movement. The movement of these elements can then operate a direct reading gauge or an electrical transmitter. The sensing elements commonly used are diaphragms, capsules, bellows and bourdon tubes.

Diaphragms.
Diaphragms, like the one shown in *Figure 13.7*, consist of corrugated circular metal discs which are secured at their edge, and when pressure is applied they are deflected.

Diaphragms are used to measure relatively low pressures.

Capsules.
Capsules, similar to the one shown in *Figure 13.8*, are made up of two diaphragms placed together and joined at their edges.

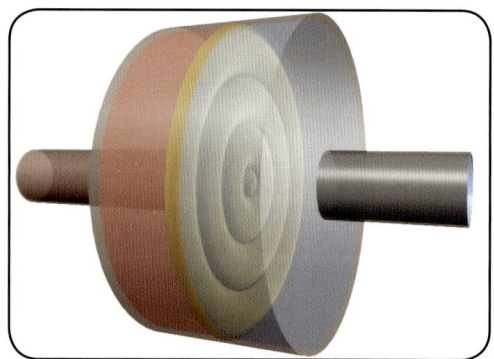

Figure 13.7 A Diaphragm.

The device thus constructed can then be used to form either a sealed chamber, which is called an aneroid capsule, or a chamber which is communicated to a pressure source, which is called a pressure capsule. Capsules, like diaphragms, are also used to measure low pressure, but capsules are more sensitive to small pressure changes.

Figure 13.8 A Capsule.

Bellows.
The bellows type element, which is shown in *Figure 13.9*, can be considered as an extension of the aneroid capsule principle. It may be used for high, low or differential pressure measurement. Note: "Aneroid" means "without liquid".

Figure 13.9 A Bellows Element.

CHAPTER 13: ENGINE INSTRUMENTS

The Bourdon Tube.

The Bourdon tube, which is represented in *Figure 13.10*, is probably the oldest of the pressure-sensing methods.

The element is essentially a length of metal tube which has an elliptical cross section. The tube is shaped to represent the letter C. One end of the tube is sealed; this is called the free end. The other end is connected to the pressure source and fixed so that it cannot move in relation to the instrument base. When pressure is applied to the tube, it tries to straighten. This movement is then magnified by levers and used to drive an indicator pointer.

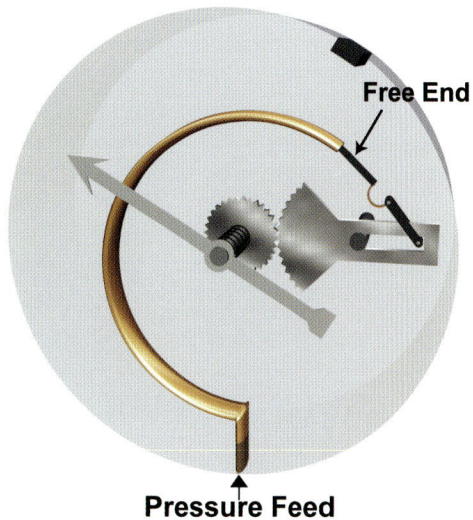

Figure 13.10 The Bourdon Tube.

The Bourdon tube can be manufactured to indicate high or low pressures, but it is normally associated with higher pressures such as engine oil pressure.

Oil Pressure Gauge.

Oil pressure is sensed at the outlet of the oil pressure pump. Normally, the oil pressure of an engine is maintained constant by an oil pressure relief valve. There are, however, situations which may affect the engine or the oil to the extent that it is beyond the ability of the pressure relief valve to maintain the oil pressure within the prescribed limits. In this situation, the oil pressure gauge, if it is used in conjunction with the oil temperature gauge, can indicate to the pilot the best course of action to retrieve the situation, (see chapter on "Lubrication".)

Figure 13.11 Oil Presure Gauge.

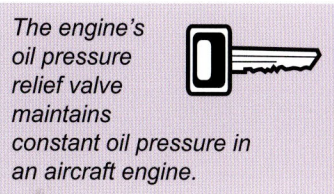

The engine's oil pressure relief valve maintains constant oil pressure in an aircraft engine.

Manifold Pressure Gauge.

The Manifold Absolute Pressure Gauge of a piston engine, like the one shown here in *Figure 13.12*, uses two bellows to measure both ambient atmospheric pressure and the pressure in the inlet manifold. Note that this gauge measures absolute pressure and in american aircraft is usually calibrated in inches of mercury (in. Hg).

When the engine is running, the manifold pressure gauge indicates less than atmospheric pressure.

Figure 13.12 The Manifold Absolute Pressure Gauge.

CHAPTER 13: ENGINE INSTRUMENTS

Earlier versions of this gauge were calibrated to read 'Boost' in pounds per square inch and called Boost Pressure Gauges.

When the engine is not running, both types of gauge, the Manifold Air Pressure Gauge and the Boost Gauge, read ambient atmospheric pressure. While the aircraft is stationary on the ground, this particular indication is called static boost.

Fuel Pressure Gauge.
A Fuel Pressure Gauge can be fitted in fuel injection fuel systems which indicates metered fuel pressure, and, by suitable calibration, will enable the mixture to be adjusted according to altitude and power setting.

FUEL CONTENTS GAUGE.

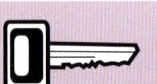
The simple float system fuel contents gauge of a light aircraft Is calibrated to be accurate at the low and empty positions.

The measurement of the quantity of fuel in the tanks of an aircraft fuel system, and its accurate indication to the pilot, is an essential requirement. The simplest form of volume indication is a float system. Early aircraft had a float which sat on the top of the surface of the fuel. Attached to the float was a piece of wire that protruded out the top of the fuel tank. As the fuel level reduced, so the wire disappeared from view.

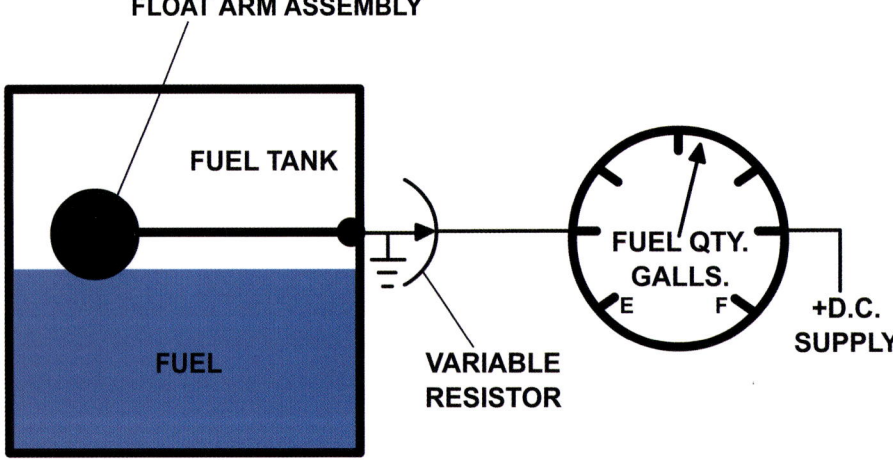

Figure 13.13 Contents Gauge System.

There have been many variations of this system. On modern light aircraft, the most common of these uses a float moving to position a wiper on a variable resistor which alters the current supplied to an indicator displacing a pointer over a scale calibrated to indicate fuel volume in gallons or litres (*Figure 13.13*).

The disadvantage of this system is that the indication is not linear, and there is no provision for making adjustments for system accuracy. The gauge is set to be accurate at the low and empty positions. The system is also subject to errors whenever the aircraft manoeuvres and the attitude changes.

CHAPTER 13: ENGINE INSTRUMENTS

FUEL FLOWMETER.

As well as measuring the quantity of fuel contained in the tanks, instruments can also indicate the rate of fuel flow. The Fuel Flowmeter can display volume flow or mass flow.

A simple flowmeter *(Figure 13.14)* can be an adaptation of a pressure gauge. This system is used in many light aircraft piston engine fuel injection systems.

THE TACHOMETER OR RPM GAUGE.

Figure 13.14 A Fuel Flowmeter.

The mechanical tachometer works on the principle of a magnetic field being induced in a drag-cup. This creates a torque which rotates a shaft attached to the pointer on the dial of the instrument.

The measurement of engine speed is of vital importance, enabling accurate control and monitoring of the engine by the pilot. On piston engines, it is crankshaft speed that is measured, in revolutions per minute (RPM). The RPM indicator is often called a Tachometer. The basic instrument for measuring engine rotational speed on piston engines is the mechanical (or magnetic) tachometer.

Mechanical Tachometer.

The mechanical tachometer consists of a flexible drive shaft and the RPM indicator. One end of the flexible drive shaft is connected to the RPM indicator in the cockpit. The other end of the drive shaft is connected to the accessory drive casing on the engine, where it is driven through gears from the crankshaft.

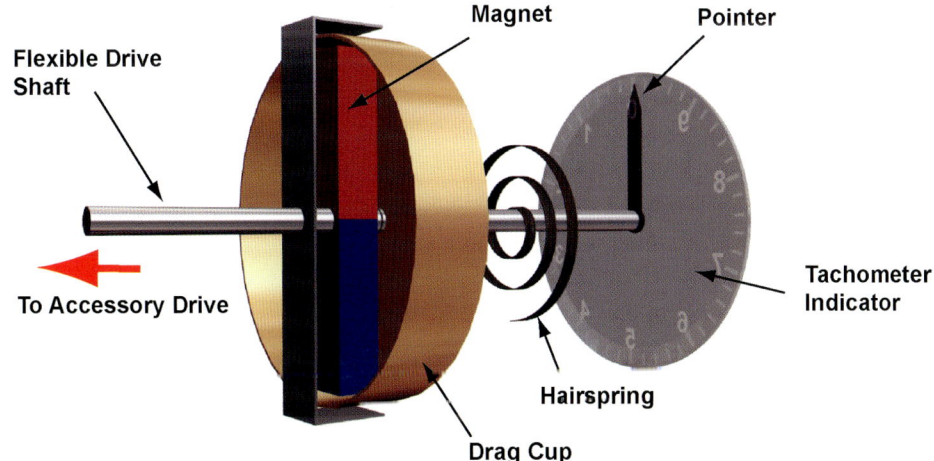

Figure 13.15 A Mechanical Tachometer.

The input drive causes a magnet to rotate inside a copper or aluminium drag-cup, inducing eddy currents in the cup.

Eddy currents are caused by the magnetic field of the moving magnet acting on the electrons of any metal in the vicinity of the magnet. The eddy currents themselves generate a magnetic field which interacts with the magnetic field of the magnet itself. This interaction causes a torque, or turning moment, which turns the drag-cup in the same direction as that of the permanent magnet's rotation.

195

A shaft extends from the drag-cup and is connected to a pointer on the dial of the RPM gauge. The turning motion of the pointer takes place against the tension of a hairspring which controls the drag-cup position and hence the position of the pointer. The flexible drive is driven slower than true engine RPM, but true RPM will be shown on the indicator. The RPM indicator incorporates compensation devices for change in temperature.

Representative PPL - type questions to test your theoretical knowledge of the Engine Instruments.

1. Where in the engine is the oil temperature read by the temperature probe which is connected to the engine's oil temperature gauge?

    a. Inside the hot sections of the engine
    b. As the oil leaves the oil tank
    c. Before the oil has passed through the oil cooler
    d. After the oil has passed through the oil cooler but before it reaches the hot sections of the engine

2. The exhaust gas temperature gauge:

    a. Is an engine instrument designed to protect the engine from excessive heat
    b. Can indicate whether the air-fuel mixture being drawn into the combustion chamber is too lean or too rich
    c. Requires power from the D.C. bus-bar
    d. Does the same job as the cylinder head temperature gauge

3. The cylinder head temperature gauge:

    a. Obtains its temperature information from the hottest engine cylinder, by means of a probe consisting of two dissimilar metals joined together
    b. Is primarily a fuel management instrument
    c. Requires alternating current to power the instrument needle
    d. Obtains its information from a probe which is installed about four inches from the cylinder head on the exhaust system

4. A simple float-system fuel-contents gauge of a light aircraft:

    a. Is designed to be accurate at all stages of flight
    b. Is totally linear throughout its entire range
    c. Is calibrated to be accurate at the low and empty positions
    d. Accurately indicates the weight of fuel in the tank, only while the aircraft is either in straight and level flight, or parked on level ground

CHAPTER 13: ENGINE INSTRUMENTS QUESTIONS

5. The mechanical tachometer:-

   a. Uses the friction generated in a drag-cup to rotate a shaft, which is connected to a pointer, against the pressure of a hairspring
   b. Is driven directly from the prop shaft. Gears reduce the speed of rotation so that a generator can be used to produce a voltage proportional to shaft speed which is indicated on a gauge calibrated in RPM
   c. Is driven directly from the alternator drive
   d. Works on the principle of a magnetic field being induced in a drag-cup and creating a torque which rotates a shaft attached to the pointer on the dial of a tachometer

Question	1	2	3	4	5
Answer					

The answers to these questions can be found at the end of this book.

CHAPTER 14
PRESSURE INSTRUMENTS

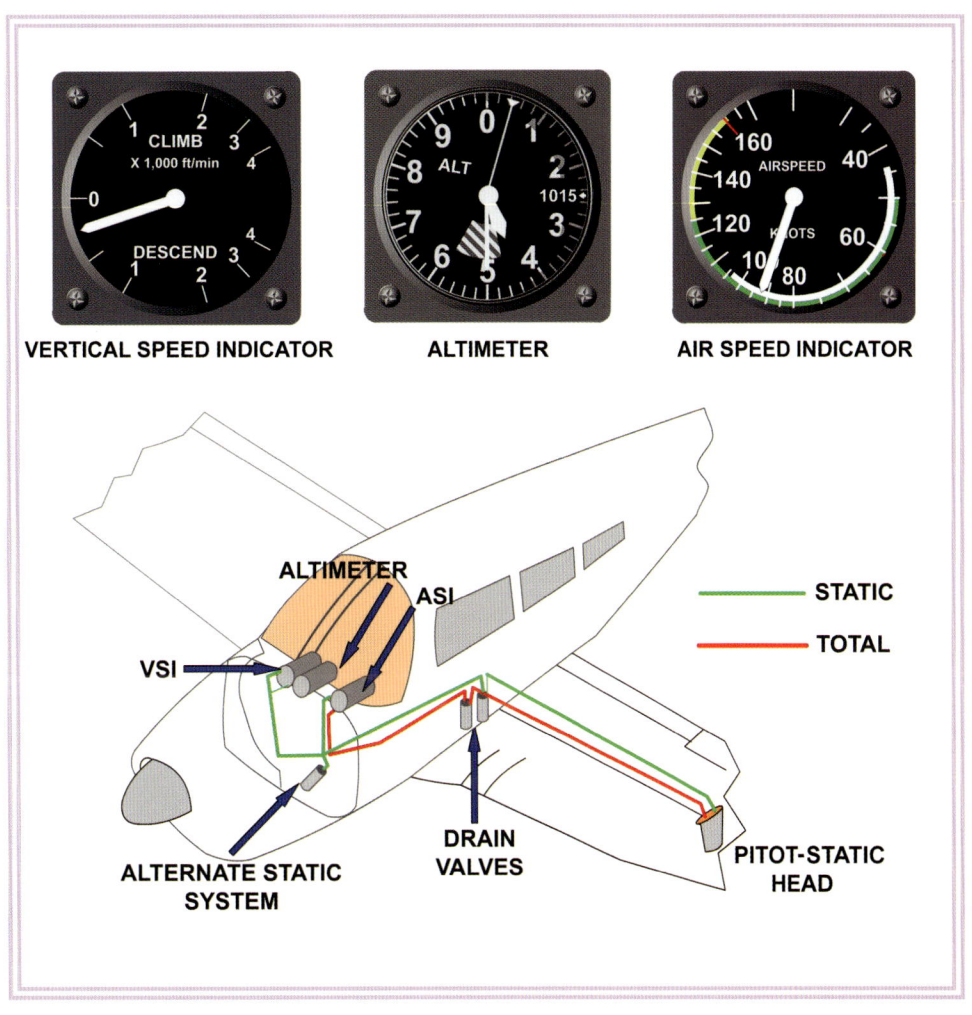

CHAPTER 14: PRESSURE INSTRUMENTS

CHAPTER 14: PRESSURE INSTRUMENTS

INTRODUCTION.

Pressure instruments are so-called because they rely on variations in air pressure in order to function. The pressure instruments are the Airspeed Indicator, the Altimeter, and the Vertical Speed Indicator.

The air pressure sensed by these instruments is either **atmospheric (static) pressure**, or **dynamic pressure** (generated by moving air), or a combination of both. (**Static pressure** + **dynamic pressure** is called **total pressure**).

An aircraft at rest on the ground, in still air, is subject to normal atmospheric pressure, which acts equally in all directions and, therefore, exerts an equal pressure on all parts of the aircraft, as illustrated in *Figure 14.1*. This atmospheric pressure is known as **static pressure**.

An aircraft in flight at a given airspeed, while still subject to the **static pressure** which prevails at its flight level, experiences an additional pressure on the leading edges due to the velocity of the air relative to the aircraft.

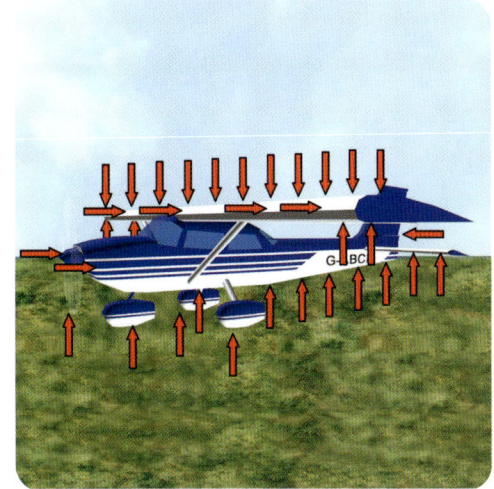

Figure 14.1 Static Pressure acts in all directions.

The leading edges of a wing, in flight, encounter a pressure consisting of static pressure plus dynamic pressure, which is known as total pressure.

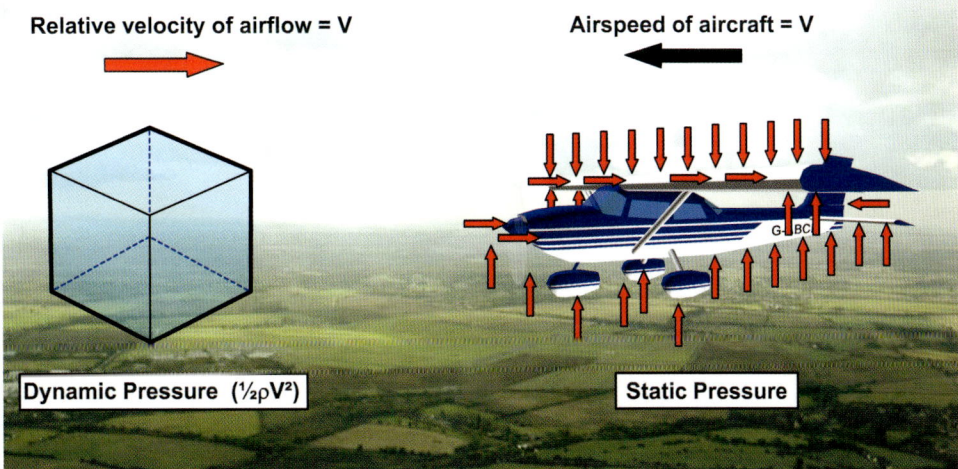

Figure 14.2 The leading edges of an aircraft in flight experience static pressure + dynamic pressure.

This additional pressure is called **dynamic pressure**. The value of dynamic pressure depends both on the speed of the aircraft through the air, and on the density of the air. The leading edges, therefore, encounter a **total pressure** consisting of **static plus dynamic pressures**. This situation is illustrated by *Figure 14.2*. You can feel this type of **"total pressure"** for yourself if you hold your hand out of a moving car with the flat of your hand facing the direction of motion.

201

CHAPTER 14: PRESSURE INSTRUMENTS

Static pressure, dynamic pressure and total pressure are sensed by the pressure instruments through the pitot-static system. ("pitot" is pronounced "pee - toe").

PITOT-STATIC SYSTEM.

The **pitot-static system**, an example of which is shown in *Figure 14.3*, transmits total and static pressures to the Airspeed Indicator (ASI), and static pressure to the Altimeter and the Vertical Speed Indicator (VSI).

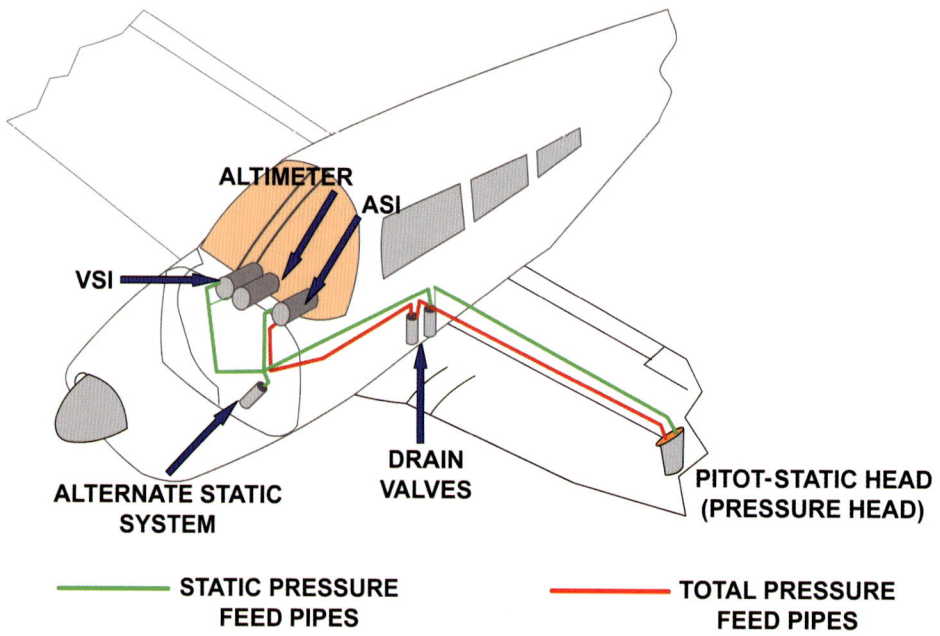

Figure 14.3 The Pitot-Static System.

Total and static pressures are sensed by what is known as a **pitot head** or **pitot-static head** *(see Figures 14.3 and 14.4)* situated where it is not likely to be affected by turbulent airflow caused by projections from the aircraft skin.

To prevent water entering too far into the system, and affecting the accuracy of the instrument readings, drain valves may be fitted at the lowest point in the pipelines. Part of the pre-flight check should involve opening these valves to allow any moisture to escape. Ensure that the valves are closed properly after the check. Let us now look more closely at how **total pressure** and **static pressure** are sensed.

Note: The **pitot tube** is named after Henri Pitot, who invented the instrument in 1732.

Pitot Heads.
An open-ended tube parallel to the longitudinal axis of the aircraft is used to sense the **total pressure** (**static** plus **dynamic**). This device is called a **pitot tube** which is mounted in the **pitot head**.

The open end of the tube *(see Figures 14.4 and 14.5)*, faces into the moving airstream, while the other end leads to the airspeed capsules in the air speed indicator. The moving airstream is thus brought to rest in the tube.

CHAPTER 14: PRESSURE INSTRUMENTS

The airstream generates the extra dynamic pressure which together with the static pressure already in the tube provides the required total or pitot pressure *(see Figure 14.5)*. An electric anti-icing heater coil is usually incorporated in the pitot tube which is controlled from a switch in the cockpit.

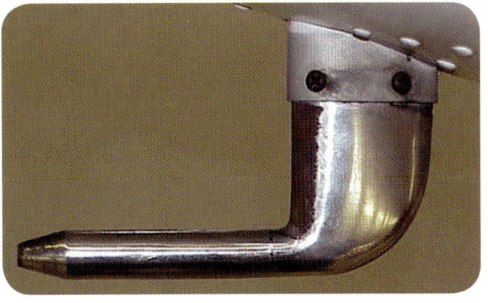

Figure 14.4 Pitot Head.

Static Sources and the Pitot Static Head.

Static pressure sources are often incorporated in the total pressure measuring head, which is then known as a **pitot-static head** or **pressure head** *(see Fig 14.5)*. The static holes take the form of holes drilled in the side of the Pitot-Static Tube and are connected with separate pressure lines leading to all the pressure instruments. (In many aircraft, static pressure is also sensed by static vents located in the sides of the fuselage, as shown in *Figure 14.6*.) Total pressure and static pressure pipelines leading from the **pitot-static head** and passing through the wing and fuselage, transmit the pressure to the gauges on the instrument panel.

If the alternate static source of an unpressurised aircraft is from within the cockpit, then the pressure sensed will normally be lower than normal outside static pressure, due to aerodynamic suction.

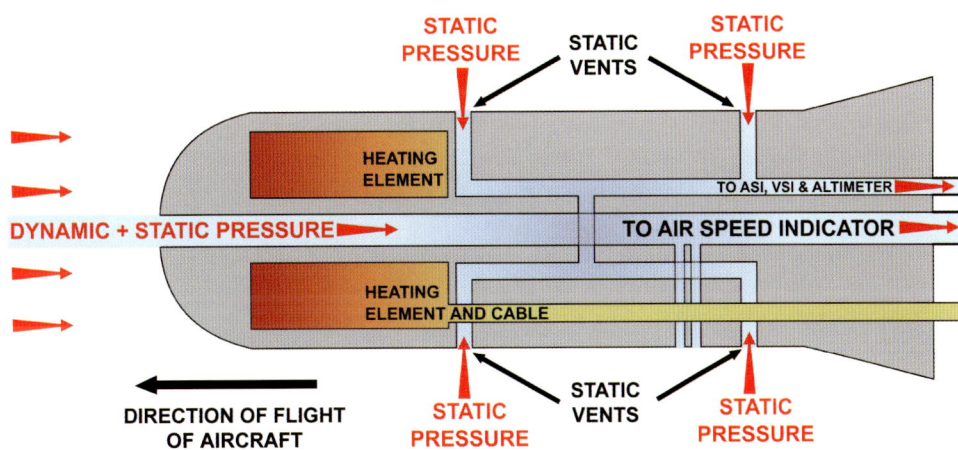

Fig.14.5 Total Pressure and Static Pressure Sensing in a Pitot-Static Head (Pressure Head).

With an unpressurised aircraft, if the alternate static source is within the cockpit, the pressure sensed will normally be lower than external static pressure because of aerodynamic suction.

Position Error.

You will doubtless appreciate that if, due to turbulent airflow in the region of the pressure sources, the pressures sensed are not representative of the true value of total and static pressures, the pressure-dependent instruments will not read correctly. This type of error is called position error (or alternatively 'pressure' error). Approximately 95% of the position error associated with a pitot-static head is produced by turbulence about the static vents.

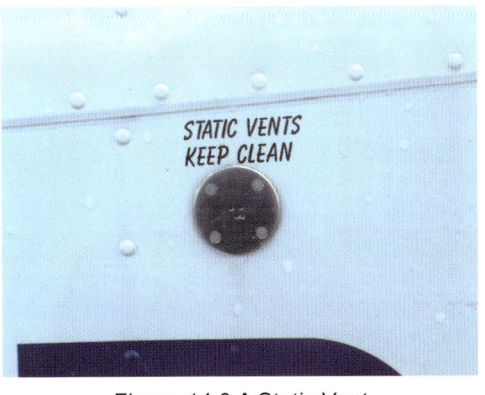

Figure 14.6 A Static Vent.

It was in order to minimise position error due to turbulence that static vents, located in the fuselage sides, were introduced as a source of static pressure instead of the pitot-static head. About 90% of the combined pressure head position error is eliminated by using a separate total pressure head and static vents. A fuselage mounted static vent is shown on the previous page in *Fig.14.6*.

There is usually some place on the airframe, quite often on the side of the fuselage, where true (or nearly true) static pressure can be sensed over the whole speed range of the aircraft.

AIRSPEED INDICATOR (ASI).

Principles of Operation of the ASI.
Earlier in this chapter we learnt that, whereas an aircraft on the ground in still air is subject only to static pressure, the leading edges of the aircraft in forward flight are subject to an additional pressure which we called dynamic pressure. This results in a total pressure on the leading edges. This relationship of pressures can be expressed mathematically as:

The total pressure sensed by the forward facing hole in the pitot tube on an aircraft in flight consists of dynamic pressure plus static pressure.

Total Pressure = Dynamic Pressure + Static Pressure

or P_{total} = Dy + S

Both total pressure and static pressure are fed to the airspeed indicator (ASI). The ASI is, in fact, a differential pressure gauge which measures the airspeed as a function of dynamic pressure. Within the ASI, dynamic pressure is "isolated" from total pressure in order to indicate airspeed. Dynamic pressure is a measure of airspeed, because of the mathematical relationship:

Dynamic Pressure (Dy) = $½ρV^2$

where **V** is true airspeed and **ρ** is the density of the surrounding air. So the ASI measures airspeed by measuring dynamic pressure, and displaying the result (usually in knots) on a suitably calibrated scale. You can see from the equation how indicated airspeed is hardly ever equivalent to true airspeed. Though the indicated airspeed, which is given by the dynamic pressure, is a function of true airspeed (**V**), it is also a function of the air density (**ρ**). But air density decreases with altitude, so at any given airspeed, **V**, the indicated airspeed will decrease with altitude, as **ρ** decreases. We will look at this more closely later on.

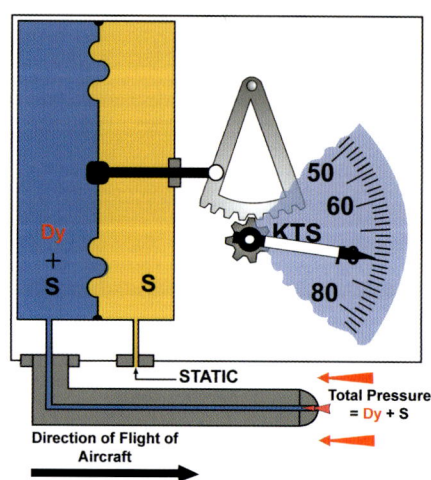

Figure 14.7 A Simple Air Speed Indicator.

Construction of The Airspeed Indicator (ASI).
In principle, the simple ASI can be considered as an airtight box divided by a flexible diaphragm, with total pressure from the pitot head (**Dy +S**) fed into one side of the diaphragm and static pressure, **S**, to the other side, as shown in *Figure 14.7*.

CHAPTER 14: PRESSURE INSTRUMENTS

The pressure difference across the diaphragm is therefore the dynamic plus the static pressure (total pressure), minus the static pressure, which leaves the dynamic pressure as the resultant pressure acting on the diaphragm.

Accordingly, the diaphragm is deflected by an amount proportional solely to this dynamic pressure, its movement being transmitted by a system of levers to the indicating needle on the face of the ASI. Note that static pressure is common to both sides of the diaphragm, and so does not influence diaphragm movement.

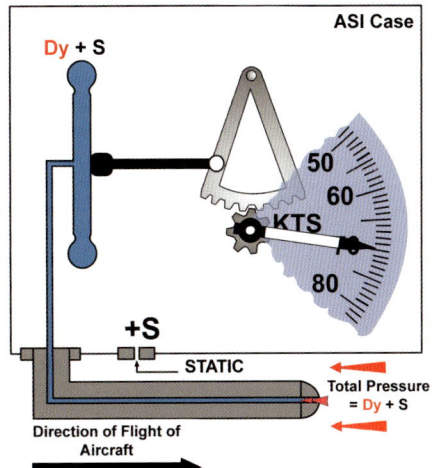

Figure 14.8 A Practical Airspeed Indicator (ASI).

In practice, as shown in *Figure 14.8*, the static pressure is fed into the hermetically-sealed case of the ASI, the total pressure **(Dy + S)** being piped to a thin metal capsule capable of expansion and contraction.

Note that the pressure differential between the inside and outside of the capsule is exactly the same as it was across the diaphragm in *Figure 14.7*. Expansion or contraction of the capsule will, therefore, be proportional to the changes in dynamic pressure produced by changes of airspeed.

The capsule movements are transmitted by a temperature-compensated magnifying linkage to the ASI pointer which indicates airspeed on the face of the instrument.

Airspeed Indicator Calibration.

We mentioned earlier that the dynamic pressure of the air, which is recorded as airspeed by the ASI, is equal to $\frac{1}{2} \rho V^2$. From this relationship we can see that dynamic pressure depends not only on the speed of the airflow but also on the air density, ρ. This density varies with temperature and pressure and, thus, with altitude.

Even ignoring any instrument or position errors, the ASI will indicate the true airspeed of an aircraft in only ISA, sea-level conditions.

The ASI is calibrated to read true airspeed (TAS) at an air density of 1 225 grammes per cubic metre which would prevail in ICAO Standard Atmosphere (ISA) mean sea level conditions; that is, at a pressure of 1013.25 millibars (hectopascals) and a temperature of +15° Celsius, in dry air conditions. No allowance is made in the calibration of the ISA for the change in density which occurs with change of altitude.

It follows that, even if there were no other errors, the ASI will indicate TAS only when ISA mean sea level air density exists at its flight level; that is to say when the aircraft is flying in air having a density of 1 225 grammes per cubic metre. This density value can be found only at, or close to, sea level, depending on how much the actual atmospheric conditions deviate from ISA. Thus, a pilot always has to calculate his true airspeed by correcting the indicated airspeed by a factor which depends on his altitude and the ambient temperature.

Airspeed Indicator Errors: Instrument Error.

Manufacturing imperfections can result in small instrument errors which may be determined on the ground, under laboratory conditions, by reference to a datum instrument. A correction card can then be produced for the speed range of the instrument.

Airspeed Indicator Errors: Position Error.

Position error arises mainly from the sensing of incorrect static pressure, because of turbulence, as indicated in *Figure 14.9*.

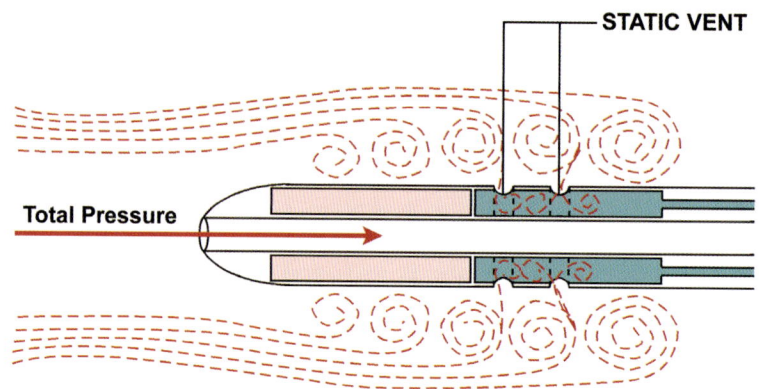

Figure 14.9 Position Error in a Pitot-Static Tube.

Position errors throughout the speed range are determined by the aircraft manufacturer during the test flying programme for a particular aircraft type. It is not unusual to compile a joint correction card for position and instrument errors and place it in the aircraft near the Airspeed Indicator (ASI), unless the errors are very small. **Indicated airspeed** corrected for instrument error and position error is known as **calibrated airspeed**.

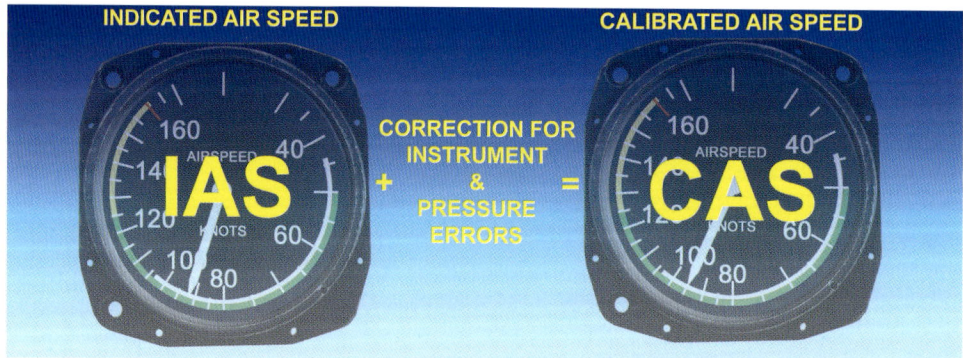

Figure 14.10 Indicated Airspeed (IAS) and Calibrated Airspeed (CAS).

Indicated Airspeed and Calibrated Airspeed.

The Indicated Airspeed (IAS) plus or minus instrument error correction and position error correction gives us the Calibrated Airspeed (CAS). Often, for practical purposes, IAS is treated by pilots as CAS, when no error table is fitted on the instrument panel.

Airspeed Indicator Errors: Density Errors.

Unless the air around the aircraft is at the calibration density of 1 225 grammes per cubic metre, which can only occur near sea level, the Airspeed Indicator (ASI) cannot correctly indicate True Airspeed (TAS).

CHAPTER 14: PRESSURE INSTRUMENTS

From the formula: **Dynamic Pressure = ½ρV²**, we know that dynamic pressure is proportional to density, **(ρ)**, as well as airspeed, **(V)**. So, at altitude, where **ρ** is less than at sea level, the dynamic pressure generated by a given airspeed will be less than that for the same airspeed at sea level. ASI capsule expansion will consequently be proportionately less, and the IAS will be lower than TAS. The difference between IAS and TAS is called density error. This density error will, therefore, cause the ASI to 'under read' at altitude.

True Airspeed (TAS).
It is possible, using a navigation computer, to correct for density error, computing **TAS** from the **CAS**, which we mentioned earlier.

TAS = CAS ± Density Error.

A pilot must use TAS for his navigation calculations, not IAS. You will learn how to calculate TAS in the "Navigation and Radio Aids" volume.

Colour Coding on the Airspeed Indicator.
The aerodynamic loads on an airframe are a function of Indicated Airspeed (IAS) only. Therefore, ASIs have coloured arcs on their dials to indicate specific speed ranges (*Figure 14.11*).

Figure 14.11 Colour Coding on the Airspeed Indicator.

The white arc denotes the flap operating range, from stall speed at maximum all up weight in the landing configuration, up to the 'maximum flaps extended speed' which is known as V_{FE}.

A climb with a blocked static source and normal pitot air will result in the ASI under-reading.

The green arc denotes the normal operating speed range, from stall speed at maximum all up weight, with flaps up and wings level, up to V_{NO}. V_{NO} is usually called the normal operating limit speed or, sometimes, maximum structural cruising speed. V_{NO} should not be exceeded, except in smooth air conditions.

Operations at indicated air speeds in the green arc should be safe in all conditions, including turbulence.

The yellow arc at the higher end of the scale denotes the caution range, extending from V_{NO}, up to V_{NE}, which is the never exceed speed. The aircraft should be operated at indicated air speeds in the caution range in smooth air only.

A red radial line denotes V_{NE}.

CHAPTER 14: PRESSURE INSTRUMENTS

BLOCKAGES AND LEAKS OF THE ASI CIRCUIT.

The Pitot Tube.

If a pitot tube becomes blocked, the ASI will constantly indicate the airspeed at which the aircraft was flying at the moment the pitot tube became blocked. Subsequent changes in actual airspeed, then, will not be recorded on the ASI.

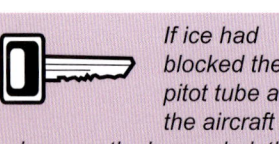
If ice had blocked the pitot tube and the aircraft subsequently descended, the readings on the Altimeter and the VSI would read correctly but the ASI would under-read.

In level cruise, a pitot tube blockage will lock in the existing total pressure and any change in actual airspeed will not be registered. However, a slow leakage in the pitot pipeline is likely, so that the Indicated Airspeed may gradually decrease.

If an aircraft with a blocked pitot tube and a clear static source is climbing, the Indicated Airspeed will increase because the pressure locked inside the ASI capsule remains constant while the static pressure of the air surrounding the capsule decreases.

Conversely with a blocked pitot tube, the Indicated Airspeed will decrease during a descent with blocked pitot tube.

A leak in the pitot tube causes the ASI to under-read, in all phases of flight.

The effect of a leak in a static pipeline is normally to make the ASI over-read. This is because, almost inevitably, the pressure surrounding the pipeline will be lower than static, because of aerodynamic suction.

Note that readings of the Altimeter and Vertical Speed Indicator will not be affected by a blocked pitot tube. These instruments will continue to read correctly, as their operation depends only on static pressure read from the static vents.

Blocked Static Vents.

A static vent in a pitot head is more exposed to icing conditions and is, therefore, more likely to become obstructed than is a fuselage-mounted static vent.

A blocked static source during descent will mean that the previous (higher altitude) static pressure surrounding the ASI's total pressure capsule will be lower than it should be, so that the ASI will over-read. This could be dangerous, because the aircraft could be nearer stall speed than the ASI is indicating.

A climb with blocked static source will result in the ASI under-reading.

ASI SERVICEABILITY CHECKS BEFORE FLIGHT.

The following checks of the ASI and pressure heads and/or vents should be made before flight.

- Pitot head covers and static vent plugs must be removed and stowed aboard the aircraft.

- The pitot tubes and static vents should be checked to ensure that they are free from obvious obstructions such as insects.

- The pitot head heater must be checked to see that it is operating normally.

- The instrument dial glass of the ASI must be clean and undamaged.

(Remember that, during the initial part of the take-off run, the ASI needs to be checked to ensure that it is registering an airspeed. If it is not, the take-off should be aborted.)

THE ALTIMETER.

Principle of Operation.

The pressure altimeter is a simple, reliable, pressure gauge calibrated to indicate height, altitude or flight level above a pressure datum which is set on the altimeter subscale.

The pressure at any level within the atmosphere depends on the weight of the column of air which extends vertically upwards from that level, to the outer limit of the atmosphere. The higher an aircraft is flying, the shorter is the column of air above it and, consequently, the lower is the atmospheric pressure acting on the aircraft.

Figure 14.12 The Altimeter.

So, by measuring the atmospheric (static) pressure, the altimeter measures the aircraft's vertical distance above the set datum level.

The relationship between pressure and height is not a linear one, so calibration of the altimeter is not a simple matter.

Calibration of the Altimeter.

With all the variables and changing relationships that abound in the atmosphere, it becomes necessary to assume certain average or 'standard' atmospheric conditions. We can then base the altimeter calibration formulae on these, and apply corrections appropriate to the deviations from standard conditions which occur with position and time. The conditions used for calibration are usually those assumed for the ICAO Standard Atmosphere (ISA) which are illustrated in *Figure 14.13, overleaf*.

Several assumptions are made in constructing the ISA. The first assumption is that at mean sea level (MSL) the pressure is 1013.25 millibars, the temperature is +15° Celsius, while the density is 1 225 grams per cubic metre.

The second assumption is that from mean sea level up to 11 kilometres, or 36 090 feet, the temperature falls at a rate of 6.5° Celsius per kilometre or 1.98° Celsius per 1 000 feet.

CHAPTER 14: PRESSURE INSTRUMENTS

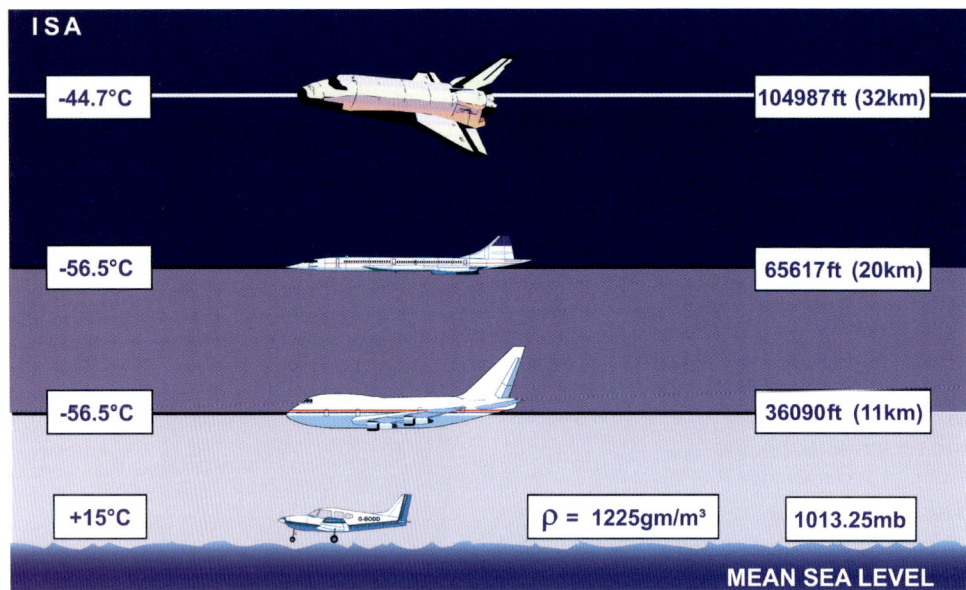

Figure 14.13 The ICAO Standard Atmosphere (ISA).

The third assumption is that from 11 kilometres to 20 kilometres, or from 36 090 feet to 65 617 feet, the temperature is constant at - 56.5° Celsius. And finally, from 20 kilometres to 32 kilometres, or from 65 617 feet to 104 987 feet, ISA conditions assume that the temperature rises at 1° Celsius per kilometre, or at 0.3° Celsius per 1 000 feet. Having made these assumptions, the pressure corresponding to any given level in the ISA can be calculated from standard calibration formulae.

Graphs or tables can be produced showing height in terms of pressure under standard conditions. These tables can be used for the manufacturer's calibration of the altimeter scale. Basically, the laboratory calibration consists of applying a series of pressures to the altimeter and checking that the instrument indicates the respective levels which correspond to these pressures in the ISA. Any discrepancies, if within certain agreed tolerances, would be listed over the operating height ranges as instrument errors. In the lower atmosphere where most light aircraft operate, pilots may assume atmospheric pressure falls at the rate of approximately 1 millibar for every 30 feet gain in altitude.

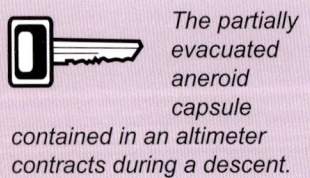 *The partially evacuated aneroid capsule contained in an altimeter contracts during a descent.*

Construction of the Simple Altimeter.

Atmospheric pressure is fed into the case of the instrument from the static source.

As height increases, static pressure decreases and the sealed, partially evacuated, aneroid capsule expands under the control of a leaf spring. Conversely, as height decreases, static pressure increases and the capsule contracts.

A mechanical linkage magnifies the capsule's expansion and contraction and converts them to a rotational movement of a pointer over the height scale on the dial. *Figure 14.14* shows how the linkage of a simple altimeter works, but the actual arrangements are, of course, much more complex.

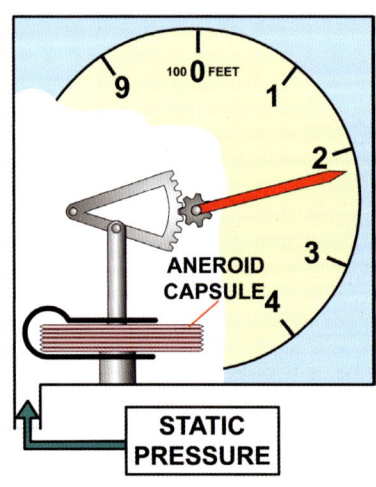

Figure 14.14 A Simple Altimeter.

CHAPTER 14: PRESSURE INSTRUMENTS

Altimeter or Subscale Setting Knob.
The simple altimeter has a setting knob which is geared to the pointer. With this knob the pointer may be set to read zero with the aircraft on the ground, so that, when airborne, the altimeter indicates height above aerodrome elevation.

Alternatively, the pointer can be set, (before flight) to the aerodrome elevation so that, when airborne, the instrument shows the aircraft's vertical distance above mean sea level (MSL). Vertical distance above MSL is known as altitude.

The Sensitive Altimeter.
Most aircraft are now equipped with the sensitive type of altimeter, the mechanism of which is similar to that depicted in *Figure 14.15*. The principle of operation of the sensitive altimeter is similar to that of the simpler altimeter but there are some refinements, as defined in *Figure 14.15*.

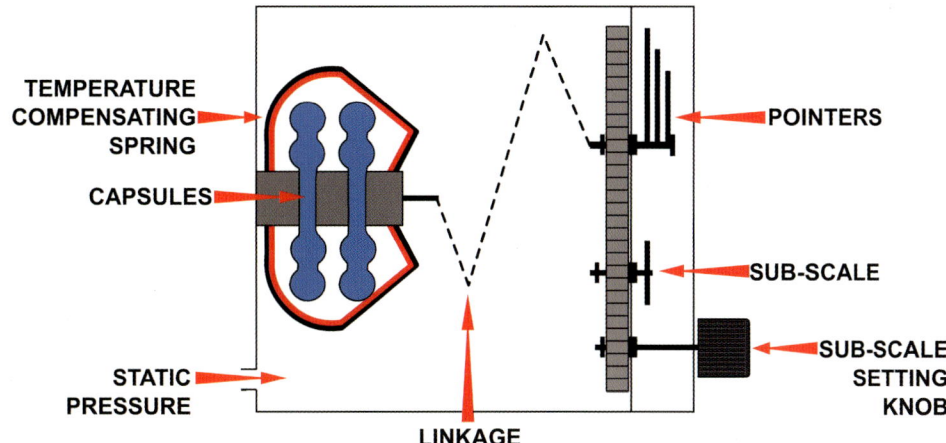

Figure 14.15 A Sensitive Altimeter Mechanism.

For instance, in the sensitive altimeter, a bank of two or three capsules gives the increased movement necessary to drive the counters and pointers. Also, jewelled bearings are fitted in the linkage, reducing friction and, thus, the associated lag in indication.

Finally, and probably most importantly, a variable datum mechanism, or subscale, is built in. This, with the aid of a setting knob, enables the instrument to be set to indicate vertical distance above any desired pressure datum.

The variable datum mechanism can be used to set the desired pressure level (say, 1005 millibars) on a pressure sub-scale on the face of the instrument. As the pilot turns the subscale setting knob, the altimeter reading changes until, when the procedure is completed with the subscale showing the desired 1005, the altimeter indicates the aircraft's vertical distance above this pressure level.

A change in altitude or surface pressure has no direct effect on the reading of the subscale; the subscale reading changes only when the pilot turns the setting knob. British altimeters have a subscale setting range between 800 and 1050 millibars.

CHAPTER 14: PRESSURE INSTRUMENTS

Reading Accuracy.

The type of three-pointer instruments shown in *Figure 14.16* give a much more sensitive indication of height or altitude than the single pointer altimeter, but they suffer from the disadvantage that they can be easily misread. The altimeters pictured are reading 24 300 feet.

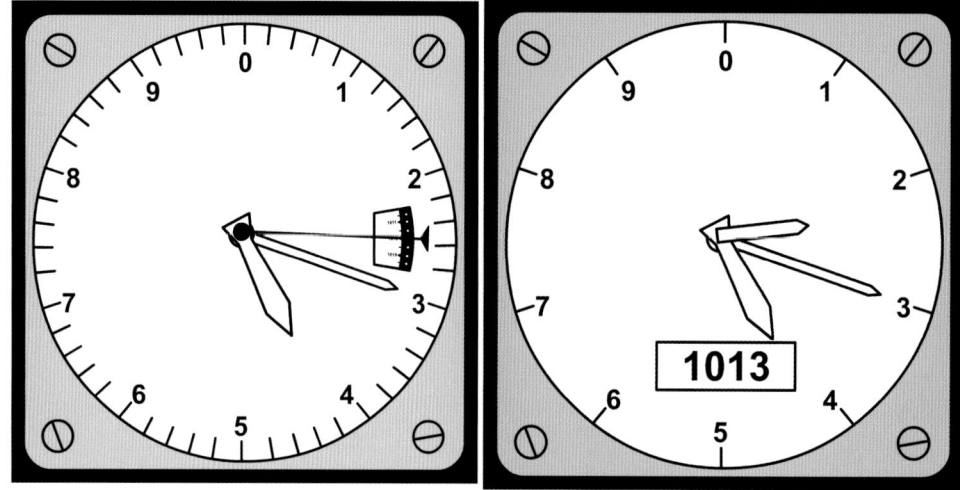

Figure 14.16 Three Pointer Altimeters.

It is not difficult for the pilot to make a reading error of 10 000 feet on the three-pointer altimeter, particularly during a rapid descent under difficult conditions with a high workload. Although a light-aircraft pilot is not likely to find himself in such a situation, accidents have occurred as a result of such altimeter misreading at lower altitudes. Various modifications to altimeter pointers, and the incorporation of warning systems in some aircraft, have consequently been tried with the objective of preventing accidents. For instance, for commercial aircraft, and aircraft which habitually fly at higher altitude, a striped warning sector appears as the aircraft descends through the 16 000 foot level *(see Figure 14.18)*.

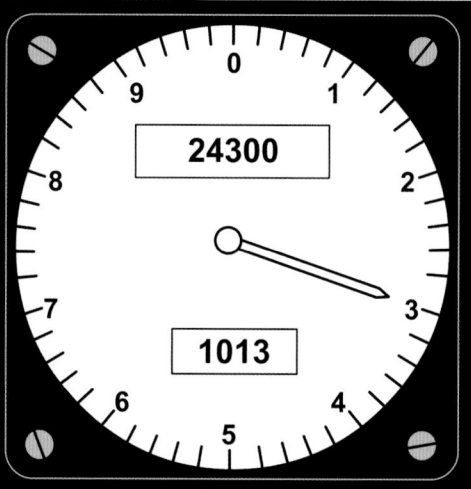

Figure 14.17 Counter Pointer Altimeter.

However, the greatest safety advance for commercial aircraft has been the introduction of the counter-pointer altimeter, shown in *Figure 14.17*, which gives a much more positive indication than either of the three-pointer dials shown in *Figure 14.16*. Compare the simplicity of this altimeter's indication, which is also showing 24 300 feet. Although this altimeter has only one pointer, the main reading is digital, and the pointer indicates only hundreds of feet. Evidently, this type of altimeter is designed for high-altitude flight only. In light aircraft, the 3-pointer altimeter is still the most commonly used. So take great care that you do not misread your height or altitude.

CHAPTER 14: PRESSURE INSTRUMENTS

ALTIMETRY DEFINITIONS.

There follow several common definitions used in the subject of altimetry.

Transition Altitude.

Figure 14.18 defines the differences between Transition Altitude, Level and Layer The Transition Altitude is the altitude at, or below which, the vertical position of an aircraft is expressed and controlled in terms of altitude. An altimeter reads altitude when the correct QNH or Regional Pressure Setting is set in the altimeter subscale.

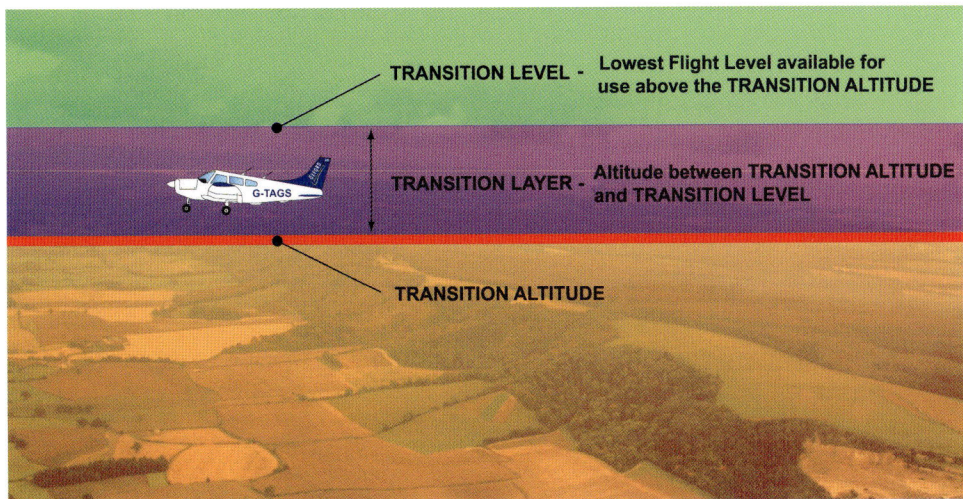

Figure 14.18 Transition Altitude, Transition Layer and Transition Level.

In the United Kingdom, the transition altitude is 3 000 feet except in or beneath airspace specified in the UK AIP, for example, in the London TMA, the transition altitude is 6000 feet.

Transition Level.

The Transition Level is the lowest Flight Level available for use above the Transition Altitude. At and above Transition Level, vertical position is expressed as a Flight Level. The altimeter reads Flight Level when the Standard Pressure Setting (SPS) of 1013.25 hectopascals (millibars) is set in the altimeter subscale.

Transition Layer.

This is the space between Transition Altitude and Transition Level. When climbing through Transition Layer, the aircraft's vertical position is expressed in terms of Flight Level; when descending through the Transition Layer the aircraft's vertical position is expressed in terms of altitude. Pilots must not assume that separation exists between the Transition Altitude and the Transition Level.

Flight Levels.

Flight Levels are surfaces of constant pressure related to the SPS of 1013.25 hectopascals (millibars). Flight Levels are separated by specified pressure intervals. In the United Kingdom, these intervals are 500 feet between Transition Level and Flight Level 245, while from Flight Level 250 upwards the intervals are 1 000 feet. A Flight Level is expressed as the number of hundreds of feet which would be indicated, at the level concerned, by an ISA-calibrated altimeter on which the subscale is set to 1013.25 millibars, or 29.92 inches of mercury. For example, at 4 500 feet the Flight Level would be FL 45.

CHAPTER 14: PRESSURE INSTRUMENTS

ALTIMETER SETTINGS.

It is important to understand that the altimeter indicates vertical distance above the pressure level set on its subscale. In the UK, pressure settings are expressed in millibars(mb). The unit commonly used throughout Europe is the hectopascal (hPa). The mb and the hPa are identical in value. The hPa is the standard JAA unit. There are four altimeter pressure settings: QFE, QNH, Regional Pressure Setting (RPS) and the Standard Pressure Setting (SPS): 1013.25 hPa (mb).

QFE.

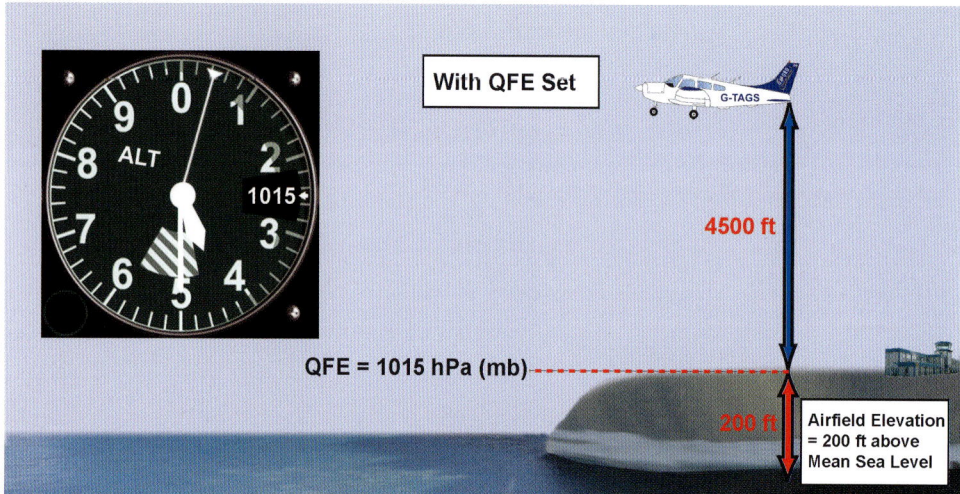

Figure 14.19 With QFE set, altimeter reads height.

QFE is the aerodrome level pressure which, when set on the altimeter subscale, will cause the altimeter of an aircraft on the ground to read zero, assuming there is no instrument error.

In flight, with QFE set, the altimeter will indicate **height** above the aerodrome QFE reference datum, provided ISA conditions prevail between aerodrome level and the aircraft, and that there are no other altimeter errors. In practice, QFE is used mainly for circuit-flying and for flight in the immediate vicinity of a pilot's home aerodrome.

QNH.

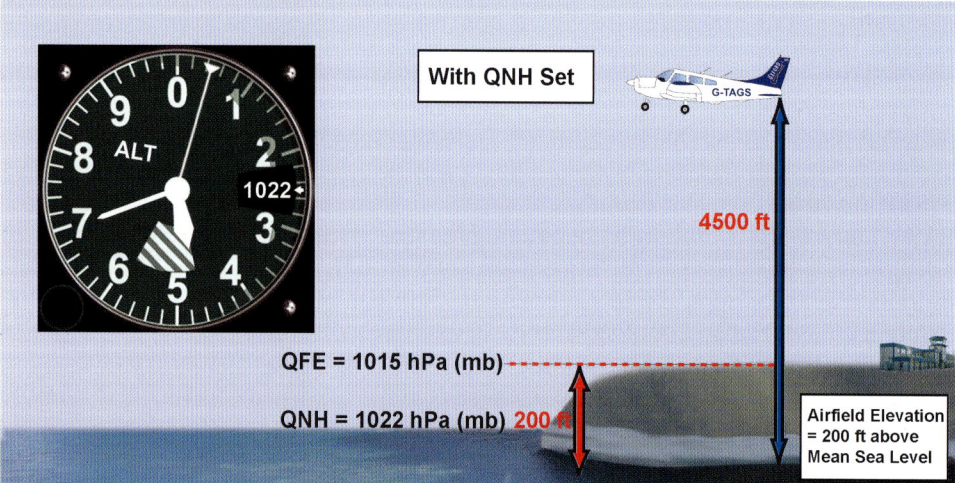

Figure 14.20 With QNH set, altimeter reads altitude.

214

CHAPTER 14: PRESSURE INSTRUMENTS

Aerodrome QNH is the observed aerodrome pressure converted to the pressure of Mean Sea Level in accordance with the ICAO Standard Atmosphere.

With aerodrome QNH set on the subscale, the altimeter of an aircraft on the ground at the aerodrome indicates **elevation**, that is, the height of that part of the aerodrome above Mean Sea Level.

With QNH set, the altimeter of an aircraft, in flight, will indicate **altitude**, that is, vertical distance above Mean Sea Level.

Regional Pressure Setting (or Forecast QNH).
With QNH set, the altimeter reads the vertical distance of the aircraft above Mean Sea Level in the local area. Because the number of aerodromes reporting actual QNH is limited, the UK is divided up into Altimeter Setting Regions, *(see Figure 14.26, p220).*

The Met Office forecasts the lowest QNH for each of these regions every hour, and sends these Regional Pressure Setting forecasts to Air Traffic Service Units. When flying cross-country below the Transition Altitude, a pilot will normally set the Regional Pressure System for the area he is transiting, for example, Cotswold Regional Pressure System.

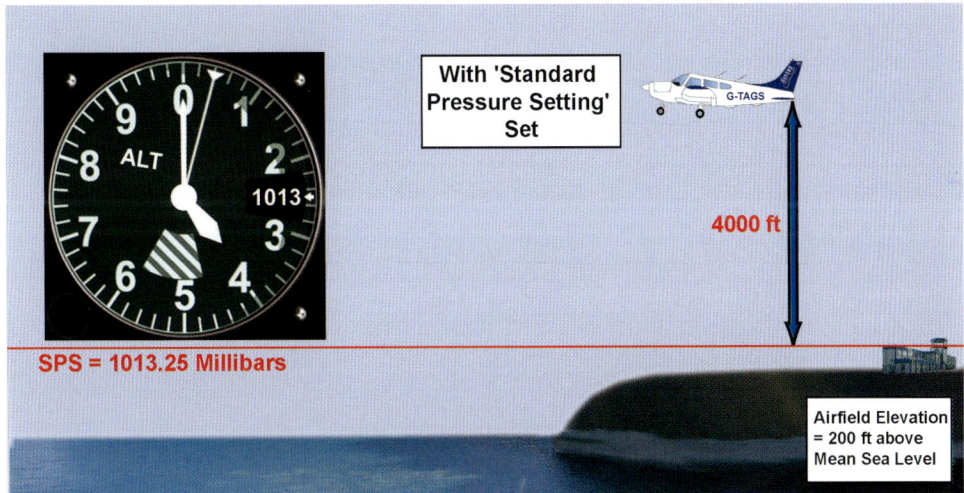

Figure 14.21 Altimeter Reading with SPS Set.

Standard Pressure Setting (SPS).
When the Standard Pressure Setting of 1013.25 hectopascals or millibars is set on the subscale, the altimeter shows the aircraft's vertical separation from that pressure level wherever it may lie. This setting is used in the United Kingdom above the Transition Altitude or Transition Level. An aircraft's vertical separation from the 1013.25 hectopascal pressure level is known as its "pressure altitude". The "pressure altitude" of an aircraft is expressed in terms of Flight Levels as already detailed on page 213. With all aircraft above the Transition Level having their altimeter subscales set to 1013, air traffic controllers can ensure safe vertical separation between aircraft under their control.

CHAPTER 14: PRESSURE INSTRUMENTS

ALTIMETER ERRORS.

Time Lag.
With many types of altimeter, the response to change of altitude is not instantaneous. This causes the altimeter to under-read in a climb and over-read in a descent. The lag is most noticeable when the change in altitude is rapid and prolonged.

Instrument Error.
Manufacturing imperfections, including friction in the linkage, cause errors throughout the operating range. The errors are kept as small as possible by adjustments within the instrument, and the calibration procedure ensures that they are within permitted tolerances. Residual errors may be listed on a correction card.

Position (or Pressure) Error.
Position error is largely due to the inability of the altimeter to sense the true static pressure outside the aircraft. The error is usually small. Position Error is covered on Page 203.

When flying in air which is warmer than the ICAO Standard Atmosphere, the altimeter will under-read.

Manoeuvre-induced Error.
Manoeuvre-induced error is caused mainly by transient fluctuations of pressure at the static vent during change of pitch attitude.

Temperature Error.
Even with no other errors at all, the pressure altimeter will not indicate the true altitude unless the surface temperature and lapse rate of the column of air are those which were assumed in the calibration of the altimeter, (i.e. ISA conditions).

When flying in air which is colder than the ISA, the altimeter will over-read.

When flying in air which is warmer than the ISA, the altimeter will under-read.

If a static vent became blocked during level flight in icing conditions and the aircraft subsequently climbed, the ASI would under-read and the readings on the Altimeter and the VSI would remain unchanged.

Where the temperature at cruising level deviates from ISA assumptions, an approximate correction can be made with most navigational computers. The correction will, however, only be approximate since vertical temperature variations are not known.

Density Altitude.
Density altitude can be defined as the altitude in the ICAO Standard Atmosphere at which the density prevailing at the location of measurement would occur. It is a convenient parameter by which to measure engine performance.

If an unpressurised aircraft has an alternate static source within the cockpit, the alternate static pressure will be lower than the outside static source.

Density altitude can be obtained by use of an airspeed correction chart or by navigational computer.

If the prevailing density decreases, the location at which the density is measured will correspond to a greater altitude in ISA. Thus, density altitude increases.

Blockages And Leaks.
If the static source becomes blocked, the altimeter will not register any change in altitude. In the case of a static source blockage, the altitude at which the blockage occurred will remain the indicated altitude, regardless of any climb or descent.

CHAPTER 14: PRESSURE INSTRUMENTS

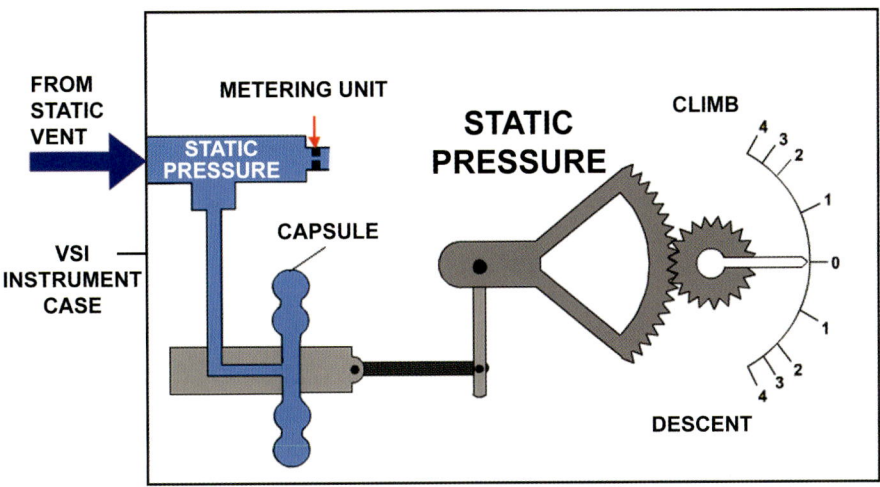

Figure 14.22 A VSI-indicated level flight.

A fracture or leak in the static line within the cockpit of an unpressurised aircraft will normally result in the altimeter over-reading. The pressure in the cockpit will be lower than ambient pressure because of aerodynamic suction.

Checks Before Take-off.

The following checks of the altimeter should be made before flight.

The instrument dial glass must be clean and undamaged and the correct altimeter setting must be set on the subscale.

If you are operating from a controlled aerodrome, Air Traffic Control will pass you the correct altimeter setting, normally aerodrome QNH.

THE VERTICAL SPEED INDICATOR.

The Vertical Speed Indicator (VSI) senses static pressure, like the altimeter but is so constructed that it indicates rate of climb or descent in hundreds, or thousands of feet per minute.

Principle of Operation of the VSI.

The construction of the VSI is shown in *Figure 14.22*. When an aircraft departs from level flight, the static pressure acting on an aircraft changes accordingly. The VSI measures the pressure difference between each side of a metering unit within the instrument case. In level flight, the pressures on each side of the metering unit are the same, (see Figure 14.22). But whereas, during a climb or descent, the static vent immediately senses the change of atmospheric pressure, the static pressure in the VSI instrument case changes at a lower rate because of the presence of the metering unit. The difference in pressure across the metering unit will last throughout a climb or descent, causing a rate of climb or descent to be indicated. Once the aircraft is in level flight again, the pressure across the metering unit equalises and the VSI indicates 0; that is, level flight.

The principle of operation of the vertical speed indicator is that it compares static pressure, sensed through a direct static vent, with that in the instrument's case, sensed through a metered vent.

The Construction of the VSI.

As is shown in *Figure 14.22*, static pressure from the static vent is fed to a capsule located within the airtight case of the VSI instrument. The instrument case itself is also fed with static pressure from the same vent, but this feed comes through a restricted metering unit. Thus as the static pressure changes, the pressure within the case surrounding the capsule changes at a slower rate than that within the capsule.

For example, if the aircraft is climbing, because of the action of the metering unit the pressure in the capsule will be less than that in the VSI instrument case. The capsule will, therefore, be compressed, this compression being converted by a suitable linkage to a pointer which indicates the rate of climb. On the other hand, if the aircraft is descending, the pressure in the case will be less than the pressure in the capsule, causing the capsule to expand. This expansion will move the linkage so that the pointer indicates the rate of descent on the VSI instrument face.

VSI Presentation.

Two types of presentation are available: a linear scale and a logarithmic scale. It will be obvious from comparing the two instruments depicted in *Figure 14.23*, that the logarithmic scale, shown on the right, is easier to read at the lower rates of climb and descent.

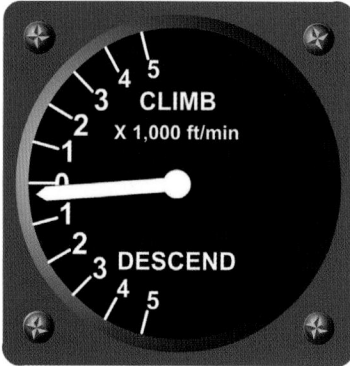 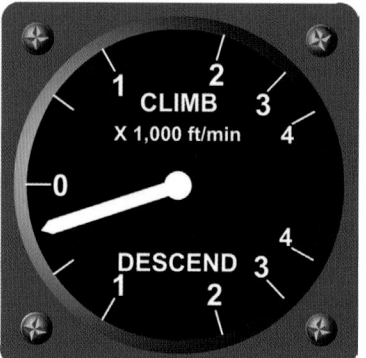

VSI with linear scale reading 250 ft/min descent.   **VSI with logarithmic scale reading 250 ft/min descent.**

Figure 14.23 Presentation of the VSI.

THE ERRORS OF THE VSI.

Instrument Error.
Instrument error is due to manufacturing imperfections.

Position (or Pressure) Error.
If the sensing of static pressure changes is subject to position error, the Vertical Speed Indicator will wrongly indicate a climb or descent when speed is suddenly changed. This error is most noticeable during take-off acceleration.

Manoeuvre-induced Error.
Any fluctuations in pressure at the static vent during attitude changes will cause the instrument to indicate a false rate of climb or descent. Consequently, most VSIs have a small counterbalance weight included in the linkage, the inertia of which causes delays in the indications of changes in vertical speed during manoeuvres.

Time Lag.
The VSI pointer takes a few seconds to steady because of the time taken to build up a steady pressure difference during climb or descent.

There will also be a time lag when the aircraft transits to level flight because of the time taken for the pressures to equalise. This error is most noticeable after a prolonged climb or descent, especially at a high rate.

The Instantaneous VSI

To overcome the problem of lag, the instantaneous, or IVSI, incorporates an accelerometer unit which responds quickly to a change of altitude. In a descent, as shown in *Figure 14.24*, the piston in the vertical acceleration pump immediately rises in the cylinder and increases the pressure in the capsule.

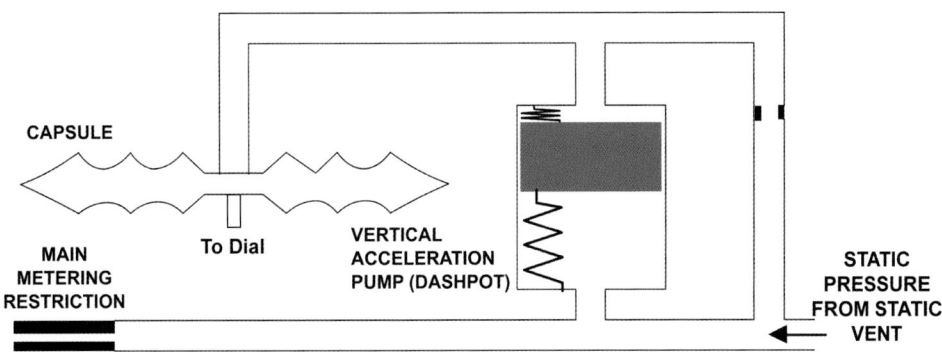

Figure 14.24 ISVI Mechanism showing Descent.

The capsule therefore, expands almost immediately and the pointer will give an instant indication of descent. If the vertical acceleration ceases, after a few seconds the piston will slowly descend to its original position, but by this time the correct differential pressure between the capsule and the case will have been set up and the correct rate of descent will continue to be shown.

> If the static vent leading to the Vertical Speed Indicator becomes blocked while an aircraft is descending, the indicator will return to zero after a short delay.

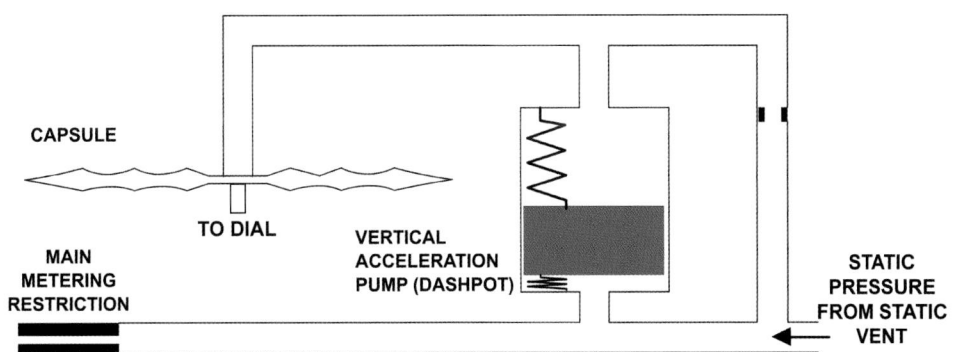

Figure 14.25 The Mechanism in a Climb.

In a climb, as shown in *Figure 14.25*, the piston in the vertical acceleration pump immediately falls in the cylinder and decreases the pressure in the capsule. The capsule contracts and the pointer will give an instant indication of climb. If the vertical acceleration ceases, after a few seconds the piston will slowly rise to its original position. But by this time the correct differential pressure between the capsule and the case will have established itself and the correct rate of climb will continue to be shown.

Blockages and Leaks.

Any blockages of the static line or vent will cause the needle to return to zero after a short delay. If the supply of air to the VSI is blocked, it is highly probable that the other pressure instruments, the Air Speed Indicator and the Altimeter, will also be affected.

Checks Before Take-off.

The following checks of the vertical speed indicator should be made before flight.

CHAPTER 14: PRESSURE INSTRUMENTS

- The instrument dial glass must be clean and undamaged and the instrument should read zero.

- In flight, the accuracy of the VSI may be checked against the altimeter and a stop watch during a steady climb or descent.

- The VSI should indicate zero when in level flight.

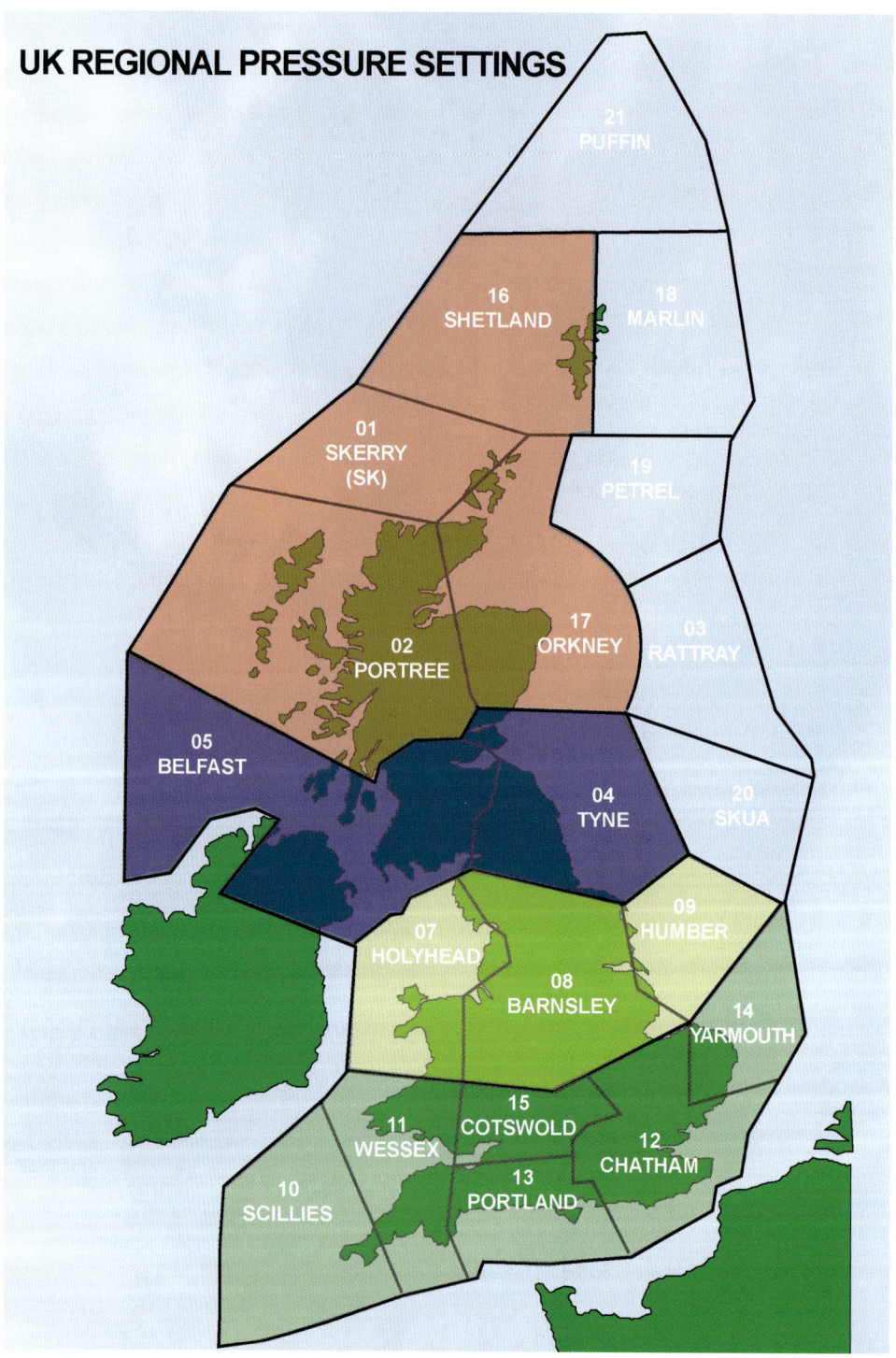

Figure 14.26 UK Regional Pressure Settings (RPS).

CHAPTER 14: PRESSURE INSTRUMENTS QUESTIONS

Representative PPL - type questions to test your theoretical knowledge of Pressure Instruments.

1. If, while an aircraft is descending, the static vent leading to the Vertical Speed Indicator becomes blocked, the indicator will:

    a. continue to show the same reading
    b. indicate a climb
    c. indicate a descent
    d. show a zero reading, after a short delay

2. When an aircraft is in flight, the pressure sensed by the forward facing hole in the pitot tube is:

    a. static pressure only
    b. total pressure plus dynamic pressure
    c. dynamic pressure plus static pressure
    d. dynamic pressure only

3. The principle of operation of the Vertical Speed Indicator (VSI) is that it:

    a. compares static pressure in a capsule, sensed through a direct static vent, with that in the instrument's case, sensed though a metered vent. The VSI is, thus, able to detect the rate of change of static pressure with height
    b. compares total pressure from the pitot tube with static pressure from the static vents. The VSI is calibrated to show the difference between the two as a vertical speed in feet per minute
    c. compares dynamic pressure from the pitot tube with static pressure from the static vents. The VSI is calibrated to show the difference between the two as a vertical speed in feet per minute or metres per second
    d. senses total pressure only, from the pitot tube, and converts the change in total pressure with height into a rate of climb or descent, measured either in feet per minute or metres per second

4. If, during descent, the static sources to the Airspeed Indicator and Altimeter become blocked by ice:

    a. the Airspeed Indicator will over-read and the Altimeter will under-read
    b. the Airspeed Indicator will under-read and the Altimeter will over-read
    c. both instruments will over-read
    d. both instruments will under-read

5. Ignoring any instrument or position errors, in what conditions will the Airspeed Indicator indicate the True Airspeed of an aircraft?

    a. at any altitude or temperature
    b. in ICAO Standard Atmosphere, sea-level conditions only
    c. at any altitude, provided that the temperature lapse rate is in accordance with ISA
    d. at any altitude, but only when ISA conditions prevail

CHAPTER 14: PRESSURE INSTRUMENTS QUESTIONS

6. If an unpressurised aircraft has an alternate static source within the cockpit, the alternate static pressure:

   a. must be selected immediately there is any fluctuation of the Airspeed Indicator
   b. will be higher than the outside static source
   c. will be unreliable because of ingress of moisture from the pitot head
   d. will be lower than the outside static source

7. An Altimeter:

   a. contains a barometric capsule, connected to a total pressure source, that contracts during a descent
   b. contains an aneroid capsule connected to a static pressure source. The capsule contracts during a descent
   c. contains a barometric capsule that expands during a descent
   d. contains a partially evacuated capsule that expands during a descent

8. If a static vent became blocked during level flight in icing conditions and the aircraft subsequently climbed, the readings on the altimeter, the VSI and the ASI would:

	Altimeter	VSI	ASI
a.	remain unchanged	remain unchanged	under-read
b.	remain unchanged	under-read	over-read
c.	under-read	remain unchanged	over-read
d.	over-read	over-read	under-read

9. If the power supply to the pitot heater failed during flight in icing conditions and the aircraft subsequently descended, the readings on the Altimeter, the VSI and the ASI would, if ice had blocked the pitot (total pressure) tube:

	Altimeter	VSI	ASI
a.	read correctly	under-read	over-read
b.	under-read	read correctly	over-read
c.	read correctly	read correctly	over-read
d.	read correctly	read correctly	under-read

Question	1	2	3	4	5	6	7	8	9
Answer									

The answers to these questions can be found at the end of this book.

CHAPTER 15
GYROSCOPIC INSTRUMENTS AND THE MAGNETIC COMPASS

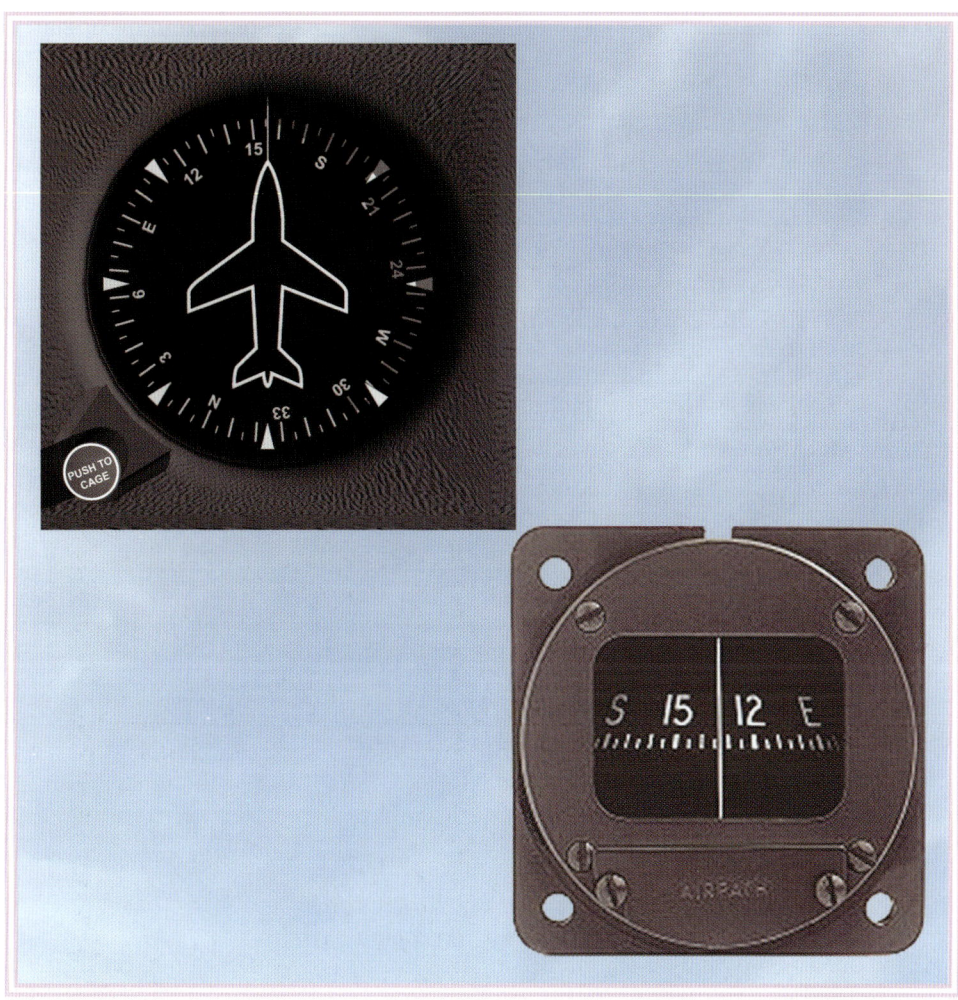

CHAPTER 15: GYROSCOPIC INSTRUMENTS & THE MAGNETIC COMPASS

CHAPTER 15: GYROSCOPIC INSTRUMENTS & THE MAGNETIC COMPASS

THE GYROSCOPE.

A **gyroscope** is a spinning **rotor** or **wheel** whose spin axis is, itself, free to rotate in one or more directions. Any rotating body exhibits gyroscopic phenomena. The Earth is a gyroscope, spinning about an imaginary axis passing through the geographic poles. A child's 'top' is a gyroscope and so is an aircraft's propeller when it is turning. The rotor which forms an aircraft instrument gyroscope may be little more than an inch in diameter, spinning at perhaps 25 000 RPM.

Gimbal Rings and Freedom of Movement.

Gimbal rings, or **gimbals**, are the rotor supports which give the rotor's spin axis its own freedom of movement.

Figure 15.1 shows a **rotor** mounted in two gimbal rings, the **outer gimbal** being supported by a fixed frame. The rotor itself is a metal disc which rotates about its axis (marked as **x-x** in the diagram). The rotor spin axis is supported by bearings in a ring called the **inner gimbal**. The **inner gimbal** is in turn supported by bearings mounted inside the **outer gimbal**. Both the **inner gimbal** and the **outer gimbal** are free to rotate within the fixed frame.

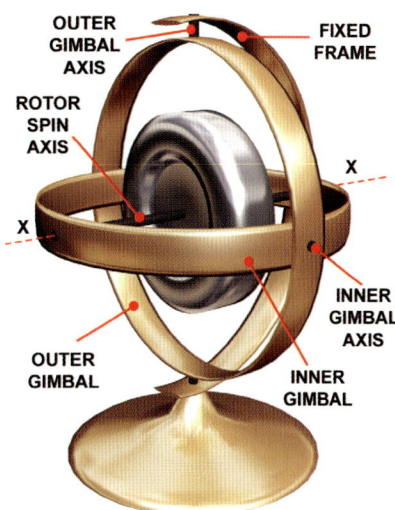

Figure 15.1 A Gyroscope.

The three **axes** of the **rotor**, **inner gimbal** and **outer gimbal** run **perpendicularly** to one another. The **outer gimbal** has **one degree of freedom**, but its **axis** has **none**. The **inner gimbal** has **two degrees of freedom**, while its **axis** has **one degree of freedom**. The **rotor**, itself, has **three degrees of freedom**, and its **axis** has **two**. It is the **interaction of these three axes** together with the gyroscopic phenomena of **rigidity** and **precession** (see below) which allow the gyroscope to be used in aircraft instruments which indicate **turning**, **attitude** and **position**.

THE FUNDAMENTAL PRINCIPLES OF THE GYROSCOPE.

Rigidity.
A spinning gyroscope at all times tends to maintain its axis pointing in a fixed direction in space. Wherever a **gyroscope** is moved, its **spin axis** will continue to point in the same direction, unless acted upon by an external force. This property is called **rigidity** or **gyroscopic inertia**. **Rigidity** is a measure of the gyroscope's tendency to resist changes to its orientation in space. This resistance to directional change is a function of the gyroscopes's angular momentum.

> A gyro maintains its axis pointing in a fixed direction in space unless it is acted on by an external force. This is called 'rigidity in space'.

Factors Affecting Gyroscopic Rigidity.
There are three factors, shown in *Figure 15.2 overleaf*, which affect the **rigidity** of a gyroscope. They are the **rotor mass**, the **effective radius** at which the mass acts and the **speed of rotation**. An increase in **mass**, **effective radius** and **rotational speed** will all increase the **rigidity** of the gyroscope.

> There are three factors which affect the rigidity in space of a gyroscope. They are the rotor mass, the effective radius at which the mass acts and the speed of rotation.

CHAPTER 15: GYROSCOPIC INSTRUMENTS & THE MAGNETIC COMPASS

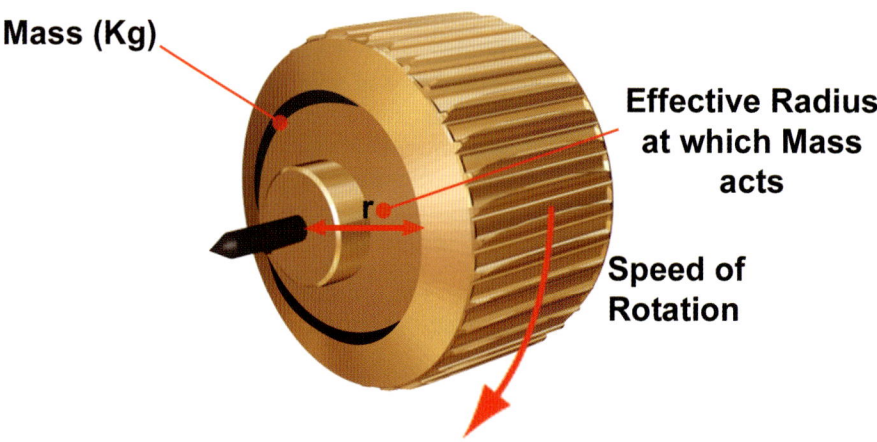

Figure 15.2 Factors affecting Rigidity.

In order to increase the **effective radius** at which the mass acts, the material of the rotor is distributed so that the greater part of its mass is near its rim.

Gyroscopic Precession.

 *If a force is applied to change the direction of the gyroscope rotor spin axis, the gyroscope resists angular movement in the plane of the force applied and, instead, moves in a plane at right angles to that of the applied force, the resulting movement being called 'precession'.*

Any spinning body, or **gyroscope**, will resist movement when a force is applied to it. If you were to hold the two ends of the axis of a wheel spinning towards you (when viewed from above), you would notice that if you attempted to tilt the axis, by lowering one end, the axis would not move very far in the direction you wished it to, but would instead move in the horizontal plane as if you had tried to push the end of the axis away from you *(see Figure 15.3)*. This phenomenon is known as **gyroscopic precession**. The result of **gyroscopic precession** is that the line of action of any force applied to the spin axis moves through 90° in the direction of spin, before taking effect.

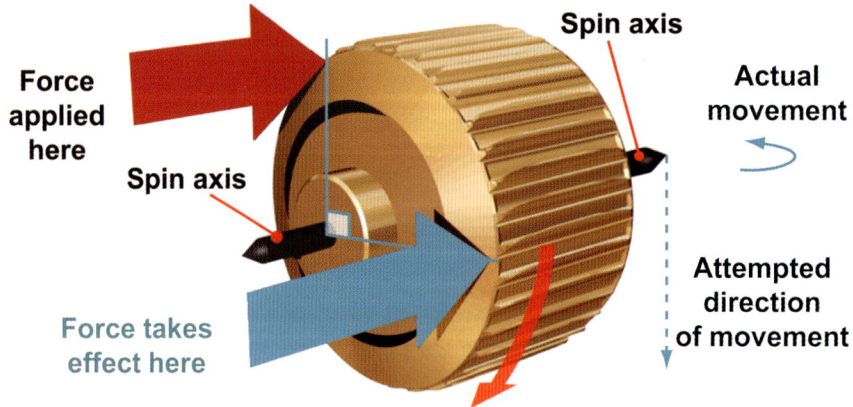

Figure 15.3 Precession in a gyro rotor.

Rate Gyroscopes.

Rate gyroscopes are used to measure **rate of angular displacement**. In a **rate gyroscope** the gimbal in which the rotor is mounted is free to move in one plane only. This means that the rotor spin axis has only one degree of freedom. **Turn Indicators** are fitted with a **rate gyroscope**.

CHAPTER 15: GYROSCOPIC INSTRUMENTS & THE MAGNETIC COMPASS

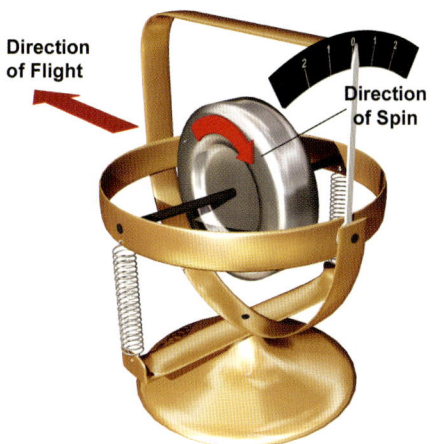
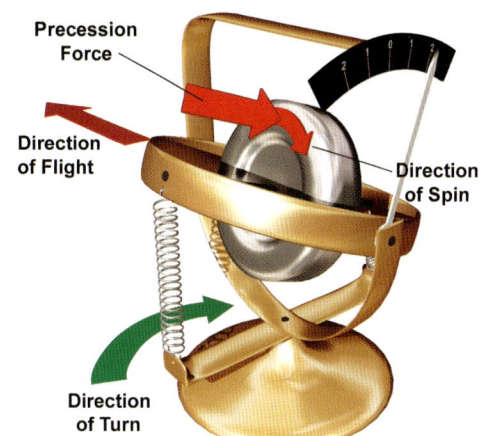

Figure 15.4a A Turn Indicator in an aircraft in straight flight.

Figure 15.4b A Turn Indicator indicating an established turn to the right.

Figure 15.4a depicts a simplified Turn Indicator as it would appear in an aircraft in straight flight. *Figure 15.4b* depicts the Turn Indicator, indicating a turn to the right. The gimbal in which the rate gyroscope spins is free to rotate in the vertical plane only. The needle of the Turn Indicator is attached to the gimbal by an appropriate mechanism (not shown here).

A turn to the right causes a force to be applied to the gyroscope assembly, as indicated by the green arrow. **Precession** causes the **line of action of that force** to move through 90° in the direction of rotation of the rotor, to become the force shown by the blue arrow labelled "**precession force**". The greater the rate of turn of the aircraft, the greater the **precession force**. The gimbal will tilt to the right, increasing its tilt until stopped by the restraining spring. The needle indicates the **rate of turn** of the aircraft on the dial.

When the aircraft stops turning, the **precession force** disappears, the springs level the gimbal, returning the gyroscope to the vertical position, and the needle once again indicates straight flight.

THE TURN AND SLIP INDICATOR.

The **Turn and Slip Indicator** *(shown in Figure 15.5)*, incorporates two measuring devices, **the turn indicator** and a simple pendulous device known as the **"ball"**.

The Turn Indicator.
The **Turn Indicator** employs a **rate gyroscope**, whose operation is described above, to measure the rate at which an aircraft changes direction in turning flight. The **rate of turn** is indicated by a needle on the face of the instrument. Most **Turn Indicators** on light aircraft have a scale which will show a maximum rate of turn of '**Rate One**'. A **Rate One Turn** is **3° per**

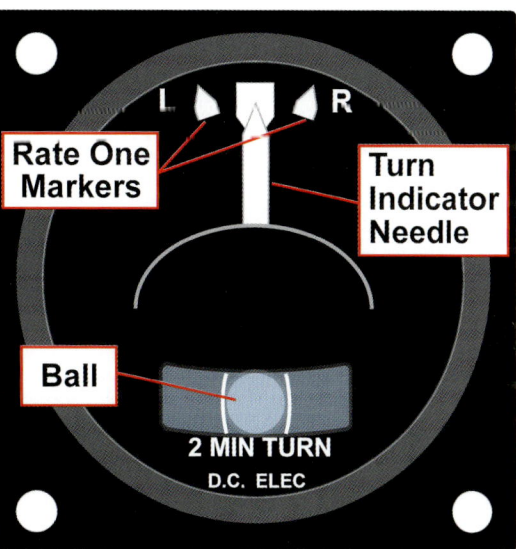

Figure 15.5 The Turn and Slip Indicator.

227

CHAPTER 15: GYROSCOPIC INSTRUMENTS & THE MAGNETIC COMPASS

second, or a complete **360° turn in 2 minutes**. A **Rate One Turn** is the rate used in instrument flying procedures.

Construction of the Turn Indicator.
Either vacuum or electrically-driven types of **Turn Indicator** are fitted to light aircraft. With the former, an engine-driven pump or venturi tube is used to apply suction to the instrument case to drive the rate gyroscope.

Effect of Varying Rotor Speed.
If the suction to an air-driven instrument is inadequate, a condition which can occur as a result of either high altitude or a choked filter, or even perhaps a leaking suction tube, **gyroscope rigidity** will be lowered because the gyroscope will rotate at a lower number of revolutions per minute than its design specifications.

> *If the gyroscope of a Turn Indicator runs at a lower rpm than its design specification, the actual rate of turn of the aircraft will be greater than the rate indicated.*

With lowered **rigidity** in space, any given **rate of turn** will cause the pointer to move by a smaller amount than if the rotor were spinning at normal speed. The **Turn Indicator** will therefore under-read. In other words, the actual **rate of turn** of the aircraft will be greater than the indicated **rate of turn**.

On the other hand, if the gyroscope were to overspeed, the **Turn Indicator** will over-read, indicating a greater **rate of turn** than the actual **rate of turn** of the aircraft. For the correct operation of vacuum-driven gyroscopic instruments, a suction of 3½ to 5½ inches of Mercury should be indicated. If the vacuum gauge indicates less than 2½ inches of Mercury, there is a risk that gyroscope indications will be erroneous. In flight, a pilot can check the accuracy of the **rate of turn** indicated by the **Turn Indicator** with his stopwatch.

The Ball and the Balanced Turn.
The other device within the **Turn and Slip Indicator**, the **"ball"**, is a very simple pendulous device which is used mainly to show whether or not a turn is **balanced**, and, if the turn is <u>not</u> balanced, to indicate the extent of **slip** or **skid**.

Turns should be properly **balanced**, with no **side-slip** or **skid**. A balanced turn implies that the **angle of bank** should be correct for the **air speed** and the **rate of turn**.

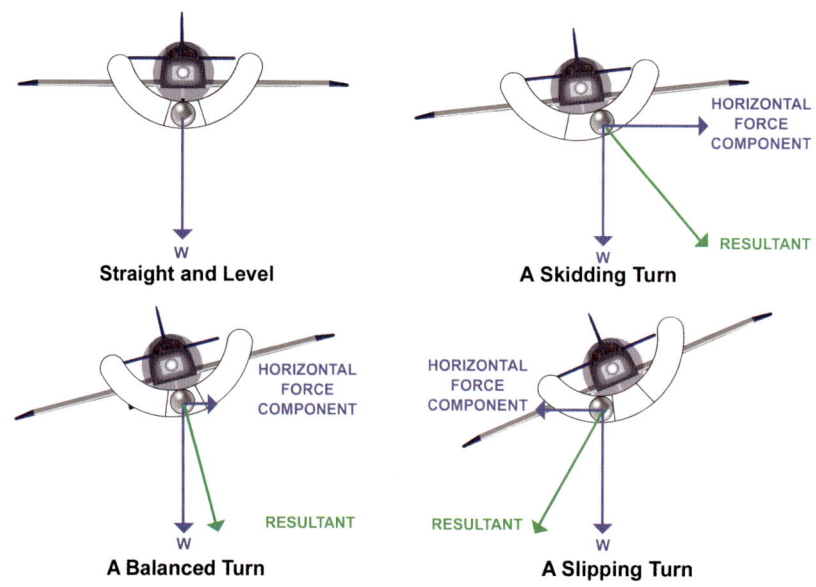

Figure 15.6 The Ball as a Slip and Skid Indicator.

CHAPTER 15: GYROSCOPIC INSTRUMENTS & THE MAGNETIC COMPASS

In **balanced flight**, the **ball** will be 'in the middle' of the curved tube between the two vertical lines. If the aircraft is **out of balance** (if, for instance, **yaw**, **slip** or **skid** is present), the **ball** will be displaced to one side or the other of the tube as shown in *Figure 15.6*.

> To estimate the angle of bank, in degrees, required for a Rate 1 turn, divide the indicated air speed by ten and add seven.

If a pilot is turning with too little bank or too much rudder, the aircraft will be **skidding** and the **ball** will be displaced towards the outside of the turn. If there is too little rudder or too much bank, the **ball** will be displaced towards the centre of the turn, indicating a **slip**.

Balanced Flight.

Your flying instructor will teach you how to fly **in balance**. Basically, an aircraft is in **balanced flight** if the relative airflow meets the aircraft parallel to its longitudinal axis. If the relative airflow is meeting the aircraft's longitudinal axis at an oblique angle, yaw is present and the aircraft is either **slipping** or **skidding** through the air, causing the **ball** of the **slip indicator** to be displaced to one side. If the **ball** is out to the right, in order to return the **ball** to the middle, that is, to return the aircraft to **balanced flight**, an appropriate amount of right rudder is applied. If the **ball** is displaced to the left, left rudder is applied to return to **balanced flight**.

The Rate One Turn.

As you have learnt, a **Rate One Turn** is a turn at **3° per second** change in direction. **(360° in 2 minutes)** The following is a good rule of thumb for calculating the **angle of bank** required to give a balanced **Rate One Turn** at a given **airspeed**. To achieve a **Rate One Turn**, take one tenth of the indicated **airspeed** in knots and add seven to give approximately the required **bank angle** in degrees. For example, at an **airspeed** of **110 knots**, **bank angle** should be **11 + 7 = 18°**. This rule gives reasonable accuracy for **Rate One Turns** for **airspeeds** between **100** and **250 knots**.

THE TURN COORDINATOR.

The **Turn Coordinator**, shown in *Figure 15.7*, is a development of the Turn Indicator. The primary differences between the Turn Indicator and the **Turn Co-ordinator** are in the setting of the appropriate axis of the **Rate Gyroscope**, and in the method of display. The **Rate Gyroscope** in the **Turn Coordinator** is mounted in such a way as to make the gyroscope sensitive to banking of the aircraft as well as to turning.

The **Turn Coordinator**, therefore, will indicate rate of roll, as well as rate of turn. The **Turn Coordinator** does not, however, indicate **angle of bank**, neither does it give pitch information. When the wing tip of the white aeroplane shown on the **Turn Co-ordinator** is against either one of the lower white marks on the instrument scale, the aircraft is executing a **Rate One Turn** - that is, a turn of **180° per minute**, or **360° in 2 minutes** (hence the annotation **'2 min'** on the instrument face.)

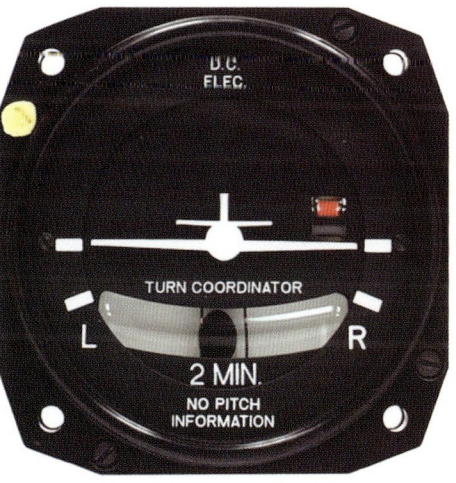

Figure 15.7 A Turn Coordinator.

CHAPTER 15: GYROSCOPIC INSTRUMENTS & THE MAGNETIC COMPASS

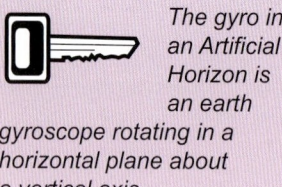

The gyro in an Artificial Horizon is an earth gyroscope rotating in a horizontal plane about a vertical axis.

Pilot Serviceability Checks.

The basic serviceability of both the **Turn Indicator** and **Turn Coordinator** can be checked by the pilot during taxying, prior to take-off. While the pilot is turning the aircraft to check correct operation of the rudder bar and differential brakes, he should verify that the **Turn Indicator**, or **Turn Coordinator**, shows a left turn when the aircraft is turning left (with the ball being displaced to the right), and a right turn when the aircraft is right (with the ball being displaced to the left.) In the air, the pilot can check the accuracy of the **Rate One Indication**, using his stop-watch.

INTRODUCTION TO THE ARTIFICIAL HORIZON.

Shown in *Figure 15.8* is the **Artificial Horizon** - or **Attitude Indicator** as it is sometimes called. The **Artificial Horizon** provides the pilot with information on the aircraft's attitude, both in pitch and roll. It is a primary instrument, replacing the natural horizon in poor visibility.

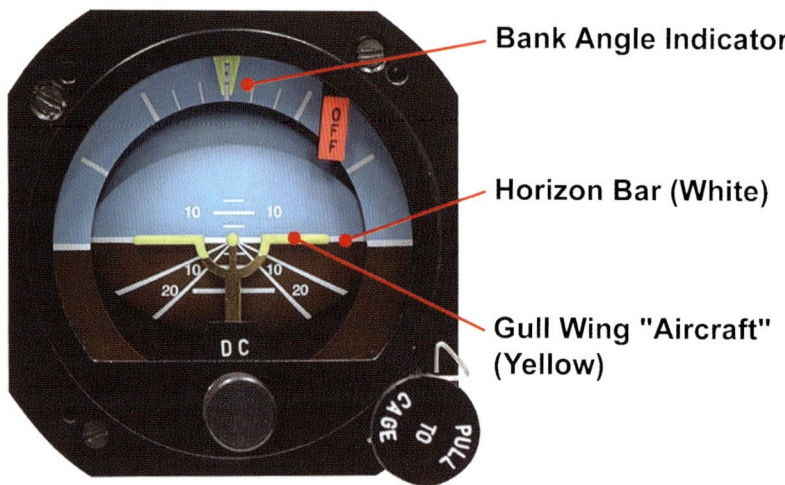

Figure 15.8 The Artificial Horizon.

The attitude display consists of a miniature aircraft shape or gull-wing attached to the front of the instrument case. Behind this symbolic aircraft is a picture of the horizon, linked to the gyroscope in such a way that the picture of the horizon is gyro-stabilised parallel to the true horizon. A pointer at the top of the instrument indicates angle of bank. So once the pilot has established the relationship between airspeed, angle of bank and rate of turn, the **Artificial Horizon** can also be used to fly a given rate of turn. The **Artificial Horizon** may be suction-driven or electrically driven.

Construction of the Artificial Horizon.

The **Artificial Horizon** uses an **Earth gyroscope** in which the spin axis is maintained in the Earth's vertical axis, because of **gyroscopic rigidity**. This means that the plane of the rotor rotation is horizontal, thus providing the stable lateral and longitudinal references required.

An engine-driven suction pump (or venturi tube in some light aircraft) is used to create a suction of about **4 or 5 inches of Mercury** in the instrument case of the air-driven **Artificial Horizon**. Replacement air, drawn in by this suction via a filter, is ducted through the outer and inner gimbals to enter the rotor case as a jet which spins the rotor at up to **15 000 revolutions per minute**. After driving the rotor, the air passes into the instrument case through slots at the base of the rotor housing.

CHAPTER 15: GYROSCOPIC INSTRUMENTS & THE MAGNETIC COMPASS

When the aircraft is manoeuvring, the whole aircraft, including the instruments and the symbolic aircraft, moves around the gyroscope with its attached horizon picture. Consequently, the **Artificial Horizon** is able to display both pitch attitude and bank angle to the pilot.

Limitations of the Artificial Horizon.
Be aware that the **Artificial Horizon** indicates **pitch attitude** and **bank attitude**, but it does not indicate aircraft performance. **For instance, the Artificial Horizon will indicate a nose-high attitude irrespective of whether the aircraft is climbing or about to stall**.

The amount the **Artificial Horizon** instrument case can move relative to the gyroscope is controlled by fixed stops. With older designs, **typical limits are ± 60° in pitch** and **110° each way in roll**. In modern instruments, there is **complete freedom in roll and up to ±85° in pitch**.

If the instrument's **limits** are exceeded, the gyroscope **'topples'**, causing violent and erratic movements of the horizon bar. Unless a fast re-erection system is incorporated, accurate indications will not be obtained from the **Artificial Horizon** until the gyroscope has re-erected itself over a period of 10 to 15 minutes.

Artificial Horizon Control Systems.
The rotor assembly is made very slightly bottom-heavy in order to keep to a minimum the time taken for initial erection when the gyroscope is first started up. A complex control system is required to maintain the rotor axis vertical in flight.

Pilot Serviceability Checks.
When manoeuvring on the ground prior to take-off, and when the gyroscope is up to speed, check that the horizon bar takes up a **laterally level position** with the **correct pitch indication** for the aircraft type. The correct **pitch attitude** for your aircraft type can be set on the **Artificial Horizon**, before take-off, by an adjusting knob. If a **caging device** is fitted, the instrument should be uncaged at least five minutes before take-off to ensure that the rotor axis has had time to reach alignment with the true vertical.

If a caging device is fitted to an Artificial Horizon, the instrument should be uncaged at least five minutes before take-off to ensure that the rotor axis has had time to reach alignment with the true vertical.

In flight, the **Artificial Horizon** should give an immediate and correct indication of any change in pitch or roll attitude.

When carrying out taxying checks, a pilot should ensure that the horizon bar remains horizontal when the aircraft is turned to the left and right during verification of ground steering. Check also that the vacuum gauge is showing sufficient suction for correct operation of the **Artificial Horizon**.

DIRECTIONAL GYROSCOPE INDICATOR.

Introduction.
The **Directional Gyroscope Indicator**, which is also called the **Heading Indicator**, **Directional Gyro**, **Direction Indicator**, or simply, the **DI**, provides a stable directional reference in azimuth for **maintaining accurate headings** and for **executing precise turns**. There is no magnetic element in the **Direction Indicator**, so it is not north-seeking and **it must initially be synchronized with the Magnetic Compass**.

CHAPTER 15: GYROSCOPIC INSTRUMENTS & THE MAGNETIC COMPASS

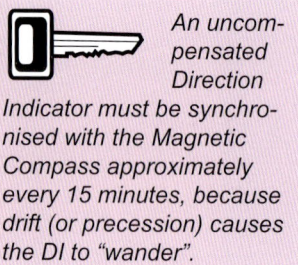

An uncompensated Direction Indicator must be synchronised with the Magnetic Compass approximately every 15 minutes, because drift (or precession) causes the DI to "wander".

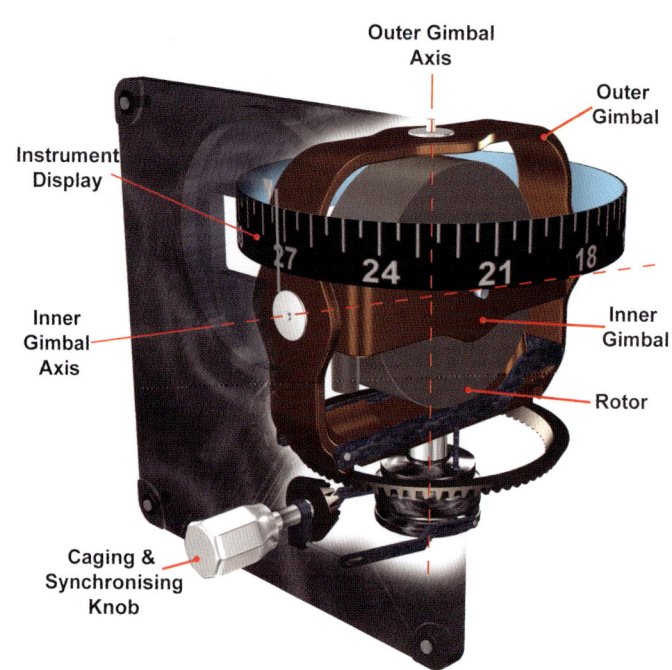

Figure 15.9 The Direction Indicator.

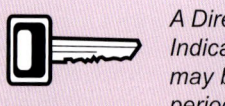

A Direction Indicator may be periodically aligned with the magnetic compass when the wings are level by using the caging knob to rotate the DI azimuth card.

Remember that the **Magnetic Compass** is the primary indicator of direction in most light aircraft. The **synchronisation** of an uncompensated **Direction Indicator** with the **Magnetic Compass** must be checked at regular intervals of about **15 minutes**. This is because mechanical errors and **apparent gyroscopic wander**, sometimes called **gyroscopic drift** or **precession** cause the **Direction Indicator** to drift away from accurate alignment with the Compass.

The **Direction Indicator** does not replace the Compass; but, having no magnetic element, the **Direction Indicator** does not suffer from the Compass turning and acceleration errors, making it easier for the pilot to roll out accurately on a desired heading. The outer gimbal permits the rotor to rotate through 360° in the horizontal plane. The outer gimbal also has a ring scale attached to it, usually graduated in 5° intervals, which provides the instrument display of the **Direction Indicator**.

The Principle of Operation and Construction of the Directional Gyroscope Indicator.

The **Direction Indicator** employs a **tied gyro**, that is to say, a gyroscope having freedom of movement in three planes mutually at right angles to each other, but with the rotor axis maintained in the horizontal plane. Because of its gyroscopic rigidity, the rotor provides the datum from which heading can be measured.

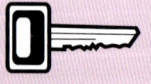

A tied gyroscope has freedom of movement in three planes which are at right angles to each other, but has its axis in the horizontal or yawing plane of the aircraft.

During a turn, the aircraft and the instrument case turn on the vertical axis bearings of the outer gimbal, whilst the gyroscope rotor, gimbals and ring-scale all remain fixed in azimuth because of gyroscopic rigidity.

In the type of **Direction Indicator** shown in *Figure 15.10a*, heading is indicated on the ring-scale by a lubber line painted on a glass window in the instrument case.

232

CHAPTER 15: GYROSCOPIC INSTRUMENTS & THE MAGNETIC COMPASS

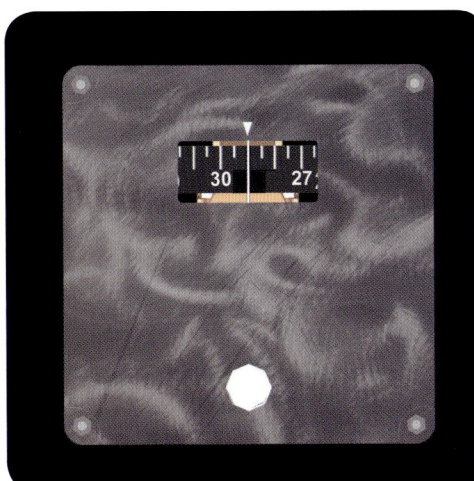
Figure 15.10a

Figure 15.10b

Two types of Direction Indicator display.

Another type of **Direction Indicator** display, shown in *Figure 5.10b*, has a circular, vertical-card indicating scale geared to the outer gimbal, instead of the cylindrical scale. In this type of display, the heading is indicated by the nose of the aeroplane-shaped pointer.

The Control System - Suction Gyroscopes.

With earlier designs of **Directional Indicators**, the rotor is driven by twin jets of air applied from the outer gimbal ring as shown in *Figure 15.11*.

Suction is applied to the case of the instrument, and replacement air enters the case through a filter and is ducted to the jets on the outer gimbal which act on 'buckets' cut in the rotor.

The jets not only spin the rotor but also serve to maintain, or 'tie', the rotor axis in the yawing plane of the aircraft.

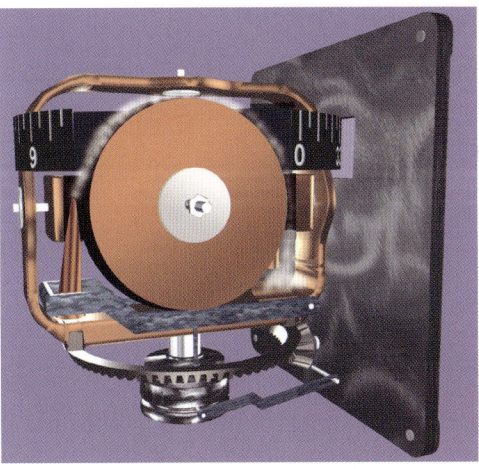
Figure 15.11 Suction Gyro.

Pilot Serviceability Checks for the Direction Indicator.

Before take-off, but after engine start, check that the vacuum gauge is indicating sufficient suction for the gyroscope rotor to operate at the correct rotational speed. As soon as practicable, set the **Direction Indicator** heading to the compass magnetic heading. While taxying, check that the **Direction Indicator** shows an increasing reading when the aircraft is turned to the right, and a decreasing reading when the aircraft is turned to the left.

CHAPTER 15: GYROSCOPIC INSTRUMENTS & THE MAGNETIC COMPASS

DIRECTION INDICATOR ERRORS - GYROSCOPIC WANDER.

If the axis of a gyroscope rotor departs from its set direction, it is said to **wander**, or **precess**.

If the axis of the gyroscope rotor **wanders** in the horizontal plane, as indicated by the horizontal arrow in *Figure 15.12*, it is said to drift.

A weight hung on the gimbal at point A will produce **drift**.

If, on the other hand, the rotor axis **wanders** in the vertical plane, it is said to **topple**.

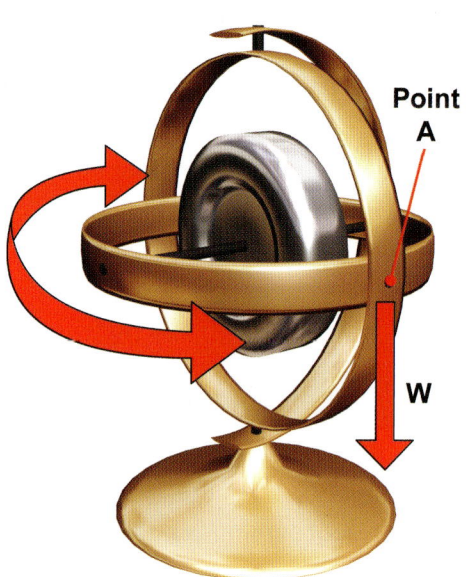

Figure 15.12 Gyroscopic Drift.

Mechanical Wander or Drift.
Manufacturing imperfections in a gyroscope cause small rates of **random precession**. Other terms given to this precession are **balance wander** or, if the precession is in the horizontal plane, **mechanical wander**.

The imperfections concerned are uneven rotor bearing friction, unbalanced gimbals, and friction in gimbal bearings. In-flight turbulence may increase the effect of these imperfections.

Apparent Wander or Drift.
Consider a **Direction Indicator** such as the one depicted in *Figure 15.13*, with the rotor axis horizontal and aligned with the geographic meridian. The rotor axis is causing the **Direction Indicator** to indicate **True North** on the Earth and is also aligned with a point at an infinite distance in space.

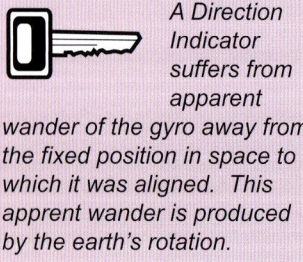

A Direction Indicator suffers from apparent wander of the gyro away from the fixed position in space to which it was aligned. This apprent wander is produced by the earth's rotation.

Figure 15.13 The Effect of Apparent Wander on a 'Free' Gyro.

Five hours later when the Earth has rotated through 75° on its axis, the gyroscope rotor axis is still aligned with the same fixed point in space (assuming no other disturbing forces) and the **Direction Indicator** no longer indicates the direction of North on the Earth. The **Direction Indicator** appears, therefore, to have changed

CHAPTER 15: GYROSCOPIC INSTRUMENTS & THE MAGNETIC COMPASS

its alignment, as seen by an observer on Earth: by 75° in the case illustrated, from 360°(0°) to 285°. This type of **wander** is called **apparent wander**, or **apparent drift**. **Apparent Wander** is due only to the rotation of the Earth about its axis.

THE MAGNET.

Even in ancient times the oxide of iron called **magnetite**, shown here in *Figure 15.14*, was observed to attract small pieces of iron. This property is known as **magnetism**.

Another property which the ancients recognised in **magnetite** was that, if it was mounted on a piece of wood to allow it to float on water, it would swing round and align itself in a roughly **north-south direction**, so acting as a primitive **compass**.

Figure 15.14 Magnetite.

> The end of a magnet which points north is called the North-seeking pole. The other end is the South-seeking pole of the magnet.

In more modern times, it was found that the magnetic properties of magnetite could be transferred to certain metallic materials. Magnetized materials of this kind were called **magnets**.

Magnetic Fields.

The field of a **magnet** is the space around it in which its magnetic influence is felt. We may get a picture of a **magnetic field** by placing a piece of card over a bar magnet and scattering iron filings on it. When the card is shaken or tapped the filings will adopt the pattern of the **magnetic field** as shown in *Figure 15.15*.

The Poles of a Magnet.

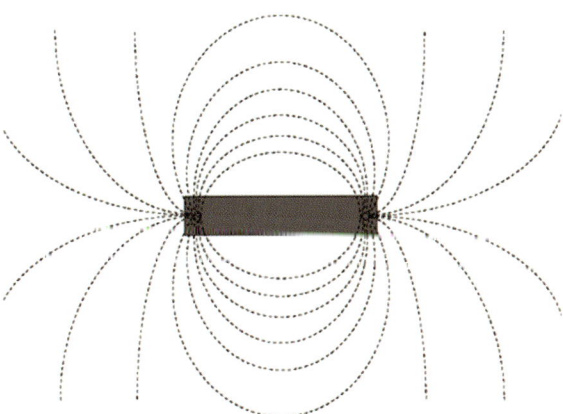

Figure 15.15 The Magnetic Field of a Bar Magnet.

Figure 15.15 also illustrates that the lines of force traced by the iron filings are closer together in the small areas near the ends of the **magnet**. These two areas are called the **poles** of the **magnet**. It is at the **poles** of a **magnet** that a **magnet's magnetism is most intense**. **Magnets** can be made in various shapes **but every magnet has two poles. A unit pole cannot exist**. If a **magnet** is cut into two pieces, each piece will have two **poles**.

235

CHAPTER 15: GYROSCOPIC INSTRUMENTS & THE MAGNETIC COMPASS

North Seeking and South Seeking Poles.

A freely suspended magnet in the Earth's magnetic field will align itself roughly **North-South** as depicted in *Figure 15.16*.

One end of the **magnet** points to the **Earth's North Magnetic Pole**. This end of the magnet is known as a **North-seeking pole** or, simply, the **magnet's North Pole**. The other end is a **South-seeking pole** more commonly called the **magnet's South Pole**.

By convention, a magnet's **North-seeking pole** is coloured red, and the **South-seeking pole** is coloured blue.

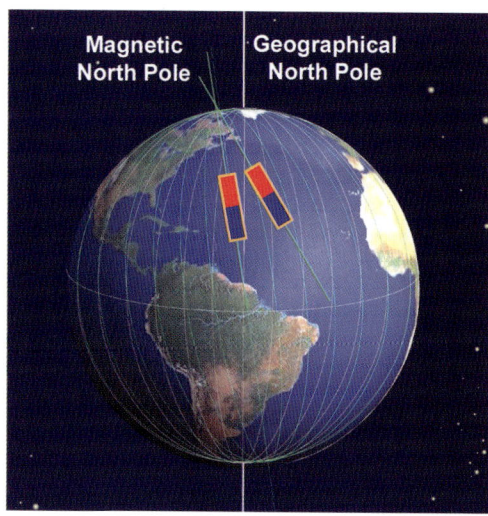

Figure 15.16 A freely suspended Magnet will align itself roughly North-South in the Earth's Magnetic Field.

Terrestrial Magnetism.

The Earth behaves as though a huge permanent magnet were situated near its centre, producing a **magnetic field** over the surface of the earth. The Earth rotates about an axis passing through its geographical North and South Poles. *Figure 15.17* shows that the poles of the hypothetical Earth-magnet do not lie on the Earth's spin axis. The **North** and **South Magnetic Poles** are not coincident with the **Geographical North** and **South Poles**.

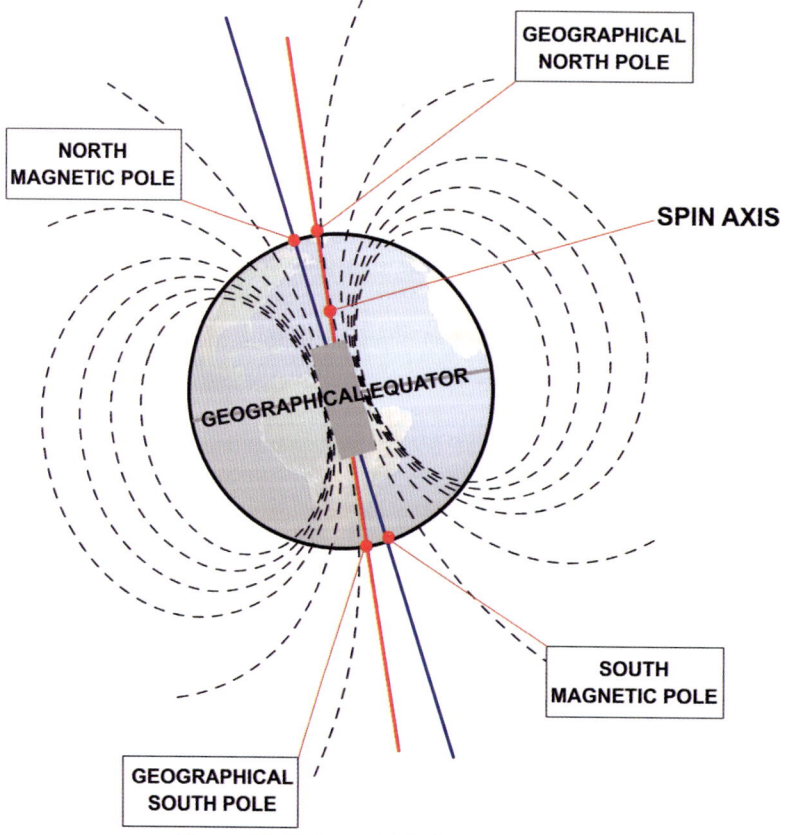

Figure 15.17 Terrestrial Magnetism.

CHAPTER 15: GYROSCOPIC INSTRUMENTS & THE MAGNETIC COMPASS

The **Earth's magnetic poles** have been given the names **Magnetic North** and **Magnetic South**, because they are not too far distant from the **Earth's geographical poles**.

The **Earth's Magnetic North Pole**, lies at present (2006) beneath Northern Canada in the area around 70°N 95°W. The **Magnetic South Pole** is currently below Antarctica near South Victoria Land.

The angular difference between the locations of the magnetic and geographic poles, as measured at any given point on the Earth's surface is called **magnetic variation** *(see Figure 15.20)*.

THE MAGNETIC COMPASS.

An instrument which is found in all aircraft, from the simplest light aircraft to the most modern glass cockpit airliner, is the simple **Magnetic Compass**.

A **compass** is an instrument designed to indicate direction on the surface of the Earth, **relative to the Earth's magnetic poles**.

In ideal conditions, the magnet at the heart of the aircraft's **Magnetic Compass**, will point at all times to the **Earth's Magnetic North and South Poles**. Theoretically as the aircraft changes direction the **compass magnet** remains aligned to the two **Magnetic Poles**. Because of this property of the magnet, the pilot is able to read off his aircraft's **magnetic heading** from the compass. As we shall learn later in this chapter, however, there are several reasons why the **compass magnet** may not always lie **North-South**, leading to errors in compass indications.

The purpose of a **magnetic compass** in an aircraft, then, is to indicate **heading**: the direction in which the aircraft is pointing.

Magnetic influences, such as those produced by iron or steel components, electric currents etc., cause local distortions in the Earth's magnetic field which lead to errors in the compass reading. This type of error is called **compass deviation**.

The rules for applying corrections for **magnetic variation** and **deviation** to the **compass heading indication** in order to determine an aircraft's **heading** with respect to **Geographical North** (otherwise known as **True North**) are discussed later in this Chapter

Direct Indicating Magnetic Compass.
This part of the chapter deals with the **Direct Indicating**, or **Direct Reading Magnetic Compass**, where the pilot directly reads his **heading** in relation to a pivoted magnet assembly.

There are two basic types of **Direct Reading Magnetic Compass** used in aircraft: the **Simple Magnetic Compass** and, less commonly, but still found in older aircraft, the **Grid Ring Compass**.

The Simple Magnetic Compass.
The **Simple Magnetic Compass** - sometimes referred to as the E-2B or **standby compass**, shown on the next page in *Figure 15.18*, is the **direct reading compass** in general use in most aircraft. The **Simple Magnetic Compass** is usually the main

CHAPTER 15: GYROSCOPIC INSTRUMENTS & THE MAGNETIC COMPASS

magnetic heading reference in light aircraft, and the **standby compass** in larger aircraft. The **Simple Magnetic Compass** consists of a circular compass card attached directly to a magnet assembly. This combined unit is suspended within the compass bowl.

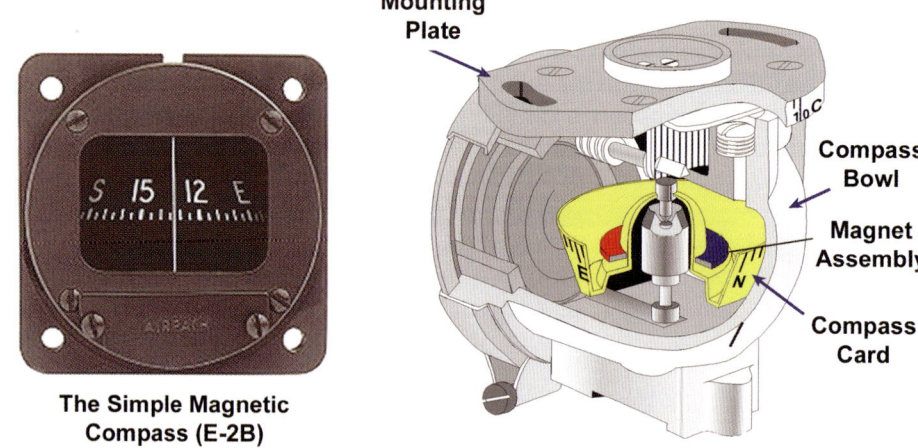

Figure 15.18 The Simple Magnetic Compass.

A vertical **lubber line** on the glass window of the bowl enables the **heading** to be read from the compass card.

The Grid Ring Compass.

The **P-type compass** or **Grid Ring Compass**, illustrated in *Figure 15.19*, is found on older aircraft, such as the De Havilland Chipmunk. It is more accurate than the **Simple Magnetic Compass** and is more stable.

The **Grid Ring Compass** is, however, heavier, bulkier and more expensive. In addition it can only be read in straight and level flight, as the grid ring has to be unclamped and aligned with the North reference before a reading can be taken against the **lubber line**.

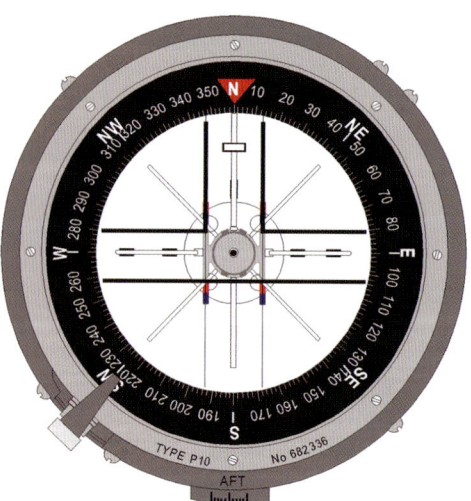

Figure 15.19 The Grid Ring Compass.

MAGNETIC VARIATION.

The Earth behaves as though a huge permanent magnet was situated near its centre, producing a **magnetic field** over its surface, as seen in *Figure 15.17*.

As we have said, the direction of that **field** at any given point can be indicated by a freely suspended magnet. Such a magnet will align itself, roughly, in a North - South direction.

CHAPTER 15: GYROSCOPIC INSTRUMENTS & THE MAGNETIC COMPASS

However, the **poles** of the **Earth's magnetic field do** move and are seldom coincident with the Earth's spin axis. The position of the **North Magnetic Pole** is moving at about 22 nautical miles per year. Since it was first located in 1831 it has moved approximately 625 miles. The **North Magnetic Pole** is presently close to Ellesmere Island in the Canadian Arctic Islands, which is 650 miles west of the **Geographic North Pole**. Consequently, **the lines of force of the Earth's magnetic field lie at an angle to the true meridians**, and so, a freely suspended magnet will align itself as shown in *Figure 15.20*.

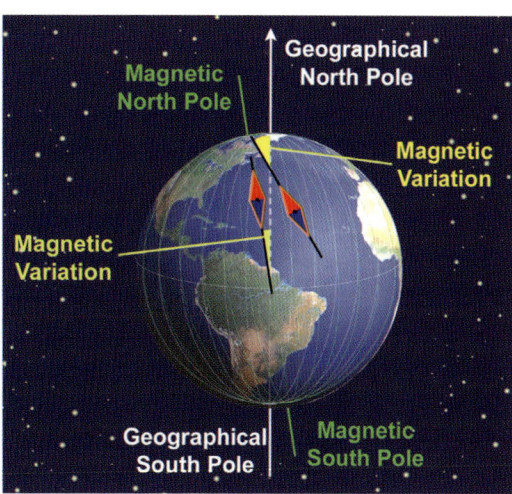

Figure 15.20 Magnetic Variation.

The angle, measured in the horizontal plane, between the magnetic meridian at any point on the Earth's surface, and the true meridian at the same point is known as magnetic variation.

The angle, measured in the horizontal plane, between the **magnetic lines of force** at a given point on the Earth's surface, and the **true meridian** at the same point is known as the **magnetic variation**. Magnetic Variation is designated **West** or **East** depending on whether the **magnetic pole** lies to the **West** or to the **East** of **True North**, relative to the point from which the **variation** is measured.

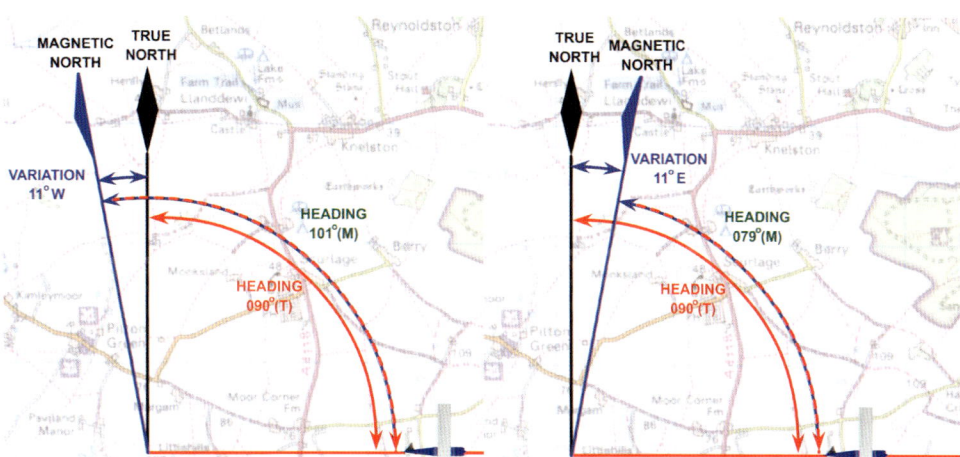

Figure 15.21 Magnetic Variation West.   *Figure 15.22 Magnetic Variation East.*

Magnetic Variation can have any value from zero to 180°, the latter occurring on the true meridian linking the **North Geographic Pole** with the **North Magnetic Pole**.

When **magnetic direction** is the same as **true direction**, the **variation** is nil; otherwise **Magnetic North** direction may lie either to the **West** or **East** of **True North**. A simple rhyme helps in working out which way to apply **variation** to your **heading**:- "Variation West, Magnetic best, Variation East, Magnetic least".

In *Figure 15.21*, an aircraft is flying due **East (090° True)** by reference to points on the ground, and **variation** is **11° West**. Therefore, the pilot has had to **add** the **magnetic variation** to his planned **true heading** to obtain the correct **magnetic heading of 101°** which he must fly in order to track due East **(090° True)** over the ground.

Conversely, as shown in *Figure 15.22*, if the variation is 11° East, then the pilot must subtract the variation from his planned **true heading** to get the correct **magnetic heading of 079°** which he must fly to track **090° True** over the ground. Remember: **"Variation West, Magnetic Best, Variation East, Magnetic Least."**

Remember, "variation west, magnetic best, variation east, magnetic least."

CHAPTER 15: GYROSCOPIC INSTRUMENTS & THE MAGNETIC COMPASS

Isogonals.

Some navigational charts are marked with lines called **Isogonals**. **Isogonals** join places on the Earth's surface of the **same magnetic variation** *(see Figure 15.23)*. You will find **Isogonals** on the 1:500 000 charts.

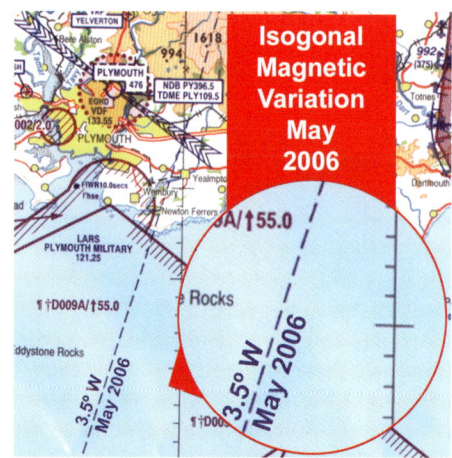

Figure 15.23 An Isogonal (Line of Constant Magnetic Variation) on a Chart.

DEVIATION.

The **Magnetic Compass** is, of course, not only sensitive to the Earth's magnetic field but also to the magnetic fields of **electrically driven instruments** and **metallic objects** within the cockpit. The presence of these "secondary" magnetic fields within the cockpit will cause the **Magnetic Compass** to deviate from pointing towards **Magnetic North**.

The angle between the local magnetic meridian and the direction in which the compass-magnets are lying, because of secondary magnetic influences within the cockpit, is called the **angle of deviation** or, simply, **deviation**.

Figure 15.24 Compass Deviation Card.

> The compass reading is the magnetic heading plus or minus the deviation on that particular heading.

Deviation can be **East** or **West** of **Magnetic North**.

Deviation varies with indicated magnetic heading, so it has to be measured on a series of different headings. This is usually done by conducting a **compass swing**. Measured **deviation** is then eliminated as far as possible by making adjustments to the compass itself by means of a correcting screw. Once **deviation** has been reduced as far as possible, the **residual deviation** is recorded on a **compass deviation card**, which is located in close proximity to the compass. During the compass swing, normal flying conditions should be simulated as far as possible, with engines running, electrical / radio services switched on, and the aircraft in a level flight attitude. It is obviously most important that no ferromagnetic objects such as tools, or watches are placed near the compass as this would introduce unknown amounts of **deviation**.

> The purpose of the compass deviation card is to indicate the discrepancy between the heading shown on the compass and the actual magnetic heading.

In *Figure 15.24* the aircraft's compass reading is **269 degrees**. The **compass reading** is the **magnetic heading** plus or minus the **deviation** on that particular heading. The **deviation card** makes it easy for a pilot to fly an accurate magnetic

CHAPTER 15: GYROSCOPIC INSTRUMENTS & THE MAGNETIC COMPASS

heading. Look closely at the **deviation card** in *Figure 15.24*; the card tells the pilot that if he wishes to fly 270° Magnetic, he must steer 269°.

The Compass Swing.

The basic method of determining deviation is to compare the aircraft's compass reading with a very accurate magnetic heading obtained from the reading of a high quality 'land' or 'datum' compass *(see Figure 15.25)*. This comparison is called a **compass swing**. The **compass swing** is carried out in an area selected specifically for this purpose. Major compass deviation errors are corrected by adjusting small magnets mounted in the aircraft's compass system. As already explained, residual errors that remain are shown on a **compass deviation card** displayed in close proximity to the compass in the cockpit, as illustrated in *Figure 15.24*.

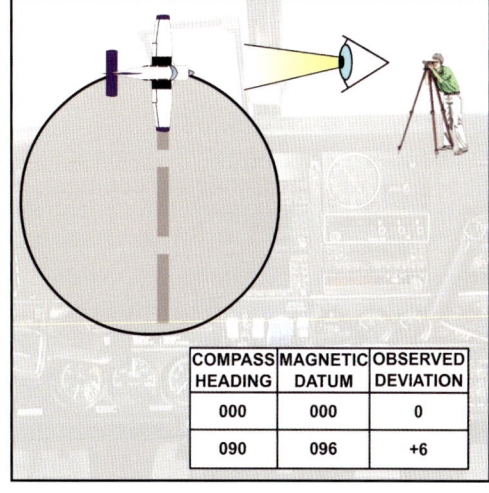

Figure 15.25 The Compass Swing.

> When a compass swing is being carried out the aircraft's compass reading is compared with readings from a 'land or datum' compass.

There are several occasions when an aircraft might require a **compass swing**. Among these are:

• When compass components are installed or replaced.

• Whenever the accuracy of the compass is in doubt.

• After a maintenance inspection, if required by the schedule.

• After a significant aircraft modification, repair or replacement involving magnetic material.

• If the aircraft has been struck by lightning.

Magnetic Dip.

Except near the Earth's 'magnetic equator', where the lines of force are parallel to the Earth's surface, one end of the freely-suspended magnet will **dip** below the horizontal, pointing to the **nearer pole**. To the **North** of the **Magnetic Equator**, the magnet's **north-seeking pole** will **dip**, as shown in *Figure 15.26*, whereas to the **South** of the **Magnetic Equator** the **south-seeking pole** will dip.

The angle, measured in the vertical plane, between the axis of the magnet and the horizontal is called the **angle of dip**.

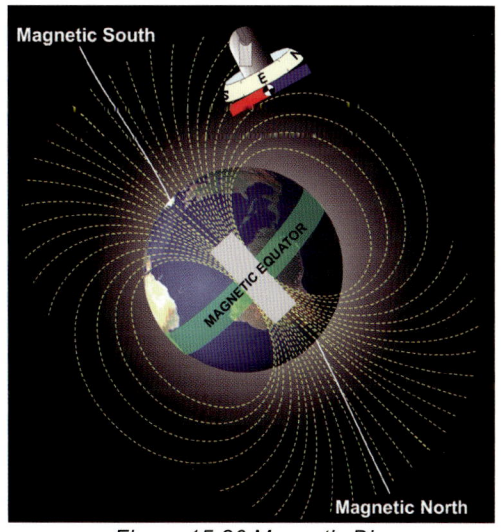

Figure 15.26 Magnetic Dip.

241

CHAPTER 15: GYROSCOPIC INSTRUMENTS & THE MAGNETIC COMPASS

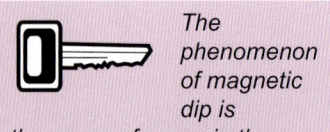

The phenomenon of magnetic dip is the cause of errors in the indications of the magnetic compass when an aircraft is accelerating or turning.

The further **North** or **South** of the **Magnetic Equator** a freely-suspended magnet is located, the greater will be the **magnetic dip**, reaching about 66° in the United Kingdom. Over the Earth's **magnetic poles**, the **dip** is **90°**. The phenomenon of **magnetic dip** is the cause of **errors in the indications** of the **magnetic compass** when an aircraft is **accelerating** or **turning**.

COMPASS ERRORS.

Acceleration Errors.

Direct reading **magnetic compasses** are subject to **errors** during **linear acceleration**, **linear deceleration**, or during a **turn**, which, of course, involves **centrifugal acceleration**.

Most manoeuvres which cause the centre of gravity of a freely-suspended magnet assembly to move away from its normal position (which is almost directly below the pivot) will produce an **error** in the indication of a compass so as to show an **apparent turn** when no turn is present.

However, if the manoeuvre displaces the centre of gravity to the north or south of its usual position beneath the pivot, so that the centre of gravity and pivot are still in the plane of the magnetic meridian, the magnet assembly merely changes its north-south tilt angle, with no rotation in azimuth, and consequently no error. There are, therefore, no **linear acceleration errors** in compass indications when the aircraft is on a heading of **360°** or **180°**. Conversely, as you might expect, **linear acceleration errors** are greatest when the aircraft is heading **090°** or **270°**.

Note, that **turning** and **linear acceleration errors** occur only where there is significant **magnetic dip**, so that except for a small liquid swirl effect in turns, the **errors** are non-existent near the **Magnetic Equator**.

When **dip** is present, the **centre of gravity** of the **pendulously suspended magnet** is not directly under the **pivot** *(see Figure 15.27)*. Therefore, when an aircraft **accelerates** on an **Easterly** or **Westerly heading**, the **inertial reaction** at the magnet's **centre of gravity** causes the suspended magnet to be "left behind" giving rise to a turning moment which acts on the magnet's **centre of gravity** while the **acceleration** lasts.

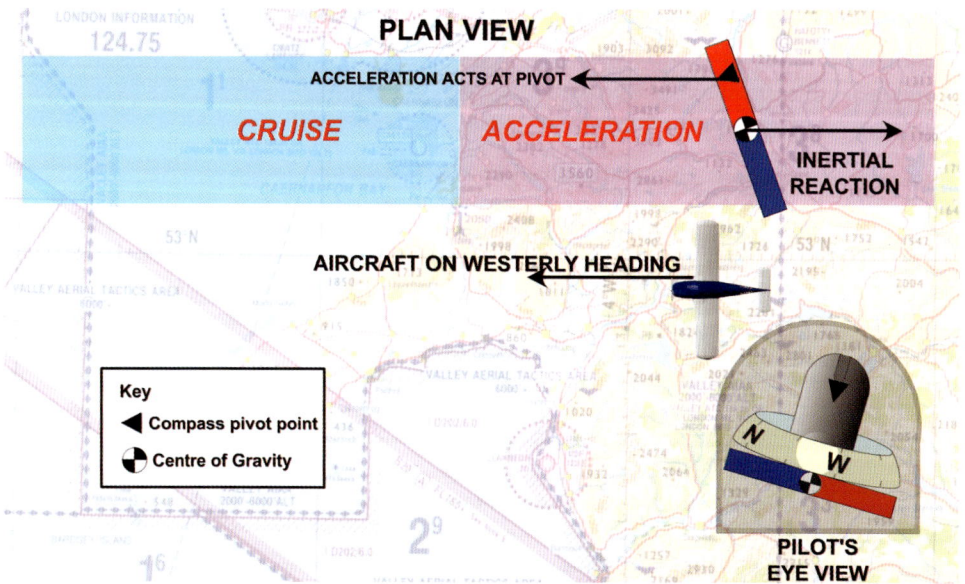

Figure 15.27 Compass indicates an apparent turn towards North.

CHAPTER 15: GYROSCOPIC INSTRUMENTS & THE MAGNETIC COMPASS

This action causes the magnet to rotate a little and indicate a turn. Once **linear acceleration** is complete and the aircraft is again flying at constant speed, no **acceleration** force acts on the magnet's **centre of gravity**, and the compass reading is again steady and correct.

Accelerating West.
Figure 15.27 shows both a plan view and a pilot's eye view of a pendulously suspended magnet (with residual dip) in the **Northern Hemisphere** with the aircraft **accelerating** on a **westerly heading**. Note that the **pivot point** and the magnet's **centre of gravity** do not lie on the same vertical line. The magnet is dipping towards the nearer pole: **Magnetic North** in this case.

The magnet is attached to the aircraft at the **pivot point**. When the **pivot** is being **accelerated**, the magnet will lag behind because of its **inertia**. The **inertial force** acts at the magnet's **centre of gravity**. The result will be that, even though the aircraft is flying in a straight line, the magnet will rotate (in this case anticlockwise) indicating a turn towards **North**.

Cruise Phase (Westerly Heading).
When the aircraft is in **cruising flight**, there is no **acceleration**; the magnet, therefore, moves back to its original position on a **Westerly heading**, and once more indicates the correct reading. This situation is illustrated in *Figure 15.28*.

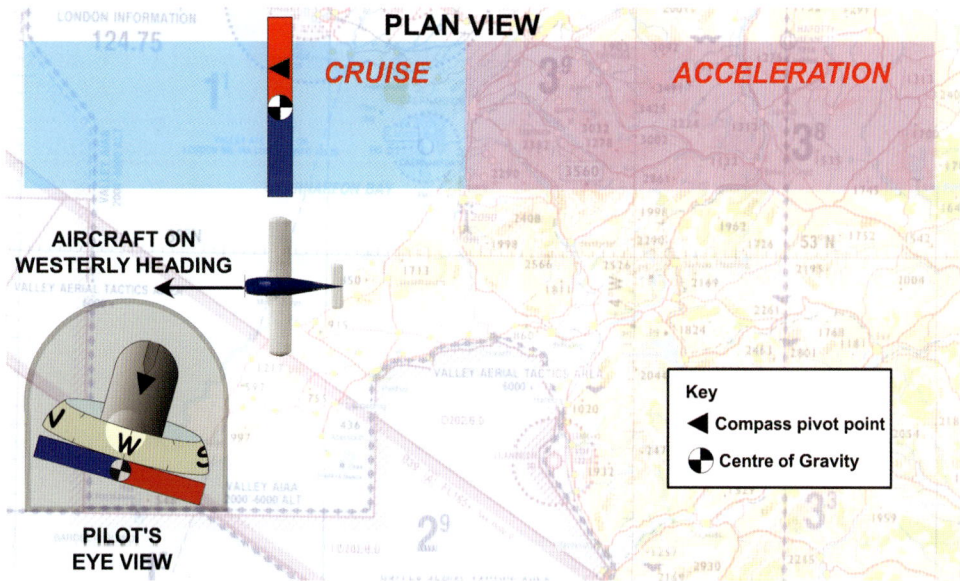

Figure 15.28 The compass reading is again correct.

Deceleration (Westerly Heading).
If the aircraft **decelerates** while maintaining a **Westerly heading**, the pendulous magnet assembly will move ahead of the compass pivot, inducing the compass to indicate an apparent turn towards the South.

Accelerations and Decelerations on Easterly Headings.
By analogous reasoning, an **acceleration** and **deceleration** on an **Easterly heading** will, likewise, cause the compass to indicate an apparent turn towards North and South, respectively. **Acceleration errors on Easterly headings are therefore identical to those on Westerly headings**. During cruising flight at constant airspeed, the compass will read correctly.

CHAPTER 15: GYROSCOPIC INSTRUMENTS & THE MAGNETIC COMPASS

The table below summarises the acceleration errors of the magnetic compass in the Northern Hemisphere.

LINEAR ACCELERATION ERRORS		
Heading	Acceleration	Deceleration
Northerly	No Error	No Error
Southerly	No Error	No Error
Easterly	Indicates apparent turn North	Indicates apparent turn South
Westerly	Indicates apparent turn North	Indicates apparent turn South

Figure 15.29 Table of linear acceleration errors in the magnetic compass.

Acceleration Errors on **Easterly** and **Westerly** Headings in the **Northern Hemisphere** can be memorised by using the mnemonic ANDS: Acceleration North, Deceleration South. In the **Southern Hemisphere**, **compass acceleration errors are the opposite** to those shown in the table. **Remember, there are no linear acceleration errors on Northerly and Southerly Headings**.

Turning Errors.

A **turning error** in a compass indication is a specialised type of **acceleration error**. When an aircraft turns at a constant speed it is subject to **centripetal acceleration** towards the centre of the turn. This **acceleration**, which is a result of the aircraft continuously changing direction, is caused by the **centripetal force** generated by the banked wings of the aircraft. The **centripetal force** acts on all parts of the aircraft, including the **centre of gravity** of the compass magnets and on the magnet pivot points. **This situation leads to the magnetic compass displaying indication errors during turns.**

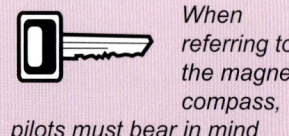
When referring to the magnetic compass, pilots must bear in mind that turning errors are maximum when turning through north and south, and minimum when turning through east and west.

Turning errors are maximum when turning through North and South, and, ignoring liquid swirl, zero when turning through East and West. The basic theory of **turning errors** is much the same as that for the linear acceleration errors that we have just covered.

Away from the regions of the magnetic equator, due to the effect of **magnetic dip**, the compass's **centre of gravity** will be **displaced** from a position directly beneath the **pivot point**. In a **turn**, the aircraft **accelerates** towards the **centre of the turn**, and therefore an **acceleration force** acts through the **pivot** towards the centre of the turn, while the **inertial reaction force** acts outwards through the **centre of gravity**. This situation results in the magnet assembly tending to 'swing out' from the turn, rotating the magnet assembly around the pivot point and producing a **turning error**.

Turning errors are usually more significant than linear acceleration errors for two reasons. Firstly, because they are inherently of greater magnitude, resulting from the greater displacement of the magnet assembly in turns; and secondly, turns are likely to be more prolonged than linear accelerations.

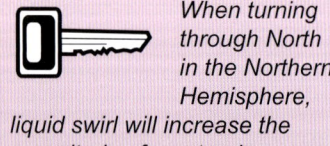
When turning through North in the Northern Hemisphere, liquid swirl will increase the magnitude of any turning error.

Liquid Swirl.

During a turn, the liquid in contact with the inside of the compass bowl tends to be dragged around with the bowl, so producing small eddies in the liquid which drift inwards from the circumference and deflect the magnet assembly in the direction of the turn. Therefore the liquid tends to **swirl** - and rotate the magnet assembly with it - in the same direction as the aircraft's turn.

CHAPTER 15: GYROSCOPIC INSTRUMENTS & THE MAGNETIC COMPASS

When turning through **North** in the **Northern Hemisphere**, **liquid swirl** will increase the magnitude of any **turning error** (in which the assembly turns in the same direction as the aircraft).

The size of the **turning error** when turning through **South** in the **Northern Hemisphere** (where the assembly turns in the opposite direction to the aircraft) will be reduced. In the **Southern Hemisphere**, the **swirl** effect will be in the **opposite sense**.

Note that at the **Magnetic Equator** where there is no **magnetic dip**, **liquid swirl** is the sole source of **turning error**; with most compasses this effect is only slight.

Turning through North, South, East and West.
Turning errors are **maximum** when turning through **Magnetic North or South**, decreasing to zero when passing through East or West.

Turning error increases with increase in magnetic latitude. At the **Magnetic Equator** the only **turning error** is due to **liquid swirl**.

Whenever the pilot turns through the **nearer pole** (that is the **North Pole** in the **Northern Hemisphere**, or the **South Pole** in the **Southern Hemisphere**) **the aircraft and compass magnet rotate in the same direction**. In this situation, the relative movement between the compass card (attached to the magnet) and the compass housing will be small, and the compass card will appear to react **sluggishly. Therefore, the pilot must roll out of the turn early, just before the indicated heading is reached** *(see Figures 15.30 and 15.31)*.

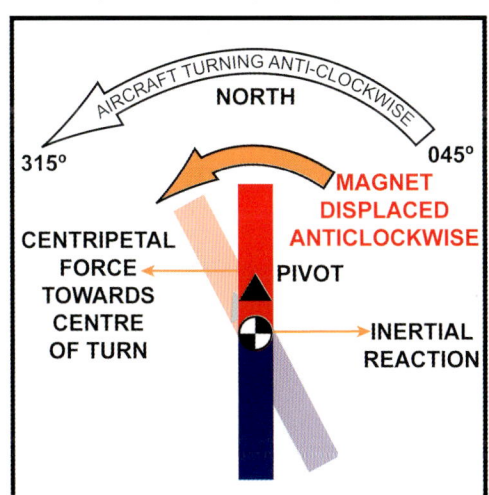
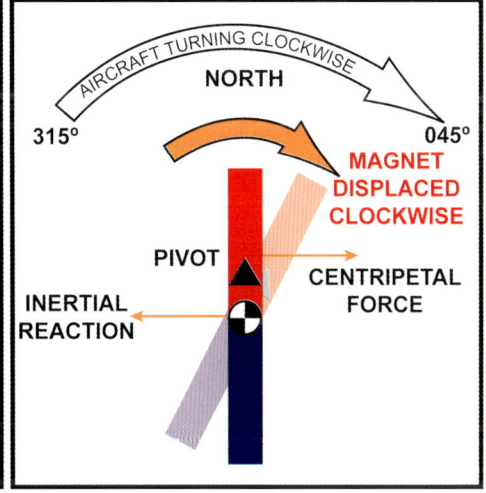

Figure 15.30 Turning from 045° to 315° (Northern Hemisphere).   *Figure 15.31 Turning from 315° to 045° (Northern Hemisphere).*

Whenever the pilot turns through the **further pole** (that is the **South Pole** in the **Northern Hemisphere**, or the **North Pole** in the **Southern Hemisphere**) the **aircraft and the compass rotate in opposite directions**. In this situation, the relative movement between the compass card and the compass housing will be large and the compass card will react **in a lively manner. Therefore, the pilot must roll out of the turn just after the indicated heading is reached** *(see Figures 15.32 and 15.33 overleaf)*.

CHAPTER 15: GYROSCOPIC INSTRUMENTS & THE MAGNETIC COMPASS

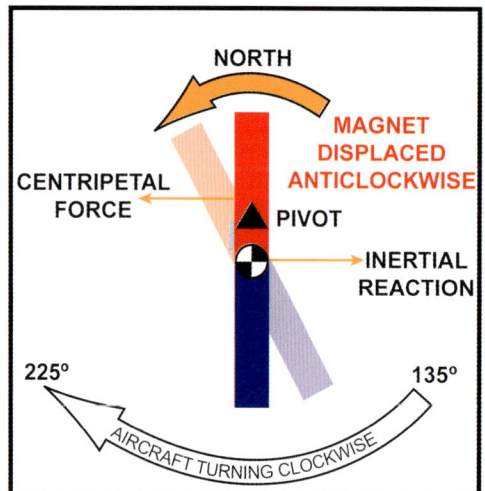
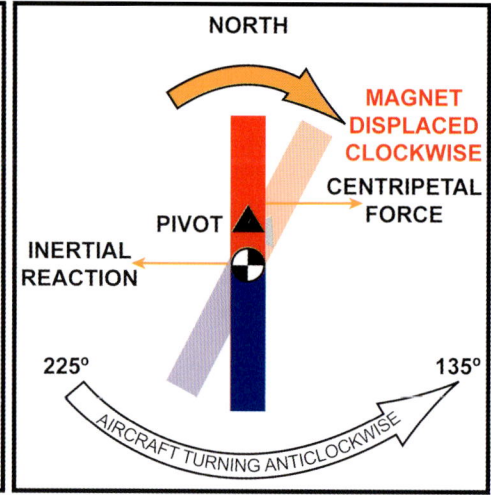

Figure 15.32 Turning from 135° to 225° (Northern Hemisphere).

Figure 15.33 Turning from 135° to 225° (Northern Hemisphere).

In the **Northern Hemisphere**, when rolling out of a turn onto a magnetic heading, using a **direct indicating magnetic compass**, the pilot should memorise the mnemonic **NESL** (NORTH (rollout) EARLY, SOUTH (rollout) LATE).

SYNCHRONISING DIRECTION INDICATOR AND MAGNETIC COMPASS.

Having learned about the **indication errors** to which the **magnetic compass** is susceptible, you are now in a position to appreciate why the aircraft must be flown at a constant speed, with wings level, whenever the **Direction Indicator** is to be synchronised with the **Magnetic Compass**.

COMPASS SERVICEABILITY CHECKS.

Prior to take off, the following checks of the **Magnetic Compass** should be carried out. The checks are done before engine start, during taxying or after lining up on a runway, as appropriate.

Prior to Engine Start.
Check that there is no obvious damage to the compass body or glass, such as dents or cracks, and that the compass is securely mounted.

Check that the compass liquid is free from sediment and discolouration, either of which would indicate corrosion, resulting in increased pivot friction.

The compass liquid should also be free from bubbles, which would probably indicate a leaking seal. Turbulence and manoeuvres would cause any bubbles to move about, creating eddies which could disturb the magnet system.

The compass reading can also be checked for gross errors when you first enter the aircraft by verifying that the compass is giving a sensible reading.

CHAPTER 15: GYROSCOPIC INSTRUMENTS & THE MAGNETIC COMPASS

During Taxying.
Check the compass reading while taxying the aircraft. The compass readings should decrease when turning left, and increase when the aircraft is turning right.

After lining up.
Just before take-off, check the compass reading against the runway heading.

CHAPTER 15: GYROSCOPIC INSTRUMENTS & THE MAGNETIC COMPASS QUESTIONS

Representative PPL - type questions to test your theoretical knowledge of Gyroscopic Instruments and the Magnetic Compass.

1. What is the purpose of the ball in the Turn and Slip Indicator or Turn Coordinator?

    a. The ball indicates rate of turn
    b. The ball indicates angle of bank
    c. The ball indicates slip and skid
    d. The ball indicates rate of descent in a turn

2. A magnetic heading:

    a. is the sum of the true heading, and magnetic deviation
    b. is the sum of the magnetic deviation and the magnetic variation
    c. is always referenced to true north
    d. is the sum of the compass reading and compass deviation

3. If the variation is west of true north:

    a. add it to the desired true track to get the correct magnetic heading
    b. add it to your aircraft's magnetic heading to get the desired true track
    c. subtract it from the desired true track to get the correct magnetic heading
    d. the angle of dip will be greatest

4. The turning errors of the magnetic compass are such that :

    a. They are zero when turning through North and South
    b. They are maximum when turning through North and South, requiring the pilot to roll out on heading early when turning through the nearer pole and late when turning through the further pole
    c. They are maximum when turning through East and West
    d. They are maximum when turning through North and South, requiring the pilot to roll out on heading early when turning through the further pole and late when turning through the nearer pole.

5. The gyroscope in an artificial horizon is:

    a. an Earth gyroscope rotating in a vertical plane about the aircraft's lateral axis
    b. an Earth gyroscope rotating in a horizontal plane about a vertical spin axis
    c. an Earth gyroscope rotating in a vertical plane about the aircraft's longitudinal axis
    d. a tied gyroscope rotating in a horizontal plane about the aircraft's longitudinal axis

CHAPTER 15: GYROSCOPIC INSTRUMENTS & THE MAGNETIC COMPASS QUESTIONS

6. The rigidity in space of a gyro:

    a. keeps its axis pointing in a fixed direction in space unless it is acted on by an external force
    b. is decreased by manufacturing the rotor from brass
    c. is maximum at the magnetic equator
    d. is minimum at the magnetic equator

7. A Direction Indicator should be aligned with the magnetic compass; approximately every 15 minutes:

    a. to minimise the effect of magnetic dip
    b. to offset the affect of acceleration during a turn
    c. because of the effect of liquid swirl
    d. in order to compensate for precession and apparent wander, by using the caging knob to rotate the DI azimuth card when the wings are level and the aircraft is in unaccelerated flight

8. A Direction Indicator:

    a. is badly affected by acceleration in a turn
    b. suffers from apparent drift of the gyroscope from the fixed position in space to which it was aligned, produced by earth rotation
    c. is not affected by drift produced from mechanical friction in the gyroscope gimbal bearings
    d. provides a stable reference in elevation in order to indicate accurate pitch attitudes

9. The purpose of the compass deviation card is to:

    a. compensate for the influence of non-ferrous material carried on the person of the pilot and/or passengers
    b. indicate the discrepancy between the heading shown on the compass and the actual magnetic heading
    c. indicate the discrepancy between the aircraft's track and magnetic north
    d. indicate the discrepancy between the aircraft's track and true north

10. When referring to the magnetic compass, pilots must bear in mind that:

    a. turning errors are maximum when turning through north and south, and minimum when turning through east and west
    b. turning errors are maximum when turning through east and west, and minimum when turning through north and south
    c. turning errors increase, the nearer the aircraft is to the magnetic equator, and diminish as the aircraft approaches the magnetic poles
    d. acceleration errors decrease the nearer the aircraft is to the magnetic poles, and increase as the aircraft approaches the magnetic equator

CHAPTER 15: GYROSCOPIC INSTRUMENTS & THE MAGNETIC COMPASS QUESTIONS

11. If the gyroscope of a turn indicator runs at a lower RPM than its design specification, how will the actual rate of turn of the aircraft compare to the rate of turn shown on the turn indicator?

    a. the actual rate of turn of the aircraft will be same as the rate indicated
    b. the actual rate of turn of the aircraft will be less than the rate indicated
    c. the turn indicator will not indicate a rate of turn
    d. the actual rate of turn of the aircraft will be greater than the rate indicated

12. When a compass swing is being carried out:

    a. the location of the aircraft must coincide with a suitable isogonal
    b. it will enable the aircraft's variation to be determined
    c. the aircraft's heading compass reading is compared with readings from a highly accurate 'land' or 'datum' compass
    d. the whole aircraft must be electrically dead

13. If there are metallic objects close to an aircraft's magnetic compass:

    a. they should have no effect on compass indications
    b. they will have a significant effect on magnetic variation
    c. the Direction Indicator will not be able to be synchronised with the compass
    d. they will cause errors in the indications of the compass

Question	1	2	3	4	5	6	7	8	9	10	11	12
Answer												

Question	13
Answer	

The answers to these questions can be found at the end of this book.

CHAPTER 16
AIRWORTHINESS

CHAPTER 16: AIRWORTHINESS

CHAPTER 16: AIRWORTHINESS

INTRODUCTION.

The United Kingdom Air Navigation Order stipulates that all United Kingdom registered aircraft should meet specific airworthiness requirements. The most important airworthiness documents, as far as the private pilot is concerned, are:

- The Certificate of Registration.

- The Certificate of Airworthiness.

- The Flight Manual.

- Maintenance Documents.

Illustrations of these documents are to be found on this and the following pages.

Certificate of Registration.

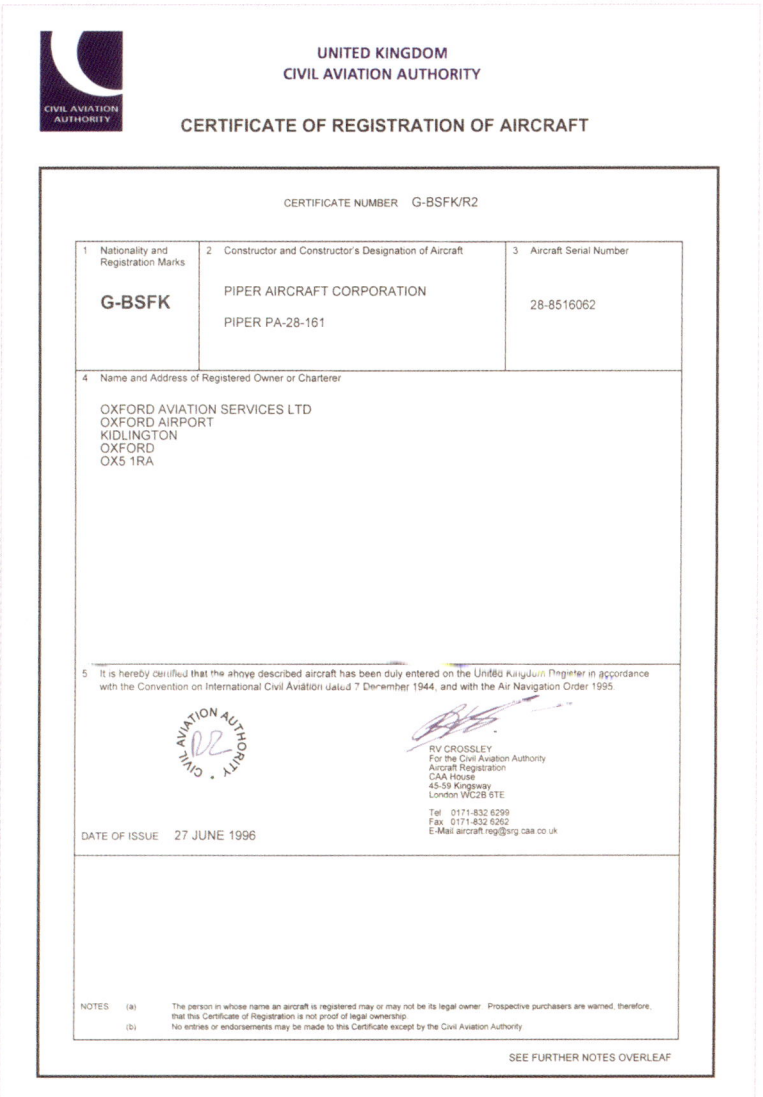

Figure 16.1 Certificate of Registration.

Certificate of Airworthiness.

UNITED KINGDOM
CIVIL AVIATION AUTHORITY

CERTIFICATE OF AIRWORTHINESS

Certificate No: 034612/005

Nationality and Registration Marks	Constructor and Constructor's Designation of Aircraft	Aircraft Serial Number
G-BSFK	PIPER AIRCRAFT CORPORATION PIPER PA-28-161	28-8516062

TRANSPORT CATEGORY (PASSENGER)	Date of Expiry: 10 July 2005

This Certificate of Airworthiness is issued pursuant to the Convention on International Civil Aviation dated 7 December 1944, and to the Civil Aviation Act 1982, and the Orders and Regulations made thereunder, in respect of the above-mentioned aircraft which is considered to be airworthy when maintained and operated in accordance with the foregoing and the pertinent operating limitations. The CAA Approved Flight Manual forms part of this Certificate.

Date of Validity: 11 July 2002

for the Civil Aviation Authority

Note: Following replacement, this Certificate of Airworthiness will cease to be in force and should be returned to the address below.

No entries or endorsements may be made on this Certificate except by an authorised person. If this Certificate is lost, the Civil Aviation Authority should be informed at once. Any person finding this Certificate should forward it immediately to the Civil Aviation Authority, Safety Regulation Group, Aviation House, South Area, Gatwick Airport, West Sussex, RH6 0YR.

CA958NR
310398

Figure 16.2 Certificate of Airworthiness.

Flight Manual.

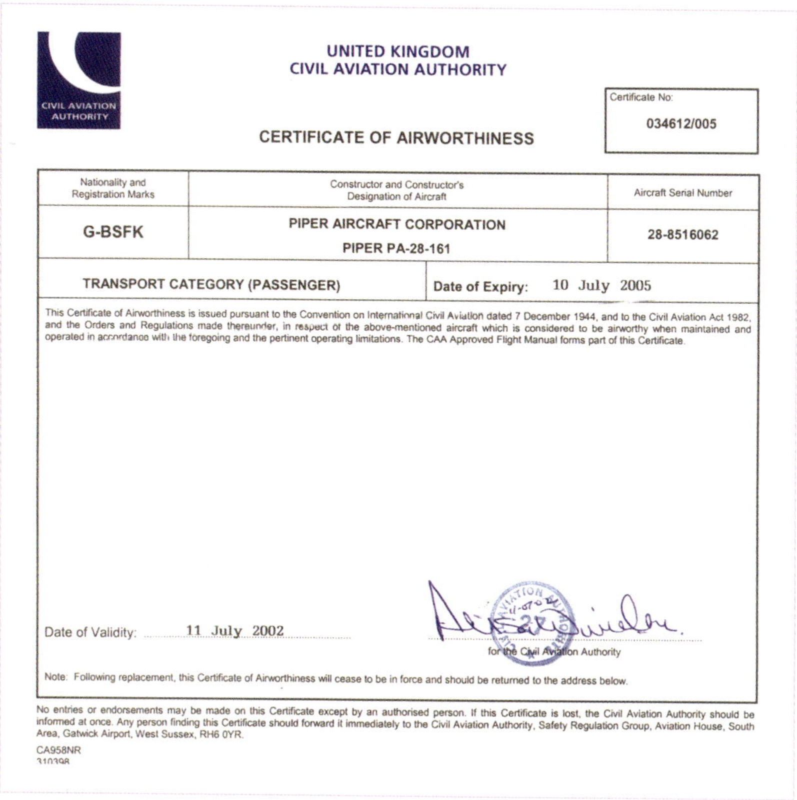

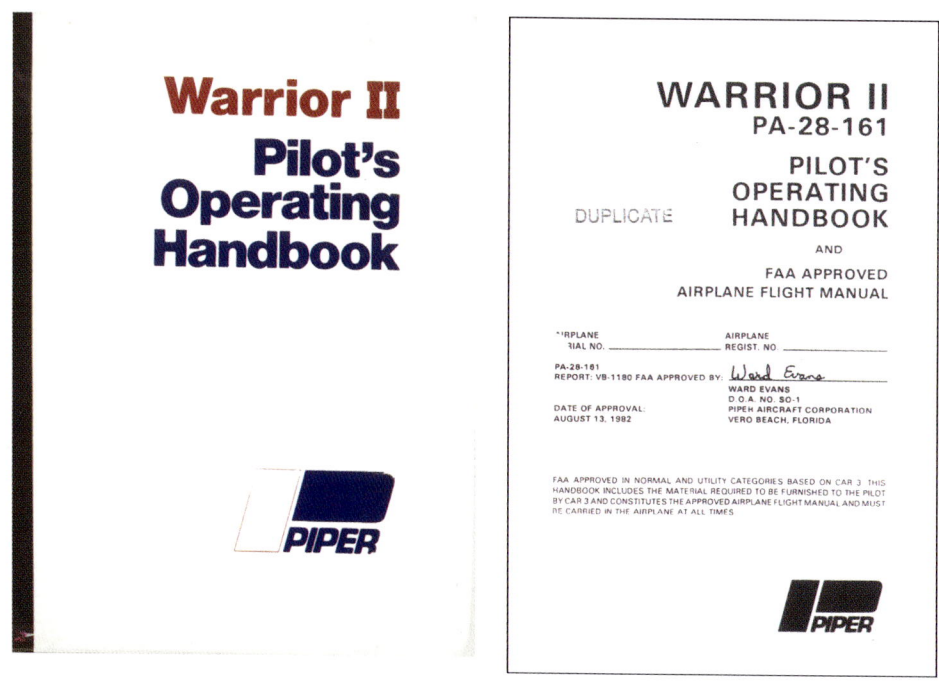

Figure 16.3 Pilot's Operating Handbook/Flight Manual.

Maintenance Documents.

CSE AVIATION
OXFORD AIRPORT, KIDLINGTON, OXFORD OX5 1RA.
T: +44 (0)1865 844 200 F: +44 (0)1865 379 123

MAINTENANCE STATEMENT AND Serial No SCH/04/032
SCHEDULED MAINTENANCE INSPECTION CERTIFICATE OF RELEASE TO SERVICE

Aircraft Type PA28-161 Registration Mark G-BTRY

Scheduled Maintenance Inspection / Check ANNUAL was completed at 6791.25 airframe hours, on the 18-03-2004 To Sch. Ref:- MS/~~MP~~/ LA/n

Category	Licence / Authority Approval No.	Signature
'A' Airframe	CAA00027 (105)	
'C' Engine	CAA00027 (105)	
'R' Radio	CAA00027 (31)	
'X' Electrics		
'X' Instruments		
'X' Autopilots		
'X' Compasses		

Certifies that the work specified except as otherwise specified was carried out in accordance with JAR-145 and in respect to that work the aircraft / aircraft component is considered ready for release to service.

The next Scheduled Maintenance Inspection / Check is a B/ONE

due at 6891.25 Hrs., or Midnight on the 17-06-2004 whichever is the sooner.

The following out-of phase inspections / component changes are due before the next Scheduled Maintenance Inspection / Check specified above:

Item	Due Hrs.	Due Date	Sector Log Reference on Completion
3 Year Compass Swing		30/5/04	3 YEARLY COMPASS SWING
			CARRIED OUT AT KIDLINGTON
			ON 28/5/2004 COMPASS
NIL			DEVIATION CARDS FITTED.
			W/O K03851 TASK CODE D01
			(56)
			CAA 00027

Retain until 06-12-2004 CERTIFICATE OF MAINTENANCE REVIEW

Aircraft Type PA28-161 Registration Mark G-BTRY

Certified that a Maintenance Review of this aircraft and such of its equipment as is necessary for its airworthiness has been carried out in accordance with the requirements of the Air Navigation Order for the time being in force.

THE NEXT MAINTENANCE REVIEW IS DUE ON THE 06-12-2004

Signature .... Date 18-03-2004

J.A.A. Approval Reference / Licence No CAA00027 (105)

Figure 16.4 Certificate of Release to Service.

CERTIFICATE OF TYPE APPROVAL.

When an aircraft manufacturer wishes to put a new type or model of aircraft on the market, he must first obtain a Certificate of Type Approval from the aviation authority in the country of manufacture. Before a Certificate of Type Approval can be issued, the prototypes of the particular aircraft type must pass many stringent tests. The tests themselves cover a multitude of aspects, such as safety, engineering, reliability and aircraft performance. The Certificate of Type Approval is not passed to the aircraft owner, but is retained by the aircraft manufacturer.

The United Kingdom Civil Aviation Authority (UK CAA) does not normally carry out a UK Type Certification for foreign aircraft of conventional design that weigh less than 6 000 lb, (2730 kg), but accepts the aircraft on the basis of the foreign Certificate of Type Approval.

CHAPTER 16: AIRWORTHINESS

If an aircraft's Certificate of Airworthiness is not maintained in accordance with the approved maintenance schedule, the Certificate of Airworthiness will be rendered invalid, until such time as the required maintenance is completed.

The UK CAA carries out a validation exercise in accordance with the procedures detailed in British Civil Airworthiness Requirements (BCARs). The level of UK CAA investigation of the aircraft depends on the intended operation and certification category, and the associated equipment fit and performance information.

CERTIFICATE OF REGISTRATION.

The United Kingdom Civil Aviation Authority requires that all United Kingdom owned or operated aircraft be registered with them. A Certificate of Registration *(see Figure 16.1)* is then issued to the owner, and the aircraft is assigned its nationality and registration marks, by which it may be recognised.

In the United Kingdom there are four registration letters which follow the United Kingdom nationality mark 'G', such as the letters shown on Golf Tango Alpha Golf Sierra, in *Figure 16.5*. Nationality and Registration marks must be displayed permanently and clearly on the aircraft, and be kept clean and visible.

Figure 16.5 Registration Letters.

CERTIFICATE OF AIRWORTHINESS.

An aircraft's Certificate of Airworthiness is valid for the period specified in that Certificate of Airworthiness.

The Certificate of Airworthiness, shown in *Figure 16.2*, is usually referred to in its shortened form as the C of A. It is issued to a particular aircraft by the National Civil Aviation Authority for a specific period, normally three years for an aircraft of less than 6 000 lb (2 730 kg). The C of A confirms that the aircraft is certified to an internationally acceptable standard in terms of safety, design, construction and performance etc.

A C of A is issued to an aircraft to allow it to operate within a specific category, as long as it complies with the appropriate airworthiness requirements. *Figure 16.2* illustrates a C of A which certifies an aircraft to fly in the Transport Category (Passenger).

Unless the aircraft has a Permit to Fly, or is undergoing a test flight, it cannot fly without a valid Certificate of Airworthiness.

Unless the aircraft has a Permit to Fly, which will be mentioned later, or is undergoing a test flight, it cannot fly without a valid C of A.

The C of A states any restrictions and conditions of issue.
The Flight Manual and the Certificate of Maintenance Review are documents associated with the C of A.

Ignoring any of the restrictions or conditions laid down in the C of A, or the procedures and limitations in the Flight Manual, or exceeding the period of validity, will automatically invalidate the C of A. Failure to maintain and operate the aircraft in accordance with the C of A will also render the C of A invalid.

CHAPTER 16: AIRWORTHINESS

CATEGORIES AND PURPOSES OF AIRCRAFT.

Aircraft are certified to operate in one of the following categories:-

Transport (Passengers) - any purpose.

Transport (Cargo) - any purpose other than the public transport of passengers.

Aerial Work - any purpose except public transport.

Private - any purpose except public transport or aerial work.

Special - any purpose, other than public transport, specified on the C of A, but usually precluding the carriage of passengers.

Aircraft are further categorised according to the manoeuvres that they are allowed to perform and certain other design criteria. Three categories relevant to aircraft (below a Maximum Take-Off Mass of 5700kg or less) likely to be flown by the private pilot are:-

Normal category - Manoeuvres limited to stalls and steep turns of 60°. Typical limit load factors are +2.5g and -1.0g.

Utility category - as for Normal Category, plus limited aerobatics. Typical limit load factors are +4.5g and -1.8g.

Acrobatic category - fully aerobatic
Typical limit load factors are +6.0g and -3.0g.

FLIGHT MANUAL.

The Flight Manual, (*Figure 16.3*), forms part of the Certificate of Airworthiness for a particular aircraft. The United Kingdom Civil Aviation Authority (UK CAA), certifies an aircraft for use within its area of responsibility, and may produce amendments to the Flight Manual.

These amendments are issued in a Flight Manual Supplement. A pilot must comply with all the requirements, procedures and limitations set out in the Flight Manual, as amended by the Flight Manual Supplement, with respect to the operation of the aircraft.

A UK CAA Flight Manual Supplement overrules the information in the original Flight Manual or Pilot's Operating Handbook.

The Flight Manual and the UK CAA Flight Manual Supplement must be carried in the aircraft at all times. In order that the pilot may have a readily available reference to the data applicable to his aircraft, the Pilot's Operating Handbook has been derived from the Flight Manual.

The same procedures, techniques, limitations and performance standards which are contained in the Flight Manual are to be found in the Pilot's Operating Handbook. However, the Pilot's Operating Handbook does not have the legal standing of the Flight Manual.

The Flight Manual and the UK CAA Flight Manual Supplement must be carried in the aircraft at all times.

A Flight Manual Supplement, issued by the CAA, deals with additional limitations which are to be complied with, even when they conflict with those published in the flight manual.

CHAPTER 16: AIRWORTHINESS

PERMIT TO FLY.

If a British registered aircraft is unable to satisfy the requirements for the issue of a Certificate of Airworthiness (C of A), it may instead be issued with a United Kingdom Permit to Fly. The Permit to Fly is a national 'permission to fly' issued by the UK CAA for use within the United Kingdom only, and does not satisfy the requirements for international flight.

The type of aircraft which operate on a Permit to Fly include:
- Amateur-built aircraft.
- Ex-military aircraft.
- Microlight aircraft.
- Vintage aircraft.

Although the European Aviation Safety Agency (EASA) will, in the future, assume many of the functions currently undertaken by national aviation authorities, aircraft which have been flying in the United Kingdom on a Permit to Fly issued by the UK CAA will, generally, remain subject to national requirements.

In the United Kingdom the inspection and maintenance requirements of aircraft which have a Permit to Fly are in the main managed by approved organisations such as the Popular Flying Association (PFA), and the British Microlight Aircraft Association (BMAA).

A Permit to Fly restricts the operation of the aircraft as follows:

Firstly, the aircraft shall be used for recreational purposes only, i.e., not for public transport or for aerial work such as aerial photography or banner towing. The one exception, however, is that aircraft may be flown for public exhibition or demonstration, such as at airshows, even when this does constitute aerial work.

Secondly, except to the extent necessary in order to take-off and land in accordance with normal aviation practice, aircraft with Permits to Fly are not allowed to fly over any assembly of persons or congested area, at any height.

Thirdly, Permit to Fly aircraft are permitted to fly in daytime and under Visual Flight Rules flight conditions only. i.e., not at night and not in accordance with Instrument Flight Rules. As stated earlier, a Permit to Fly permits flight in the United Kingdom only: however, every Permit to Fly carries an Exemption which allows the aircraft to leave UK airspace, which the Air Navigation Order would otherwise prohibit. Note, however, that this exemption still does not represent a permission to enter the airspace of another country. Full details of the Permit to Fly are currently contained in the UK CAA publication, CAP 733.

MAINTENANCE SCHEDULE.

All aircraft in the Transport, Aerial Work and Private Categories are to be maintained in accordance with either an approved Maintenance Schedule, or, if its Maximum Take-off Weight Authorised does not exceed 6 000 lb (2 730 kg), the Light Aircraft Maintenance Schedule. Both these schedules require that a system of regular checks and inspections be carried out by licensed and approved persons. Furthermore, logbooks must be kept in respect of the engine and the airframe, and if the aircraft is fitted with a constant speed propeller, it too must have a logbook.

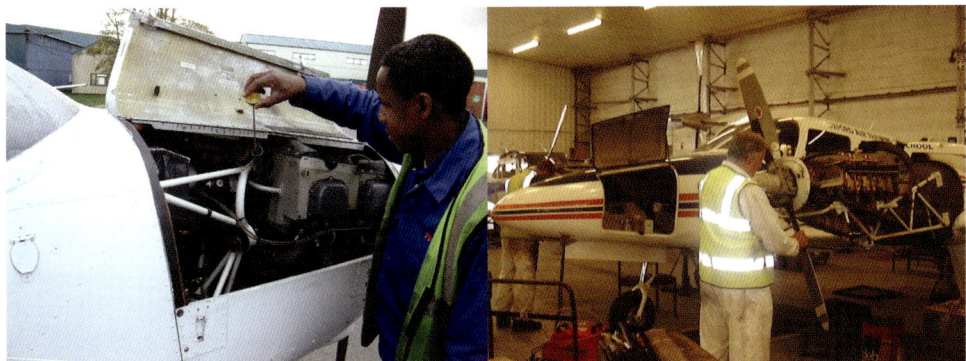

Figure 16.6 Part of the Daily Inspection, or Check A.

Figure 16.7 150-Hour Inspection.

A typical maintenance schedule will include:-

- The daily inspection, sometimes called the Check A. This is a thorough pre-flight inspection carried out by the pilot. (see *Figure 16.6*).
- A 50-hour inspection, (or 6 month inspection - whichever is earlier).
- A 150-hour inspection, (*Figure 16.7*), which is much more detailed than the 50-hour check.
- The annual inspection, which is a major inspection of the engine, the airframe and all of the aircraft systems and components.
- The 'Star Annual' inspection, which is an expanded annual inspection carried out every three years. This inspection includes a test flight to ensure that the aircraft is performing to the standards set out in its Flight Manual.

CERTIFICATE OF MAINTENANCE REVIEW.

A valid Certificate of Maintenance Review, which is shown in *Figure 16.8.*, must be in force for an aircraft with a Transport Category Certificate of Airworthiness. The Certificate of Maintenance Review confirms:

- that the aircraft has been maintained in accordance with its Maintenance Schedule
- that any Airworthiness Directives released within the previous 12 months have been complied with

Retain until 06-12-2004 CERTIFICATE OF MAINTENANCE REVIEW

Aircraft Type PA28-161 Registration Mark G-BTRY

Certified that a Maintenance Review of this aircraft and such of its equipment as is necessary for its airworthiness has been carried out in accordance with the requirements of the Air Navigation Order for the time being in force.

THE NEXT MAINTENANCE REVIEW IS DUE ON THE 06-12-2004

Signature J R Bradley Date 18-03-2004

J.A.A. Approval Reference / Licence No CAA00027 (105)

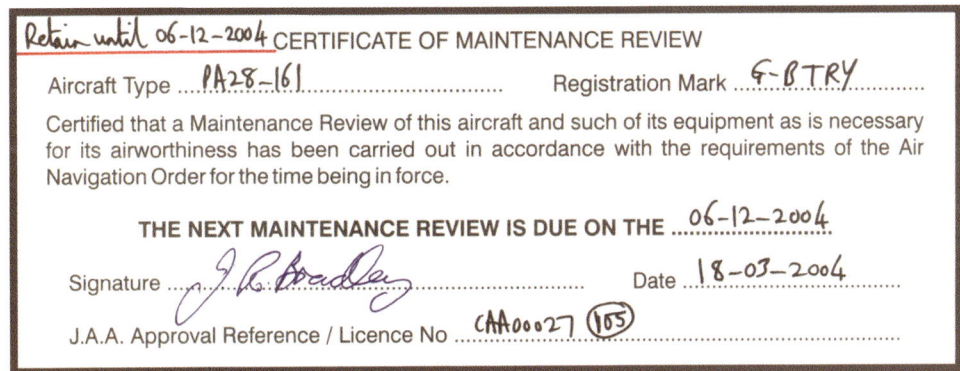

Figure 16.8 Certificate of Maintenance Review.

- that any Manufacturer's Service bulletins which have been released during the same period have also been complied with. Airworthiness Directives may often be used to make a Manufacturer's Service Bulletin compulsory.

TECHNICAL LOG.

An example of a Technical Log is shown in *Figure 16.9*. An aircraft with a Transport Category Certificate of Airworthiness must have a Technical Log.

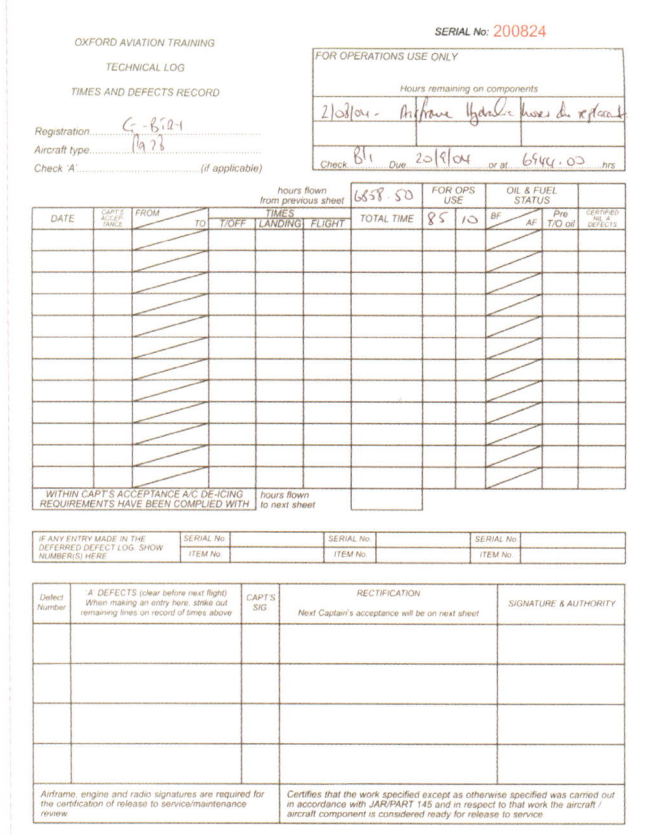

Figure 16.9 Technical Log.

The Technical Log is used by the pilot to record take-off and landing times, and it must be signed by the pilot after each flight. Any defects in an aircraft which become apparent during the flight should be entered in the Technical Log. The maintenance staff will also use the Technical Log to record any work carried out to rectify aircraft defects.

CERTIFICATE OF RELEASE TO SERVICE.

Following any maintenance carried out on an aircraft that has a Certificate of Airworthiness, a Certificate of Release to Service, an example of which is shown in the top half of *Figure 16.4*, is issued by a licensed engineer.

This certifies that the work carried out on the aircraft has been done in accordance with both the Civil Aviation Authority's and the manufacturer's procedures.

Work carried out by a pilot or the owner of the aircraft does not require a Certificate of Release to Service.

Maintenance Allowed by Pilots.

Although, in general, all maintenance on an aircraft with a United Kingdom Certificate of Airworthiness must be carried out and inspected by a licensed aircraft engineer, the Civil Aviation Authority has made provision for certain minor repairs and servicing to be performed by owners or operators who are not licensed engineers.

Figure 16.10 Replacing Wings which are Designed for Disassembly.

Certain types of repairs and servicing can be carried out by pilots who are owners or operators of aircraft if their aircraft weighs less than 6 000 lb (2 370 kg) and is in a Category other than Public Transport. A list of those tasks allowed to be performed by a Private Pilot's Licence holder who is not a licensed engineer is published in the Air Navigation (General) Regulations, N° 16. That list is reproduced below:

> Aircraft maintenance carried out by a private pilot in accordance with the pilot's legal entitlement is to be entered in the aircraft's log book and certified by the pilot who carried out the maintenance.

- Replacement of landing gear tyres, landing skids or skid shoes.

- Replacement of elastic shock absorber cord units on landing gear where special tools are not required.

- Replacement of defective safety wiring or split-pins excluding those in engine, transmission, flight control and rotor systems.

- Patch-repairs to fabric not requiring rib stitching or the removal of structural parts or control surfaces, if the repairs do not cover up structural damage and do not include repairs to rotor blades.

- Repairs to upholstery and decorative furnishing of the cabin or cockpit interior when repair does not require dismantling of any structure or operating system or interfere with an operating system or affect the structure of the aircraft.

- Repairs, not requiring welding, to fairings, non-structural cover plates and cowlings.

- Replacement of side windows where that work does not interfere with the structure or with any operating system.

- Replacement of safety belts or safety harnesses.

- Replacement of seats or seat parts not involving dismantling of any structure or of any operating system.

- Replacement of bulbs, reflectors, glasses, lenses or lights.

- Replacement of any cowling not requiring removal of the propeller, rotors or disconnection of engine or flight controls.

CHAPTER 16: AIRWORTHINESS

- Replacement of unserviceable sparking plugs.

- Replacement of batteries.

- Replacement of wings and tail surfaces and controls, the attachments of which are designed to provide for assembly immediately before each flight and dismantling after each flight, *(Figure 16.10)*.

- Replacement of main rotor blades that are designed for removal where special tools are not required.

- Replacement of generator and fan belts designed for removal where special tools are not required.

- Replacement of VHF communication equipment, being equipment which is not combined with navigation equipment.

In addition to this list, the holder of a Private Pilot's Licence may also carry out the 50 hour inspection of an aircraft in the Private Category, if he is the owner or operator of the aircraft.

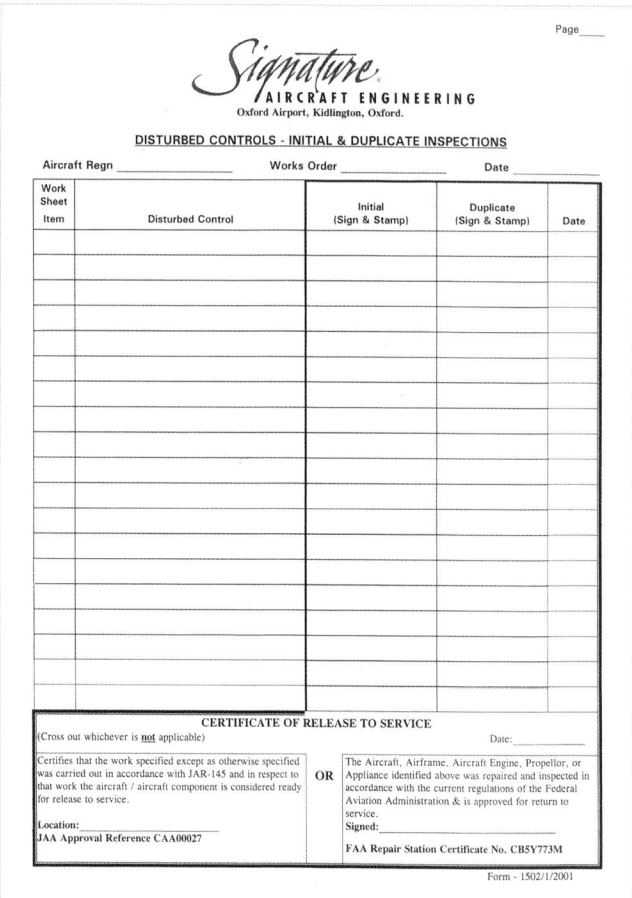

Figure 16.11 Inspection of Disturbed Controls.

Aircraft maintenance carried out by a private pilot in accordance with the pilot's legal entitlement is to be entered in the aircraft's log book and certified by the pilot who carried out the maintenance.

CHAPTER 16: AIRWORTHINESS

DUPLICATE CONTROL SYSTEM INSPECTION.

If any adjustments are made to the flight controls or the engine controls, these adjustments would normally be required to be checked by two licensed personnel, either engineers or inspectors, to confirm that the work has been properly carried out and that the controls are functioning properly. This is termed a Duplicate Control System Inspection.

However, British Civil Airworthiness Requirements state that should a minor adjustment of a control system be necessary when the aircraft is away from base, and where the initial part of the inspection has been done by a licensed engineer, the second part of the inspection can be carried out and certified by a pilot licensed for the type of aircraft concerned. Subsequent to the inspection, a form similar to that shown in *Figure 16.11* must be completed.

British Civil Airworthiness Requirements (BCARs) state that the second part of a duplicate inspection on an aircraft's control system, which has had a minor adjustment away from the aircraft's home airfield, may be carried out by a pilot, type-licensed for the aircraft concerned.

DAILY INSPECTION (CHECK A).

The Daily Inspection, also known as the 'Check A' in the United Kingdom, must be carried out prior to the first flight of the day, although in practice it is carried out before each flight . This check may be carried out by the pilot.

INSURANCE DOCUMENTATION.

The pilot must confirm that the aircraft he or she is about to fly has valid insurance cover. Although a Certificate of Insurance is not part of the Certificate of Airworthiness, it is only common sense that a pilot should ensure that he and his aircraft are covered for any eventuality. *Figure 16.12* is an example of the sort of document to look out for if you are searching for your aircraft's Certificate of Insurance.

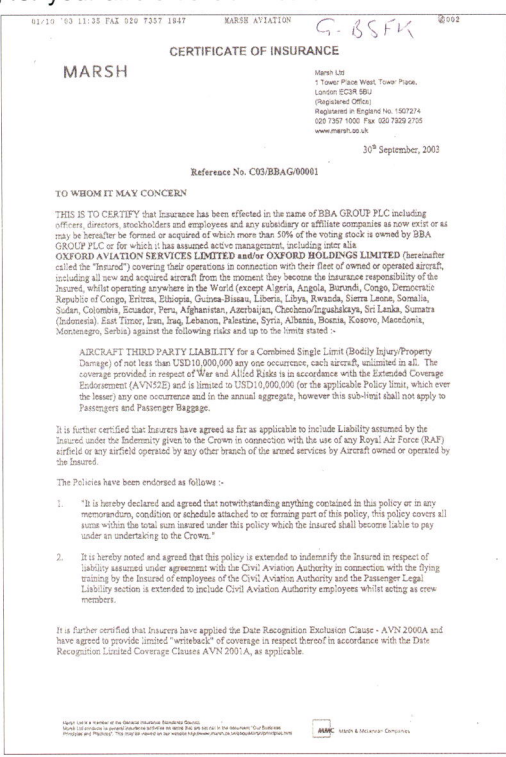

Figure 16.12 The Certificate of Insurance.

CHAPTER 16: AIRWORTHINESS QUESTIONS

Representative PPL - type questions to test your theoretical knowledge of Airworthiness.

1. A Flight Manual Supplement issued by the CAA deals with additional limitations:

    a. it will contain only limitations not dealt with in the manual published by the aircraft manufacturer
    b. the limitations apply only to in-flight tests carried out for the purpose of amending the Certificate of Airworthiness flight test
    c. the limitations are to be complied with, even where they conflict with those published in the aircraft manufacturer's manual
    d. it can be disregarded as long as the limitations in the original aircraft manufacturer's manual continue to be complied with

2. Aircraft maintenance carried out by a private pilot in accordance with the pilot's legal entitlement:

    a. is to be entered in the aircraft's log book and certified by a licensed engineer
    b. need not be logged or recorded
    c. is to be entered in the aircraft's log book and certified by a CAA approved inspector
    d. is to be entered in the aircraft's log book and certified by the pilot who carried out the maintenance

3. The consequence for the validity of an aircraft's Certificate of Airworthiness (C of A) if the aircraft is not maintained in accordance with the approved maintenance schedule detailed in the C of A will be that:

    a. the aircraft owner must apply to the CAA for an exemption from the required maintenance schedule
    b. the C of A will be rendered invalid until such time as the required maintenance is completed
    c. the C of A must be renewed before the aircraft may fly
    d. the validity of the C of A will not be affected

4. The second part of a duplicate inspection, required by Chapter A6-2 of BCARs, on an aircraft's control system which has had a minor adjustment away from its home airfield, may be:

    a. delayed until the aircraft returns to its home airfield
    b. carried out by a type-licensed engineer only
    c. carried out by a pilot type-licensed for the aircraft concerned
    d. postponed until the next convenient opportunity

CHAPTER: 16 AIRWORTHINESS QUESTIONS

5. An aircraft's Certificate of Airworthiness (C of A):

    a. is valid for the period specified in the C of A
    b. expires only when the aircraft is removed from the British register
    c. is valid indefinitely, provided that the aeroplane is maintained in accordance with the requirements specified in the C of A
    d. is valid for 6 months

Question	1	2	3	4	5
Answer					

The answers to these questions can be found at the end of this book.

AIRCRAFT (GENERAL) SYLLABUS

JAR-FCL PPL THEORETICAL KNOWLEDGE SYLLABUS.

AIRCRAFT (GENERAL).

The table below contains the principal topics and subtopics from the current outline syllabus for the theoretical examination in **Aircraft (General)** for the **Private Pilot's Licence**, as published in **JAR-FCL 1**. In this book, the subject of **Aircraft (General)** is covered in the section on **Aeroplanes**. Syllabuses may be modified, so always check the latest examination documentation from your **national civil aviation authority**, or from **JAR-FCL/EASA**.

In the United Kingdom, **Aircraft General** is examined in the same paper as **Principles of Flight**.

AIRCRAFT (GENERAL)	
AIRFRAME	
Airframe structure:	components; fuselage, wings, tailplane, fin; primary flying controls; trim and flap/slat systems; landing gear (nose wheel, including steering; tyres, condition; braking systems and precautions in use; retraction systems).
Airframe loads:	structural strength; safety factor; control locks and use; ground/flight precautions.
POWERPLANT	
Engines – general:	principles of the four stroke internal combustion engine; basic construction; causes of pre-ignition and detonation; power output as a function of RPM.
Engine cooling:	air cooling; cowling design and cylinder baffles; design and use of cowl flaps; cylinder head temperature gauge.
Engine lubrication:	function and methods of lubrication; lubrication systems; methods of oil circulation; oil pump and filter requirements; qualities and grades of oil; oil temperature and pressure control; oil cooling methods; recognition of oil system malfunctions.
Ignition systems:	principles of magneto ignition; construction and function; purpose and principle of impulse coupling; serviceability checks, recognition of malfunctions; operational procedures to avoid spark plug fouling.
Carburation:	principles of float type carburettor; construction and function; methods to maintain correct mixture ratio; operation of metering jets and accelerator pump; effect of altitude; manual mixture control (maintenance of correct mixture ratio; limitation on use at high power; avoidance of detonation); idle cut-off valve; operation and use of primary controls; air induction system; alternate induction systems; carburettor icing, use of hot air; injection systems, principles and operation.
Aero engine fuel:	classification of fuels (grades and identification by colour; quality requirements); inspection for contamination; use of fuel strainers and drains.
Fuel systems:	fuel tanks and supply lines; venting system; mechanical and electrical pumps; gravity feed; tank selection; system management.
Propellers:	propeller nomenclature; conversion of engine power to thrust; design and construction of fixed pitch propeller; forces acting on propeller blade; variation of RPM with change of airspeed; thrust efficiency with change of speed; design and construction of variable pitch propeller; constant speed unit operation; effect of blade pitch changes; windmilling effect.

AIRCRAFT (GENERAL) SYLLABUS

Engine handling:	starting procedures and precautions; recognition of malfunctions; warming up, power and system checks; oil temperature and pressure limitations; cylinder head temperature limitations; ignition and other system checks; power limitations; avoidance of rapid power changes; use of mixture control.
SYSTEMS	
Electrical system:	installation and operation of alternators/generators; direct current supply; batteries, capacity and charging; voltmeters and ammeters; circuit breakers and fuses; electrically operated services and instruments; recognition of malfunctions; procedure in the event of malfunctions.
Vacuum system:	components; pumps; regulator and gauge; filter system; recognition of malfunction; procedures in the event of malfunctions.
INSTRUMENTS	
Pitot/static system:	pitot tube, function; pitot tube, principles and construction; static source; alternate static source; position error; system drains; heating element; errors caused by blockage or leakage.
Airspeed indicator:	principles of operation and construction; relationship between pitot and static pressure; definitions of indicated, calibrated and true airspeed; instrument errors; airspeed indications, colour coding; pilot's serviceability checks.
Altimeter:	principles of operation and construction; function of the sub-scale; effects of atmospheric density; pressure altitude; true altitude; international standard atmosphere; flight level; presentation (three needle); instrument errors; pilot's service ability checks.
Vertical speed indicator:	principles of operation and construction; function; inherent lag; instantaneous VSI; presentation; pilot's serviceability checks.
Gyroscopes:	principles; rigidity; precession.
Turn indicator:	rate gyro; purpose and function; effect of speed; presentation; turn co-ordinator; limited rate of turn indications; power source; balance indicator (principle; presentation); pilot's serviceability checks.
Attitude indicator:	earth gyro; purpose and function; presentations; interpretation; operating limitations; power source; pilot's serviceability checks.
Heading indicator:	directional gyro; purpose and function; presentation; use with magnetic compass; setting mechanism; apparent drift; operating limitations; power source; pilot's serviceability checks.
Magnetic compass:	construction and function; earth's magnetic field; variation and deviation; turning, acceleration errors; precautions when carrying magnetic items; pilot's service ability checks.
Engine instruments:	principles, presentation and operational use of: oil temperature gauge; oil pressure gauge; cylinder head temperature gauge; exhaust gas meter; manifold pressure gauge; fuel pressure gauge; fuel flow gauge; fuel quantity gauge(s); tachometer.
Other instruments:	principles, presentation and operational use of: vacuum gauge; voltmeter and ammeter; warning indicators; others relevant to aeroplane type.
AIRWORTHINESS	
Airworthiness:	certificate to be in force; compliance with requirements (periodic maintenance inspections; compliance with flight manual or equivalent, instructions, limitations, placards); flight manual supplements; provision and maintenance of documents (aeroplane, engine and propeller log books; recording of defects); permitted maintenance by pilots.

ANSWERS TO THE AEROPLANES QUESTIONS

ANSWERS TO THE AEROPLANES QUESTIONS

ANSWERS TO THE AEROPLANES QUESTIONS

Chapter 1   Airframes.

Question	1	2	3	4	5	6	7	8	9	10	11	12
Answer	c	b	a	c	d	b	a	b	c	b	b	d

13	14	15	16
b	c	a	b

Chapter 2   Landing Gear, Tyres and Brakes.

Question	1	2	3	4	5	6	7	8	9
Answer	c	a	b	c	a	a	d	b	d

Chapter 3   Engines General

Question	1	2	3	4	5	6	7	8	9
Answer	a	d	a	d	b	c	b	a	d

Chapter 3A   Aero Diesel Engines

Question	1	2	3	4	5
Answer	b	a	d	d	c

Chapter 4   Engine Cooling

Question	1	2
Answer	d	c

Chapter 5   Lubrication

Question	1	2	3	4	5
Answer	b	a	c	c	d

Chapter 6   Ignition Systems

Question	1	2	3	4	5	6	7	8	9	10	11
Answer	a	a	c	b	d	c	d	b	c	b	a

Chapter 7   Carburation

Question	1	2	3	4	5	6	7	8	9	10	11	12	13
Answer	d	c	a	c	a	b	d	a	a	c	b	c	d

ANSWERS TO THE AEROPLANES QUESTIONS

Chapter 8 — Aero Engines and Fuel Systems

Question	1	2	3	4	5	6	7
Answer	c	a	b	d	a	d	c

Chapter 9 — Propellers

Question	1	2	3	4	5	6	7
Answer	c	d	a	b	c	d	c

Chapter 10 — Engine Handling

Question	1	2	3	4	5	6
Answer	a	b	a	b	d	a

Chapter 11 — Electrical System

Question	1	2	3	4	5	6	7	8	9	10
Answer	c	d	a	c	a	b	a	b	d	b

Chapter 12 — Vacuum Systems

Questions	1	2	3	4	5
Answer	c	b	d	b	a

Chapter 13 — Engine Instruments

Question	1	2	3	4	5
Answer	d	b	a	c	d

Chapter 14 — Pressure Instruments

Question	1	2	3	4	5	6	7	8	9
Answer	d	c	a	c	b	d	b	a	d

Chapter 15 — Gyroscopic Instruments and the Magnetic Compass

Question	1	2	3	4	5	6	7	8	9	10	11	12	13
Answer	c	d	a	b	b	a	d	b	b	a	d	c	d

Chapter 16 — Airworthiness

Question	1	2	3	4	5
Answer	c	d	b	c	a

Index

A

Absolute Pressure	192
Accelerator Pump	104
Acrobatic Category	257
Adjustable-pitch Propellers	138
Ailerons	8
Airframes	3
Airspeed Indicator (ASI)	204
- Airspeed Indicator Errors	206
- Airspeed Indicator Serviceability Checks	208
Air Bleed Mixture Control	103
Air Cooling	65
Air Filter	104
Air Intake	104
Alternate Static Source	203
Alternating Current	159
Alternators	162
- Alternator Failure	174
Altimeter	209, 211
- Altimeter, Calibration of	209
- Altimeter Settings	214
Ammeters	166
Anti-surge Valve	77
Apron	18
Aquaplaning	30
Artificial Horizon	230
Asymmetric Blade Effect	136
Atmosphere	209
AVGAS	117
AVTUR	117
Awl Vents	29
Axes	7

B

Balance	9
Batteries	162
- Battery, Charging	165
Battery Circuit	172
Bellows	192
Bending Stresses	6
Bernoulli's Theorem	99
Biplanes	5
Blade Geometry	129
Bottom Dead Centre	41
Bourdon Tube	193
Braced Monoplane	5
Bracing Wires	5
Braking Systems	32

INDEX

Bulkheads	4
Busbars	161

C

Calibrated Airspeed	206
Cantilever Monoplane	5
Capacitor	86
Capsules	192
Carbon Reinforced Plastic	6
Carburettor	98
Carburettor Icing	106
Castoring	26
Certificate	253
Certificate of Airworthiness	256
Certificate of Maintenance Review	259
Certificate of Registration	256
Certificate of Release To Service	260
Certificate of Type Approval	255
Checks	16
Check A	259
Chemically Correct Ratio	95
Common-rail Fuel Injection	55
Common-rail Fuel Injection Principle	53
Common-rail Fuel Injection Systems	57
Compass	237
- Acceleration Errors	242
- Compass Errors	242
- Compass Serviceability Checks	246
- Deviation	240
- Direct Indicating Magnetic Compass	237
- E-2b	237
- Liquid Swirl	244
Composite Materials	6
Compound Oils	78
Compression Ratio	47, 55
Compression Stroke	40
Connecting Rod	43
Constant-speed Propeller Controls	139
Controls	8
Control Column	8
Control Locks	13
Control Movement	9
Cooling	73
Cooling Systems	66
Crank-pins	44
Crankshaft	44
Crank Throw	44
Creep	29
Cylinder	40
Cylinder Head	45
Cylinder Head Temperatures	68

INDEX

D

Daily Inspection	259
Daily Inspection (Check A)	263
Dead Cut Check	87
Design Limit Load	13
Design Ultimate Load	13
Detonation	95
Diesel Engines	53
Diesel Engines, Advantages	53
Diffuser	101
Diode-rectifier	169
Directional Gyro Indicator	231
Directional Stability	7
Direct Current	159
Direct Fuel Injection	55
Distributor	86
Dry-sump System	75

E

Electrical Faults	167
Electrical System	159
Electrical Wiring Diagram	171
Electrodes	163
Elevators	8
Emergency Drills	16
Empennage	7
Engine Construction	42
Engine Icing	105
Engine Performance Indicators	189
Engine Systems Check	149
Exhaust Gas Temperature	98
Exhaust Gas Temperature Gauge	190
Exhaust Stroke	41

F

Fin	7
Fire Extinguishers	14
Fixed Pitch Propellers	137
Flap	11
Flight Levels	213
Flight Manual	257
Flight Manual Supplement	257
Flight Navigation Computer	32
Float Chamber Carburettor	99
Flutter	9
Flying Controls	8
Forward And Aft Limits	9
Four Stroke Cycle	40
Friction	73

INDEX

Fuel	117
- *Additives*	78
Fuel Contamination	120
Fuel Contents Gauge	194
Fuel Flowmeter	195
Fuel Pump	122
Fuel Systems	117
Fuselage	3
Fuses	168

G

Gasoline	117
Generators	162
Gimbal Rings	225
Glow Plug	55
Grades of Oil	78
Gudgeon Pin	43
Gyroscope	225
- *Gyroscopic Precession*	
- *Gyroscopic Wander*	234

H

Helix Angle	131
Horizontal Stabiliser	7
Hydraulicing	79

I

ICAO Standard Atmosphere	209
Idle Cut-off	153
Idle Cut-off Valve	102
Impulse Coupling	87
Indicated Airspeed	206
Indicated Horse Power	47
Indicator Diagram	46
Induction Stroke	40
Induction System	104
Inlet Manifold Suction	182
Instrument Error	206
Insurance Documentation	263
Internal Combustion Engine	39
Interplane Struts	5
ISA	209

J

Jet A1	117

INDEX

L

Landing Gear	25
Lateral Axis	8
Life Jackets	15
Longerons	4
Longitudinal Axis	8
Longitudinal Stability	7
Lubrication System	73

M

Magnetic Field	235
Magnetos	85
Magneto Dead-cut Check	149
Mainplanes	5
Maintenance Allowed by Pilots	261
Maintenance Schedule	258
Main Gear	26
Malfunctions In The Electrical System	172
Manifold Pressure Gauge	193
Manoeuvrability	6
Mass Balancing	9
Mechanical Tachometer	195
Mixture Control	98, 103, 152
Mixture Range	95
Mixture Strengths	96
MOGAS	119
Monoplane	5
Multigrade Oils	78

N

Normal Axis	8
Normal Category	257
Nose Gear	26
Nose Wheel Steering	26

O

Oil	73
Oil Cooler	77
Oil Pressure	79
Oil Pressure Gauge	193
Oil System Malfunctions	80
Oil Temperatures	68
Oil Temperature Gauge	190
Oleo-pneumatic Struts	25
Overheating	65

INDEX

P

Permanent Magnet Generator	86
Pilot's Operating Handbook	257
Piston	43
Piston Engine	39
Piston Rings	43
Pitch	8
Pitot-static System	202
Ply Rating	29
Pneumatic Tyres	27
Popular Flying Association	258
Position Error	203
Power Absorption and Efficiency of Propellers	133
Power Stroke	41
Pressure Lubrication	73
Primary Cells	163
Primary Flying Controls	8
Priming Pump	122
Principles of Operation of the ASI	204
Propellers	
- Angle of Attack	132
- Chord	130
- Chord Line	130
- Solidity	133
- Thrust	129
Propeller Diameter	133

Q

QFE	214
QNH	214

R

Regional Pressure Setting (or Forecast QNH)	215
Retractable Landing Gear	27
Ribs	6
Rigidity	226
RPM Gauge	195
Roll	8
Rudder	9
Ruddervator	11

S

Secondary Cells	163
Semi - Monocoque Construction	4
Shimmy	27
Slow Running Systems	101
Society Of Automobile Engineers' Or SAE	78

INDEX

Spars	6
Splash Lubricated	73
Stabilator	8
Stabilising Surfaces	7
Standard Pressure Setting (SPS)	215
Starter Circuit	171
Starter Motor	171
Starter Relay	171
Static Sources	203
Step-Up Transformer	86
Straight Oil	78
Stringers	6
Structural Safety	6
Struts	5
Suction Pumps	181
Systems Check	149

T

Tachometer	195
Tailplane	7
Tail Unit	7
TAS	207
Technical Log	260
Thermal Efficiency	65
Thermal Shock	68
Timing	41
Top Dead Centre	41, 42
Torsion	13
Torsion Box	6
Trailing Edge Flaps	10
Transition Altitude	213
Transition Layer	213
Transition Level	213
Trim Tabs	10
True Airspeed	207
Turning Errors	244
Turn and Slip Indicator	227
Turn Co-ordinator	229
Twisting Forces	13
Two-Pitch Propellers	138
Type Certificate	255
Tyres	27

U

Undercarriage	25
Utility category	257

INDEX

V

Vacuum Gauge	183
Vacuum Pumps	183
Vacuum Warning Light	184
Valves	45
Valve Guides	45
Valve Seat	45
Valve Springs	45
Variable Pitch Propellers	138
Variable Resistor	194
Venturi Tubes	182
Vertical Speed Indicator	217
Vertical Stabiliser	7
Voltage	160
Voltage Regulator	170
Voltmeters	167

W

Wet-sump system	74
Wings	5

Y

Yaw	8

SKILLS · FOR · FLIGHT

Mass and Balance

6

OXFORD
AVIATION TRAINING

TABLE OF CONTENTS

MASS AND BALANCE

CHAPTER 1: MASS & BALANCE	1
CHAPTER 2: CENTRE OF GRAVITY CALCULATIONS	15
MASS & BALANCE EXAMINATION SYLLABUS	45
ANSWERS TO MASS & BALANCE QUESTIONS	47
MASS & BALANCE INDEX	49

TABLE OF CONTENTS

CHAPTER 1
MASS & BALANCE

CHAPTER 1: MASS AND BALANCE

CHAPTER 1: MASS AND BALANCE

INTRODUCTION.

Figure 1.1 Mass and Balance calculations must be carried out before every flight.

Mass and Balance calculations affect both the safety and performance of your aircraft and must never be neglected. An overloaded aircraft may fail to lift off during the take-off run while an aircraft whose centre of gravity is out of limits may be unstable and difficult to control. In the subject of **Mass and Balance**, the word **mass** refers, of course, to the mass of the aircraft, either empty or loaded, and the word **balance** refers to the position of the **centre of gravity**.

During the early stages of your flying training, your flying instructor will take responsibility for the **Mass and Balance** calculations for the aircraft. But, in the later stages of your training, and, certainly, in order to pass the ground examinations and skills test for the Private Pilot's Licence, you will be required to demonstrate your understanding of the principle of **Mass and Balance** by successfully answering questions in a multiple-choice examination paper, and by practically presenting your instructor and examiner with **Mass and Balance** data for actual flights. This chapter and the chapter on '**Centre of Gravity Calculations**' aim to provide you with the theoretical knowledge that you require to achieve these important objectives.

During flying training and on the skills test, your flying instructor or examiner has the obligation to ensure that you correctly perform the **Mass and Balance** calculations for the aircraft; but once you have obtained your licence, the responsibility is yours alone. Both **good airmanship** and **regulations** require that the Pilot-in-Command of an aircraft registered in the United Kingdom satisfy himself that, before the aircraft takes off, the **weight (mass)** of the aircraft is within limits, and that any load is so distributed that the **centre of gravity** of the aircraft is also within limits.

The **Pilot's Operating Handbook** for your aircraft will provide you with the specific information that you need to ensure that your aircraft is safely loaded.

> *The pilot-in-command has a legal responsibility for the safe loading of his aircraft.*

MASS OR WEIGHT?

You will often hear the subject **Mass & Balance** referred to as **Weight & Balance** although there is a crucial conceptual difference between the concepts of **mass** and **weight**. The change of ground subject title occurred when pilot licences changed

CHAPTER 1: MASS AND BALANCE

from purely UK CAA licences to JAA licences. The word **Mass** was substituted for **Weight** in the title of the subject, but the authorities gave no explanation of why the change was made.

As we explain below, although when considered scientifically, **weight** and **mass** are two different concepts, as far as the **subject Mass and Balance** is concerned, **mass** and **weight** are treated as having the same meaning. Some text books call the subject **Weight and Balance**, others call it **Mass and Balance**. The following paragraphs explain why **mass** and **weight** may be considered as meaning the same thing for aircraft balance and performance considerations.

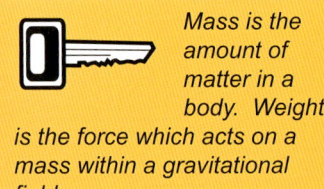
Mass is the amount of matter in a body. Weight is the force which acts on a mass within a gravitational field.

Figure 1.2 On the Earth's surface, an astronaut has a certain Mass and Weight. In space, his Mass will be the same as it was on Earth, but his Weight will be effectively zero.

The difference between **mass** and **weight** is fully explained in the **Principles of Flight** volume in this series. Basically, however, **mass** is the **amount of matter** in a body, while **weight** is the **force** which acts on a **mass** when the **mass** is **located in a gravitational field**. A body will always possess **mass** but if there is no gravity the body will have no **weight**. (*See Figure 1.2*)

For us Earth dwellers, **weight** is the force acting on a body of a given **mass** due to the Earth's force of gravity; the **direction of the weight force is always towards the centre of the Earth**. In *Figure 1.3* on *page 6,* you see that the aircraft's weight is acting vertically downwards.

When we consider aircraft **accelerations** in the horizontal plane, it is **mass** which is the relevant concept; when we consider **lifting the mass of the aircraft against the force of gravity**, it is the concept of **weight** which is in play.

Of course, in a **gravitational field of constant strength** (as we may consider the Earth's to be in the realms where aircraft fly) **weight is directly proportional to mass,** so we can use the concepts of **weight** and **mass** interchangeably and get away with it. Nevertheless, the subject might more accurately have been styled 'Weight, Mass and Balance'. But **Mass and Balance** is the title of the subject we have been given, so in this section we use the words **weight** and **mass** largely interchangeably.

Be aware, when referring to aircraft handbooks, that American handbooks are almost certain to refer to an aircraft's **weight**, whereas European handbooks will invariably refer to **mass**. British aircraft handbooks are likely to use either **mass** or **weight**. JAA/EASA refers almost exclusively to **mass**, and, so, that will be our practice here. Just remember that for this groundschool subject, **Mass and Balance**, **mass** and **weight are treated as the same concept.**

Where the distinction between **mass** and **weight** is important for your understanding, the difference will be pointed out.

CHAPTER 1: MASS AND BALANCE

FUNDAMENTAL DEFINITIONS OF AIRCRAFT MASS.

A number of fundamental definitions are used when referring to standard aircraft **mass**. The fundamental definitions are:

Basic Empty Mass.
The **Basic Empty Mass** of an aircraft refers to the **mass** of the **airframe**, **engine**, all standard, **fixed equipment**, **unusable fuel**, **full oil contents**, and the of any other item which is used on **all flights** of the aircraft concerned.

The **Basic Empty Mass**, which does not include the weight of the pilot, payload (referred to as **traffic load** by the JAA), ballast or usable fuel, is the **mass** of the aircraft which a pilot uses as the starting point for **all load and centre of gravity calculations**, prior to a flight.

The Empty Mass.
The **Empty Mass** is the same as the **Basic Empty Mass** except that the **mass** of the oil contents is limited to the **unusable oil**. The **Empty Mass** of the aircraft is the **mass** used for the initial calculation of the **Centre of Gravity** entered in the aircraft's **Flight Manual** or **Pilot's Operating Handbook**.

Gross Mass (All-Up Mass).
The **Gross Mass** or **All-Up Mass** of the aircraft is the **total mass of the aircraft and all its contents** at any given time. The **Gross Mass** must never exceed **Maximum Take-Off Mass** for any given take-off, whether structurally or performance limited, nor must it exceed the **Maximum Landing Mass** for any given landing, again irrespective of whether that landing is limited by structural or performance considerations. (A given aircraft may have different maximum **gross mass** limitations depending on what category – e.g. Normal or Utility – it is permitted to operate in.)

An increase in gross mass (weight) will lead to an increase in an aircraft's stall speed, take-off run and landing run.

An increase in **Gross Mass** will cause an increase in stall speed, and an increase in the take-off and landing run required.

The Zero Fuel Mass.
The **Zero Fuel Mass** is equal to an aeroplane's **Gross Mass less the usable fuel** in the aircraft's tanks. **Zero Fuel Mass**, then, does include pilot, payload and ballast, but only **unusable fuel**.

MASS AND BALANCE LIMITATIONS.

Aircraft are designed to carry a prescribed maximum **mass**. Furthermore, the **force** acting on the aircraft's **mass** (i.e. its **weight**) must also act through a point (the aircraft's **centre of gravity**), which lies within prescribed limits along the fore and aft axis of the airframe structure.

The point through which the weight acts is called the Centre of Gravity .

To operate legally in the United Kingdom (UK), an aircraft must have a valid **Certificate of Airworthiness** or **Permit to Fly**. These documents, directly, or by reference to an approved **Flight Manual** or **Pilot's Operating Handbook,** lay down various **limitations** on **mass,** and the **range of Centre of Gravity (CG) positions**, within which the aircraft must be operated.

5

CHAPTER 1: MASS AND BALANCE

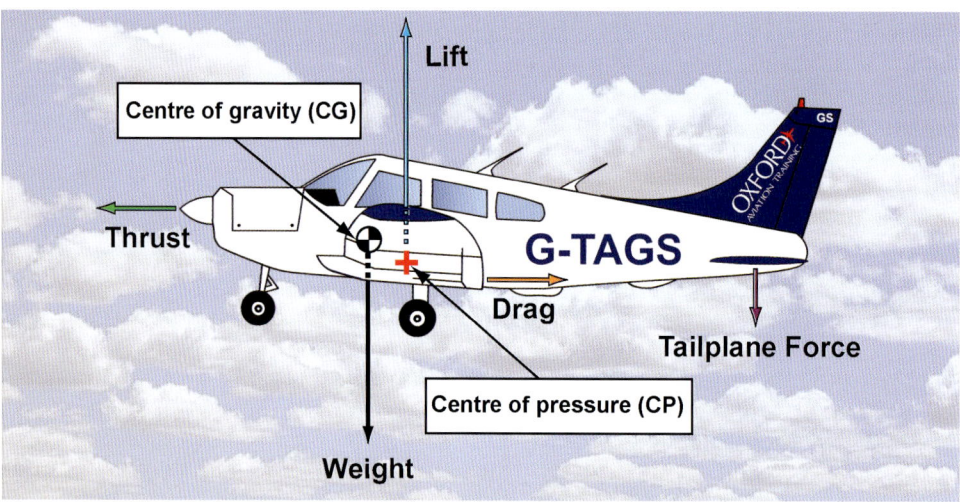

Figure 1.3 Weight is the force acting on the aircraft's mass. Weight acts vertically downwards through the aircraft's Centre of Gravity.

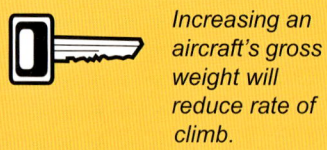

Increasing an aircraft's gross weight will reduce rate of climb.

The **limitations on mass** are set in order to ensure adequate margins of safety with regard to the strength of the airframe structure and so that the aircraft can meet the in-flight performance specified by the designer.

Limitations on the **CG position** ensure adequate **stability** and **controllability** of the aircraft.

Flight performance is also affected by **CG position** because of changes in drag which arise as **CG position changes**.

If an aircraft exceeds the **mass limit**, the aircraft is said to be **overloaded**. If the **CG** is not within the specified range, the **CG** is said to be **out of limits**. Both situations would be detrimental to flight safety.

The effects of **overloading** an aircraft are as follows.

- **Structural safety** margins will be reduced.

- **Reduced acceleration** and increased speed and distance required on take-off.

- Flight performance is reduced, with reductions in **rate** and **angle of climb**, **service ceiling**, **maximum speed**, **range** and **endurance**.

- **Manoeuvrability** and **controllability** will be impared.

- **Stalling speed** of the aircraft will be increased.

- Increased **landing speed** and **landing run**.

- **Excessive loading on the undercarriage** will also increase wear on tyres and brakes.

Because of the dangerous consequences of **overloading** an aircraft, maximum

CHAPTER 1: MASS AND BALANCE

mass or weight limits are applied to aircraft, depending on their structural strength, their operational role, and even for specific manoeuvres.

The Pilot-in-Command has a legal obligation to ensure that **mass limitations** are not exceeded and that the aircraft's **CG** is within limits.

MAXIMUM TAKE-OFF MASS (MTOM).

The maximum limits of **mass** for flight which are permitted for a particular aircraft will be stated in the **Certificate of Airworthiness**, **Permit to Fly** or **Pilot's Operating Handbook**.

The Pilot-in-Command has a legal obligation to ensure that the aircraft's Maximum Authorised Take-Off Mass is not exceeded, and that the CG is within limits.

Figure 1.4 Maximum Take-Off Mass (MTOM) is the maximum permissible total mass of the aircraft at the beginning of the take-off run.

All definitions of mass limitations may be examined in the PPL ground examination.

The **Maximum Take-Off Mass (MTOM)** is defined as **the maximum permissible total aircraft mass at the beginning of the take-off run**.

It may be permissible for the **MTOM** to be exceeded by a small amount, while the aircraft is parked on the ramp or while taxing to the take-off point. This level of mass is known as **Maximum Ramp Mass**. The extra mass, above **MTOM**, is carried as fuel. During taxi, this fuel is burnt off and the aircraft arrives at the start of the take-off run at its prescribed **MTOM**. Not all aircraft have a specified **Maximum Ramp Mass**, usually only commercial aircraft; but you need to be aware of the term and its definition.

NB.: Taking off from a given aerodrome in given runway, atmospheric and weather conditions may impose a performance-related Maximum Take-Off Mass, quite independent of the structurally-imposed Maximum Take-Off Mass.

Remember that operations from grass airfields, especially where the grass is long and/or wet, will impose performance limitations which must be considered along with MTOM. If a runway has a pronounced slope and the temperature and altitude are high, further performance considerations are imposed.

7

CHAPTER 1: MASS AND BALANCE

MAXIMUM LANDING MASS (MLM).

The **Maximum Landing Mass (MLM)** is defined as **the maximum permissible total mass of the aircraft upon landing, under normal circumstances.** MLM does not apply in the case of an emergency. On most light aircraft, the **MTOM** and **MLM** are the same. It is the the Pilot-in-Command's responsibility to check both **MTOM** and **MLM**.

Figure 1.5 Maximum Landing Mass (MLM) is the maximum permissible total mass of the aircraft on landing, under normal circumstances.

NB.: Landing at a given aerodrome in given runway, atmospheric and weather conditions may impose a performance-related Maximum Landing Mass, quite independent of the structurally-imposed Maximum Landing Mass.

MAXIMUM ZERO FUEL MASS (MZFM).

The **Maximum Zero Fuel Mass (MZFM)** is not a term commonly used when referring to light aircraft. **MZFM** is more important for larger aircraft. However, some light aircraft may have a **MZFM** specified, and you should be familiar with this expression.

The following paragraph explains the thinking behind the concept of **MZFM**.

Lift produced by an aircraft's wings produces **bending moments** which are at a maximum at the wing roots. Consequently, **fuel** is often carried in tanks located in the wings to help **reduce** resultant **bending moments,** in flight. If there were no fuel in the wing tanks, there would, of course, be no reduction in **bending moments** at the wing roots. An aircraft, therefore, may have a **maximum empty mass** imposed, before fuel is uploaded, which must not be surpassed.

Maximum Zero Fuel Mass includes any fuel in the **aircraft fuel system that is unusable**, the **mass of the pilot, passengers** and **any baggage** and **equipment** carried on the aircraft.

BALANCE - EFFECTS OF OUT-OF-LIMIT CENTRE OF GRAVITY POSITION.

The **Centre of Gravity (CG)** must lie between prescribed **forward** and **aft limits**. If the **CG** is **outside limits**, control forces, stability, manoeuvrability and performance will all be affected.

The following paragraphs give an indication of the consequences which might result from the **CG** being out of limits.

CG Outside Forward Limit.

When aircraft are manoeuvred, they rotate about their **Centre of Gravity (CG)**. The major significance of the **CG** being further forward than the forward limit is that the aircraft's tailplane, which provides the aircraft's longitudinal stability, has a longer than usual moment arm, making the tailplane even more effective. The aircraft's **longitudinal stability is, therefore, increased**, and will be more than usually resistant to movement in the pitching plane when the pilot operates the elevators, especially at low airspeed, when the elevators are, in any case, less effective.

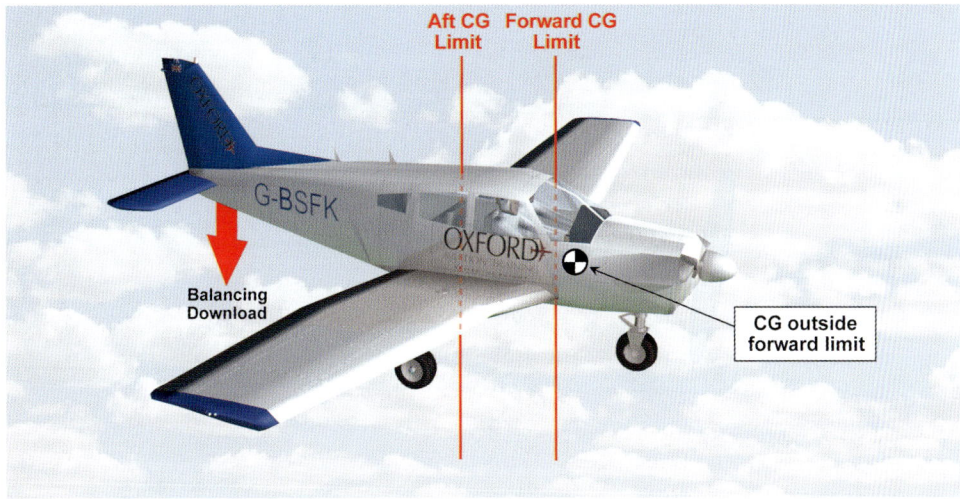

Figure 1.6 Aircraft with CG outside its forward limit.

Furthermore, with the **CG** outside the forward limit, the elevators may have to be permanently displaced upwards in order to provide sufficient balancing download from the tailplane for straight and level flight. This situation leads to **increased form drag** from the control surfaces and, because of the **increased wing lift** required to balance the tailplane download, **increased induced drag**, too.

Reductions in aircraft performance resulting from a **CG outside its forward limit** are:

- **Stalling speed** will be increased because of the increased wing-lift required.

- **Longitudinal stability** is **increased**, leading to a requirement for higher stick forces in pitch.

- **Range** and **endurance** are **decreased** because of the increased form and induced drag.

> When an aircraft's CG is outside its forward limit, longitudinal stability is increased leading to a requirement for higher stick forces.

CHAPTER 1: MASS AND BALANCE

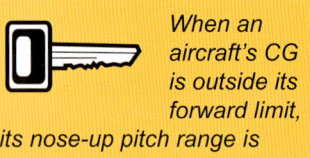
When an aircraft's CG is outside its forward limit, its nose-up pitch range is decreased.

- The **nose-up pitch range is decreased** because some elevator deflection has already been used to trim the aircraft for straight and level flight.

- **Decreased elevator authority**, especially at low forward speed. This is especially important for rotation and round-out on take-off and landing.

CG Outside Aft Limit.

With the **CG** further aft than the aft limit the tailplane's moment arm is shorter than usual, making the tailplane less effective. **The aircraft's longitudinal stability is, therefore, decreased**, and the aircraft will, consequently, become more sensitive in the pitching plane when the pilot operates the elevators, especially at low airspeed.

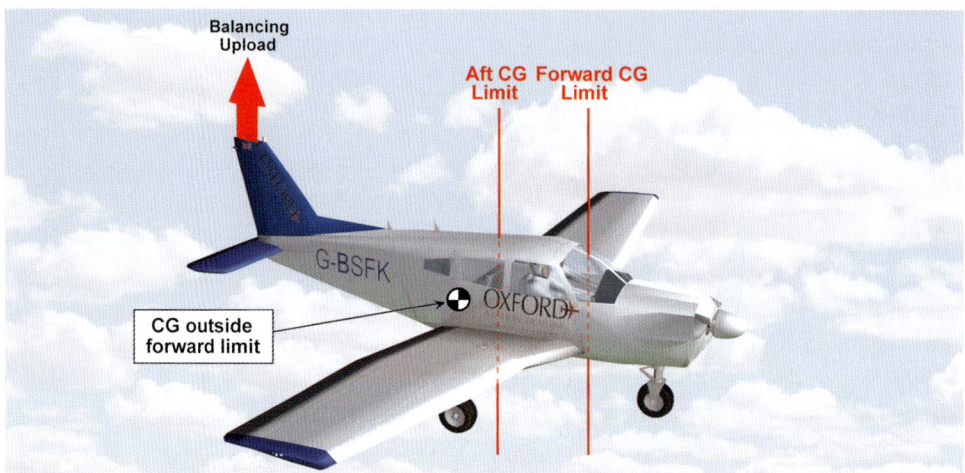

Figure 1.7 Aircraft with CG outside of its aft limit.

Furthermore, with the **CG** outside its aft limit, the elevators may have to be permanently displaced downwards in order to provide sufficient balancing upload from the tailplane for straight and level flight. This will increase form drag.

The principal effects on performance from a **CG** outside the **aft limit** are:

- **Longitudinal stability is reduced.**

- If the **CG** is **too far aft**, the aircraft will become **sensitive in the pitching plane**. Stick forces in pitch will be light, and a small elevator movement will produce a larger than normal change in pitch attitude.

When an aircraft's CG is outside its aft limit, elevator forces will be light, the aircraft may be unstable and show a greater tendency to spin.

- The aircraft will tend to pitch up at low speed and high power setting. This may lead to over-rotation on take-off, or to an inadvertent stall in the climb.

- The aircraft will be difficult to trim, especially at high power settings.

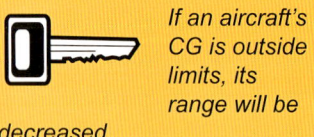
If an aircraft's CG is outside limits, its range will be decreased.

- The aircraft will be more difficult to recover from a spin.

- **Range** and **endurance** will usually **decrease** due to the increased form drag from the elevator.

GENERAL OBSERVATIONS ON MASS & BALANCE LIMITATIONS.

It must be understood that although an aircraft may be fitted with four seats and have an additional baggage area, it is **not generally possible** to fill all the seats, the baggage area and the fuel tanks without exceeding maximum **mass limitations** and **CG** limits.

Figure 1.8 Tandem seat aircraft may specify from which seat the aircraft must be flown solo.

Likewise, if flying an aircraft solo, although it is unlikely that the maximum **mass limitations** will be exceeded, the **CG** may well be out of limits if the pilot neglects to carry out **Mass and Balance calculations**. Solo flight may even necessitate ballast being carried if the crew-weight (mass) does not reach a minimum value. Some aircraft which have tandem seating may stipulate, in their **Pilot's Operating Handbook,** from which seat the aircraft must be flown solo.

Always remember that an aircraft is designed to fly within certain **mass** and **CG position** limits. Consequently, an aircraft may be unsafe to fly for two principal reasons:

- The aircraft's mass(weight) is out of limits.

- The aircraft's CG position is out of limits.

It is the responsibility of the Pilot-in-Command, when preparing his aircraft for flight, to ensure that both mass and CG position are within limits.

Representative PPL - type questions to test your theoretical knowledge of Mass and Balance.

1. If an aircraft's C of G is at or beyond its aft limit:

    a. The aircraft will be more stable longitudinally
    b. The aircraft will be difficult to rotate on take-off
    c. The aircraft's stall speed will decrease
    d. The aircraft's range will be reduced

2. An aircraft loaded in a dangerous manner, so that its C of G is beyond its forward limit, will:

    a. require less effort to flare when landing
    b. require less effort to rotate on take off
    c. have both an increased longitudinal stability and stalling speed
    d. have both an increased range and endurance

3. The flight characteristics of an aircraft which has its C of G at the forward limit will be:

    a. insensitivity to Pitch Control and little Longitudinal Stability
    b. sensitivity to Pitch Control and little Longitudinal Stability
    c. sensitivity to Pitch Control and great Longitudinal Stability
    d. insensitivity to Pitch Control and great Longitudinal Stability

4. The consequences of operating an aeroplane with the C of G beyond the aft limit will be:

    I. on the ground the aircraft would be tail heavy and passenger or crew movement or fuel usage could make it tip up
    II. the flying controls would be too sensitive, increasing the risk of a tail strike at rotation
    III. the tendency to stall would increase and it may be impossible to achieve "hands off" balanced flight
    IV. recovery from a spin would be much more difficult

    a. All statements are correct
    b. Only statement I is correct
    c. Only statements I and IV are correct
    d. Only statements II and III are correct

5. When calculating the MZFM (maximum zero fuel mass), the following are included:

    a. pilot, passengers & baggage, unusable fuel
    b. pilot, passengers, baggage & operating fuel
    c. pilot, unusable fuel, but less passengers and baggage
    d. pilot, passengers, operating fuel but less baggage

CHAPTER 1: MASS AND BALANCE QUESTIONS

6. Complete the following sentence. If an aircraft is loaded such that its C of G is approaching the aft limit:

    a. the stall speed increases
    b. the aircraft's longitudinal stability will decrease
    c. range and endurance increase
    d. stick forces increase

7. Assuming the aircraft is at rest on the ground, what term best describes image 'A'? (*See Picture 1, page 14*).

    a. Zero Fuel Mass
    b. Take Off Mass
    c. Maximum All Up Mass
    d. Empty Mass

8. Assuming the aircraft is at rest on the ground, what "mass expression" best describes image 'D'? (*See Picture 1, page 14*).

    a. Zero Fuel Mass
    b. Basic Empty Mass
    c. Empty Mass
    d. Maximum All Up Mass

9. What name is given to the total mass of an aeroplane, including its total load that it is carrying, at any given time?

    a. Zero Fuel Mass
    b. Gross Mass
    c. Basic Empty Mass
    d. Maximum Landing Mass

10. What effect will increase in the gross mass of an aeroplane have on its stall speed and take-off and landing run?

    a. Increase the stall speed, but decrease the take-off and landing run
    b. No effect
    c. Decrease the stall speed and increase the take-off and landing run
    d. Increase the stall speed and increase the take-off and landing run

11. What effect will an increase in the landing mass have on an aircraft's landing run at any given approach speed and flap setting:

    a. A decrease in landing run
    b. No effect
    c. Length of landing run is independent of mass
    d. Increase in landing run

CHAPTER 1: MASS AND BALANCE QUESTIONS

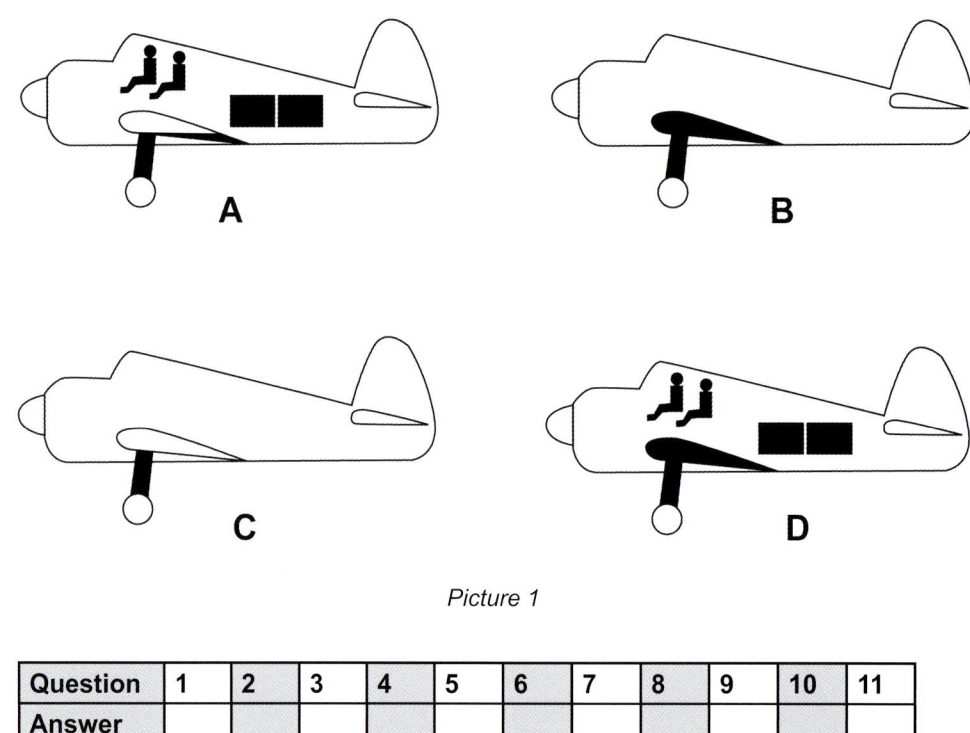

Picture 1

Question	1	2	3	4	5	6	7	8	9	10	11
Answer											

The correct answers to these questions can be found at the end of this book.

CHAPTER 2
CENTRE OF GRAVITY CALCULATIONS

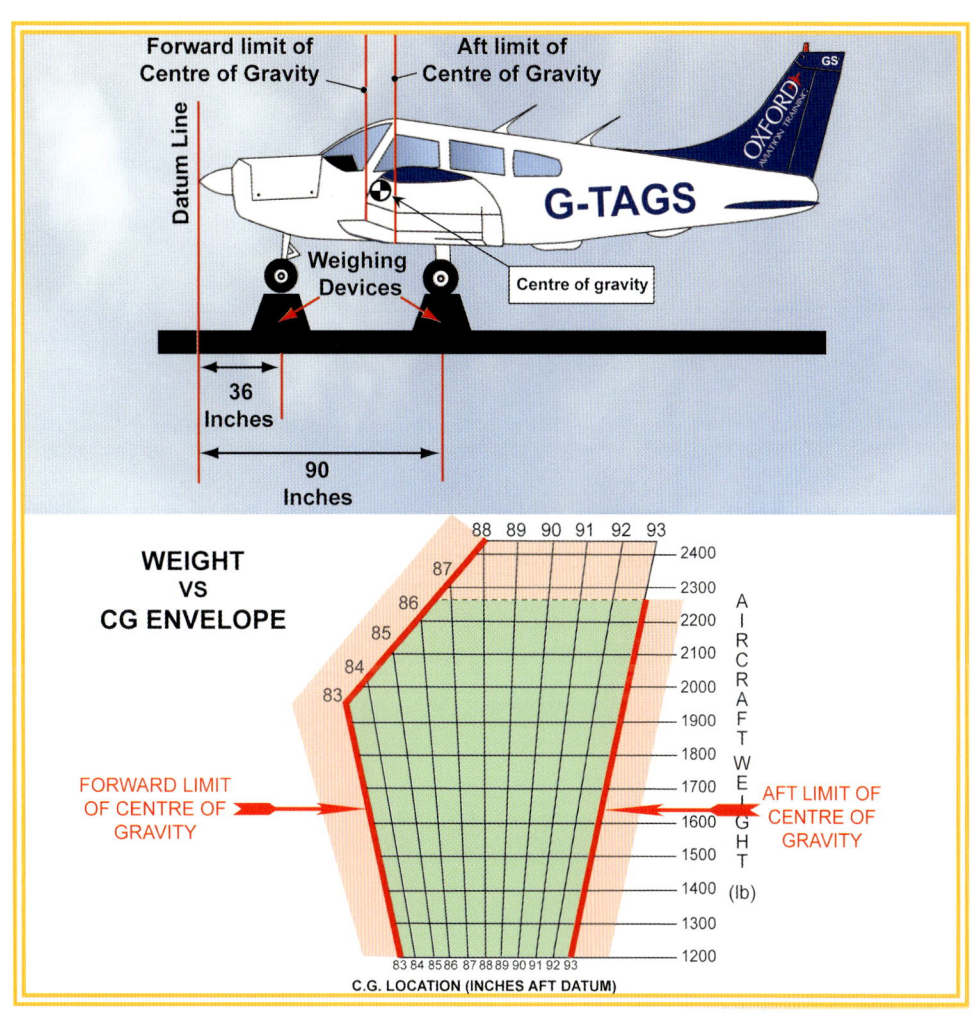

CHAPTER 2: CENTRE OF GRAVITY CALCULATIONS

CHAPTER 2: CENTRE OF GRAVITY CALCULATIONS

INTRODUCTION.

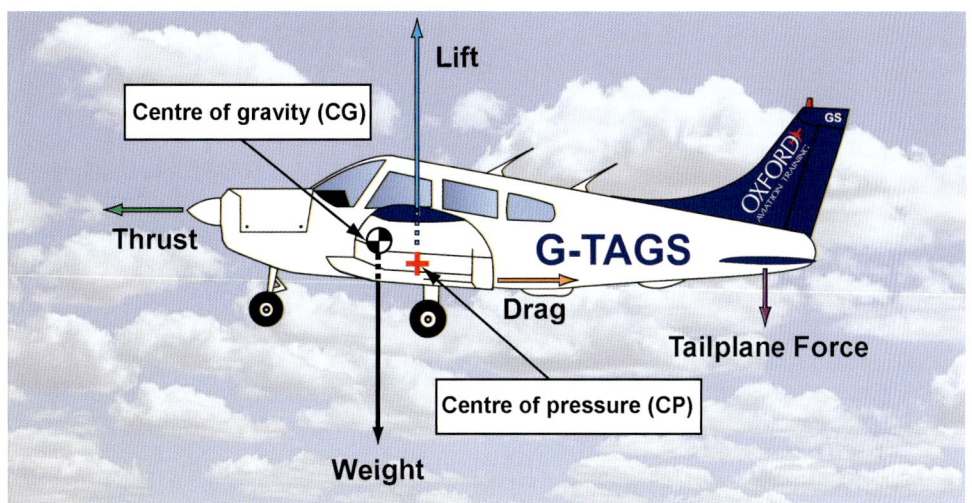

Figure 2.1 Weight is the force acting on the aircraft's mass. Weight acts vertically downwards through the aircraft's centre of gravity.

The **centre of gravity (CG)**, is the point within a body of a given **mass** through which the **force of gravity**, acting on that **mass**, is considered to act. The magnitude of the **force of gravity** acting on the body's **mass** is called the body's **weight**. **Weight** always acts vertically downwards (*See Figure 2.1*) towards the centre of the Earth. If an aircraft were to be suspended by a single force, say a *rope*, attached to the aircraft's **CG**, we could place the aircraft with its longitudinal axis horizontal, and the aircraft would remain horizontal in perfect balance, as depicted in *Figure 2.2*.

The magnitude of the force of gravity acting on a body's mass is called "weight". Weight acts through a body's centre of gravity.

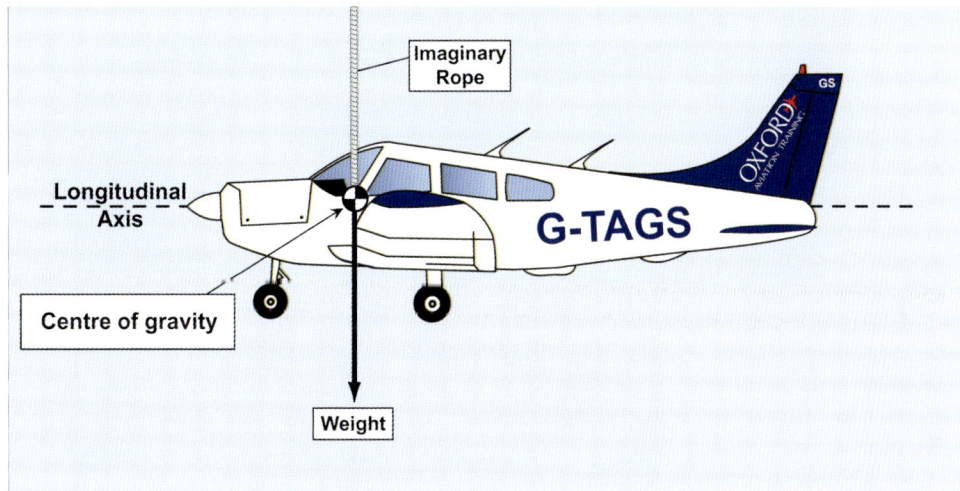

Figure 2.2 If an aircraft could be suspended by its CG, it would remain in any attitude in which it were placed.

In fact, if the aircraft were suspended exactly through its **CG**, we could put the aircraft **in any attitude we wished**, and it would remain in that attitude, because there could be no out-of-balance force or moment to make it move.

CHAPTER 2: CENTRE OF GRAVITY CALCULATIONS

When manoeuvring, in flight, an aircraft rotates about its CG.

In flight, an aircraft, when manoeuvred, rotates about its **CG**, but the aircraft's **weight always acts vertically downwards towards the centre of the Earth**. The **magnitude of the weight force** of the basic aircraft and of every constituent of the aircraft's load is of considerable importance because of the effect both on aircraft structural integrity and the position of the **CG**.

All aircraft have published **masses**, such as Basic Empty Mass, Maximum Gross Mass, Maximum Zero Fuel Mass, Maximum Take-off Mass, Useful Load (Payload and Fuel), Maximum Landing Mass, etc. Furthermore, because, during the flight, the aircraft consumes fuel, the **mass** (and, therefore, **weight**) of the aircraft constantly changes. As fuel tanks empty, the distribution of the **mass** throughout the aircraft will change, and, thus, the position of the aircraft's **CG** will change, too.

The position of the Centre of Gravity of an aeroplane is of crucial importance to its stability, controllability and safety.

As you have learnt, the position of the **centre of gravity CG**, measured horizontally along the aircraft's longitudinal axis, is of crucial importance to the aircraft's **longitudinal stability, controllability, performance,** and, ultimately, **safety**.

Consequently, there are **forward and aft limits** (*see Figure 2.3*) to the **CG**, calculated by the aircraft's designer, within which the **CG** must remain throughout a flight.

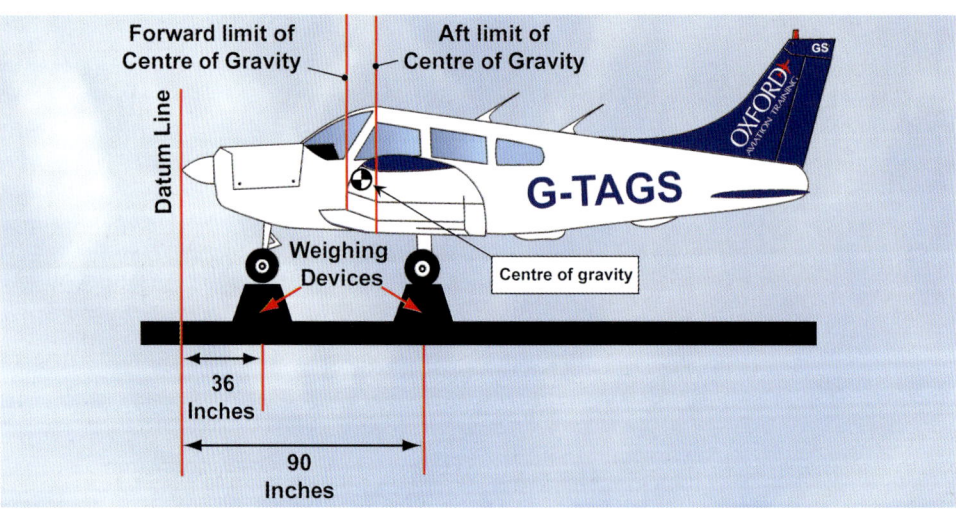

Figure 2.3 The CG limits are measured with respect to a datum line.

Fore and aft Centre of Gravity limits are measured with respect to a defined datum.

The **CG limits** are measured with respect to a **datum line**. *Figure 2.3* depicts representative forward and aft **CG limits** for a PA28. The **datum line** is an imaginary line which may be located either inside or outside the actual body of the aircraft. In the example above, the **datum line** is shown coincident with the tip of the propeller spinner.

In addition to the aircraft's basic mass, the mass (weight) of fuel, passengers, baggage, and other loads, must be taken into account when calculating an aircraft's permissible mass and **CG** position.

Therefore, alongside such information as Maximum Gross Mass, and Maximum Take-Off Mass, the **Pilot's Operating Handbook (POH)** will contain separate details of crew and passenger mass, and of the mass which may be loaded in the aircraft's baggage compartment. The pilot must not neglect to include crew and fuel loads in his **Mass and Balance** calculations because carrying too great a load could move the **CG** out of limits, even if the Maximum Take-Off Mass is not exceeded.

The **POH** will also specify such details as minimum crew mass for solo flight.

It is one of the pilot's major responsibilities, when preparing his aircraft for flight, to confirm that mass limitations are respected and that the **centre of gravity** is situated within the limits stipulated in the **Pilot's Operating Handbook**.

CALCULATING THE POSITION OF AN AIRCRAFT'S CENTRE OF GRAVITY.

Now that you have learnt how crucial the position of an aircraft's **centre of gravity** (**CG**) is to the safety of the aircraft, let us learn how a pilot calculates the **position** of the **CG** so that he may check whether the **CG** lies within the prescribed **forward** and **aft limits**.

We already know that the aircraft manufacturer defines the **CG limits** in terms of their distance from a **defined datum line**. The **datum line** may be positioned anywhere that the aircraft designer chooses. (**datum** is a Latin word which means "that which is given or defined"). For the aircraft that we are going to examine, we will assume that the **datum line** is a vertical line which is coincident with the point of the aircraft's propeller spinner, as depicted in *Figure 2.4*

Figure 2.4 The Datum Line with respect to which the CG limits are defined.

The **CG limits**, then, are set by the aircraft designer. The responsibility of the Pilot-in-Command is to ensure that the **CG** always remains within these limits.

CG for the Aircraft's Basic Empty Mass.
Let us see how the position of the aircraft's **CG** is calculated for the aircraft's **Basic Empty Mass**.

Consider the diagram at *Figure 2.5*. The diagram illustrates the aircraft being **weighed** with its main and nose-wheel undercarriage legs placed upon **weighing devices** positioned at the indicated distances behind the **datum line**.

CHAPTER 2: CENTRE OF GRAVITY CALCULATIONS

It is here that we see the difference between **weight** and **mass**. When we weigh an aircraft, we are measuring the force which is pulling the aircraft to the centre of the Earth. So it is the aircraft's **weight** that is being recorded. However, in a **constant gravitational field, weight is proportional to mass**, so we can record **mass** if we so choose. (This is what JAA/EASA urges us to do. In many aircraft **POHs**, however, **weight** is still referred to.)

The **masses** recorded at each undercarriage leg are recorded in a table, such as the one shown in *Figure 2.5*, along with the distances behind the **datum** of the line of action of the **weight** acting on each **mass**.

Notice that the table at *Figure 2.5* also has a column marked **Moment**. The **Moment** column, you will see, has the units "pound-inches" (lb-ins). In this column we enter the figure for the **mass** recorded at each undercarriage leg multiplied by the **distance from the datum** of the line of action of the force acting on each undercarriage leg. Many American-made aircraft still use **Imperial Units** so manufacturers record the **mass** in pounds (lb) and the **distance from the datum**, at which the **mass** is effective, in inches (ins). The **moment** of each **mass** reading, then, is given in **lb-ins**.

As you will learn presently:

Moment (lb-ins) = Mass (lb) × distance from datum (ins).

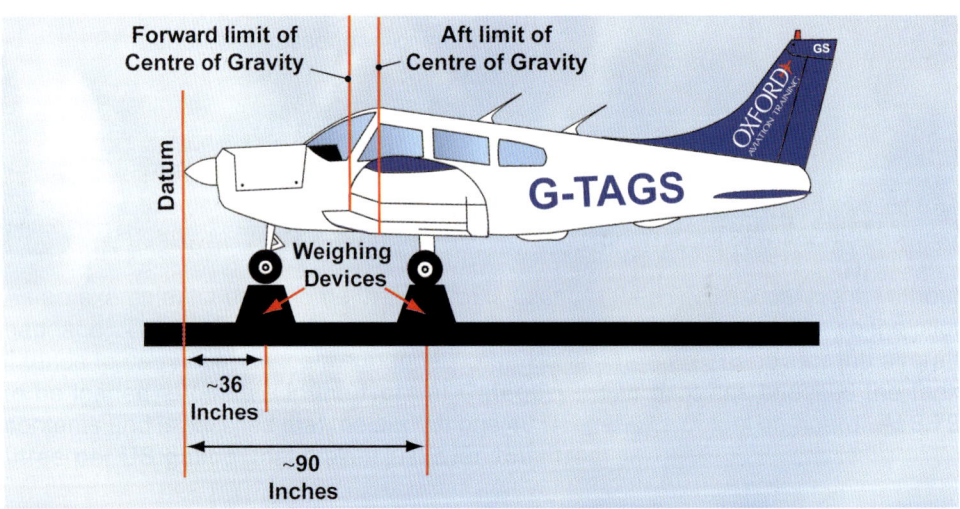

ITEM	MASS (lb)	ARM (ins)	MOMENT (lb-ins)
Nosewheel			
Left Main Wheel			
Right Main Wheel			
TOTAL			

Figure 2.5 Calculating the Position of the Centre of Gravity.

The distance of each **mass** reading, behind the **datum**, is commonly called the **"moment arm"**. That is why the column in *Figure 2.5*, in which the distances are recorded, is labelled **"ARM"**.

Before proceeding further, however, we must take a closer look at the concept of **"moments"**.

THE PRINCIPLE OF MOMENTS.

The **moment of a force** acting on a **mass** is defined as the **turning effect that the force exerts about any defined axis, pivot point, or fulcrum.**

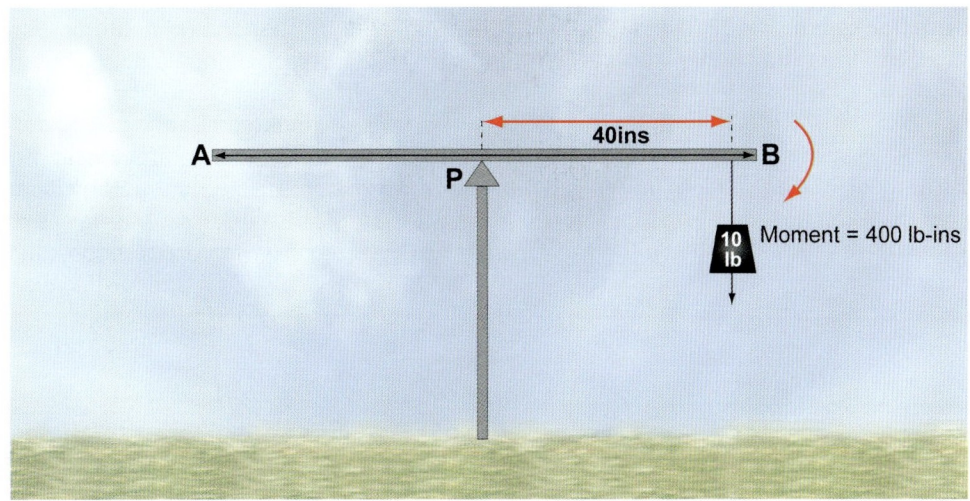

Figure 2.6 A moment of 400 lb-ins acting clockwise on a 10 lb mass.

In *Figure 2.6*, we see a **10 lb mass** suspended at **40 ins** from a **pivot-point**, **P**.

For practical purposes, the **weight** of the **mass** may also be taken to be **10 lbs**, so the **turning effect**, or **moment**, of the **mass** about the pivot, **P**, is quantified as being: **10 lbs × 40 ins = 400 lb-ins**.

This **moment** of **400 lb-ins** will, quite obviously, cause the beam, to which the **mass** is attached, to **rotate clockwise**.

The moment of a mass is equal to the force acting on that mass times the distance of the mass from the pivot point, i.e. the point of rotation.

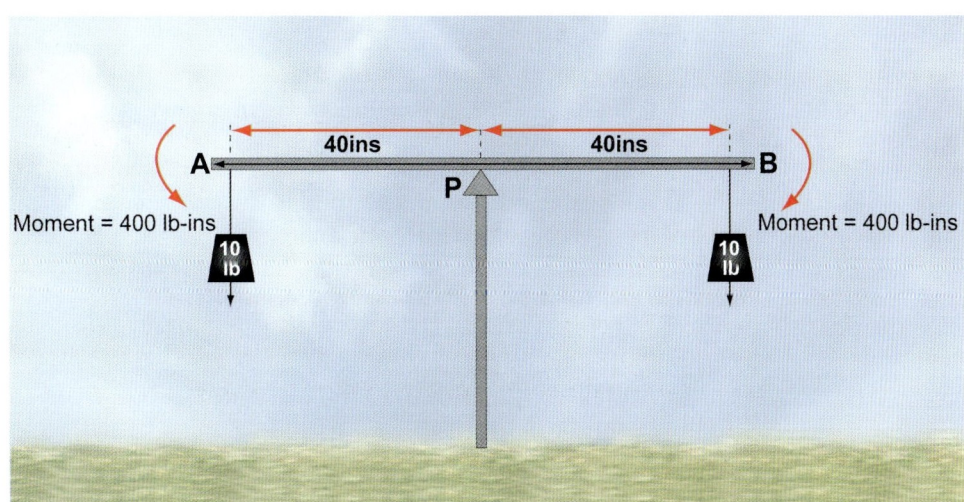

Figure 2.7 Two moments of 400 lb-ins balancing each other.

CHAPTER 2: CENTRE OF GRAVITY CALCULATIONS

We can prevent that **clockwise rotation** by applying to the beam an equal and opposite **turning moment** of **400 lb-ins** acting **anti-clockwise**. This could be achieved by hanging an identical **10 lb mass** at **40 ins** from the pivot, **P**, from the left hand side of the beam, as depicted in *Figure 2.7*.

However, the <u>essential</u> matter in balancing the original **400 lb-ins clockwise moment** is <u>not</u> to have an <u>identical mass</u> suspended at an <u>identical distance</u> on the other end of the beam, but to create, in whatever way we can, a **balancing moment acting anti-clockwise**, of **400 lb-ins**. This could be achieved by suspending a **20 lb** mass at **20 ins** from the pivot, **P**, on the left hand side of the beam, as depicted in *Figure 2.8*.

The **20 lb mass**, then, suspended at **20 ins** from the pivot-point, **P**, has the **same turning effect** as a **10 lb mass** suspended at **40 ins** from the pivot-point. Both

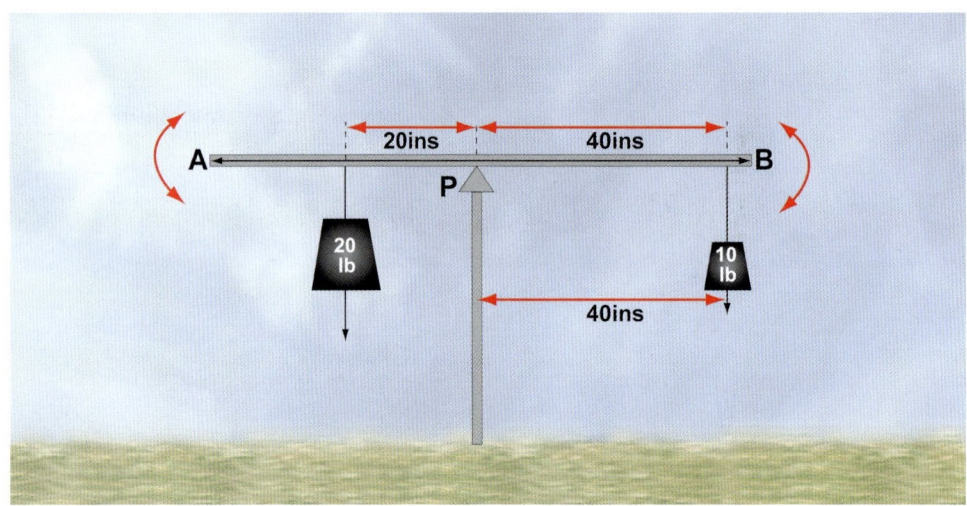

Figure 2.8 Two balancing moments, each of 400 lb-ins.

masses have a turning effect or **moment** of **400 lb-ins**. So a **mass** of **20 lb** with a **moment arm** of **20 ins** has the same **moment** as a **mass** of **10 lb** with a **moment arm** of **40 ins**.

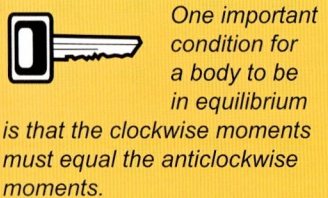

One important condition for a body to be in equilibrium is that the clockwise moments must equal the anticlockwise moments.

We could have found, <u>by trial and error</u>, hat the **20 lb mass** needed to be placed at **20 ins** from the pivot, **P**, in order to balance the beam, or we could have **calculated** its position. Let us look at the calculation.

In order to balance the **clockwise moment** of **400 lb-ins**, we know we need an **anticlockwise moment** of the same value. So, for balance:

$$\text{Clockwise moment} = \text{Anti-clockwise moment}$$

So, $\quad 400 \text{ (lb-ins)} = 20 \text{ (lb)} \times x \text{ (ins)} \quad \text{.......} \quad \mathbf{1}$

where x is the unknown **moment arm** at which the **20 lb** mass must be placed to achieve balance.

By simple mathematical transposition we can see from equation **1** that:

$$x \text{ (ins)} = \frac{400 \text{ (lb-ins)}}{20 \text{ (lb)}}$$

Therefore, $x = 20$ ins

So, to find the **moment arm** of the **20 lb mass**, required to balance the beam, we simply divided the clockwise moment, **400 lb-ins**, by the mass, **20 lb**.

Calculating the Position of the Pivot-Point P.

There is one, final, important matter to note. Because, in *Figure 2.8*, the beam is in **equilibrium** and the total magnitude of the downward acting force (**weight**) acting on the two **masses** is **30 lb**, an **upwards acting force of equal magnitude, 30 lb**, must act at the **pivot-point**, as depicted in *Figure 2.8b*. If it did not, the beam would fall to the ground.

> For a beam to be in equilibrium, the clockwise moments must equal the anticlockwise moments, and the upwards acting forces must equal the downwards acting forces.

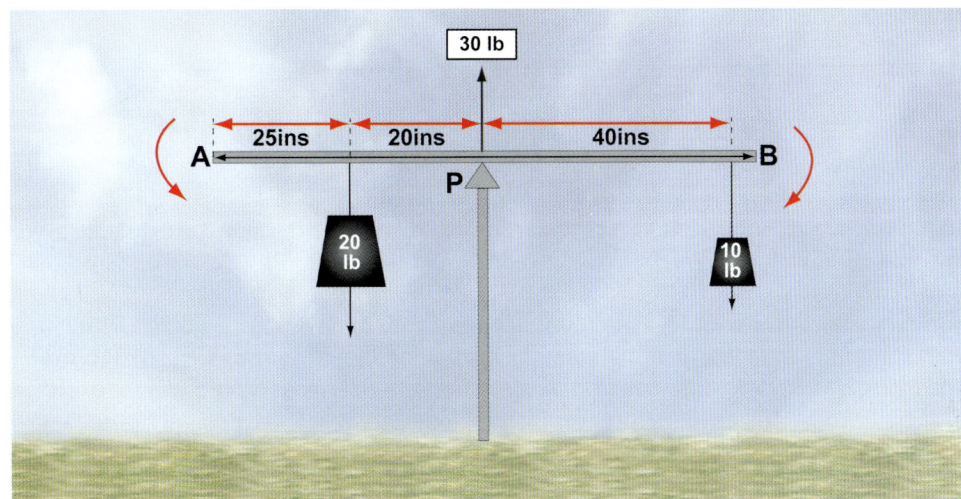

Figure 2.8b An upwards-acting force of 30 lb, at P, balances the 30 lb force (20 lb + 10 lb) acting downwards.

We can see, then, that when the beam is not rotating (that is, when the beam is in **equilibrium**), the **moments balance each other out**, the clockwise moment having the same magnitude as the anticlockwise moment, and the downward-acting forces are equal to the upward-acting forces.

For **equilibrium**, it is not important that a particular **mass** be placed at a particular distance from the **pivot-point**. Whatever **mass** we use, and wherever we **position** it, it only matters that the **moment** should be of the **correct magnitude** and act in the **correct direction**. We have seen that a **10 lb mass** hung at **40 ins** from a **pivot-point** produces the same **moment** (turning effect) as a **20 lb mass** hung at **20 ins** from the **pivot-point**.

Because the beam is in **equilibrium** and not turning, with the clockwise and anti-clockwise moments **in balance, we could, if we wished, take moments about any datum point** to express this state of **equilibrium. The datum point need not even lie on the beam.**

CHAPTER 2: CENTRE OF GRAVITY CALCULATIONS

Let us try out this theory. Let us take **moments** about **Point A**, in *Figure 2.8b)* at the left-hand end of the beam. We will assume that **Point A** is **25 ins** from the **20 lb mass**.

For **equilibrium**, of course:

clockwise moments = anticlockwise moments

Let us see if this is, in fact, true, by taking moments about **Point A**. First, we will calculate the **clockwise moments**.

clockwise moments = (20 lb × 25 ins) + (10 lb × 85 ins)
   = 500 lb-ins + 850 lb-ins
   = 1 350 lb-ins

Now we will take the **anticlockwise moments**. This will be the moment caused by the **30 lb** upward-acting force at the **Pivot P**.

anticlockwise moment = 30 lb × 45 ins = 1 350 lb-ins

As we see, the **anticlockwise moment** <u>does</u> equal the **clockwise moments**, both having a magnitude of **1 350 lb-ins**. So, our theory is proven:

To check for equilibrium, then, we may take moments about any datum we choose.

In fact, using this principle, we could calculate the value and position of **P**, for any combination of masses. For instance, if we replace the **20 lb mass** by a **15 lb mass** and move it to a position **20 ins** from **A** *(see Figure 2.8c)*, what **would the magnitude of P have to be for equilibrium**, and what distance must **P** be positioned from **A**?

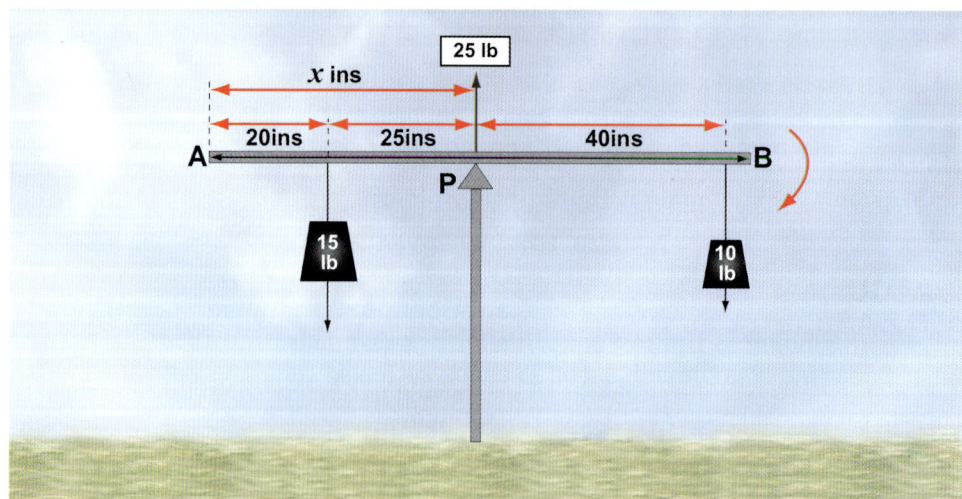

Figure 2.8c Calculating the distance of P from A.

Well, we can easily calculate the **magnitude** of **P**. The total downward acting force (**weight**) is now **25 lb**, so, **P**, the pivot-point, must be **pushing upwards** with a **force of 25 lb**. Now, what about the position of **P** with respect to **A**?

For equilibrium

clockwise moments = anticlockwise moments

Taking moments about **Point A**:

clockwise moments = (15 lb × 20 ins) + (10 lb × 85 ins)
= 300 lb-ins + 850 lb-ins
= 1 150 lb-ins

anticlockwise moment = 25 lb × x ins, where x is the distance of **P** from **A**.

Therefore, for equilibrium   25 × x lb-ins = 1 150 lb-ins

So, $x = \dfrac{1\ 150 \text{ lb-ins}}{25 \text{ lbs}}$ = 46 ins

So, **P**, the pivot-point, must now be at **46 ins** from **A**.

This, then, is the **Principle of Moments**. We can use the **Principle of Moments** to calculate the position of the **centre of gravity of an aircraft** in exactly the same way that we calculated the position of **P** from **A**, for a beam in **equilibrium**.

When we **weigh** an aircraft, as depicted in *Figure 2.9 overleaf*, the aircraft is static and motionless, and, so, is in **equilibrium**. Just as the **pivot-point, P**, exerts a force equal to the magnitude of the combined value of the forces acting on all the **masses** on the beam, the combined forces acting on all the **masses** making up the aircraft's structure, equipment and loads will act through the aircraft's **centre of gravity**, giving us the aircraft's total **weight**.

If you examine the inset to *Figure 2.9*, you see that we have a measured **reaction force** acting upwards on the **nose wheel** of **100 lb**, and a measured **reaction force** acting upwards on each of the two **main-wheels** of **725 lb**. This means that the aircraft's total weight acting downwards through its **centre of gravity** is **1550 lb**.

The **moments** of all the aircraft's constituent masses, therefore, can be entered into a **Principles of Moments** calculation to determine the aircraft's **centre of gravity**.

CALCULATION OF AN AIRCRAFT'S CENTRE OF GRAVITY FOR ITS BASIC EMPTY MASS.

Overleaf, we reproduce the diagram and table that we need to calculate the aircraft's **centre of gravity (CG)** for its **Basic Empty Mass**. This table is called the aircraft's **load sheet**.

We can now complete the **load sheet, overleaf**.

CHAPTER 2: CENTRE OF GRAVITY CALCULATIONS

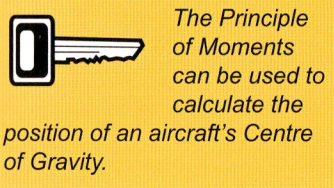

The Principle of Moments can be used to calculate the position of an aircraft's Centre of Gravity.

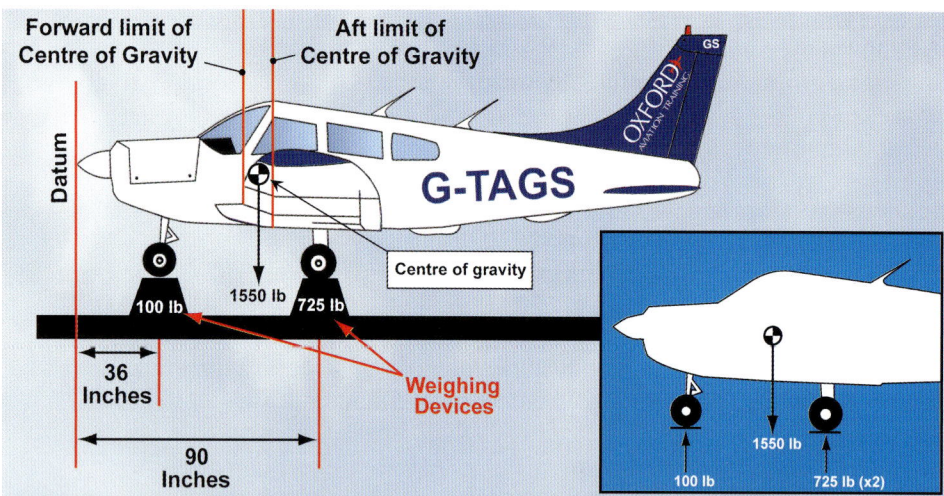

ITEM	MASS (lb)	ARM (ins)	MOMENT (lb-ins)
Nosewheel	100	36	3 600
Left Main Wheel	725	90	65 250
Right Main Wheel	725	90	65 250
TOTAL	1 550		134 100

Figure 2.9 Calculating the aircraft's CG for its Basic Empty Mass.

The **moment** about the **datum** of the **upward reaction force** acting on the nose-wheel is **100 (lb) × 36 (ins) = 3 600 lb-ins**. Similarly, the **moment** about the **datum** of the **upward reaction force** acting on the left main-wheel is **725 lb × 90 ins = 65 250 lb-ins**. The main right-wheel will, of course, exert the same **moment** of **65 250 lb-ins** about the datum.

We can see, then, that there are three forces being measured by the **weighing devices**: the **upward reaction forces** acting on the **nose-wheel** and on the **two main-wheels**. We can also see from the table that the **moment** about the **datum** has been calculated for each one of these **forces**.

So, knowing that the **total weight** acting on the aircraft's **total mass** will act downwards through the aircraft's **centre of gravity (CG)**, we can now calculate the position of the **CG**, by calculating the **moment** it would have about the **datum**, that would be equal to the **three moments** that we have already calculated.

From the table at *Figure 2.9*, we can easily find the **total mass** of the aircraft by adding together the readings from all three weighing devices. The total mass is **1 550 lb**. The force acting on this **mass** is the **weight** of the aircraft, also expressed as **1 550 lb**, which, as we have seen, acts downwards throught the **CG**.

We can also find the **total, anticlockwise moment** of the aircraft about the **datum** by adding up the three individual **moments** acting at each undercarriage leg. The total moment is **134 100 lb-ins**.

Now, because the aircraft is in **equilibrium**, the force acting on the total mass of the aircraft, **1 550 lb**, must exert an equal and opposite **clockwise moment** of **134 100 lb**.

We can now, therefore calculate the distance (**moment arm**) of the aircraft's **CG** from the **datum:**

$$\text{moment (lb-ins)} = \text{mass (lb)} \times \text{moment arm (ins)}$$

We can see, therefore, from simple mathematical transposition that:

$$\text{moment arm (ins)} = \frac{\text{moment (lb-ins)}}{\text{mass (lb)}}$$

Consequently, the **moment arm** for the **total weight** of the aircraft acting on its **total mass** is given by:

$$\text{moment arm (ins)} = \frac{134\ 100\ \text{(lb-ins)}}{1\ 550\ \text{(lb)}} = 86.5\ \text{ins}$$

86.5 ins, then, is the **distance behind the datum** of the **CG** of the aircraft, through which the aircraft's **total weight** acts on the aircraft's **total mass** (by definition).

The completed **load sheet** for the aircraft's Basic Empty Mass is at *Figure 2.10*.

ITEM	MASS (lb)	ARM (ins)	MOMENT (lb-ins)
Nosewheel	100	36	3 600
Left Main Wheel	725	90	65 250
Right Main Wheel	725	90	65 250
TOTAL	1 550	86.5	134 100

Figure 2.10 The completed load sheet for the aircraft's Basic Empty Mass, showing its CG position: 86.5 ins aft of the datum.

This **CG position** for the **Basic Empty Mass (BEM)** is calculated by the aircraft manufacturer and will be entered in the **Flight Manual** and **Pilot's Operating Handbook**. The manufacturer will, of course, ensure that this **BEM CG position** is **within** the permissible **forward and aft limits** for the **CG**. It is the pilot's reponsibility to ensure that the **CG** remains within the permissible limits when the aircraft is carrying fuel, crew, baggage, etc.

The aircraft manufacturer defines the fore and aft limits of the Centre of Gravity. It is the pilot's responsibility to ensure that the position of the Centre of Gravity remains within the limits.

CHAPTER 2: CENTRE OF GRAVITY CALCULATIONS

MASS - CENTRE OF GRAVITY ENVELOPE.

At the end of the design and testing process for a new aircraft, the manufacturer will produce a **MASS - CENTRE OF GRAVITY ENVELOPE** for the aircraft, which makes it relatively straight forward for the pilot to ensure that his aircraft's **mass** and **CG position** stay within limits at all times. A representative **MASS - CENTRE OF GRAVITY ENVELOPE** for a light aircraft is depicted at *Figure 2.11*.

Notice that *Figure 2.11* is called a **WEIGHT - CENTRE OF GRAVITY ENVELOPE**. This is because the example is taken from an American **Pilot's Operating Handbook**. But do not let this fact concern you. The words **weight** and **mass** are interchangeable in this subject, as we have discussed.

The **MASS - CENTRE OF GRAVITY ENVELOPE** shows us that the **permitted CG limits** are between **83 ins** and **93 ins aft of the datum** for operations as a **Normal Category** aircraft and that maximum permissible gross mass for **Normal Category Operations** is **2 325 lb**.

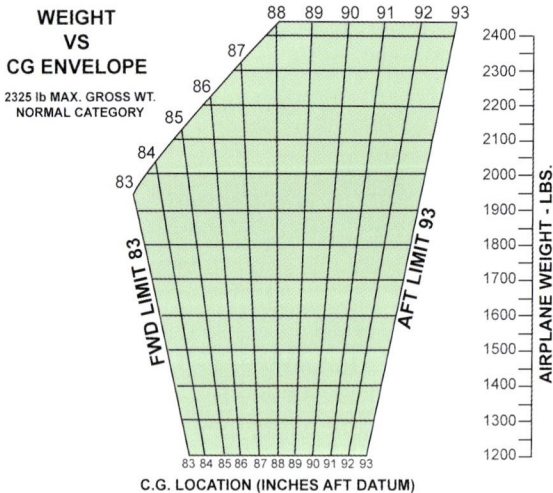

Figure 2.11 A Mass-Centre of Gravity Envelope for a Light Aircraft.

CALCULATION OF CG POSITION FOR A LOADED AIRCRAFT.

Once the **CG position** for the aircraft's **Basic Empty Mass** has been calculated, the **CG position** and **mass limits** for a **loaded aircraft** can be calculated in the same manner, so that the pilot can check that his aircraft is within limits for both take-off and landing.

This calculation can be made using a **load table** such as the one shown in *Figure 2.12*.

CHAPTER 2: CENTRE OF GRAVITY CALCULATIONS

ITEM	MASS (lb)	ARM (ins)	MOMENT (lb-ins)
Aircraft Empty Mass	1 550	86.5	134 075
Front Seat (1)	190	80.5	15 295
Front Seat (2)	200	80.5	16 100
Rear Seat (1)	100	118.1	11 810
Rear Seat (2)	-	118.1	-
Baggage (200 lb max)	65	142.8	9 282
Fuel	210	95.0	19 950
TOTAL	2 315		206 512

Figure 2.12 Calculation of CG position for a loaded aircraft.

We see that an aircraft is to carry a pilot and two passengers, plus baggage.

The **load table** contains, in the top line, the information that we already have concerning the aircraft's **mass and CG position, empty**. The other lines in the table contain **moment arms** for the front seats, rear seats, and fuel tanks. The **Pilot-in-Command** enters the actual **mass (weight) values** depending on the weight of **crew, passengers, lugagge** and **fuel uptake.**

With all figures entered into the table, the pilot completes the **moment column** for the **individual loads**, adds up the **masses** (the **payload**) and the **moment arms** and can then calculate the **CG position** for the **loaded aircraft**.

He does this by dividing the total of all the moments **206 512 lb-ins** by the total mass of the aircraft **2 315 lb**, including **payload**, to get the **CG moment arm of 89.21 ins**. That is, **89.21 ins aft of the datum**. The pilot checks this figure against the **permissible CG limits** in the **MASS - CENTRE OF GRAVITY ENVELOPE** and sees that it is, indeed, within the limits stipulated, between **83 ins** and **93 ins** aft of the datum (*See Figure 2.13*).

He also sees that the **total mass** of his loaded aircraft, at **2 315 lb**, is within limits (*See Figure 2.13*).

Both the total mass of the aircraft, and the position of its Centre of Gravity must be within the limits laid down by the manufacturer.

CHAPTER 2: CENTRE OF GRAVITY CALCULATIONS

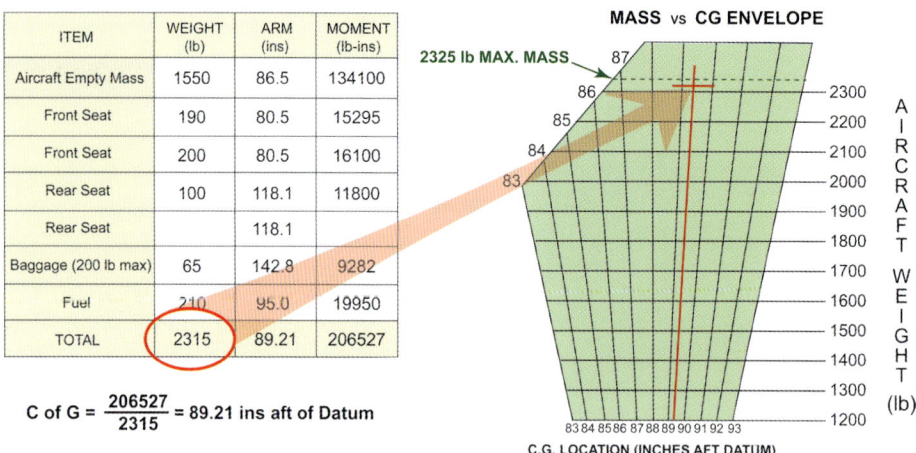

$$C \text{ of } G = \frac{206527}{2315} = 89.21 \text{ ins aft of Datum}$$

Figure 2.13 The loaded aircraft has its mass and CG position within limits.

CALCULATING THE CG POSITION ON LANDING.

Having determined that the aircraft's **mass** and **CG position** are within limits for the proposed flight, a prudent pilot will also check that the **CG position** will still be within limits **for the landing**, following the **planned fuel consumption**.

In order to make this calculation, the pilot needs to calculate the **moment** about the datum of the **fuel** that he plans will be **consumed** during the flight.

We must be very careful in making these calculations, because **fuel consumption** for American-made aircraft is often given in **US gallons per hour**, whereas fuel bowsers and pumps in the United Kingdom and Europe deliver fuel in **litres**. It is vital, therefore, that a pilot should know how to **convert** between **Imperial**, **American** and **Metric Units**. These conversions can be easily made using your **Flight Navigation Computer** (See Volume 3 **'Navigation and Radio Aids'** and *Figure 2.17*).

However, to keep matters simple for our **CG** calculations, we will refer to fuel consumption in mass, using the unit **lb**. The **lb** will be quoted in the **Pilot's Operating Handbook** for many American aircraft, such as Pipers and Cessnas. Obviously, it is straight forward to convert lb into kg (kilogram).

Let us assume that the pilot calculates that he will use **150 lb** of fuel for his planned flight. Given the calculations already made above, will the aircraft's **CG** still be within limits on landing?

Well, we know from the **load table** at *Figure 2.12* that the location of the fuel tanks gives the fuel a **moment arm** of **95 inches**. The **moment** for the fuel planned to be consumed during the flight will, therefore, be:

> **moment of fuel consumed = 150 lb × 95 ins = 14 250 lb-ins.**

In order to calculate the new position of the aircraft's **CG** on landing we must do the following:

CHAPTER 2: CENTRE OF GRAVITY CALCULATIONS

- Substract the mass of fuel used, **150 lb**, from the **take-off mass** of the aircraft, **2 315 lb**.

- Substract the **moment of the fuel used** from the **total take-off moment** of the aircraft.

- Calculate the **new CG position** by **dividing** the **total moment on landing** by the **mass of the aircraft on landing**.

This calculation is shown below in *Figure 2.14*.

Landing CG Moment Arm = $\dfrac{\text{Landing Moment}}{\text{Landing Mass}}$ = $\dfrac{19\,2262 \text{ lb-ins}}{2\,165 \text{ lb}}$ = 88.8 ins

We see then, **from the MASS vs CG ENVELOPE,** that the **landing CG position** of **88.8 ins aft of the datum**, is still within the permissible **CG limits** for the aircraft.

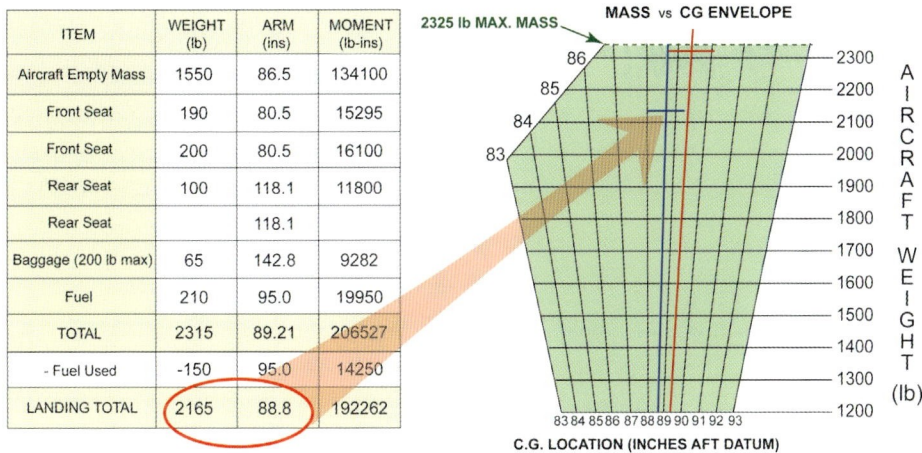

Figure 2.14 Landing CG Moment Arm.

Remember, the **CG must** lie between forward and aft limits.

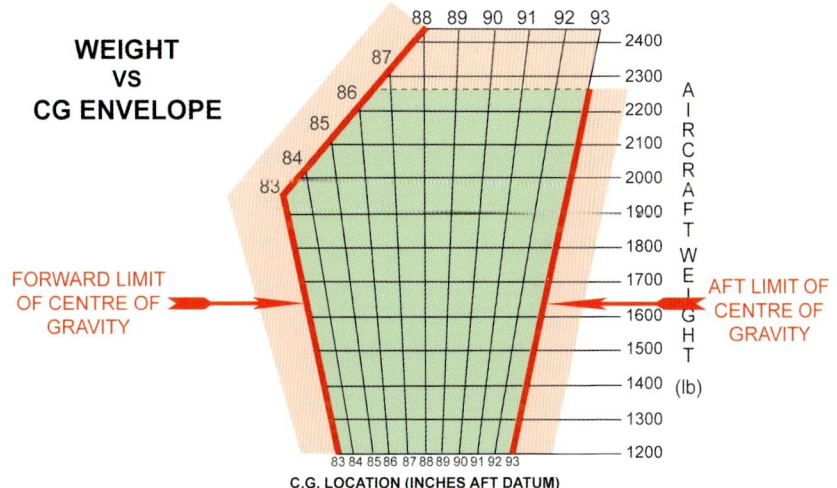

Figure 2.15 The aircraft's CG must lie between the permissible forward and aft limits.

CHAPTER 2: CENTRE OF GRAVITY CALCULATIONS

If the **CG** is **out of limits**, **stability**, **control forces** and **performance**, will all be affected. More importantly, the **safety** of the aircraft may be compromised.

The Pilot-in-Command must always ensure that his aircraft is within permissible mass and CG limits, before every flight.

FUEL LOADS AND CONVERSION FACTORS.

In order to calculate the effect of **fuel up-take** and of **fuel consumption** on the **weight** (**mass**) of your aircraft, in terms both of **maximum permissible take-off mass** and of **CG position**, you must familiarise yourself with the **conversion factors** which relate fuel capacity, in **gallons** or **litres**, to fuel **weight** (or **mass**), in **pounds** or **kilograms**.

A table summarising these relationships appears below at *Figure 2.17*. Full instruction on these **conversions** is given on the Flight Navigation Computer Training CD-ROM which comes with Volume 3 of this series: **'Navigation and Radio Aids'**.

Conversions using the **Flight Navigation Computer** (illustrated in *Figure 2.16*) are very easy to make.

You should use the **Computer** for all **conversions** that are asked for in the PPL ground examination questions. The table and worked examples which follow are meant, purely, to demonstrate to you the principles of converting from capacity to mass, and vice-versa, and from one system of units to another.

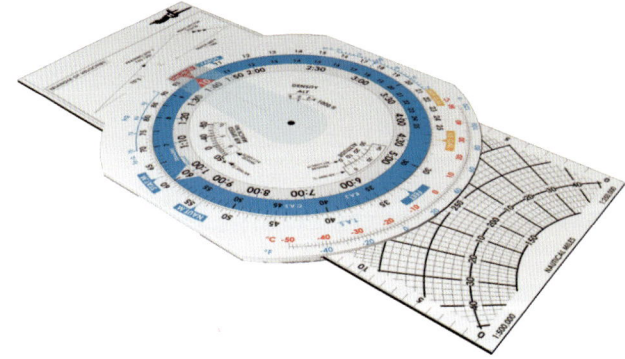

Figure 2.16 Flight Navigation Computer.

Learn the most common conversion factors.

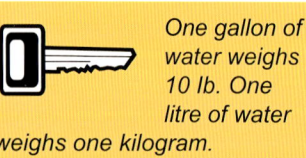
One gallon of water weighs 10 lb. One litre of water weighs one kilogram.

1 litre of water weighs 1 kilogram (kg)

1 litre of AVGAS at a Specific Gravity of approximatelly 0.72 weighs 1kg × 0.72 = 0.72kg

1 kg is equal to 2.2 lb, approximately.

1 Imperial gallon = 4.55 litres, approximately.

1 Imperial gallon of water weighs 10 lb.

1 US gallon = 3.8 litres.

1 US gallon = 0.83 Imperial gallons.

Figure 2.17 Conversion factors for Imperial, US and Metric units.

CHAPTER 2: CENTRE OF GRAVITY CALCULATIONS

Worked Examples.

Here are some worked examples of conversions from capacity to weight (mass) and vice-versa, in both imperial and metric units.

Worked Example 1

What is the weight, in lb, of 15 Imperial gallons of AVGAS whose **specific gravity** is 0.72?

First of all, specific gravity refers to the weight of a given quantity of a fluid compared to the weight of the same quantity of water.

Therefore, as 1 Imperial gallon of water weighs 10 lb, 1 gallon of AVGAS would weigh:

$$10 \text{ lb} \times 0.72 = 7.2 \text{ lb.}$$

It follows, then, that, 15 gallons of AVGAS would weigh **15 × 7.2 lb = 108 lb**.

The specific gravity of any fluid is a dimensionless number which relates the weight of a given quantity of that fluid to the weight of the same quantity of water.

Worked Example 2

A pilot needs to upload 120 lb of AVGAS. He knows that the **specific gravity** of AVGAS is 0.72. How many Imperial gallons would he need to put into his tanks? The pilot then realises, of course, that he can only buy fuel in litres. How many litres would he need to buy?

10 lb of water makes 1 gallon.

So, if the fuel were water, 120 lb would be 12 gallons. However, AVGAS is only 0.72 times the weight of water, so there will be more gallons of fuel than there are of water.

$$10 \text{ lb of AVGAS} = \frac{1}{0.72} = 1.39 \text{ gallons}$$

Therefore, **120 lb of AVGAS = 12 × 1.39 gallons = 16.7 gallons**

But, **1 gallon = 4.55 litres**

It follows, then, that: **16.7 gallons = 16.7 × 4.55 litres = 76 litres**

Worked Example 3

What is the weight, in lb, of 290 litres of AVGAS whose specific gravity is 0.72?

1 litre of water weighs 1 kg.

Therefore, 290 litres of water would weigh 290 kg. However, AVGAS weighs only 0.72 as much as water. So 290 litres of AVGAS weighs 290 kg × 0.72 = 208.8 kg.

Now 1 kg = 2.2 lb, approximately.

Therefore, 208.8 kg = (208.8 x 2.2) lb = 459.36 lb. Say, 460 lb, approximately.

CHAPTER 2: CENTRE OF GRAVITY CALCULATIONS

Worked Example 4

A pilot calculates that he needs to upload 15 US gallons of AVGAS. How many litres is that, and how many pounds does the fuel weigh, if its specific gravity is 0.72?

$$1 \text{ US gallon} = 3.8 \text{ litres}$$

Therefore, $\quad\quad$ 15 US gallons = 15 × 3.8 litres = 57 litres

57 litres of AVGAS, whose specific gravity is 0.72, weighs:

$$(57 \times 0.72) \text{ kg} = 41 \text{ kg}$$

Now, $\quad\quad\quad\quad\quad\quad\quad$ 1 kg = 2.2 lb

So, $\quad\quad\quad\quad$ 41 kg = (41 × 2.2) lb = 90 lb, appoximately.

Now try the questions at the end of this chapter.

NB.: Remember, learn to use your **Flight Navigation Computer** for these conversions; it is easier that way! (See CD-ROM in Volume 3: **'Navigation and Radio Aids'**).

"MASS - CENTRE OF GRAVITY ENVELOPES" FOR DIFFERENT CATEGORIES OF AIRCRAFT OPERATIONS.

You learn elsewhere in this book about different categories of aircraft (such as the **Normal**, **Utility** and **Aerobatic Categories**) and the different **load factors** that each category is designed to withstand. Well, some light aircraft, such as the PA28 Warrior, are designed to operate in **more than one category**. The Warrior, for instance, may operate in the **Normal Category**, with **load factor limits** of **+2.5** and **-1**, or in the **Utility Category**, with **load factor limits** of **+4.4** and **-1.8**.

Figure 2.18 The Warrior can operate either in the Normal or Utility Categories, depending on its operating mass.

While operating in the **Normal Category**, an aircraft may not be spun; turns are limited to 60° angle of bank, and no aerobatic manoeuvres are permitted. In the **Utility Category**, turns may be flown at bank angles in excess of 60° and spinning

CHAPTER 2: CENTRE OF GRAVITY CALCULATIONS

is permitted, if the aircraft is cleared for this manoeuvre. No aerobatic manoeuvres may be flown.

However, in order to determine in which category an aircraft may operate, different **mass** and **CG limits** are applied to the aircraft.

For example, the **MASS - CENTRE OF GRAVITY ENVELOPE** shown below, in *Figure 2.19*, which we have already used in this chapter, is for an aircraft which may be operated in the **Normal Category**.

> *When an aircraft is cleared to operate in more than one Category, the mass and Centre of Gravity limits are usually different for each Category.*

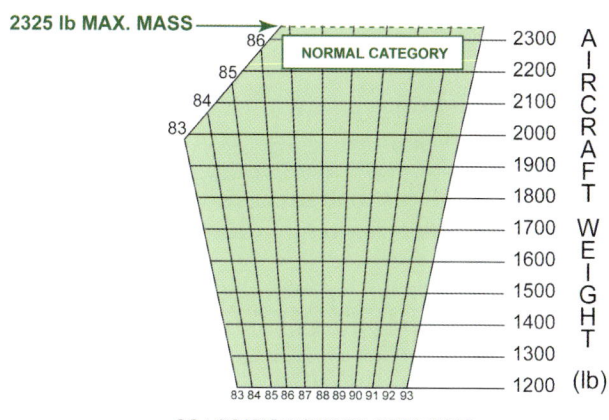

Figure 2.19 A Mass - Centre of Gravity Envelope for an aircraft operating in the Normal Category.

You can see from *Figure 2.19* that, in the **Normal Category**, the maximum take-off mass permitted for the aircraft is **2 325 lb**, with the CG position limited to between **83 ins** and **93 ins** aft of the datum.

The same aircraft, however, can be operated in the **Utility Category,** but only if different **mass** and **CG position limits** are applied. The **MASS - CENTRE OF GRAVITY ENVELOPE** for the aircraft operating in the **Utility Category** is shown below in *Figure 2.20*.

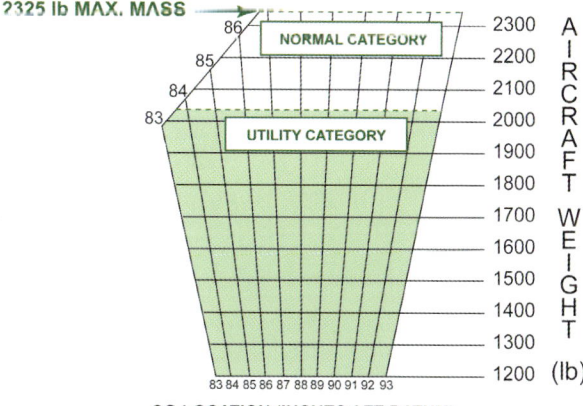

Figure 2.20 A Mass - Centre of Gravity Envelope for an aircraft operating in the Utility Category.

CHAPTER 2: CENTRE OF GRAVITY CALCULATIONS

You can see in *Figure 2.20* how the boundaries of the envelope (the green shaded area) have reduced for the **Utility Category** operations. The **Maximum Permissible Mass**, for instance, has been lowered from **2 325 lb** to **2 020 lb**. You will notice, too, that the permissible **CG limits** have also been narrowed slightly, at the **Maximum Permissible Mass,** to between **83.5 ins** and **93 ins** aft of the datum.

CALCULATING MASS AND CENTRE OF GRAVITY USING THE GRAPHICAL METHOD.

Pilot Operating Handbooks (POH) for light aircraft often contain simple **graphs** which may be used to perform **Mass & Balance calculations**, as an alternative to the arithmetical method. There are normally three steps to take using the **graphical method,** which we examine here.

Step One.
The **POH** may contain a **loading graph** similar to the one in *Figure 2.21*.

The graph has two **axes**: the **vertical axis** showing **load**, in **lb** or **kg**, and the **horizontal axis** showing the **load moment**, in **1000 ˟ lb-ins** or a metric equivalent.

From the **origin** of the graph, in the bottom left hand corner, straight lines slope upwards to the right, one for each of the following aircraft stations:

- Pilot and front passenger, or student.

- Fuel load.

- Rear passengers.

- Baggage.

As an example, let us assume that a pilot is taking a friend for a local flight, without baggage. The trip is to be of one hour's duration and air experience only, so the pilot intends to carry out only gentle manoeuvres. He is, therefore, happy for the aircraft to be loaded to operate in the **Normal Category**. The pilot has checked the tank contents and is satisfied that the aircraft has **40 US gallons** of fuel on board. At **3.79 litres per US gallon**, that makes just over **150 litres**.

The total **weight (mass)** of the pilot and front passenger, together, is **370 lb**. The pilot locates the point on the "pilot and front passenger" line corresponding to the reading of **370 lb** on the vertical axis, and, from that point, follows the vertical line downwards to where it cuts the horizontal axis. He sees that the **moment** for himself and his passenger is **28 000 lb-ins**. *(See Figure 2.21)*

At a **specific gravity of 0.72, 150 litres of fuel** will weigh (150 litres ˟ 0.72) kg = **108 kg**; that makes (108 kg ˟ 2.2) lb = **238 lb**.

Using the same method to calculate the **fuel moment** as he did for the **crew moment**, and taking care to use the straight line representing **fuel load** in order to do this, the pilot finds that the **fuel moment** is **23 500 lb-ins**.

CHAPTER 2: CENTRE OF GRAVITY CALCULATIONS

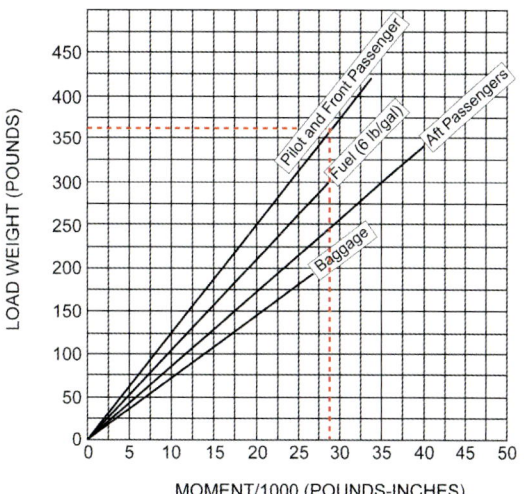

Figure 2.21 A typical light aircraft loading graph. The red dotted line shows that a front seat crew mass of 370 lb gives a Moment of 28 000 lb-ins.

Step Two.

The pilot now takes the **load sheet** for the aircraft, as depicted in *Figure 2.22*, and completes it for the planned flight. The pilot notes that he just has to fill in the **mass** and **moment** columns as he has been able to read the **moment for crew and fuel** directly from the graph.

ITEM	MASS (lb)	ARM (ins)	MOMENT (lb-ins)
Aircraft Empty Mass	1550	86.5	134 075
Front Seat (1)	185	80.5	14 000
Front Seat (2)	185	80.5	14 000
Rear Seat (1)			
Rear Seat (2)			
Baggage (200 lb max)			
Fuel	238	95.0	23 500
TOTAL	2 158		185 575

Figure 2.22 Load Sheet

From the **load sheet**, the pilot quickly sums up the **aircraft empty mass**, the **crew mass**, and the **fuel mass** in the **mass column**, and sees that the **total mass for the flight** is (1 550 lb + 370 lb + 238 lb) = **2 158 lb**.

Adding up the **moment arms**, he arrives at the figure of:
(134 075 lb-ins + 28 000 lb-ins + 23 500 lb-ins) = **185 575 lb-ins** for the total moment.

Step Three.

Referring to the **POH**, the pilot now merely has to relate **total aircraft mass** and **total moment** for his flight, to a simple diagram contained in the **POH**, known as the **Centre of Gravity - Moment Envelope**, in order to determine whether aircraft will be within **mass and centre of gravity limits** for the flight. (*See Figure 2.23*).

CHAPTER 2: CENTRE OF GRAVITY CALCULATIONS

For the aircraft to be **in-limits**, the point of intersection of the values for **mass** (**weight**) and **moment** must fall <u>**within the envelope**</u>.

Using the **Centre of Gravity - Moment Envelope** (*See Figure 2.23*), the pilot locates the **total take-off mass of 2 158 lb** on the vertical axis, and the **total moment of 18 5575 lb-ins**, on the horizontal axis. He notes that where the lines from these two points intersect is **inside the Envelope** *(See Figure 2.23)*, showing the pilot that the **aircraft's total mass** and **total moment** are **within limits** for the aircraft to operate in the **Normal Category**; that is, with turns limited to a maximum bank angle of 60°, no spinning and no aerobatics.

Calculating Mass and CG Position, on Landing.

The pilot has also calculated that, in one hour, he will use about **10 US gallons** of fuel; that makes just under **40 litres** of fuel. Taking the figure of **40 litres**, he calculates that at a **specific gravity of 0.72**, the amount of fuel consumed will weigh **29 kg**, or **64 lbs**.

From the table at *Figure 2.22*, the pilot sees that the **moment of this weight of fuel** is **6 500 lb-ins**.

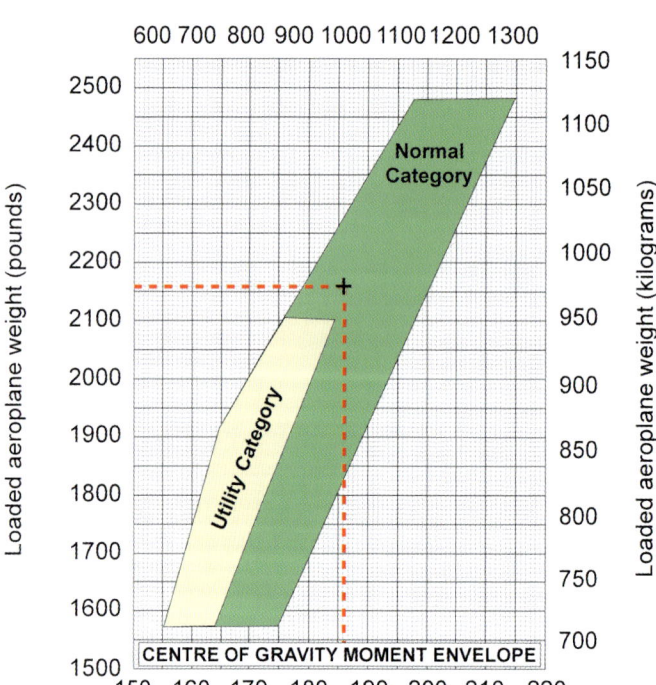

Figure 2.23 A typical Centre of Gravity - Moment Envelope for a light aircraft. The total mass and total moment must fall within the shaded area, depending on aircraft category.

Subtracting these **fuel-burn figures** from the aircraft's **total take-off mass and moment**, the pilot calculates that the **landing mass and moment** for the aircraft will be **2 094 lb** and **179 075 lb-ins**, respectively.

CHAPTER 2: CENTRE OF GRAVITY CALCULATIONS

Referring to the aircraft's **Centre of Gravity - Moment Envelope**, the pilot sees that the aircraft's mass and moment on landing will still be within limits, so is happy to proceed with the flight.

You should note that if the aircraft's mass and/or moment figures put the load and/or centre of gravity position out of limits, either for take-off or for landing, you will have to re-plan the loading of the aircraft.

DANGEROUS GOODS.

There are many goods which should not be carried in aircraft. Some goods are illegal and some goods, while legal, are better not carried. The following is a list of some of the **dangerous goods** which are hazardous to aviation:

- explosives.

- flammable goods.

- radioactive materials.

- infectious substances.

- corrosive substances.

- magnetic materials.

Note, too, that different nations have different rules on the import/export of live animals, plants and seeds.

Figure 2.24 Dangerous Goods Labels.

CHAPTER 2: CENTRE OF GRAVITY CALCULATIONS.

LOAD RESTRAINT.

All loads carried in an aircraft must be secured to prevent movement in flight. Acceleration and deceleration, on take-off and landing, during manoeuvres, and when the aircraft is exposed to turbulence, would cause an unsecured load to shift its position and endanger the safety of the aircraft. If loads were to move in flight, some of the consequences might be:

- Injury to personnel in the aircraft, particularly those forward of the cargo.

- Movement of the **CG** position outside the permissible limits.

- Structural damage to the aircraft.

- Blockage of emergency exits.

- Damage to other cargo items.

Small items of miscellaneous cargo may be safely secured by a net draped over them which, in turn, is secured to the aircraft structure. But bulky and heavy items must be more positively secured. This type of security is carried out by the use of special equipment known collectively as **tie-down equipment**. All cargo aircraft are provided with tie-down points which are part of the aircraft structure and to which items of cargo can be secured.

CHAPTER 2: CENTRE OF GRAVITY CALCULATIONS QUESTIONS

Representative PPL - type questions to test your theoretical knowledge of Mass and Balance.

1. An aircraft weighing 2 000 lb with a total C of G moment of 169 400 lb-ins uplifts 440 lb of fuel. If the effective arm of the fuel is 88.5 inches aft of the datum, what will be the aircraft's new mass and C of G moment?

    a. 1 560 lb   208 340 lb-ins.
    b. 2 440 lb   169 488.5 lb-ins.
    c. 1 560 lb   169 488.5 lb-ins.
    d. 2 440 lb   208 340 lb-ins.

2. Your aircraft has:

    A Take-off Mass   =   2 353 lbs
    A calculated C of G for departure   =   89.75 inches aft of the datum
    An estimated fuel burn   =   200 lb with a C of G 85.00 inches aft of datum.

    The position of the C of G on landing will be?

    a. 90.19 inches aft of the datum
    b. 82.52 inches aft of the datum
    c. 105.98 inches aft of the datum
    d. 96.97 inches aft of the datum

3. Your aircraft has an oil reservoir, with a capacity of 3 Imperial gallons, which is positioned 20 inches aft of the datum. Given that the oil weighs 9.1 lb/gal, the reservoir will possess a moment of:

    a. 60 lb-ins
    b. 27.3 lb-ins
    c. 182 lb-ins
    d. 546 lb-ins

4. The Maximum Take off Mass of an aircraft may be limited by:

    a. structural design load limits and or runway length, altitude and temperature
    b. the authorised performance category of the aircraft, i.e. utility / normal / aerobatic
    c. the airworthiness condition of the aircraft
    d. all of the above

5. At what mass and C of G position would it be safe to operate the aircraft represented by the attached Mass vs C of G Envelope? *See Graph 1, Page 43.*

    a. 2 250 lb   86.00 inches aft of the datum
    b. 2 000 lb   84.00 inches aft of the datum
    c. 1 900 lb   82.00 inches aft of the datum
    d. 2 300 lb   86.00 inches aft of the datum

CHAPTER 2: CENTRE OF GRAVITY CALCULATIONS QUESTIONS

6. At what mass and C of G moment would it be permissible to operate, in the Normal Category, the aircraft represented by the Centre of Gravity / Moment Envelope at *Graph 2, Page 43*?

	Mass	Moment
a.	2 100 lb	75 000 lb-ins
b.	2 300 lb	110 000 lb-ins
c.	2 275 lb	98 000 lb-ins
d.	2 400 lb	93 000 lb-ins

7. At what mass and C of G moment would it be permissible to operate, in the Utility Category, the aircraft represented by the Centre of Gravity / Moment Envelope at *Graph 2, Page 332*?

	Mass	Moment
a.	1 900 lb	63 000 lb-ins
b.	1 700 lb	83 000 lb-ins
c.	2 000 lb	69 000 lb-ins
d.	2 050 lb	75 000 lb-ins

8. In which Category, Utility or Normal, would you expect to operate the aircraft represented by the attached C of G / Moment Envelope at *Graph 2, Page 43*, if its mass is 2 100 lb and its C of G moment 90 000 lb-inches?

   a. Utility
   b. Normal
   c. Both
   d. Neither

Question	1	2	3	4	5	6	7	8
Answer								

The answers to these questions can be found at the end of this book.

CHAPTER 2: CENTRE OF GRAVITY CALCULATIONS QUESTIONS

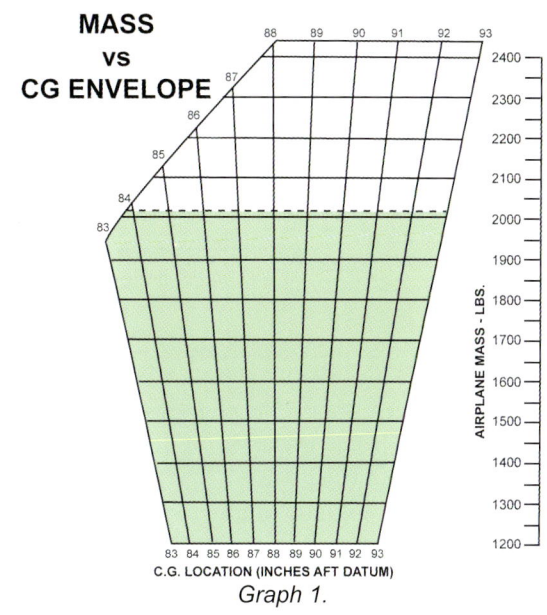

Graph 1.

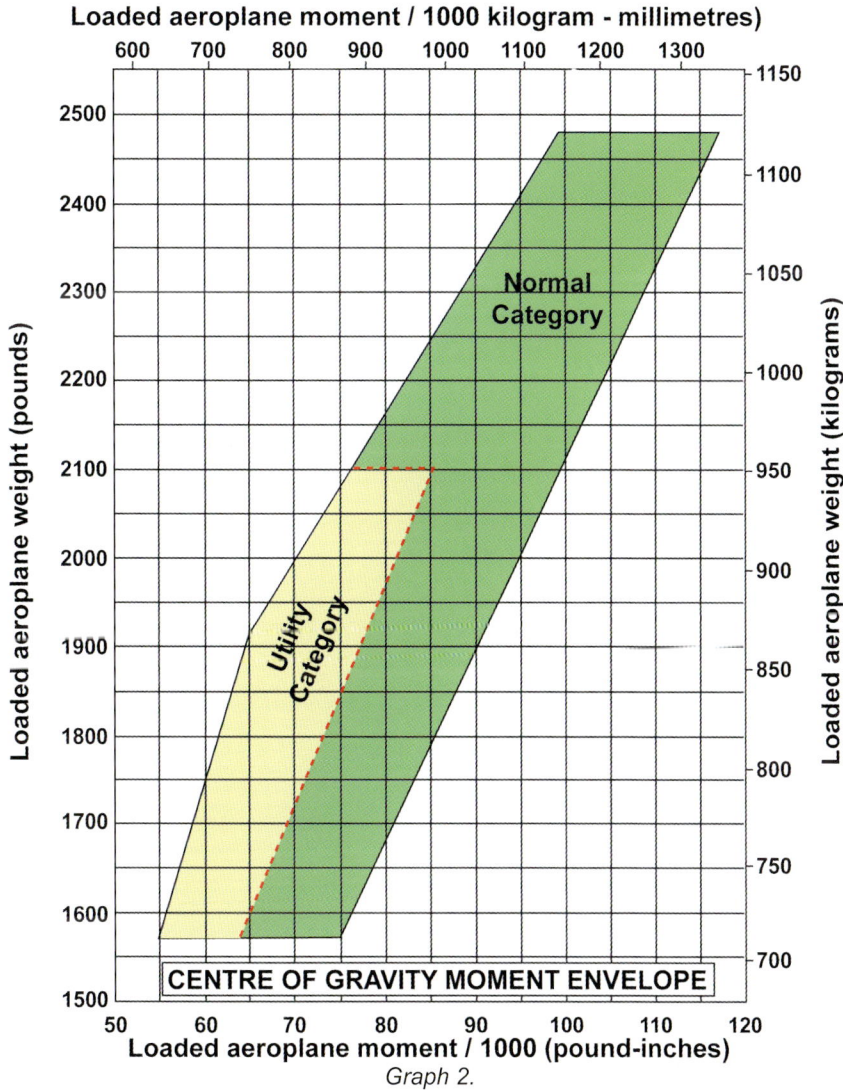

Graph 2.

JAR-FCL PPL THEORETICAL KNOWLEDGE SYLLABUS

MASS & BALANCE

The table below contains the principal topics and subtopics from the current outline syllabus for the theoretical examination in **Mass & Balance** for the **Private Pilot's Licence**, as published in **JAR-FCL 1**. Syllabuses may be modified, so always check the latest examination documentation from your **national civil aviation authority**, or from **JAR-FCL/EASA**.

In the United Kingdom, **Mass & Balanace** is examined in the same paper as **Flight Performance and Planning**. In this series of text books **Flight Performance and Planning** is covered in the section **Aeroplane Performance**, in **Volume 5**.

MASS AND BALANCE	
Mass and Balance:	• limitations on maximum mass; • forward and aft limits of centre of gravity, normal and utility operation; • mass and centre of gravity calculations; • aeroplane manual and balance sheet.

MASS AND BALANCE SYLLABUS

ANSWERS TO MASS AND BALANCE QUESTIONS

ANSWERS TO THE MASS AND BALANCE QUESTIONS

Chapter 1   *Mass and Balance*

Question	1	2	3	4	5	6	7	8	9	10	11
Answer	d	c	d	a	a	b	a	d	b	d	d

Chapter 2   *Centre of Gravity Calculations*

Question	1	2	3	4	5	6	7	8
Answer	d	a	d	a	b	c	d	b

INDEX

A
All-Up Mass — 5

B
Balance — 11
Basic Empty Mass — 5

C
Calculating Mass and Centre of Gravity
Using the Graphical Method — 25
Centre of Gravity — 5,7,19
  - *Calculation of Position of Centre of Gravity* — 19
  - *Datum*
  - *For Empty Aircraft* — 25
  - *For Loaded Aircraft* — 28,30
  — 18
  - *Forward and Aft Limits* — 18
  - *On Landing* — 30
  - *Outside Forward Limit* — 9
  - *Outside Aft Limit* — 10
Centre of Gravity Envelope — 29
Controllability — 6
Conversions Factors — 32

D
Dangerous Goods — 39

E
Empty Mass — 5

F
Flight Navigation Computer — 32
Forward and Aft Limits — 9
Fuel Loads and Conversions Factors — 32
Fulcrum — 21

G
Gross Mass — 5

I
Imperial Units — 20

L
Load Restraint — 40
Load Table — 30

MASS AND BALANCE INDEX

M
Manoeuvrability	6
Mass	
- The Difference Between Mass and Weight	6
Mass and Balance	5
Mass and Balance Limitations	6
- General Observations	11
Maximum Landing Mass (MLM)	8
Maximum Ramp Mass	7
Maximum Take-off Mass (MTOM)	7
Maximum Zero Fuel Mass (MZFM)	8
Moment	21
Moment Arm	21
Moment Of Fuel Consumed	21

N
Normal Category	38

O
Overloading	6

P
Pivot-Point	21
- Calculation of	23
Planned Fuel Consumption	32
Principle of Moments	21

S
Stalling Speed	6
Structural Safety	7

U
Utility Category	35

W
Weight	6
- The Difference between Weight and Mass	
Weighing an Aircraft	26

Z
Zero Fuel Mass	5